By the same author

BIOGRAPHY
Brendan Behan
Oliver St John Gogarty
Celtic Dawn: A Portrait of the Irish
Literary Renaissance
Biographers and the Art of Biography

POEMS AND PLAYS
Life Styles
All Things Counter
One is Animate
Three Noh Plays
Execution
Poems of the Damned: Translations from Baudelaire

OTHER BOOKS
Irish Tales and Sagas
A Critic at Large
The Campbell Companion (with memoir)
The Yeats Companion (with memoir)
Sport is My Lifeline
The Troubles (Ireland 1912–22)
Brian Friel: Crisis and Commitment

The Ulick O'Connor Diaries

1970–1981

A Cavalier Irishman

Foreword by Richard Ingrams

JOHN MURRAY

© Ulick O'Connor 2001
Introduction © Richard Ingrams 2001

First published in 2001 by John Murray (Publishers)
A division of Hodder Headline

Paperback edition 2003

1 3 5 7 9 10 8 6 4 2

A CIP catalogue record for this title is available from the British Library

ISBN 0-7195-5674-0

Typeset in Monotype Bembo by Servis Filmsetting Ltd, Manchester
Printed and bound in Great Britain by Clays Ltd, St Ives plc

John Murray (Publishers)
338 Euston Road
London
NW1 3BH

Contents

Illustrations   vi
Foreword by Richard Ingrams   vii
Author's Preface   xiii
Acknowledgements   xiv

1970   3

1971   65

1972   103

1973   129

1974   163

1975   183

1977; and December 1977–January 1978,
     Tangier   207

1978   249

1980–1981   281

APPENDICES

1. Table-talk of Eoin O'Mahony ('The Pope')   315

2. Requiem for a Nanny   317

Notes on Frequently Mentioned Persons   319
Index   323

Illustrations

1. With Mariga and Desmond Guinness, Leixlip Castle, 1959
2. Nanny
3. Anne Brady
4. Billy Wicklow, 8th Earl of Wicklow
5. Bob Bradshaw
6. With Sarah Churchill before the first night of *Counterparts*
7. Judge at Trinity College races, College Park, Dublin, May 1970
8. Playing in Selected International XV vs The President's XV, October 1971
9. Georgian Society cricket match
10. Rathgar *circa* 1900
11. Micheál MacLiammóir in Anouilh's *Ring Round the Moon*
12. With John Hume, Derry, 1972
13. Viva Superstar
14. With Stephen and Jean Kennedy Smith, New York, April 1977
15. With Monk Gibbon, Christopher Sinclair-Stevenson and Jack Lynch at the launch of *A Terrible Beauty is Born*, 1975
16. With Mary Ure at the launch of *Irish Liberation*, 1974
17. Playing Oliver St John Gogarty in the RTE film *An Offering of Swans*, 1977
18. At the National Boxing Stadium, 1950, after knocking out an opponent in four seconds
19. Sparring with British lightweight champion Charlie Nash, 1980

The author and publishers thank the following for their permission to reproduce copyright photographs: Pat Maxwell (3, 8); Sir Charles Fergusson, Bart (4); Sheila Bradshaw (5); the Gate Theatre, Dublin (11); the Kobal Collection (13); Leslie Keating, Dublin (15); William V. Carson, Pennyburn-Derry (19)

Foreword by Richard Ingrams

Some years ago when I had only recently begun writing a weekly column for the *Observer*, I received a furious letter from Ulick O'Connor, a name I knew only slightly having previously met him at a literary quiz game on Granada TV in Manchester. Ulick objected vigorously to what I had written about Northern Ireland, assuming that like most British journalists I was a supporter of the Union. Obviously I had failed to make myself clear – not for the first time. At any rate I wrote back explaining that as far as 'the Troubles' were concerned he and I were allies. Thus a friendship was born. Not long afterwards, when I was in Ireland with my wife, we visited Ulick at his home in Rathgar (a house, I remember, filled with books and mementoes of writers he has known). Later we were treated to a tour of Dublin by this most erudite of guides and a man for whom, as for many Irishmen, the past is as vivid as the present.

I cannot claim to be an expert on Ireland. But I have gathered enough about it from personal experience to know that, from an Englishman's point of view, it is a foreign country – as foreign as France or Germany. Even on a superficial level you can tell after only a few days amongst the Irish that they are not like us. One of my earliest Irish memories is of listening to conversations involving friends and relatives, the majority of whom were either in lunatic asylums or undergoing treatment for alcoholism. (Such conversations were needless to say accompanied by a prodigious intake of alcohol.) They were not like us, more notably in their obvious love of talk and especially of gossip. It was not only the drink that flowed but the conversation as well. Everyone seemed to know everyone else – as you quickly discovered if you walked down Grafton Street with an Irishman. They were different above all in that politics and religion, the two topics that were traditionally supposed to be out of bounds at an English dinner table, were here regarded as matters of vital importance.

So the appeal to me of Ireland was first and foremost that it was different despite being so close. And it was this view that all along coloured my attitude to the so-called Irish problem. The Irish of North and South had much more in common with one another than they ever had with the English. Gerry Adams and Ian Paisley were brothers under the skin, united, though neither of them would have said as much, by a dislike and distrust of British politicians. That finding of mine was confirmed when some time after our first meeting I joined up with Ulick at a debate on the Irish question at Trinity College Dublin. I remember feeling very left out of things listening to the committed Nationalist Ulick and the Unionist politician Ken MaGinnis engaged in an animated and obviously friendly discussion about rugby football.

The eldest of five children, Ulick O'Connor was born in 1929 in the house in which he still lives in Fairfield Park, Rathgar. It is a quiet suburb of Dublin, three or so miles from the centre of the city in an area of two-storey Georgian houses, the home traditionally of Dublin's prosperous middle class. Ulick's father, Dr Matthew Harris-O'Connor, was one of the heads of the new Irish army's medical corps and later became Professor of Pathology and Dean of the faculty in the Royal College of Surgeons in Ireland. His wife Eileen (née Murphy) was the daughter of a senior civil servant. She was a well-educated and cultured woman, an excellent violinist who took a degree in Celtic Studies at University College Dublin. The O'Connors differed from most of their neighbours only in that they were Catholics – though this was never, in Dublin, a cause of friction as it would have been north of the border.

Another major point of difference with the Irish is their passion for sport, a result, perhaps, of the country never having been an industrial one. Both of Ulick's parents were keen sports people, his father excelling at rugby, cricket and tennis, his mother the captain of the UCD Women's hockey team. When Ulick went to the day school St Mary's, he found himself under the tutelage of the Holy Ghost Fathers, a body of monks whose devotion to God was matched by their passion for rugby football – sport being, in their eyes, not merely a recreation but an important character-forming exercise. 'If you didn't tackle or go down on the ball,' remembers Ulick, 'you were regarded as a moral leper . . . nothing was impossible if you really believed it could be done.'

By the time he went to University, to read philosophy and law, all his energy was going into sport, athletics, cricket, boxing and rugger. He was the University College wicket-keeper, the British Universities welter-weight boxing champion (he still holds the record for the quickest knock-out in Dublin's National Stadium, four seconds from the start of the fight) and at the age of eighteen, while still at school, he became the Irish men's pole vault champion at the same time as he was playing in first-class rugby.

It might seem a strange background for a writer to emerge from, but in Ireland, the combination of sport and literature (or sport and politics, for that matter) is by no means unusual. Parnell and Samuel Beckett were both keen cricketers, the poet Patrick Kavanagh was a sports writer on the side, while the subject of Ulick's first biography, Oliver St John Gogarty, combined an extraordinary career not only as a champion athlete, but as a poet, airman, journalist and surgeon all rolled into one.

That book was commissioned as a result of a chance meeting with the famous publisher Jonathan Cape in 1954, though it was not published for another ten years. During this period, Ulick worked not only as a barrister in Dublin and on the Western circuit but as a sports columnist for the *Observer* as well as anonymous drama critic for the London *Times*. He was mixing with writers, actors and journalists on both sides of the Irish Sea, and had himself gained a reputation in the theatre, both as a playwright and as an actor. A regular column in the *Sunday Mirror* (then edited by Michael Christiansen) led to him travelling all over the world interviewing the likes of Bobby Kennedy, Muhammad Ali, Samuel Beckett and Simon Wiesenthal. In 1966 he had become famous in Ireland almost overnight when he began to appear regularly on Irish television as a guest of Gay Byrne's *Late Late Show*. Fan letters poured in and even today when Ulick has long since given up television, he is still recognized all over Ireland. I can remember visiting with him the Cistercian monastery at Roscrea, where he was greeted by the monks as a long-lost friend.

Such fame or notoriety, coupled with his journalism, brought Ulick into contact with a huge range of people. While mixing in sporting and literary circles, he became a close friend of Mariga and Desmond Guinness, who held court at Leixlip Castle, as well as a confidant of the famous Irish actor and playwright Micheál MacLiammóir with whom he dined regularly once a fortnight.

By the time Ulick's second biography, *Brendan Behan*, was published in 1970, the long running 'Troubles' had begun in Northern Ireland, provoking a situation in which it was hard for any Irish writer not to become involved. In Ulick's case, such involvement was inevitable since both of his biographies had already led him into the tangled history of Irish Republicanism. Gogarty had been a close friend and admirer of Michael Collins, later becoming a Senator in the Irish Free State, while Behan had at one time been imprisoned by the British for IRA activities. Such links were not unusual, almost the whole of Irish literature being inextricably woven with the troubled politics of the country. Still, when the situation in the North worsened through the Seventies there were plenty of people, politicians and writers south of the border who tried not to become involved, doing their best to turn a blind eye to a crisis that William Trevor once compared to a 'disease in the family that is never mentioned'. Some, like Ulick's *bête noire* Conor Cruise O'Brien, actually sided with the Unionists, while the majority made every effort to remain neutral in the hope that whatever else happened the people of the South would be spared the bombings and shootings which became commonplace in the North and even on the mainland.

With all his contacts in the media, Ulick proved a valuable ally to the Nationalist politicians of the North following the shootings of Bloody Sunday in 1972 and from then on became more and more active in the search for a solution. I travelled with him to Belfast in 1990 where we were granted an interview in the recently bombed Sinn Fein HQ by Gerry Adams (then *persona non grata* with the British). The visit brought home to me not just the futility of British efforts to uphold the status quo, but the naïveté of commentators who saw the Irish situation as a war between two bands of bigots which could never be resolved. Adams, I could see, was a man almost desperately eager to forge links with Protestants, an aim that he shared with Ulick. Both wanted a United Ireland for the logical reason that Irishmen were already united by history, geography – even by their love of sport. There is plenty of evidence in these diaries, evidence which may startle some readers, to confirm this – witness, for example, the close rapport which sprang up between the notorious UDA terrorist Gusty Spence and the Catholic Cardinal of All Ireland, the late Tomás O'Fiach.

Most of our famous diarists of today have circulated in a little world of their own making. Writers like Anthony Powell or James Lees-Milne were confined in one social circle, meeting only people of similar class and background. Ulick O'Connor's diary is refreshingly unusual in that he is at home in so many different worlds – society (high and low), the theatre, the world of books, politics, sport and journalism. Perhaps that is a range which only an Irishman, unaffected by the artificial barriers of English life, could achieve. Whatever the reason, readers on my side of the Irish Sea will be reminded (as they regularly need to be) of the extraordinary achievements of the tiny little country of Ireland and in particular of the host of brilliant and talented men and women it has produced – and is still producing – over the years, of whom Ulick O'Connor is one.

Author's Preface

Though I practised at the Irish bar from 1951 to 1970 and enjoyed myself hugely in Dublin's Law Library, where barristers work from, 'the best club in Dublin', it had never occurred to me that I would be anything else but a writer. However, it was some time before I would narrow my vocation to concentrate on what I instinctively accepted as my trade. I then began to keep regular diaries in order to keep an eye on myself and so as not to let material that might be useful to me as a writer be erased from memory. From time to time I would neglect to make entries and, at times for months, there are blank pages in the diaries. Despite these omissions, by the Nineties there was an accumulation of over twenty volumes in which I had more or less recorded my impressions of what had been happening over two decades. There are, in addition, hundreds of private letters, to me and from me, pocket diaries and numerous notebooks. My agent, Paul Marsh, when he learned of this material, suggested to John Murray that the diaries might be of interest if published in book form, an eventuality I had not envisaged. It was in this way that this volume, dealing with the years from 1970 to 1981 (excluding 1976 and 1979, the entries for which seem to me to be of less general interest), has come into being.

Acknowledgements

I am especially grateful to Caroline Knox of John Murray and my literary agent Paul Marsh, who between them brought the idea of these diaries to a publishing contract. Their advice, as the manuscript proceeded, was sound and unobtrusive. Patrick McEntee, Senior Counsel was most helpful in reading the manuscript for me. Antony Wood and Gail Pirkis were extremely helpful in the final editing process. Grant McIntyre encouraged the project throughout. As usual my friend Gerry O'Flaherty, during the writing of the book, exercised a stern vigilance over aberrations in syntax and literary usage if they appeared in the manuscript.

I would particularly like to thank Richard Ingrams for writing the Foreword.

Others to whom I would like to express my gratitude are: the late Gregory Corso; John Cunningham (research); the late Liam Galligan; John Kelly RHA; Lynn Kemp; Tomás MacAnna; Anna-lise MacNamara (research); Catherine McGough; Pat Maxwell; Patria Monaghan; Eve Mooney; Catherine Murphy; Leanne O'Brien; Ray O'Connell; the late Barney Rosset; and Caroline Westmore.

U.O.'C.

Grateful acknowledgement is made to the following for their kind permission to reproduce copyright material: Colin Smythe Limited on behalf of the Estate of Oliver Duane Gogarty for the poem 'Golden Stockings' and a stanza beginning 'From his dewlap only' by Oliver St John Gogarty; the Estate of Gerald Brenan, c/o Margaret Hanbury, 27 Walcot Square, London SE11 4UB for passages from two letters dated 26 February and 15 April 1971, Copyright © 2001 Gerald Brenan – all rights reserved; Alan Brien for a passage from his 'People' column in the *Sunday Times*; Desmond Elliott, Administrator of the Estate of Sir John Betjeman, for lines from the poem by Sir John Betjeman beginning 'D'ye ken Kolkhorst in his artful parlour'; A.P. Watt Ltd on behalf of Michael B. Yeats for lines from the poem 'The Statues' by W.B. Yeats (from *The Collected Poems of W.B. Yeats*, 2nd edition, Macmillan, London, 1950, p. 375) and from the play *The King's Threshold* by W.B. Yeats (from *The Collected Plays of W.B. Yeats*, Macmillan, London, 2nd edition, 1952, p. 141); and the Literary Estate of John Ryan and The Lilliput Press, Dublin for a passage from *Remembering How We Stood* by John Ryan (Gill & Macmillan, Dublin, 1975).

Every effort has been made to contact copyright-holders of material from which quotation is made, but if any have been overlooked, the author and publishers would be glad to hear from them.

I write from my house in Rathgar, Dublin, the one in which I was born. It overlooks a large square whose lawns and flowers are protected from the road by huge sycamores and other trees. It is only twenty minutes away from the beaches of Dublin Bay, and in the other direction, one can reach the foothills of the Dublin mountains in approximately the same time.

Should I slip into the city centre, I am still not cut off from hill and sea. On a clear day looking up the great Georgian boulevards you can see the mountains hung like a backdrop and discern the purple and gold of heather and gorse. The River Liffey, which flows through the city centre, is tidal and the seagulls and the smell of the salt sea signify beaches within walking distance. The architects who laid out the city knew precisely how to use hill and sky, against an urban background. They bent stone until it accommodated the clouds, thus creating an urban ambience in which a stroll through a crowded street may enhance the spirit and liberate the mind.*

---

* Alas, today pterodactyl-like cranes defile the skyline as unscrupulous developers and corrupt officials, between them, consign to dust the heritage of centuries.

1970

3 January, Dublin

Peter Sellers, the film actor, at dinner, at Aileen [the Hon. Mrs Brinsley] Plunket's, Lutterellstown Castle. Seems down after his separation from Britt Ekland. Tears stream down his cheeks.

'Knife in my heart, excuse me if I cry.'

I suggest that all men cry for the lost belief in the goodness of womanhood. Lolita. He tells me that when Britt ran out of money, he went back to her.

'I didn't kick her when she was down.'

When I told him he looked in good shape he said he worked out in the gym every day with weights. Was this wise since he had had heart surgery? He said not only was it safe but it actually improved his condition. He had always been interested in sport anyway. He talked of his uncle Brian Sellers, Captain of Yorkshire and England Selector, who he said used to take him to matches when he was a small boy. I was surprised at this because I always assumed Peter was a Bow Bells boy. Not so. I am touched by his affection for Uncle Brian and put a note about the relationship in my *Sunday Mirror* column. Later I receive an angry note from Brian Sellers denying he is related to 'that bloody little cockney'. How extraordinary to invent a sporting pedigree on the spur of the moment.

9 January

Prof. James Carney [Head of Department of Celtic Studies at the Institute of Advanced Studies] at Peter's Pub. Remarks on Brendan Behan as a Regency Buck. Met Arthur Power* later in the Bailey. Tells me his exhibition is a sellout. Discuss envy of Irish. Says every Irishman wants to be a trapeze artist, i.e. in the public eye.

Went on to Arts Club† with Power. He maintains George Moore's

---

* 1895–1985; painter and man of letters. Cavalry Officer in World War One. Lived in Paris. Friend of Modigliani and James Joyce. Returned to Ireland in 1938 and opened an antiques shop and art gallery in Balfe St. Author of *Conversations with James Joyce* (1974).
† United Arts Club, 3 Fitzwilliam St. Founded in 1906 with the aim of promoting interest in the arts. W.B. Yeats, William Orpen and Constance Gore-Booth (Countess Markiewicz) were early members.

Celibates best book of short stories ever written. I maintain *The Untilled Field* is the title of Moore's book of short stories and that from this book James Joyce got the notion for *Dubliners*. We have a bet. Arthur goes to Club library to check. Comes back. 'You're right.' Doesn't like Sean O'Faolain. Tolstoy best ever. Lifts hand in pontifical gesture as if signifying infallibility, though in the nicest possible way. Talks about Lord Dunsany,* the playwright and novelist who invented science fiction:

'Before the First War Dunsany had plays running in Moscow, Paris, London and New York in the same week.'

Arthur played cricket as a boy at Dunsany Castle, Co. Meath. Dunsany accused him once of casting spells as a wicket-keeper: then lay down on the wicket. At lunch Dunsany raised his rifle and shot the wasps hovering over the champagne bottles. Sat in hooded chair watching. During the second innings Dunsany bowled a handgrenade. He told Power the game was slowing up.

Vincent Grogan says he has been called back to be Attorney-General for the third time by the government of Ghana. We discuss Lytton Strachey. Arthur doesn't like him. Grogan catches what we are saying and puts his oar in. 'Style is all. That's why one should be a gentleman.'

23 January

Tonight hurt eye playing squash at Fitzwilliam Club. Jonah Barrington over for Irish Championship. Knew him at Trinity College as a shy skinny left-half on the soccer XI and not able to find a place on the squash side. Since then he has built himself up to be the greatest squash player in the world.

For a decade Leixlip Castle, Co. Kildare had been an escape to an enchanted world. It was acquired in 1958 by Desmond and Mariga Guinness†‡ whom I

---

* 18th Baron Dunsany (1878–1957), author and playwright. Lived at Dunsany Castle, Co. Meath; wrote over a hundred books and plays.
† The Hon. Desmond Guinness, second son of Bryan Guinness (later Lord Moyne) and Diana Mitford, decided as a young man to devote himself to the preservation of Georgian architecture in Ireland, much of which was in danger of demolition. With his wife Mariga he founded the Irish Georgian Society, which became a force in preventing the destruction of a valuable heritage. These two took the elitism out of preservation and peopled their Society with persons of all backgrounds, thus creating a formidable opposition to the market forces marshalled like Genghis Khan's army round the country ready to level

had first met on my way to lunch in Oscar Wilde's rooms at Magdalen College,
Oxford. Mistaking Desmond for a porter (the hunting cap he had on was similar
to those worn by porters at Trinity College Dublin), I had asked for directions,
and as he was going to the same lunch we went together. I saw a great deal of D
and M over the next twenty years. An invitation to dinner at Leixlip could arrive
at the last moment and I would zoom down in a taxi (Leixlip, near Dublin,
was then a country village) and often stay the night. One had no idea who would
be there. In a month one could encounter Lord Mountbatten, Mick Jagger,
Marianne Faithfull, Nancy Mitford, Sir Oswald Mosley, Lady Longford,
Mormons, dainty little Father Murphy from the parish of nearby Robertstown,
Captain Costello from the Curragh or Mrs Deirdre Fitzsimmons who owned
a flourishing pub in Dorset Street. I would often spend Christmas alone at
Leixlip with Desmond, Mariga and the children. Always it was fun, sheer fun.

24 January, Leixlip Castle

Lunch at Leixlip. Countess Mabs Moltke there. As a young and
famous New York beauty she had known the poet Oliver St John
Gogarty, whom I suspect she had a fling with. She tells us that Gogarty
used to call her Europa (presumably seeing himself in the role of the
god-bull) and wrote a long poem for her in that role. I know the poem
but decide not to recite the relevant passages as it would be hard to
judge the effect of stanzas such as:

> From his dewlap only
> Drops of water trickled,
> For she felt his back warm,
> Silky-soft and dry,

---

stately mansions everywhere. He has had much recognition for his work on architectural preservation and has written notable books on the subject. Impossibly good-
looking, he has had much success lecturing throughout the United States.

‡ Mariga Guinness (1932–89), formerly Princess von Urach of Württemberg, grand-
niece of Elizabeth, Empress of Austria, was in the tradition of the great hostesses,
Madame Récamier, Madame de Staël, Lady Londonderry, and like them had an instinct
for creating an atmosphere in which people could bring out the best in each other. A
noted beauty, she revelled in the dottiness of Ireland, where such figures as Countess
Markiewicz, Maude Gonne and Lady Gregory had set a precedent for the sort of aristocrat *engagée* that she herself became. Also extremely funny, a gift she expressed through
her own carefully created mask which concealed a natural shyness but allowed her to make
her surrealistic comments from a safe distance.

And no common bull's hide!
For it never tickled,
When she held the strong beast
Tight with either thigh.

Desmond announces he is slimming. Says he can't bear to be a fat *little* man. Patrick is going to Winchester. Nannie draws me aside.
'I always said he was clever.'

25 January, Dublin

Meet Jonah Barrington* for lunch. Talks about Mary Rand, Olympic hurdler, whom we both know. He thinks she is very sexy – rolls herself up like a ball. Claims he has broken four minutes for the mile in training, although he has never competed in the event.

Took a bus home (15 minutes) and heard this old chap behind me talking to a crony.

'That book collector fellow, Scully, is always pestering me about Maud Gonne,† he thinks the sun, moon and stars shone out of her eyeballs. Oh I remember her well enough, attired in widow's weeds for Major MacBride's funeral after his execution in the Rebellion. I suppose she'd forgotten about the ad she'd put in the *Irish Independent* five years before, "To all shops and suppliers whom it may concern, I, the under signed, will not be responsible for the debts incurred by my husband John MacBride."'‡

Much cackling and tee-heeing.
Went to the Plough Bar across the road from the Abbey Theatre. Vincent Dowling, the actor, says he will play in no more adaptations.

---

* He was the first British player to win the World Professional Squash title which he held for five years.
† Maud Gonne MacBride (1865–1953). Revolutionary, famed for her beauty. W.B. Yeats was hopelessly in love with her and wrote much of his best work inspired by this infatuation. As a political activist she was responsible for certain social reforms in the new Irish State. In 1904 she married Major John MacBride who had led a brigade under General Botha in the Boer War. The marriage was dissolved in 1908.
‡ Although not officially a member of the Volunteer Army which occupied the General Post Office in the Rebellion, MacBride had taken part in the fighting there, and perhaps because of his earlier role in the South African war on the Boer side, he was executed along with the leaders.

'That's not what the Abbey is for.'

Later, a schoolteacher friend of the playwright Brendan Behan's,* Jack O'Shea, who was interned with him during the war, tells me one I haven't heard. He was driving across the Border with Behan in 1947. The RUC man on duty was surly. Brendan reacted by dropping to his knees and crawling on the road as if looking for something. When the policeman asked him what he was at, Brendan replied:

'I'm trying to find the shaggin' Border. I thought it would be marked out like a soccer pitch.'

26 January

Out for New Year's dinner to Beatrice Glenavy† at Sandycove. The guests are Michael Campbell (her son),‡ his friend Bill Holden, friends of Beattie, Shelah Richards,§ Norah McGuinness¶ and Monk Gibbon.**

---

* 1923–64. His plays *The Quare Fellow* and *The Hostage* and his autobiography *Borstal Boy* brought him international fame. A brilliant wit and talker, he was a sort of non-drawing-room version of Oscar Wilde. He died in his early forties from alcohol-related illnesses.
† Lady Glenavy (1883–1968), wife of the second Baron Glenavy, Gordon Campbell. Born Beatrice Elvery, she had been a noted painter in her youth, having studied in Paris with Sarah Purser, Estella Solomons and other young Irish girls seeking to escape from the restraints of home. She was the mother of Patrick Campbell, the humorous essayist and television personality and Michael Campbell, the novelist. Beattie was a brilliant talker and in her youth was painted by Orpen who is said to have been her lover. From 1912 to 1920 she was part of a group of London writers and painters which included D.H. Lawrence, Middleton Murry, Katherine Mansfield, Mark Gertler and Dora Carrington.
‡ Novelist and barrister, younger brother of Patrick, whose best known novel is *Lord Dismiss Us* which is based on his days at St Columba's College, Rathfarnham, Dublin.
§ W.B. Yeats's favourite actress in the Abbey Theatre. He wrote *The Death of Cuchulain* especially for her. Married to the playwright Denis Johnston whom she divorced in 1947.
¶ 1903–80; Irish painter and member of the Royal Hibernian Academy. One heard that she was very beautiful when young, but that radiance had not stood the test of time.
**William Monk Gibbon (1896–1992). Poet, memoirist, novelist. Pandit Nehru used to say that *Mount Ida*, Monk Gibbon's account of three chaste love affairs, was his bedside book. He wrote many books in this genre including *The Climate of Love* and *The Brahms Waltz*. His verse is uneven but he wrote some fine poems which merited inclusion in *The Oxford Book of Modern Verse* from which he was excluded by his cousin W.B. Yeats. His advice to me was always valuable, that of a professional man of letters with wide experience of various literary genres. In 1964 he edited for Jonathan Cape my first book, a biography of Oliver St John Gogarty, an experience which provided a fastidious introduction to the precision and accuracy required in the profession of letters.

When I come in Beattie, as usual, is in full flow. Next year is the fifty-fifth anniversary of the 1916 Rebellion and she is going on about how useless it all was. I, of course, settle in soon and flay her in return. Really enjoy it. Here is a woman twice my age who takes me on in argument and what's more I, respecting her wit rather than her age, take her on, no punches pulled. I have just made an EP of the soldier poets of the Rebellion, so I promise to bring it out to her next time, so she can hear what their verse is like. Then Shelah Richards and Norah McGuinness arrive. Shelah sails in giving me rather a cold look. Then to Beattie:

> *Shelah:* 'I am only here because I heard you are dying.'
> *Snort from Beattie:* 'You look sixteen in that dressing gown. Who's with you?'
> *Shelah:* 'Norah McGuinness.'
> *Beattie:* 'Norah is a Belfast bitch.'

Norah hears this as she appears under the wickerwork but Beattie deftly turns it onto Michael and blames him for the remark. Shelah has been listening with attention to me talk for some time like a director watching an actor in rehearsal: 'You know you speak quite nicely. Why don't you speak that way on television instead of the awful Dublin accent you use.' Michael speaks of his aunt Haggie, a legendary Dublin figure. Daughter of a Lord of Appeal, James Campbell, she lived life to the full, manoeuvring where she could to take full advantage of the family title. Michael does her voice very well. 'Made a coup, dear,' she would tell him on the phone and ask him to meet her in Grafton Street with his car. A 'coup' was a visit to Switzers department store where she would buy vast quantities of expensive clothes, wine and food and charge them to her brother's (Gordon, Lord Glenavy's) account. Michael's car was required for the getaway. Later they would settle down for scoff.

Monk Gibbon arrives. He hands what appears to be a painting wrapped in paper to Beattie as a New Year's present. Talk restarts almost immediately and Michael and Bill Holden, his friend, are soon swept up in an argument with Gibbon about the merits of George Moore. In the middle of the spate, Monk turns round to Beattie and says:

'If you like that painting, Beattie, you can keep it. If you don't, my daughter Philly would like to have it.'

Beattie thunderstruck. We then go into dinner, Monk and Michael 'moorizing' at full lick. There is a slight sensation of thunder. The turkey comes and the dinner is bowling along when I ask Beattie does she like the painting Monk has given to her. I hear Michael mutter to himself 'Oh Jesus'. Beattie lets go with a fearful bellow:

'I have never heard of anyone being given a present on the condition that they may give it back to someone who wants it more than they do.'

Monk sits there like Lord Roberts in command of his troops. When the noise subsides he says with perfect calm:

'I have given you, Beattie, a present infinitely more precious than any painting could be, I have left you with a grievance.'

To cool things I ask Michael (who once made a century at St Columba's) the latest cricket score in the test match between England and Australia. But he has either lost interest in cricket or is too stunned to answer. He is working on his next novel but feels that he ought to type it himself, and is worried about giving it away for typing. I hasten to expound my method to him, which is to write, dictate, and then have someone else hammer it out on the machine.

27 January

Lunch at the Waldorf Pub near the Abbey Theatre with Cyril Cusack* and Father Pat Canning who has been exiled from a respectable parish to working-class high-rise flats in Ballymun. Cyril on about a bad notice of *Hadrian VII* in which he plays the lead. Very embittered. He asks me what I think his three best performances are. I say the Covey in *The Plough and the Stars*, Christy Mahon in *The Playboy of the Western World* and the uncle in *The Cherry Orchard*. He says his recent *Playboy* had certain moments – not complete. Early performance in 1945, which I saw when I was a schoolboy, better. Asks me for a solicitor to take on critics. Fr Canning says he has been joined in his tenth-floor flat in Ballymun by a Holy Ghost Father who has been expelled from Biafra. 'We go anywhere.' Canning says the Irish need to go outside and face a crisis before they can love fully. Mentions a sister in Nigeria.

---

* 1910–93; Abbey actor and film star. The actress Sinead Cusack is his daughter.

30 January

No taxis available this evening, so bus to Leixlip Castle for dinner. On the way upstairs on the double-decker, I see R.B. McDowell,* the Trinity History Professor down below, sitting all muffled up in his scarf with hat low down on his brow like an Arab in a dust storm. Then to my surprise on the top deck I find the 'Pope' O'Mahony,† the gifted genealogist with a flow of conversation that comes through his bushy white beard like a burst dyke.

The 'Pope' tells me he and McDowell never travel on the same part of the bus for Leixlip affairs, but won't say why. The reason is, I believe, they are both conversational prima donnas and are building up to unleash a tidal wave of eloquence when they will get in among the guests and seek out listeners. A confrontation with each other on the bus might blunt their style. As we go up the drive one walks on either side of me, but they don't talk to each other, only vicariously through me. Once in they will find their particular circle and begin, as Mariga flits butterfly-like from group to group, watching, out of the corner of her eye, the 'Pope' and McDowell with glee. She has 'discovered' both for Leixlip and its Georgeenians.

---

* Robert Brendan McDowell. It was typical of Mariga that she should have 'discovered' R.B. For decades of Trinity students he had been a college character, whizzing, with his gown flying behind him, around Front Square, his piercing voice extrapolating on whatever subject came to mind. Like puppets on a string, groups would follow him, mesmerized by the sheer power of his conversational thrust.

† Eoin O'Mahony (1904–70), barrister at law, Knight of Malta, genealogist and man about town. Known as the 'Pope' because at school he once claimed that this is what he would be. John Ryan, artist, author and owner of The Bailey Restaurant, once described him as 'a strolling aristocrat manqué from the courts of the Stuarts'. Without a cause to pursue, life would have had little meaning for the 'Pope'. Political prisoners of all kinds were his speciality, Irish, Breton, Spanish. He conducted his campaigns from the Graduates' Room in Trinity College (he was a Triple Gold Medallist there and Auditor of the Historical Society) with the gas fire full on, even in summer and, if it was wet, the steam coming off his clothes. A constant stream of letters poured out daily from here addressed to Foreign Offices throughout Europe, with the return address on the heading of the notepaper, the Men's Hairdressing Saloon at the Gresham Hotel. Undeterred by the problems of a dwindling private income, if he wished to travel the countryside he would simply stop a car at random on the road to take him where he wanted to go. To resolve the problem of bed and board he would arrive at night on the doorstep of sympathetic admirers and ask for a bed. A walking newspaper of gossip, and a skilled genealogist who could fill in gaps in any family pedigree, he would usually be asked to dine as well. When someone once pointed out to the poet Patrick Kavanagh that the 'Pope

On the way to train on the College Park* grass track, meet Brendan
Kennelly† who lectures here. Walk to his rooms. Asks me do I consider vulnerability. I say the artist is necessarily vulnerable, it's no big
deal for him, it helps to set off 'savage indignation' which the great
Dean himself used as a spur. Brendan says that's why he talks about
the defences he must build up against the Trinity establishment. I say
the defences should be to protect his art, not his job, which I think is
more likely what Brendan, a bit of a Kerry trimmer, is thinking of.
He tells me *The Penguin Book of Irish Verse* edited by him is coming
out, very large pre-publication sales. A translation of mine is included.

With my barrister's bag in which I carry training togs, track-suit,
running shoes etc, I head for the pavilion which rises, like the loggia
of a doge's palace, from the playing fields.

Presently emerge onto a magnificent green sward. Huge elm trees
curtain off the busy street from one of the finest cricket creases in the
world. To the right the green carpet extends till it stops at Woodward
and Deane's Venetian Gothic Museum Building, described by
Ruskin, who hired its architect to build his Oxford museum, as the
finest in the Kingdom. As I jog around to warm up it occurs to me
that I might as well be in some eighteenth-century country estate, for
all the effect the busy city outside is having on me. Trees seal the
silence. The only sound is the cooing of pigeons, and maybe I will
hear a robin or two in this early spring. Now I have done my warm-
up I have stretching to do. Then ten short sprints in quick succession,
which is the new approach to building stamina and which suits me as
I hate endless laps with your lungs pumping like a hydraulic engine.
Oh damn. Here's Fitzgerald the college groundsman coming out to

---

had to sing for his supper', Kavanagh, who resented anyone monopolizing the conversation, perpetrated a classic Irish bull: 'He would eat a damn sight better if he kept his
mouth shut.'

Alas, his type of talk is an ephemeral art, the full effect of which cannot be captured
on the page: the nearest anyone has ever come to catching a whiff of how the 'Pope'
talked is the above-mentioned John Ryan, who wrote down a conversation he had with
the 'Pope' during a train journey, reproduced in Appendix 1.

* A large green belt inside Trinity College Dublin, which contains the cricket, soccer,
athletics and rugby pitches. The University (founded by Queen Elizabeth in the sixteenth
century) is right in the centre of the city.

† Poet and academic. Became Dean of the Faculty of English, TCD in 1985. Author of
twelve volumes of poetry.

inspect his beloved wicket which he tends during the harsh winters like a mother her baby. I shall have to do my wind sprints on the rugby pitch on the other side of the footpath. As I crouch for the start the seagulls are shrieking overhead, a sign that the mackerel are in the bay. I can just glimpse the Dublin mountains edging through the Georgian skyline, the ones to which the Trinity dons, at the turn of the century, used to set out after Sunday Lunch, to clear the fug from their over-worked brains and be back in time for six o'clock Commons. Sprints done, my body is shrived and I go into the pavilion for that most perfect of balms, the hot shower peppering the body with its little stabs and that special drowsy feeling as the warmth rushes through the limbs. This is the reward that nature gives us for fulfilling her demands, which I've read recently is scientifically explained by the fact that little shots of morphine (endorphins) are released into the body after exer-cise.

A fair-haired head sticks its way through the steam from the corri-dor outside. It is my pal Trevor West,[*] to tell me to hurry up or I'll miss the match. But wait a second. Christ. What does he mean I'll be late for the match? He's been waiting on the squash-court for me for half an hour, that's what he means. Oh God. Out of the shower like a greyhound from a trap, towel myself in the dressing-room with more vigour than is necessary, partly as a protective against the bollocking that I feel I deserve, and partly to work off my personal fury at having forgotten where I should be. At last I'm on court.

'No toss. You serve.'

4 February

Meet Denis Johnston[†] in St Stephen's Green. Thanked me for recent letter in the papers. I remarked it was deliberately short. He said the shortest letter ever was from W.B. Yeats to Shelah Richards, Denis's

---

[*] Trevor West, FTCD, Professor of Mathematics, one of the youngest Fellows ever, rep-resented Trinity in the Senate (Irish Upper House) for twelve years. He is in the tradition of all-rounder Trinity dons, athletes as well as intellects, such as Mahaffy, Macran, Traill and Leland Lyons. Author of the definitive biography of Sir Horace Plunkett, who played a leading role in the emergence of the new Ireland before the creation of the Irish Free State in 1922. In encouraging Trevor to complete this important work I wondered some-times if by doing so I had hindered his progress in a mathematical school which included Sir William Rowan Hamilton, J.L. Synge and Ernest Walton amongst its teachers.

[†] 1901–84. Johnston was primarily a playwright, but he had been a multitude of other things: lawyer, actor, play director, war correspondent, teacher, scholar, and literary critic.

wife. Yeats, thinking she was getting too thin, is supposed to have written:

> Dear Shelah
>
> Fatten.
>
> Yours sincerely,
>
> W.B. Yeats

Denis persuaded her to write back:

> Dear WB
>
> Button.
>
> Yours sincerely,
>
> Shelah Richards

16 February, London

Jonah Barrington at Lansdowne Club. Of course, murdered me on the squash-court. Rested in Park Lane Hotel. Then to dinner with Desmond Gorges, public relations man with the O'Brien Agency, who will be handling the publicity for my Brendan Behan biography. He tells me his ancestors owned the state of Massachusetts. One of them was related to Anne Boleyn. Desmond also has an Irish connection. His aunt (a Flanagan) was married to W.T. Cosgrave, the first President of the Irish Free State. The White Anglo-Saxon Protestant strain of his ancestor Admiral Gorges, whom he claims as one of the founders of the English navy, mixes merrily with the anarchic Flanagan genes.

18 February

Evening, John Lawrence, Arts Editor of *The Times*. John as usual his own loveable self. Gavin his son has given up sprinting to go to art

---

Educated at St Andrew's in Stephen's Green, Merchiston in Edinburgh, and Cambridge. His plays include *The Moon in the Yellow River*, *A Bride for the Unicorn* and *The Old Lady Says 'No'*. The last-mentioned is one of the first Expressionist plays in English and helped to establish the reputation of the Dublin Gate Theatre in the Thirties.

lectures at the Tate. Over the years I have been trying to find out who the other people are besides myself who write as 'Our Special Correspondent' in the various arts columns of the *The Times*. I have ascertained that Lindsay Anderson and Ken Loach write anonymously on films and Roy Strong on painting. There are still others I want to tease out but John won't budge.* With his bald head he looks very much older than he is. In fact, he is under fifty and flew with Bomber Command during the War. An unusually mild man, he nonetheless is apt to suddenly bring his fists down with a crash on the table and declare in ferocious tones: 'Bomber Harris was right.'

19 February

Lunch today at La Popotte, laid on by Desmond Gorges. Princess Anne and Andrew Lyttelton there. Also Liz Anson. Princess Anne says she has relatives in Antrim. The McDonnells. Likes Dublin better than Belfast. Her current reading includes *The Godfather* by Mario Puzo. Witty. Liz Anson has just written a piece about the anti-bloodsports organization which has protested against the shooting of pigeons which the farmers describe as vermin. Anne suggests they should change the name of the well-known dish to 'Vermin Pie'. The Princess gives the impression she knows that people assume that as a royal she isn't all that bright but in fact seems on the ball but too decent to push it.

Desmond Gorges regales us afterwards with stories about his 'Uncle Willie', W.T. Cosgrave, President of the Irish Free State after being condemned to death in the 1916 Rising as Vice-Commandant of the South Dublin Union. He married the immensely rich but somewhat plain daughter of a Dublin rancher and market gardener, Miss Louie Flanagan. Desmond spent much of his early boyhood in the embattled house of President Cosgrave which was constantly under threat from post civil war opponents. Des talks a lot about his Aunt Louie swinging her rosary and the fact that his Uncle Willie went to three masses every day to make up for polishing off a number of his best friends during the civil war. Des maintains he was often shanghaied from his bed at 7.00 am to serve first mass in Cosgrave's private chapel. As he knelt at the foot of the altar he would see the black sheep of the

---

* *The Times* tradition was that critics were not named.

family, Meehawl (who should have been serving mass), slipping upstairs after a night on the town. Des really has things in hand over here. There is hardly anyone he can't get to and the Establishment revere him. He even has the editor of the *Evening News* in his pocket. Once Des collared a review of a book of mine for the literary pages. When I nagged him to finish the review he said he was very busy and asked me to do him a favour and write the review myself. After I had written it, I handed him the copy. He simply wrote at the end of it 'the best book I've read in a decade' and handed it in to the *Evening News* editor.

23 February, Dublin

Lunch with Mariga at 50 Mountjoy Square. Some years ago, she and Desmond formed a trust to buy seven Georgian houses in this great eighteenth-century square which were about to be demolished. Mountjoy is the finest of Dublin's Georgian squares, but because it is on the north side of the river has become run-down. Developers moved in and it was with them that M and D negotiated the deal that saved some of the houses. The deal, however, didn't save the ones on either side of No. 50 from being demolished and leaving it on its own like a lone tooth in a gaping jaw. Mariga has just obtained a court order requiring that supports be erected on either side of the house. Now she is ensconced like her ancestor King Ludwig in her own castle surrounded by the wreckage of her enemies.

Paddy Rossmore also there, an ascetic earl with whom I play squash at the Kildare Street Club. Has the look of a fine-boned medieval monk. I think Paddy reads a lot but his range is restricted and when Mariga and I discuss the clever adaptation of Baron Corvo's marvellous *Hadrian VII* at the Abbey last night with Cyril Cusack in the lead, it turns out that he has not heard of book or play. Mariga's present concern is about Frascati, 'the temple by the sea' about seven miles from here in Blackrock which was the home of Lord Edward Fitzgerald and his wife Pamela (daughter of the Pompadour). It is in good nick at present, but the news is that the developers are in full cry. Mariga announces she has received £72,000 to help her preserve No. 50. I remark that it would be a good thing if she were to take steps to preserve herself because I hear she was nearly strangled in this house last week. She pooh-poohs this, but claims she was rescued by circling 'helicopterists' who heard her cry for help. A number of the rooms in No. 50 have a specific cause apportioned to them. One is the Frascati room; then there is the Save the Bianconi House room; downstairs there are posters for Maretimo House in Blackrock.

Mariga gets on famously with her tenement neighbours, some of whom live in one room with marble mantelpieces and ceilings by the likes of Michael Stapleton. She believes that they are influenced by the beauty which surrounds them and are not as concerned as one would imagine with installing 'improvements' like central heating and inside lavatories. One rosy-cheeked oul' one whom officials wish to relocate to a council flat has told her 'that central heating would spoil my complexion' and said that 'a council box' wouldn't be able to house all the things that she has found space for in her vast tenement room. Mariga says that when their outside lavatories are out of order she has asked them to come in and use hers, but they just come in to look at it.

When we go out on the street the twilight is coming down and the great towering houses are losing the rose-red colour of their brick and stand against the sky like triumphant galleons. The silhouette of the bare trees in the square adds a slightly Japanese effect. 'You know,' says Mariga, 'I've always wondered if this really is a square. I'll measure it next week and let you know.'

2 March

From the early Sixties I had gone on Sundays to afternoon tea at Monk Gibbon's house Tara Hall at Sandycove, about seven miles from the city, where writers, painters and composers would gather. In the Gibbons' high airy drawing room, Winifred, his wife, would serve up a delicious tea. Monk Gibbon had been very much part of the Irish Literary Renaissance as a young man, and in the Twenties had sat at the feet of his cousin W.B. Yeats, George Russell, James Stephens and others. He seems to have made a bad impression on Yeats and the relationship got to the stage where it became clear that Yeats simply could not stand him. His efforts to use his cousins, Yeats's sisters Lily and Loly, as intermediaries only angered the poet further and Gibbon was left with a lifelong grudge when Yeats awarded him the Silver Medal for poetry at the 1928 Tailltean Games,* reserving first place and Gold for Oliver St John

---

* After the foundation of the Irish Free State in 1922, the Tailltean Games, a pre-Christian festival held at Taillte, Co. Meath under the auspices of the High King of Ireland, were revived to run in tandem with the Olympic Games, continuing until 1932. As well as athletic events, they included competitions in poetry and music.

Gogarty. Also, Yeats included seventeen of Gogarty's poems in his Oxford Book of Modern Verse, *while poor Monk didn't even get one in. It was greatly to Monk's credit that in 1962 he accepted an offer from Jonathan Cape to edit my biography of Oliver St John Gogarty, and did so without a hint of the grievance he must have felt at having once again to take second place to Gogarty.*

Monk Gibbon's at 3.30. The idea is to have a cup of tea and then at four-thirty head off for Beattie Glenavy's house which is on the Bay about five minutes away. When I arrive Monk is in the sitting room. He has been rereading George Moore's* *A Mummer's Wife*,† and is ecstatic at the quality of the prose. As he knows I too am a faithful devotee he wants to share his enthusiasm and has the book at hand to launch his barrage.

'Listen to this for prose,' he says as soon as I've settled myself:

'At the bottom of the valley, right before her eyes, the white gables of Bucknell Rectory, hidden amid masses of trees, glittered now and then in an entangled beam, that flickered between chimneys, across brick banked squares of water, darkened by brick walls. Behind Bucknell were more desolate plains, full of brick, pit and smoke and beyond Bucknell, an endless tide of hills rolled upwards and onwards. Through a drifting veil of smoke, the sloping sides of the hills where all the fields could be seen sleeping under great shadows or basking in the light.'

Monk: 'Now who today evokes a scene like Moore does?'
Me: 'The extraordinary thing is, though the old boy wrote magic prose, he made a pig's ear out of any poems he tried to write.'
Monk: 'I have never read any.'

---

* Though he was acknowledged at the height of his power as the first novelist of his time, by the time he'd died in 1933, George Moore's light had dimmed. Joyce sent a wreath to his funeral, a rare tribute from someone who rarely expressed his debt to others. Moore once plaintively complained that he had written the first modern short stories in English, *The Untilled Field* (1903), and anticipated James Joyce's autobiographical novel, as well as providing a blueprint for Joyce's *Ulysses* with his account of life in Dublin, *Hail and Farewell* (1911–14).
† Published in 1885, this is the first naturalistic novel in English. Moore introduced Emile Zola's new approach to English readers. He described himself as a 'ricochet from Zola'.

Me: 'Yes, his only book of poetry, *Pagan Poems*, should be called *Pagan Pains*. He has lines in it like "Beyond the weak-hours' hopeless horoscope", "Fair were the dreadful days of old". But old George knew his limitations and gave up the verse to hammer out a prose style good enough to have influenced Joyce.'
Monk: 'When I met Moore in London, in Ebury Street, he talked with bright-eyed attention, like a child, and convinced me that the living moment is literature if we can find the means to transfer it to the page.'
Me: 'Well, he found a disciple. Your best work is about the living moment.'

Pleased, Monk snaps his book shut with a squeak. We rush out into the sun-filled street, turn right at Martello Lane at the end of which, on the right-hand side, is Beattie's house. When we come in, she's sitting with her coterie, which includes Shelah Richards and Eileen Ganly. Monk pauses in the door for a second and says across the floor to Beattie:

Monk: 'Beattie, how are your feet, I hear they're paining you?'
Beattie: 'Winifred has been telling tales.'
Monk: 'Already, you've fired a shot across my bows.'
Beattie: 'A gentleman never shows his sores.'

I have brought over the recently-recorded EP record as promised on which I recite poems by Patrick Pearse, Joseph Plunkett, Thomas MacDonagh, soldier poets and leaders of the 1916 Rising. When Shelah Richards asks if I would play the record now as she has to leave soon, Beattie says, rather ungraciously I think, 'The gramophone is under the wireless.' I can see her girding her loins as we turn over the disk for the second half.

Beattie: 'The way you recite poetry makes it seems dreadfully melancholy, you go down on each chord. Perhaps it's all that blood sacrifice nonsense you want to emphasize.'
Shelah: 'Don't be silly, Beattie, it's to bring up the rhythm.'
Beattie: 'As for Patrick Pearse, he would never look you straight in the eye.'
Me: 'Beattie, the poor guy had a squint.'
Monk (to calm things down): 'Talking of the 1916 Rebellion, I've

only just found out that Roger Casement* was born in the house
next-door to me.'
Beattie: 'That traitor. I turn my head away every time I pass it.
His brother was completely different – Tom. He used to say to
me in the Arts Club:† "I could trust Roddie with any woman I
introduced him to, but my dear, I like you even better than
Roddie." Which at one time or another, he used to say to every
woman under forty in the club.'

20 March

Lunch today with Micheál MacLiammóir.‡ He does a superb imita-
tion of Noël Coward in the film *In Which We Serve*, standing on the
prow of the ship as it slowly sinks.

M. is really awfully witty. Very much in the class of his hero Oscar
Wilde. As we were sitting in the restaurant Patrick Perrott, the set
designer, passed with a new partner who is Jewish. After a few slightly
condescending remarks from Perrott delivered in an imperious voice,
the pair passed on. Micheál murmured through almost closed lips,
marvellous roguish eyes sparkling with fun, 'Good God, look at the
pair of them. Pomp and circumcision.'

---

* Sir Roger Casement (1864–1916), knighted for humanitarian achievements in the
Belgian Congo and the Amazon. He was in Berlin in 1916 attempting to organize
German support for a proposed rising in Ireland. Believing that the Rising as planned was
futile, he returned to Ireland by submarine that week to try and stop it and avoid loss of
life. He was arrested on the Kerry coast, taken to London, convicted of treason and exe-
cuted on 23 May 1916. Like the other leaders of the Rising he would become an icon of
Irish Nationalism. Roger Casement was homosexual, a fact which was used by the British
Government at the time of his trial to try and smear his reputation in the United States.
† Tom Casement, brother of Roger, lived in the Dublin Arts Club, of which Beattie had
been President. A gentle easy-going man who sold life-saving equipment after he left the
Civil Service, he'd been an officer in the Merchant Navy and British Consul in
Portuguese East Africa, as well as fighting in the South African War and the First World
War. He had plenty of ability but was fond of the hard stuff. He attended international
rugby matches wearing his pyjamas under his clothes to keep him warm and to avoid
having to carry luggage.
‡ 1899–1978; founder with Hilton Edwards and Lord Longford of the Dublin Gate
Theatre. Actor, writer, director, playwright and linguist (spoke in all six languages including Gaelic and Swedish). Remembered best as an actor for Iago to Orson Welles' Othello
in the film, for his Brack opposite Peggy Ashcroft in *Hedda Gabler* and his one-man show
on Oscar Wilde, arguably the finest of its genre of the twentieth century.

He followed this up with an intriguing piece of information about show business argot. In the Edwardian theatre uncircumcized males were referred to as having 'coliseum curtains'. When we talked of Behan's sexuality, Micheál summed the matter up. 'Brendan Behan said to me once, "men are great gas but I never lost my heart, I kept that for the ladies."'

Lunching with Micheál gives one an idea of what an hour with Oscar Wilde might have been like. His long rolling sentences mount like waves in to shore, and just when you wonder where they are going, come to a calm and completely satisfactory conclusion. (As Wilde inherited the Irish storyteller tradition (*seanachaide*) from his mum, Lady Wilde, Micheál listened to the storytellers when he was learning Irish in the Aran Islands, and allied to his extraordinary achievements in set design, painting, play-writing and acting, his storytelling gift makes a conversation with him a rare experience.) You can get a year's arts course from Micheál in the space of an hour. He can talk about Gordon Craig's set design ('the first minimalist'), Aubrey Beardsley's black and white drawings ('Beardsley's drawings are a bottomless pit down which no artist should go, and from which I am presently trying to escape'), St Francis of Assisi ('They say I play St Francis as a cissy'), Orson Welles, W.B. Yeats ('my lifeline to heaven'). He speaks four languages perfectly and can break into any one of them at choice, in order to illustrate a point about a poem or song. As a young man he had astonishing good looks and was thought to be a lookalike for John Gilbert, the movie heart throb of the Twenties. He and his partner Hilton Edwards have become part of Dublin life. Their Gate Theatre[*] is a splendid counterpart to the Abbey.

I first met Micheál in 1954 when he sent me a letter inviting me to lunch after I had written a review of a season he had done at the Gate Theatre.[†] He had played during the course of a month Oedipus in *Oedipus Rex* (Yeats's version), the 'King' in Pirandello's *Henry IV* (translated by himself), and Lord Henry Wootton in *The Picture of*

---

[*] Founded in 1932. One of its aims was to bring modern European theatre before Dublin audiences.

[†] 'I hope you will forgive this because it is to say thank you many times for the things you wrote about me in *Dublin Opinion*. They cheered me a great deal. This is no country for any action over the age of 25. Ireland mistrusts maturity in art, she has developed the habit of contributing from afar. It is a candle in the Celtic Twilight (that grim reality).'

Dorian Gray, which, as well as designing sets for, he had adapted for the theatre.

Thus our friendship. We would meet every few weeks for lunch and I could test the subject of my latest enthusiasm against his astounding knowledge of ballet, theatre, paintings and literature. When he first did his one-man show on Oscar Wilde, *The Importance of being Oscar*, at the Gaiety Theatre in September 1960 it was clear that this would be the definitive version. What was particularly significant was the linking script which could have been written by Wilde himself, laced with brilliant asides and epigrammatic wit.

Today, instead of walking across Stephen's Green as we normally do, Micheál had an appointment and we took a cab to his house in Harcourt Terrace. He sat in the front with the driver as he frequently does while I sat in the back. They chatted in the ruminative way that Micheál does. After he paid the driver and got out I got into the front. The driver couldn't wait to make his comments.

'Your man MacLanamar is a genius.'

He looked at me to see how this was going down and then continued:

'But he's one of them maphrodites. He can't help it though. Glandular. God makes them that way.'

Again, a side look to see how I was taking this. Then as he stepped on the accelerator:

'You'd need to watch your jewellery all the same when he's around.'

There are four things here I think which are special to Dublin. First, the classical reference (Hermes and Aphrodite). Second, the compassion, 'God made them that way'. Third, the scientific back-up 'glandular'. Fourth, native Irish caution.

4 May, Lexilip

Spent the night at Leixlip Castle. Came down this morning to breakfast to find Mick Jagger there resplendent in dressing-gown, a book propped in front of him as he eats. It is Oscar Wilde's *Fairy Tales*. Seeks to enrol me as an enthusiast and seems a little disappointed to find I already am. Nothing is quite so overwhelming as a fan in the first flush of discovery, so inventing an excuse that I had forgotten to shave, I grab a plate of bacon and eggs from the side table and flee.

5 May, Dublin

Card from Mariga arrives, posted yesterday.

> Tried to shout that you're not at home on Saturday after
> Desmond, but he had already driven off to the airport accompa-
> nied by Mick Jagger. Such an incongroise [*sic*] pair.
>
>   Love
>   Mariga

6 May

I only heard last night that while I was away Micheál's sister Marjorie
had died. She was married to Anew McMaster the Shakespearean
actor, who toured Ireland for decades with his company. It was he
who took Micheál on board and gave him his first experience of
acting. I was a pet of hers and she always seemed determined to feed
me when I came to the house. They lived in a beautiful villa overlooking the vast sweep of Dublin Bay and its four mile strand at
Sandymount. Marjorie played a vital part in Micheál's life. As his elder
sister she formed his taste in the arts and it was through her that
Micheál first learned about the work of Wilde, Beardsley, Jarry and
Yeats. When he played as a boy actor with Noël Coward and Anew
McMaster in *The Goldfish* directed by Beerbohm Tree, it was little
Marjorie who waited every night at the stage door to bring him home.
He never forgot this in later years and every day at 4 o'clock he would
cross the city to spend an hour or so with her.

I'm sure it was because of Marjorie that I was invited to a spectac-
ular lunch in 1959 which she and Anew McMaster gave for Noël
Coward, Marie Lohr, Christopher Casson, Sybil Thorndike and Lewis
Casson. I was the only 'layman' present and had come straight from the
Law Library in dark suit and cutaway collar – decidedly unbohemian.
It was like being put in a time capsule and shot back into the Edwardian
era as they talked of Henry Irving, Oscar Asche, Elisabeth Bergner,
Beerbohm Tree, and other stars of the Edwardian age. Micheál recalled
how Sarah Bernhardt had given him a kiss when he was ten and after-
wards he hadn't washed his face for a week. Needless to say, in the
company we were in there were numerous impersonations of
Edwardian stars, just like a reunion of past pupils. Many references
to the merits of Edwardian acting. McMaster mimicked Elisabeth

Bergner speaking the ghastly line 'My whole life has been a bunch of violets.' But the voice he faultlessly reproduced in a Viennese accent lent the words the delicacy of a musical phrase.

Apparently, I had made an impact on Noël Coward ('His eyes were out on stalks and we were all watching,' Marjorie said to me the next day). After lunch, he had his chauffeur drive me into town and then asked me to come for a drink in the Shelbourne. It didn't occur to me that we would be going to his suite. He was fidgeting around for about twenty minutes while I discoursed on Theatre, Poetry, Ballet and Wit until, finally unable to contain himself, he asked me which did I like, men or women, and was clearly put out when I expressed a preference for the latter. To smooth things over I started to praise Micheál's achievements. But this only made things worse and led to Noël referring to Micheál as 'that silly old tart with the toupee up at 4 Harcourt Terrace'.* This party was only ten years ago but it drifts through the mind like the twilight I've seen settle over the sea in front of that beautiful marine villa.

18 May

Letter from an Aileen Holland.

> You know, Irish people are not yet self-educated enough to admit their true thoughts and view on anything except the weather and even at that, what is allowed an airing is usually saturated after the first shower. Until our Irish schools can produce independent, creative and critical citizens, people like you will get the knocks for trying to raise the standards and lower the habit of social conventional – 'right-words-at-the-right-time' – kind of rapport. I say, keep being yourself so long as you can stand the hurt, or are you, in fact, all granite?!

22 May

Heard Mariga on the radio today. She's just back from India where she took her Georgeenians. Asked by the interviewer about the hunger in India her reply was that the natives weren't too put out by it. 'They

---

* This was before Micheál's world success with the Oscar Wilde show, after the first night of which I sent Coward a copy of an ecstatic review in *The Times* without feeling it necessary to mention that I had written it myself (at this time *Times* notices were anonymous, 'by our special correspondent').

believe they will be reincarnated in the next world where they will have plenty to eat.' Asked was it not elitist for Georgeenians to have spent such large sums of money viewing Indian palaces, she said: 'I am a Socialist. I believe that no one has the same mind and that we must all pool what everyone is good at.'

27 May

This is a busy week – Trinity Week. Every day from Monday to Friday there is a special event. Yesterday a Trinity Cricket XI played the British Ambassador's Selection in College Park and this evening the Trinity boxing team will take on Guy's Hospital and the week will end with the Regatta at Island Bridge followed by the Trinity Ball in the Dining Hall in Front Square.

Today it's the College Races* where there will be track and field athletics and cycle racing on one of the finest grass tracks in Europe.† It's a morning suit affair which poses a problem as I have to open the Irish Water Colour Association Exhibition at lunchtime in the Molesworth Hall off Dawson Street, only about 100 yards from Trinity, and then have to switch clobber in the men's room so as to be in College Park for the races which commence at 2 pm.

The standard at the exhibition is high and there is an impressive turnout. I open with a sweetener about Nathaniel Hone, Sarah Purser, Walter Osborne, William Orpen and Evie Hone who have all been members of the Association; and then about the current ones who are keeping up the tradition in what tends to be a rather undervalued art form. Egg laid, I split. In the men's room I do my quick change and slip across the street to Trinity in full fig.

Ladies lovely, their new dresses on show, out for the first time in the May sun. National anthem played as President Eamon de Valera arrives. Fifty years ago he would not have been let inside the gate of Trinity, as he was on the run, first from the British and then from his former comrades in the civil war. Now the Provost and Fellows are fussing around him as, though quite blind, he strides vigorously across the park towards the pavilion. It's not all that long since they stopped playing God Save

---

* Up to World War One the College Races had been, from a social point of view, the outstanding outdoor gathering of the season in Ireland. At their height they attracted over 37,000 people over two days.
† Bram Stoker, later of *Dracula* fame, won many events in the 1870s.

the King at the races instead of the Soldiers' Song, though the Tricolour has long replaced the Union Jack at nearby Dublin Castle.

Afterwards, attend a reception given by the Knights of the Campanile, a club similar to Vincent's at Oxford or The Hawks at Cambridge. To be a Knight you have to have your colours (Pink) for rugby, cricket, soccer, boxing or athletics, but being pushy is not regarded as an asset for membership. Two English Knights, whom I remember as noble souls in the Fifties, are there, Paddy Burgess Watson and Barry Brewster. Have to leave at 7 pm to go down to the Trinity gym where the College are taking on Guy's in an annual event. They are short of referees so I am asked to take the job for the heavy-weight bout. This is my first time in this role and I find myself at sea quickly. When one of the boxers goes down, I forget to begin count-ing, but instead set about helping him to his feet, as it has escaped my mind for a second that I am the referee.

29 May

This afternoon in College Park, my selected XI versus Trinity College First XI at football. I have collared Paddy Mulligan, the Chelsea centre half, and Joe Haverty, the former Arsenal left wing, for the side as well as Jonah Barrington, my squash friend. Argument in the pavilion beforehand about my playing on the left wing. Joe Haverty says that that's his position on the Irish team. I argue that he's a professional who can kick just as well with both feet, whereas I can kick only with my left. Grumpily Joe agrees to change wings. In the second half he swerves inside brilliantly so that he can prime his left foot to shoot for goal which he does, dispatching the ball like a torpedo into the back of the net. I note that Jonah just cruises up and down during the match. I ask him if he *is* so fit why didn't he play more on the ball. He admits being cautious; his legs are insured, I hear, for many thousands of pounds.

Back home for a rest and then down to Trinity College at 11.00 pm for the Trinity Ball. As I am talking to a very pretty young girl student in Front Square, I suddenly feel as if I have been hit by a cannon ball on the side of the jaw between my eye and my left ear. Looking up I see that without warning the College heavyweight has slugged me from behind. I put up my hands instinctively preparing for a fight. Someone pulls him away. The lout is shouting that it was his girl I was talking to. She shrieks that she's only met him an hour ago. College proctors in their velvet jockey caps move in. I think it the best of my play to slip off. When I come out into the street in my dinner jacket, I am so hot I decide to walk home instead of getting a taxi. One of my teeth hurts but there is no blood in my mouth so, though my head is singing, I'm not worried. I walk the whole three miles home and before going to bed I take a Veganin for the ache in my tooth.

30 May

Ring my dentist, Colm O'Sullivan, who insists I come into the Dental Hospital to see him. Have to wait when I get there and write a piece of my *Sunday Mirror* column.

Probes my lower tooth and then says: 'Your jaw is broken.'

Up in an ambulance to St Mary's Hospital in the Phoenix Park. On the table for four hours. Wake up the next day with my mouth full of wire. Told no solid food for six weeks.

I was hors de combat for six weeks till the wires came off my jaw. This was barely in time for me to fly to London and prepare for the launch of my biography of Brendan Behan published by Hamish Hamilton.

Only afterwards I learned from people who came in to see me that my face was pumped up like a balloon for a day or two. Christy Brown* couldn't get in, but sent a poem instead. It's in the local tradition, a ballad on a current event.

To Ulick on hearing of his mishap

> The occasion was, as I recall,
> The night of the elegant Trinity Ball
> When some uncouth student with brutish paw
> Presented you with a broken jaw.
> Apparently because he took slight objection
> To your well known predilection
> For seeking out and exposing
> Things we would not be supposing
> Existed in other peoples' lives;
> Fornicating husbands and faithless wives,

---

* 1933–81; writer, poet, painter. He was severely handicapped at birth as a result of cerebral palsy. He learned to write and paint with his left foot as it was the one limb he could control. His best known book is his autobiography *Down All the Days* which was made into an Oscar winning film directed by Jim Sheridan with Daniel Day Lewis playing the part of Christy.

Plump bishops who gobble brandy and swear,
Stout athletic fellows who are really 'quare',
Demure sisters and drunken brothers
Ridden with fixations about fathers and mothers,
And shedding light with pitiless clarity
On those who cash in on Christian charity,
Collecting pennies for the poor
And spending it on some respectable whore.
Dear friend, you tread on sensitive toes
By digging up such secret woes
And plunging headlong into print
With here an innuendo and there a hint
That some people are not what they seem to be
Despite what in their books they dream to be.
Give up your vendetta against taxi cabs,
Middle-class hypocrites and trade union scabs;
Be a nice little journalist with proper manners,
And don't go for people with tong and hammers,
Don't advocate the distribution of french letters
And try to recognize, if not respect, your betters,
Don't dash around with silver tongue in cheek,
Scaring the panties off ladies modest and meek,
And if some brash bawdy blokes are in fact queer –
Well, really, is it either there or here?
Give up making comments contrary and terse –
How about writing some nice Catholic verse?
You may well believe in honesty and liberal law –
But really now, is it worth a broken jaw?

*

*Billy Wicklow** had been a pal since student days. I first met him when he came
to chair a debate at the Literary and Historical Debating Society at University*

---

* William Cecil James Philip John Paul Forward-Howard, 8th Earl of Wicklow, Baron
Clonmore. Succeeded as eighth Earl in 1946. Educated at Eton and Merton College,
Oxford. As Billy Clonmore was a notable figure at Oxford among the 'Brideshead' set.
Served as Captain in North Africa in the Royal Fusiliers 1940–45. After the war resided at
the family seat, Shelton Abbey, in Co. Wicklow and kept a pied-à-terre in Leeson Street,
Dublin. Began publishing as Clonmore and Reynolds and had an enjoyable two decades
circling the city in a seamless stroll, until marriage in the Sixties curtailed his lifestyle.

College Dublin in 1950. Knowing that he had taken Minor Anglican Orders before becoming a Catholic. I had attired myself in the dress of a Protestant dean, complete with wide-brimmed hat, to upbraid him for leaving our church and 'perverting' to Rome. But he joined in the charade, clapped his hands and became a friend. I didn't drink then but he did and the two of us would traipse round the pubs in the working-class areas of the city where he had become well known. 'Hello Earl,' someone was sure to say as we stepped into the wooden-floored pubs where he was looked upon as 'one of our own'.

After the war Dublin had become a culinary paradise (food was still rationed in England) and it became the in thing for many of the Oxford set of 1926–30 to visit Billy in Dublin where he would provide them with lavish scoff. They knew him as 'Cracky' Clonmore, and included the likes of Evelyn Waugh, Harold Acton, John Betjeman, Brian Howard, Christopher Hollis, Martin D'Arcy, Osbert Lancaster, Douglas Woodruff. I was installed as a sort of statutory guest for the splendid dinners he gave for his friends in the Kildare Street Club where he would introduce me as a sort of Gogarty figure biding my time as a barrister in the Law Library before ascending into art.

Billy loved the Law Library chat I would pass on, and the idea of me in a wig and gown taunting judges amused him hugely. His happiest years were just after the war when he had a pied-à-terre in Leeson Street and kept himself in ample funds by selling the occasional Canaletto or Guardi. His attempt to run the family home in Wicklow, Shelton Abbey, as a hotel had been unsuccessful, but his publishing firm, Clonmore and Reynolds, brought in dividends. The Kildare Street Club, with its excellent kitchen and rooms in Sir William Deane gothic, provided an agreeable bolt-hole.

2 July

From Billy (Wicklow) this morning.

> I am sorry to hear of your misadventure but you are now old enough to give up insults and take compliments. I hear you may not be very talkative for a month or so when I will then give Rudge a piece of my mind. Best wishes.
>
> Flogger

'Flogger' is my name for Billy and 'Rudge' his name for me after Dickens's louche character. I have named him 'Flogger' because though he was a peaceful soul, I once saw him, when threatened by a bully, give a wolf-like snarl which frightened the hell out of the lout.

These days meetings are few; Billy has been kidnapped by a middle-aged woman architect who has limited his access to the hard stuff, and has also kept his pals away from him. I have been to an occasional lunch with him in the Royal Irish Yacht Club, Dun Laoghaire, but Billy I think is scared that the new Countess may have had her spies out so now we meet in the nearby Royal Marine Hotel, for afternoon tea. In between the Earl Grey, he usually slips himself a brandy which he downs as quickly as possible, keeping an eye out to make sure the wife is not in the vicinity. The Countess's maiden name was Eleanor Butler and someone in the Kildare Street Club has said, 'Wicklow was looking for a butler and he got one.'

My dilemma these days is whether I should encourage Billy to snore away the rest of his life in a safe sitting room, or induce him to come out on the town to enjoy himself as of old. The Countess does organize his life, so he is less likely to have to do a turn from time to time in a home to give his liver a break. At one time before his marriage the situation had deteriorated so much that I set a Carmelite on him to bring him to heel. Billy has a healthy fear of hell and the monk, well trained in the fire and brimstone tradition, scared the bejasus out of him.

> Between ourselves [Billy wrote to me at the time], you may be interested to hear that to avoid anything like this happening again, I've been on a course, a very stiff one. That is why you have not seen me, but I hope to see you soon. I'm back again at work and shall be in the Central Library in the afternoons. You will find me a changed person. I hope to see you soon. Every good wish.
>
> Billy
>
> P.S. I've given up Whiskey. I'm very sorry for not answering before.

This was a satisfactory result, but there's no guarantee that it will survive his present incarceration. The city (only six miles away) still tugs at him. He has become a 'character', accepted by a citizenry discerning about those upon whom they bestow such recognition. We shall see.

15 July, London

Arrive in London for the launch of the Behan book. Staying at the Savoy. Desmond Gorges from the Toby O'Brien agency is there to meet me. It looks like being a neat campaign. I learn that the BBC's *Twenty-four Hours* is making an hour-long programme on the Dublin launch. Back in Dublin, Nanny and Annie my housekeeper,* who will appear in scenes shot around the house, are nervous about seeing themselves on the TV screen for the first time.

16 July

Great fun on BBC Radio with William Hardcastle. Recite my translation from the Irish of Brendan's poem on Oscar Wilde. Hit it off straight away with W.H.

Just as I am leaving the hotel, I am called to the phone. It is my friend Gerry O'Flaherty in Dublin to say that Beatrice Behan† has a highly snotty letter in today's *Irish Times* about the biography. She objects to it mainly on the grounds that I have devoted two pages to homosexual aspects of Brendan's life. It had become quite clear after I began to write the book that Brendan was bisexual. Being in Borstal for three years he had availed himself of whatever sexual cocktail was available. But as he was primarily heterosexual I had felt his proclivities in relation to the male sex should not be overemphasized. However, it would have been against all my ideas of what a biography should be about to have omitted a mention of this side of his character. I had had impeccable sources, I used them and did not overuse them. This thought eased my conscience as I set out for a meeting with Brian Desmond Hurst, the film director, at his Chelsea mews. He is six foot two and surprisingly has a strong Ulster accent (I did not know he was Irish). His latest film is *The Playboy of the Western World* with Siobhan McKenna which was made in Ireland. He has a hell of a movie record and I'm hoping that he might do something about buying the rights of my biography. When we sit down for a drink, I ask him about the possibility of making connections in the film world. The phone rings and Hurst takes it up:

---

* Anne Bell, who had been my Nanny, and my housekeeper Anne Brady were still in the household. Both of them had arrived before my tenth birthday, Nanny when I was five.
† See 17 July, note.

'Yes, that sounds all right. As long as his cock is as big as you say.'
Puts down the phone.

'That's my procurer from the Household Cavalry. He sends them along in batches.'

What is all this in aid of? I change the subject and ask him about the filming of *The Playboy*. Says Gary Raymond, who plays Christy Mahon, is supposed to have gypsy blood. Actually Raymond is appalling in the part. Hurst wants to give me lunch but I am allergic to onions and cream and feel it would be too much trouble to ask for 'a Ulick special'. However, he has a chef in his kitchen who omits both from the sauce and a delicious meal is served.

When I get back to the Savoy I call Derek Jameson of the *Sunday Mirror* who have bought the serialization rights to the Behan biography. Derek says he will call back in half an hour. When he does so, there are firm instructions. I'm to get out of the hotel immediately and go back to Dublin and not to answer any questions from the other newspapers. Beatrice's letter will be in tomorrow's English papers. He has spoken to Irene Joseph, my agent, and she has agreed that I won't give any interviews until the book is published.

17 July

Papers are still buzzing. I dictate a letter to the papers in reply to Beatrice.

Meet Frank Norman, another successful convict playwright, in La Popotte restaurant. He is reviewing the Behan biography in the *Sunday Times*. He is a bit sniffy about Stephen and Kathleen Behan* in his conversation. Resents Dominic. I find Norman a bit hard. No working-class friendliness. Also repetitive. Perhaps he has drink taken.

---

* Parents of the playwright Brendan Behan (1923–64). Stephen was a master house painter. Kathleen was a sister of the poet Peadar Kearney, who wrote the Irish national anthem; she was a woman of exceptional ability and was often referred to as 'the Mother of all the Behans'. Brendan had five brothers: Rory and Sean, half-brothers from a previous marriage of Kathleen's; Seamus (who worked in the printing trade in England and served in the RAF during World War Two), Dominic (author, composer and broadcaster) and Brian (playwright and author); and one sister, Carmel. In 1955 he married Beatrice, née ffrench-Salkeld, the daughter of a distinguished painter and herself an artist.

Brendan wasn't all that keen on Dominic taking up writing. When he heard that Brian was also at the job, he was furious. 'Does he think that geniuses come in litters?' he snarled to his mother.

Tells me he attended Brendan's funeral with Joan Littlewood. Says the set of his play *Fings Ain't What They Used To Be* was later used in Behan's *The Hostage* slightly adapted by the designer. I'm leaving pronto this afternoon. At the airport, although the biography should-n't yet be on sale, I thought I'd have a look on the ever-watchful W.H. Smith bookshelves. There is Brendan's face looking down at me in the midst of a huge display. I quickly buy a copy and flick through. It occurs to me that Dominic, Brendan's brother, who lives in West Sussex, might not have read it and he may think from all the press goings-on that I've written a pornographic work on his brother. Now that I have the book in my hand it seems essential somehow to get it into Dominic's possession. I go out to the taxi rank and ask a cabman would he take a parcel to Crawley. He charges me £20 but takes the package containing the book and a brief note to Dominic from myself.

18 July, Dublin

Back in Dublin. Holy murder has broken loose. Phone is going ding dong. I'm accused of having crucified Brendan. Of course practically nobody has read the book yet. I don't know what is going to happen tomorrow when the Sunday papers appear.

A nun called Sister Dunne rings. She knew Beatrice well. Says she will talk to her on my behalf. Apropos of what I am not sure. She adds that her father taught James Joyce at school in Belvedere, and that as a teenager Joyce used to be found kneeling in the college chapel with his arms stretched out before the Blessed Sacrament. Whew! John Ryan, patron of the Bailey, writer and artist, one of Behan's closest friends, rings to give sound advice. I go in to meet him and have a drink in the Bailey. He says 'Keep mum and let the storm break.' Tells me a marvellous anecdote about Brendan's father-in-law, Cecil Salkeld, which I wish I had known before the book came out. Salkeld is an artist of exceptional talent and a man of letters. He made a decision, however, in 1956 to go to bed and hasn't got up since. Beatrice's sister Celia and her mother Florrie daily cater to the 'invalid's' needs. When John went to visit him recently he was delighted to find a live canary perched on Salkeld's bald head. It had obviously acquired the status of a familiar, for when Salkeld turned his face to Ryan the canary shifted itself and dug in its little claws to readjust its stance.

The BBC were on this evening trying to put words into my mouth about Dominic. Sunday papers' news sour enough. But there is a windfall from the *Sunday Times*. In Alan Brien's 'People' column he describes how he had talked to Dominic.

First reactions from the Behans were unpromising. Brendan's brother, Dominic, for example:

'O'Connor got me on the telephone while he was writing the book and Brendan's supposed homosexuality was one of the questions he apparently wanted answered. From the time he was a child I slept with Brendan, I went to Paris with Brendan, no one was closer to him than me and I've never heard anyone suggest he was a homosexual.'

Mr Behan added that if he went to the party on Thursday it would only be 'to take Mr O'Connor by the scruff of the neck and sock him half way round London.' Understandably, the prospect of a confrontation between Mr O'Connor and the Behans has worried Mr Desmond Patrick Michael Gorges, a publicist of the O'Brien Organization which is organizing Thursday's party.

'I'm fighting the issue,' Mr Gorges said gloomily. 'I don't want these people here at all, but I presume we're going to get them. Ulick said to me yesterday he had all their addresses and was going ahead with it. I tried to talk to him at the Savoy where he was having lunch with the lady PRO and someone from the newspapers. I heard a voice in the background say 'Tell *him* I'll ring him back.'

'Well, I'm going to go to Fortnum and Mason's for my booze for the weekend and — Ulick.'

'As for the party,' says Mr Gorges, 'with the Irish Ambassador and half the Guinness tribe there, well, it'll be the wars of Limerick, that's all I can say.'

And then it came to pass, as temperatures rose, that a special messenger delivered a copy of Mr O'Connor's book to Dominic Behan's home. 'I've been up all night reading it,' Mr Behan said, contritely. 'Speaking for myself personally I think it's a good book, highly objective.'

So Thursday may be a mellow one for the Irish in London after all. For, as Mr O'Connor himself said last week: 'The Behan family are highly civilized people.'

19 July

Letter from Mariga in Holland where she is taking the Georgeenians on a tour of stately houses.

Dear Ulick,

Rushing round rainy Holland in a bus full of grumbling Georgians, the only cheerful soul being Kevin Nowlan.* Still, we have seen some marvellous things, and listened to the difficulties of cleaning inner moats, outer ones being easier. Our hosts are all still in the Williamite wars, and always say where their mothers and wives were born. Their homes are embellished with the money made by selling the Irish estates William gave them.

Then I go to my Fabian fishing huts in Norway. Would you like to go there too? The address is:

AADNEST OE
    VESTRE SLIDRE
        VALDRES.

One can telegraph to Vestre Slidre. An aeroplane is the quickest way of going to Oslo; from which there are now 2 trains, at least, to FAGERNES. From here (the train comes to an end) you could be rescued by me, or go by bus, milk lorry or even taxi. Do think of it, I shall be there all August.

Love
Mariga

I have had similar invitations from Mariga, but I haven't yet had the nerve to accept one. So far the journey sounds horrific for someone as reluctant as I am to rough it. Then the conditions are spartan in the 'Fabian fishing huts', left to her by her grandmother. No electricity, baths or inside lavatories. Shivers run up my spine. Earth lavatories terrify me and I am ill at ease without the facilities of modern life even

---

* Professor of Irish History at University College Dublin. A true Dubliner (a Belvederian) with a highly sharpened critical faculty long lost among many at his university. A real contributor to Irish life.

if occasionally I don't resort to them as often as I might. Yet I know
Mariga. The inside of the 'huts', under her management, even
without flush lavatories and heating, could well be made as comfortable as a Leixlip drawing room.

20 July

BBC at Fairfield Park today filming for the *Twenty-four Hours* programme, a special on the Behan biography. They know about Nanny
and are keen to meet her but she is not all that impressed. Thinks there
is too much attention being paid to me. 'Why are you always getting
your name up?' Annie serves tea and sandwiches to the presenter and
crew. They consult her as to what furniture can be moved. She shows
them how to open the doors between the dining room and the
drawing room. Both rooms have tall windows and high ceilings and
with the doors open, the light streams in, and the camera men smile.

As make-up worked on me, looking upwards towards the cornices,
I wondered how a hundred years ago the owners of the house would
have coped with the prospect of the interior of their room being
viewed by millions. The marble mantelpieces in the rooms, the
fireplaces in the bedrooms, the Pre-Raphaelite stained-glass in the hall
door were part of a Victorian Dublin whose inhabitants would not
have looked kindly on the idea of the world outside having a peep at
their blessed plot.

21 July, Leixlip

Tonight beside Nancy Mitford for dinner. She is presently having
radium treatment for an illness. Says it slows her up. That slight flush
which implies all is not well. The blue Mitford eyes however glow like
vestal fires. I think she is on painkillers though very sweetly she makes
an effort to perk up at things I say. Tell her I can never quite make out
what was the precise nature of the controversy about U and non-U
words in *Noblesse Oblige*. When I was growing up in Dublin many U
words were still in common use among middle- and even working-
class people, *lavatory, napkin, looking-glass, writing-paper*, while their
non-U equivalents, *toilet, serviette, mirror* and *note-paper* were looked on
as smart-alec. She says that the whole thing was a result of an article
for *Encounter*, was not meant to be scientific, and anyway has been
blown up out of all proportion.

Nancy is a devoted Mariga fan and when our hostess is out of the room has a story to tell. Apparently the last time she was here an American family, husband, wife and daughter, had knocked at the door of the Castle while Nancy and Mariga were standing at a window upstairs looking down. (Nancy does the American accent very well.)

Mariga: 'You are the friends of Mr Henry McIlhenny?'
Americans: 'Oh no, we're not his friends.'
Nancy: 'If not, then his enemies?'
Americans (nervously): 'Oh, of course not, we're sure he's ter-rific.'
Mariga (looking down the drive): 'Here comes your enemy, Mr McIlhenny.'
Americans: 'We are not his enemies, we're sure he's a lovely person.'
Mariga: 'May I introduce Mr McIlhenny? – Mr & Mrs Olivera.'
Americans: 'The name's O'Leary.'

Nancy adores the huge wood fires in her room, set by Mariga. Later in the drawing room under the huge marble mantelpiece another fire roars. Mariga's speciality. A large cat is outside the window trying to get in. 'Is it Lord Holmpatrick or Thomas Pakenham,' I ask, knowing Mariga's habit of naming cats after her friends. As she rushes to open the window she gasps, 'No, it's Mrs Beelzebub' and the cat shoots in. This is a reference to a friend of Desmond's whose name is Mrs Bielenberg, but which is mispronounced by the Guinness daughter aged six.

22 July, London

Meet Geoffrey Wheatcroft, PR from Hamish Hamilton. Seems a little wooden. But someone has got the terrific publicity the book has had and I have to assume that it is him. He runs through a list of papers and radio stations and then I ask him if he has anything to do with the *Twenty-four Hours* programme. He says he knows someone in the BBC who fixed it for him. Top marks. There is a launching party tomorrow at Brown's Hotel. Kathleen Behan is coming over for it. Also Seamus, Brendan's brother who lives in England, will be there.

Brendan's sister Carmel too.

23 July

Geoffrey has very kindly met Kathleen Behan at the airport. I went to see her at her hotel and the first thing she did was to give me an enormous kiss. I had been worried that all the fuss in the papers might have disappointed her. 'Aren't we all human' was the first comment of this splendid octogenarian. She is fond of me and calls me her seventh son.

5.30 pm the large room of Brown's Hotel is packed. Suddenly it appears to me that Brendan has risen from the grave and actually appeared in the crowd. Then I realize that it is his brother Seamus (whom I have never met before) who is a dead ringer for Brendan. Seamus is somewhat the black sheep of the family because he emigrated to England during the war and joined the RAF. The patriotic Behans including their father Stephen and mother Kathleen were not too pleased at this. But Seamus ploughed his own furrow and has made a very good living in England working as a printer. He comes up to me now with a grin, his very white teeth showing.

'You did it, warts an' all as Oliver Cromwell said to Sir Peter Lely when he was doing his portrait.'

Only a Behan could have used the hated Cromwell's name to another Irishman to make a positive point. Later Kathleen, at my request, sang a favourite song of Brendan's. She had put it together herself, taking a verse from Charles Kingsley beginning 'When all the world is young, lad' and placing it side by side with Housman's 'With rue my heart is laden.' I don't know where the blazes she got the tune from but it works like a dream.

1 August, Dublin

Card from Desmond Guinness.

> Can you come for a tennis weekend at Castletown (and retrieve
> your spongebag) on August the 5th? Sir Alfred* is coming to play
> on the 6th so I hope you'll stay.

---

* Sir Alfred Beit (1903–94). South African industrialist married to Desmond's cousin Clementine (née Mitford). An art collector internationally renowned for his acquisition of Vermeers, Velázquezes and Rembrandts which, with great generosity, he bequeathed to the Irish nation.

Castletown, the finest of the great Irish Palladian houses, was bought
for the Georgian Society by Desmond (with help from his father) four
years ago. During that time D and M have worked incredibly hard to
put it in shape and with the aid of dedicated volunteers have almost
finished. Meanwhile Desmond uses his second castle for tennis.

3 August

Met Kevin Nowlan in the street today; he has been accompanying the
Irish Georgian Society and Mariga in Holland. When I see him his
eyes light up, I know he's got a good story to tell.

'Great gas in the Netherlands. We visited a castle, just outside
Amsterdam, and were met by the lady of the house who had some
connection with minor Austrian royalty. Wasn't all that pleased to see
us . . .

'"Oh, we rarely have people here."
'I walked in front with her as she showed us around.
'"What is the name of your leader?"
'"Mariga Guinness."
'"Oh! Brewers."

'This was said with a barely disguised sniff. I let her know that
Mariga was Princess von Urach and Württemberg, whom she, as an
Austrian, might know was the grand-niece of the Empress of Austria.
This took her nibs by surprise and she almost went into a sprint to get
back to talk to Mariga. She showed us round every nook and cranny
after that, informing us that the language of the house was French,
thus distancing herself from the coarse vowels of her adopted race.'

6 August, Castletown, Co. Kildare

Turns out it is doubles at Castletown, Alfred Beit and me against
Desmond and Grey Gowrie.* A.B.it (as Desmond calls him) is doing
warm-ups beforehand, swishing his racket in sinister fashion. Clearly
no fooling with our Alf. He plays every stroke as if he'd been thinking about it for five minutes beforehand and when the ball goes into
the net – a not infrequent occurrence – you may hear a faint Afrikaans
squeak, but the face remains immobile. Silent as the tomb during play.

---

* Lord Gowrie, Irish peer, later Chairman of the Arts Council of England.

Even when one congratulates him on the occasions the ball does get over the net, there's no response. When I played with him before I found his silence irritating, with the result that now I shut up as well, which adds to the eeriness of the occasion, the only sound to be heard being Desmond's voice giving instructions to Grey Gowrie.

Changing shoes and tying my laces after the match, I look straight into Sir Alfred's stern blue eye and deliver a polite but formidable rocket. Nonplussed.

21 August, Mountstewart

This is one of the most extraordinary week-ends I have ever spent. I went up on the early train to Belfast to stay at Lord Londonderry's house, Mountstewart.* I am in deep depression over my financial condition. A collapse can come. The only way I can keep mobile is to put every debt out of my mind and replace it by some hopes I have of retrenchment. As well, Flannery† has rung to say while he might direct my Noh plays, it will take four weeks and he thinks that is not possible. I feel too that he needs six weeks to get the performance in proper shape. The best I can hope is that Brendan Smith will announce at the end of the Dublin Theatre Festival that these plays will be scheduled for next year. I rewrite my *Sunday Mirror* piece on the way up for the sixth time. This is my way. By constantly rewriting I hope that ideas will turn into agreeable words.

Monty‡ meets me at the station. He is exactly the same. Cheerful English wife who rides horses. Stop at Newtownards to buy a razor replacement. Girl overwhelms me with 'sirs'. 'Sorry to turn my back on you sir' etc. Mountstewart Georgian domestic with portico added in 1840s. Colonnade. Inside slightly Victorian. Horses on walls. A

---

* Lord Londonderry (Charles Stewart Henry Vane-Temple-Stewart, 1878–1949) was Northern Ireland Minister for Education, 1921–26, Secretary of State for Air, 1931–35, and Leader of the Lords, 1935. He was a pioneer in improving relationships between Nationalist and Unionist communities.

† James Flannery, theatre director and academic. Professor of Drama at Emory University and author of *Yeats and the Theatre*.

‡ Harford Montgomery Hyde (1907–89). Liberal Unionist MP for West Belfast, 1938–72. Barrister, biographer and journalist. Called to the English bar in 1934. Author of many biographies, the most notable of which are those on Edward Carson, Oscar Wilde and the Secret Service chief William Stephenson. As a young man Hyde was Secretary to Lord Londonderry. Afterwards, the Londonderrys were more or less his patrons.

good painting of Hazel Lavery by John Lavery. Sit on balcony watching trippers. For the first time, I feel colonial. Looking down on the natives. Only these are probably Northern Irish Protestants who would regard me as one of the natives because of my religion. At lunch we serve ourselves; devilled kidneys – and rice pudding. After lunch we sit on the balcony. (Meanwhile, I have been shown my room. It is called the Florence Room. Quite plain.) Look at the library. Presentation copies from James Stephens, Yeats, Gogarty to Lady Londonderry. Gogarty inscription strikes me as slightly sycophantic – 'To L.L. who has done more for literature than an host of authors.' A complete set of Yeats poetry. *Gould's Birds* is worth £10,000. An elaborate picture book about the visit of King Edward VII to Mountstewart. The book plate and the portraits upstairs show Lady Londonderry as a stunner. She had a salon in London as well as Mountstewart. Gogarty used to fly himself up for air displays to Newtownards airport which was built by Her Ladyship when her husband was Minister for Air in the British Coalition Government of 1931–35. She gave her inner circle titles. She was Queen of the Ark. Monty was 'Monty the Mole' because he was always burrowing after things. I wish I knew such a person as her; power, influence, intellect and beauty.

We sat out on the balcony and avoided the wasps which were everywhere. One got entangled in my hair. As there was hair spray in it, it was hard to get him out, so he buzzed away for longer than I would have cared with his nasty little sting hovering over my unprotected skull. I showed Monty a catalogue of my literary archives and his feeling was that perhaps I should sell now, as the world was in a dubious state. He says he will write to New York for me.

We join Lady Mairi Bury who is a daughter of Lord Londonderry and talk away for about two hours. There is an interesting man called Basil Kennedy here who looks a mixture between Basil Rathbone and the late Lord Brookeborough. He has a Dublin roll to his voice and seems to know about Dublin in the Forties; set designer Alpho O'Reilly, Gate Theatre actor Patrick Bedford etc. Also Davy Byrne's.* Can do Dublin accents. Actually is the son of a Limerick doctor and a mother of landed background (Stoddard). He listens

---

* Well-known Dublin pub, noted for its conversation. Provides a mise-en-scène in the Lystrygonians episode in Joyce's *Ulysses*.

attentively and later says Arizona where he lives doesn't provide conversation of the kind he hears now between authors. Lady Mairi quite
a good face. Slightly housewife but good eyes. Too much chin.
Doesn't drink now.

Go for swim with Monty. We go out along a beautiful peninsula
marked 'private'. We are on the edge of the sea at Strangford Lough.
The pool area is large, surrounded by granite walls. On the way across
the gardens, Monty explains that it is not easy to open the door of the
pool with a key. He fiddles around in a most mysterious way, very
much 'Monty the Mole'. The door of the swimming pool swings
open to reveal an enchanted garden. There is a curved swimming pool
with sea water which looks emerald. Around are verandas with stone
pillars. Very Greek. There is just enough growth to make it exotic –
yet not enough to let the place seem grotesque. Monty dives in and
swims with quite an impressive trudgeon stroke, up and down twice.
Two young people come in and evidently quite surprised by our presence go out through the other gate. They seem to know the terrain.
One is carrying a lemonade bottle. Monty and I go outside to the
grass path running along the edge of the sea to have a look. There are
some couples there who are a bit embarrassed at seeing us, thinking
we are Lords of the Manor instead of two doctors' sons, one from
Eire.

We walk back to the house for afternoon tea. I break my diet to eat
delicious cucumber sandwiches. Afterwards it is so hot, on impulse I
grab a towel and rush across the garden to the pool. Rather than fiddle
round with the key, decide to climb over the wall. I can hear the sound
of heavy knocking inside as if someone is doing damage. When I get
in, I see two entirely naked boys running out by another gate. I run
out and find one of them putting on his togs in a disused greenhouse.
I tell him this is private property. He says 'Beg your pardon' and goes
away. The irony of the situation is that I am a Taig* and he is from the
siege class. Yet he will kow-tow because I am on siege property and
therefore apparently representative of the system that protects him
(and exploits him too). Inside again, I take off my clothes and plunge
in. I bathe in the sea so seldom I feel a nip of cold despite the hot
weather. I get quite breathless from the cold as I cross the pool and I
think what a bad swimmer I am. Then I move to the sunny part of

---

* Ulster Protestant name for a Catholic. Taig is Irish for Timothy.

the pool and suddenly it is quite warm. Now I am enjoying one of my boyhood fantasies – to swim in salt water which doesn't take my breath away. It is warm, caressing and stimulating.

Monty, who was in the prosecution team in Nuremberg, says the hardest of all to sentence to death for treason after the war was John Amery[*] who had pleaded guilty. He thinks the conviction of William Joyce[†] was a bad legal decision. When a friend of Monty's went to visit Guy Burgess in Moscow, Burgess asked him to bring him curry powder. It wasn't available in the Soviet Union. Monty maintains Lloyd George destroyed the Liberal Party – corruption and coalition.

There are pictures of a Von Keppel on the wall here, an ancestor of Lady Londonderry, who was William of Orange's boyfriend and also an ancestor of Violet Trefusis.[‡] Monty went on to say one of the reasons he lost the West Belfast seat was that he had said King Billy was fond of the boys. He described his initiation into the Freemasons, obligatory then for Orangemen. He said there was a moment which was very frightening and solemn but won't tell me what it is. I find this strange as he later tells me he became an atheist after reading Gibbon when he was a schoolboy and sick for a time.

It turns out Monty knows Russian. Learnt it at Oxford. His book on Stalin I had forgotten about. He never looks at you straight. Closes his eyes as he encounters yours. Talks of 'My cousin Henry James'. I told him how the broadcaster Prionsias MacAonghusa heard Ken Topping, the Unionist MP, discussing how to do Monty in, in the election in 1952 and told Jack White of the *Irish Times* who wrote a feature on it. Monty says it did help to stop the rot. Basil K. there. His wife was with someone else when he came back from RAF. Flew 41 sorties. Now Monty says he lives in Arizona perhaps because of the presence of a homosexual colony there. Both came to Mountstewart on the day Lady Mairi Bury's daughter Annabel (now Mrs Birley) was born.

---

[*] Son of Leo Amery MP. Leo Amery made the famous speech in the House of Commons which resulted in Winston Churchill replacing Neville Chamberlain as Prime Minister. His son John remained in Germany during the war and was tried and sentenced to death in England in 1946.

[†] Known as 'Lord Haw-Haw'. He broadcast anti-English propaganda from Hamburg during the war. He was later captured and tried for treason; he was hanged in 1946.

[‡] See 5 December 1975, note.

Walk with Monty to graveyard 'Tir na nOg' laid out by Lady L. She was very into the Irish Literary Revival. Yeats and Gogarty wrote her letters. Ramsay MacDonald, Labour Prime Minister and all that he was, actually penned four hundred to Her Ladyship. Her favourite dogs and horses are buried here with appropriate gravestones.

In the morning we went up to the Temple of the Wind on a cliff above the sea. Octagonal with slightly unnecessary classical front. Down below the sea like Nice. The wind a warm breeze. Perhaps the only time in 400 years as warm and dry as this. Monty told me that William Drennan,* Lord Charlemont and Lord Londonderry used to meet here for port before dinner. Dinner was much earlier those days so they met at five. Here radicals (for Drennan was a United Irishman and a poet) met with Unionists, before the system solidified.

Visited the chapel which is very High Church with a crucifix and a Botticelli 'Mother and Child' over the altar. Her Ladyship was High Church, but I gather his nibs wasn't.

Later when I get back to Dublin I look up the manuscript for my book *A Terrible Beauty is Born*† and find that Lord Londonderry is one of the hard-line Unionists, and there will be a picture of him in the book. I must say better looking than the others though.

PS. Before I left, I noted down the servants' guide to the different rooms which was posted up in the kitchens.

Valets 20 calls   Maid 20 calls   Room 30 calls

Names of Rooms on principal rooms indicator:

  1. Her Ladyship's Bedroom
  2. Her Ladyship's Bathroom
  3. His Lordship's Dressing Room

---

* Belfast doctor, a Protestant Nationalist who took part in the 1798 Uprising against England. He was very much a product of the Enlightenment who saw no reason to separate people because of their religious beliefs.

† Published in 1975 by Hamish Hamilton and in America by Bobbs-Merrill. Its subtitle was 'Ireland 1912–1922'. It was well received and has since had seven reprints and is still in print, republished by Abacus under the title *The Troubles*. The book starts with the passing of the Home Rule Act in the House of Commons in 1912 and ends with the evacuation of the British administration in January 1922.

4. His Lordship's Bathroom
5. Billiard Room
6. Entrance
7. Dining Room
8. His Lordship's Study
9. Breakfast Room
10. Her Ladyship's Sitting Room
11. Drawing Room
12. Salon
13. Card Room
14. Lady's Maid's Bedroom
15. Captain Stopford's Bedroom
16. Butler's Bedroom
17. Ypres Bathroom
18. Cologne Bathroom
19. Moscow Bathroom
20. Leghorn Bathroom
21. Rome Bathroom
22. Versailles Bathroom
23. Paris Bathroom
24. Palermo Bathroom
25. Capt. Stopford's Bathroom
26. Visiting Maid's Bathroom
27.
28. Office
29.
30.

Guest Rooms

Calais	Paris
Lyons	Versailles
Winneux	Florence
Rome	Naples
Leghorn	Stockholm
Petrograd	Moscow
Sebastopol	Archangel
Amsterdam	Cologne
Plaque	Palermo
St Omer	Ypres

22 August, Dublin

In McDaid's* tonight a lout emerges from Paranoic's Parlour (a corner in the pub for whiskey drinkers only) and as he passes, fixes me with an Ancient Mariner eye:

'When you're livin' within the city walls, then you can write a life of Brendan Behan.'

I was talking at the time to Joey Betts, a dapper little man who sports a geranium in his buttonhole and is by profession a bookie's runner.

'Don't talk to him, Joey,' the man continued, 'you know he writes down what you say and he'll use it in a book?'

Joey looked at him with some contempt:

'Don't be an even bigger eejit than God made you – it's not the writing down that counts' (*pause*), 'it's the assembly.'

The last word was delivered with a snap like the sound of the key-stone of a Gothic arch being slid into place. Unaware that he had just paraphrased both Aristotle and Aquinas, Joey turned to me and said pointing to an unbloomed rose in my buttonhole:

'You know Ulick that's why I like you? You have panache!'

It's rumoured that though Joey Betts can read he's never learned to write which is maybe why he makes such a fine bookie's runner.

29 August

Today who do I meet coming down the steps of the Royal Hibernian Hotel but the ravishingly beautiful Miss X. She and I had gone to Sligo some months ago with Desmond and Mariga, Desmond driving, Mariga in front, and me, Marina and Miss X in the back. We returned after a few days and the day we got back, I finished up having dinner with Miss X in the Hibernian. Next day we were drinking in the lounge when she nipped off to the lavatory. I noticed the awful 'Gurrier' Mackey follow her into the ladies' loo. Later I discovered that he had been dispatched by his lord and master to hand her an air ticket

---

* Pub in Harry Street, off Grafton Street. In the Fifties and Sixties McDaid's succeeded the Bailey and Davy Byrne's (both in nearby Duke Street off Grafton Street) as the pub where artists, writers and revolutionaries met. Patrick Kavanagh, Brendan Behan, the painter Patrick Swift and Brian O'Nolan (Myles na Gopaleen) were among those who used it on a constant basis.

to London. His boss had apparently done one of his lie-down-outside-your-door-all-night stunts to impress Miss X and when this did not have any effect was now offering her a week in London at the Savoy.

Off she skipped and more power to her. Now, a year later, here she is on the Hibernian Hotel steps, albeit that I am on the step below her. I feel I should take the opportunity to remind her of the episode last year which I have not had the chance since to discuss with her.

'My dear, that was a fabulous flit you did last year when we were in the middle of our drink downstairs. You must be the first person ever to have been offered an air ticket in the ladies' lavatory – and by a man too.'

Miss X, understandably rattled by this account, pointed to the person she was with,

'This is Sir John – we're just married.'

By any reckoning a hit, a palpable one. I managed to blurt out, 'Hang in there old chap, just watch the air tickets.'

Sensing tents folded I stole away.

3 September

After running into Seamus Heaney in the Arts Club tonight, I invited him and his wife, Marie, home for a drink. He was impressed that I have plenty of wine, whiskey and gin in the cupboard, though I don't drink myself. Most amiable. I asked him about the teaching career he had embarked on. Would it harm his poetry?

'When I teach creative writing, I give away only my soft side. I keep the dangerous side for writing.'

He is at present teaching at Carysfort College in Blackrock. Thinks highly of Brian Moore's novels. I only like one, *The Lonely Passion of Judith Hearne*.

Talks of the Enlightenment at the end of the eighteenth century. After 1789 it was beginning to take root in Ireland. But he believes it died with the Act of Union which demolished the Irish Parliament and transferred it to Westminster. Peggy Jordan sings *The Rocks of Bawn*. Seamus says this is actually a recruiting song. He gives a vivid description of Leo Rowsome, the Uileann piper, pummelling his instrument to draw from it the precise sound he wanted.

Tonight at 1 am in Micheál MacLiammóir's sitting room at 4 Harcourt
Terrace I am in front of a blazing log fire. Have come to collect a
drawing for a collection of Irish tales* I am putting together for
Granada Publishing. While Micheál is rifling through his paintings
downstairs I chat to Tiger, his current masseur, who is stretched lux-
uriously on the rug in front of the fire. Tiger is in army uniform (he
is an N.C.O. in the Irish Army), and our only previous meeting has
been in the boxing ring in the National Stadium where I fought him
as a welterweight. We are discussing straight lefts and right hooks
when Micheál arrives back carrying a marvellous black and white
etching of a man kneeling down on one knee, defying the challenge
of great rolling waves coming in to engulf him. I daren't comment
that the work has a touch of Aubrey Beardsley, as Micheál is only too
well aware of his debt in that direction, maintaining that if you allow
yourself to be seduced by Beardsley's curves and swerves it is 'like
descending into a deep tunnel from which you will never return'. I
content myself with commenting how wonderful it is, muttering
something about Gustave Doré when the door bursts open and
Hilton† rushes in exhausted and drops into a chair. He had been
casting since midday for *Man of Destiny* by Shaw which is to go on in
the Gate Theatre.

It turns out that Hilton has chosen Patrick Bedford, his current
boyfriend, in the leading role. Bedford, a good-looking young man of
working-class background, had not at that time begun to show the
talent which would win him awards on Broadway ten years later in
Philadelphia Here I Come by Brian Friel. Micheál is clearly not chuffed
with the choice.

'This is preposterous Hilton. The emperor of the French did not
express himself in the accent of the Dublin quays. After all I never
asked you to let Tiger play Lady Macbeth.'

Hearing his own name mentioned, Tiger stretched himself sensu-
ously once more on the rug.

I quickly slip the marvellous drawing in a folder and going downstairs let myself out the front door.

---

* *Irish Tales and Sagas*, Granada, 1981.
† Hilton Edwards (1903–82), actor/director, Micheál MacLiammóir's partner at the Gate
Theatre.

20 September

A ferocious row with Micheál [MacLiammóir] last week. I had made
a few appointments to see him but they all misfired. I don't think his
secretary, Brian Tobin, likes me all that much and I thought maybe he
wasn't giving the messages to Micheál. I had gone down to 4 Harcourt
Tce and had a brief encounter with employees there. I may have raised
my voice a little but not enough to provoke a shenanigan of this kind.

He writes to me, 'In bed', from 4 Harcourt Terrace. He says he can't
go on saying sorry indefinitely. He feels I'm exactly like his dear
Hilton who has a habit of being completely in the right and then
reversing himself in a second, and that he (Micheál) is almost pleased
to find that this tendency is not confined to Hilton who might almost
be my twin brother in the matter. He ribs me about my habit of
attributing certain temperaments to racial origins and slyly implies
that maybe Hilton's Murphy mother, or one of his ancestors, submit-
ting to a handsome Cromwellian soldier, is the reason for the resemblance in our temperaments. Whatever the cause, he is upset at being
shouted at when he isn't well, and all his 'sangre española' comes to
the surface in anger. Only one minute before I appeared in what he
refers to as 'that lovely brown overcoat and that towering bouderie
Navrante', had he remembered our appointment.

He had hoped to talk to me about his latest Hamlet. But he has
rehearsals on the stage at dawn even though he is laid low with Asiatic
influenza, probably brought into the country, he says, by Chinese
dancers at the Gaiety.

'Still your friend if you care that it should be so.'

Ring Micheál and ask him to lunch next week.

22 September

Met Peter Robinson, a stockbroker, in the Hibernian Buttery. Told
me his brother the 'Bomber' Robinson has had a haemorrhage, and is
in Jervis Street Hospital. Cecil Robinson got his nickname the night
the Luftwaffe dropped a landmine on the North Strand killing eighty
people. The sound of the explosion travelled across the bay to
Monkstown where the Robinsons lived. His mother said when she
heard the huge thump 'I'm sure that's Cecil', and from then on he was
known as 'The Bomber'. He had, however, become seriously

addicted to the hard stuff and to cure him the mother sent him on a
trip to Egypt. He was put on the mailboat in nearby Dun Laoghaire
Harbour going to Holyhead and booked into an expensive state room.
Six weeks later he arrived back at Dun Laoghaire in a distinctly fragile
condition. Egypt didn't seem to have agreed with him because not
only was he without a sun tan but it was clear that he had been drinking heavily while away. What the Bomber had done with great
cunning was not to get off the Holyhead boat at all but to remain on
it for the whole six weeks as it went back and forth, so that he was
able to have liquid refreshment served continually in his cabin (on the
slate) throughout the voyage.

9 October, Stockholm

Arrive in Stockholm. Have arranged interviews with *Dagens Nyheter*
and other papers, as well as radio interviews, for the Swedish publication of the Behan biography. Olof Lagercrantz, the editor, has
long been a friend of mine. We met in the Fifties when he came
over to Dublin as literary editor of *Dagens Nyheter* to do a piece on
James Joyce. I took him to the Joyce Tower and various other places
connected with *Ulysses*. This was not the well-worn run then that
it became in later years and Olof was charmed to find *in situ* so
many of the places he had seen with his mind's eye when reading
Ulysses.

Check in at a good hotel near Stockholm's Old Town. When I get
on the phone it seems that everyone is away for the weekend. What
really knocks me back is that there is a pneumatic drill going full blast
outside. To my horror, it keeps up all evening. Industrious Swedes
who want to get the job done in the shortest possible time.

I make for Alexandra's, the chief night-club in the city. Pleasant
enough and an agreeable meal. The music is very loud but seraphic
compared with what I am going to have to put up with at the hotel
when I go back.

Worst fears realized. I would have slept better at the Battle of El
Alamein.

10 October

Walking through the familiar streets. Stureplan, as the city centre is
called, has become bland. Formless shops in a triangle, at the middle

of which is a small patch of weather-beaten grass. I walk up to Sturegatan where I used to stay with Gordon and Anne Elliot. It has the nineteenth-century grandeur about it which cities like Zurich, Bonn and Copenhagen still maintain. At the east side of the square is the school where Vera Volkova, who was one of the last dancers to train under Diaghilev, used to give ballet classes. One of my pals in Stockholm, Wili Sandberg, with other members of the Royal Swedish Ballet, used to attend these classes. He took me along with him once and I began, along with some others from the Royal Swedish Ballet, to take classes from her. Coming out afterwards, one felt incredibly refreshed. The vigorous exercise to music under the inspired hand of a great ballet mistress, followed by a hot shower, made it possible to greet the cold northern air outside with exhilaration. Wili told me, incidentally, that at the Royal Opera House after class everyone, ballerinas and premier danseurs like himself, shower together. Swedes pride themselves on the absence of any hang-ups.

I head down towards the Royal Theatre. A beautiful building on the edge of the bay. Then go into a café for coffee. In a corner, Edna O'Brien is sitting there all by herself. I don't know her particularly well but recognize her immediately. She is here to talk about her novel *August is a Wicked Month*. I tell her I am on a similar mission. We chat away.

When I come out of the restaurant, I notice once more how many really extraordinarily pretty girls there are in Stockholm. Of course, it's a stereotype in a way: blonde hair, perfect skin and blue eyes. But the number one sees here striding along like lithe leopards exceeds anything I have ever found in any city so far.

11 October

Walk in Skansen which is the Hyde Park of Stockholm. There are many old people sitting in the autumn sun. They all, men and women, have dark glasses. As they lean back to catch the sun's rays you get the impression of a series of skulls laid out in a line. The people taking the sun don't talk. No one seems to stride out. There is a strange quietness. This is now broken by a long piercing whine like a siren. I trace the sound to the Zoo which is part of the park. It comes from a wolf pacing up and down his inadequate cage. I feel an intense pity for the poor thing dragged from his natural habitat in Northern Sweden and now confined in this shabby prison. Later I meet Edna for coffee. Ask her about her writing routine. She is a morning bird

– a lark who works from 10.00 am to 3.00 pm. I am an owl and work at the other end of the scale into the small hours. Only happy when she is in love or at work. She thinks *Pagan Place* is her best work. Admires Ibsen and Strindberg. She says Pinter and Wesker want to write novels. She feels women are more self-centred and fundamentally more vicious than men. Takes Strindberg's *The Father* as an example. Her own boys are capable of greater loyalty, she thinks, than the girls who visit them. She finds the Swedes funny.

'They talk like apples knocking together.'

Virginia Woolf, she reminds me, took months over her essay on Joyce. Woolf had reacted badly at first to *Ulysses*, but after she'd recognized its merit, wanted to put things straight. Edna says she is apprehensive in Ireland of people moving in on her. She wants to go around the world as much as she can before going back. We talk about our favourite food. Mine: bacon and eggs, steak, cream cakes, tea and coke (rather uninspired I admit). Edna says she likes tea, figs, wine, cheese and brown bread. Works in her kitchen. It gives her a sense of power. Hangovers, she thinks, actually improve her work.

'You feel so bad, that you've got to get yourself together. The result can be psychedelic.'

She says it doesn't matter who you are in love with, you can still work. Samuel Beckett is a dream.

'You must be on a trip to reach him. You know that that section in *Krapp's Last Tape* is of his mother dying. He writes such nice letters.'

I ask her is it true she doesn't want to meet people. She says she finds it difficult to go to pubs. Once an Indian said to her. 'You are alone. I would like to join you,' sensing her isolation. Her sons help. We decide to meet later and have dinner. She tells me to keep on the turquoise shirt I am wearing. Not really a shirt but a sort of T-shirt with buttons at the neck.

Back at the hotel, I remember I have told Edna about the Literary Editor of *Dagens Nyheter*, Olof Lagercrantz, and that I will give him a call to see if he can arrange something for her in the paper. He is a poet himself and I am sure a fan of hers. I call *Dagens Nyheter* but Olof isn't back yet from the weekend. At 8 o'clock I collect Edna in her hotel and we go to a restaurant in the Old Town. It is a beautifully preserved place, winding medieval streets. Buildings that were there at the time when the Swedes ruled half of Europe and the Viking boats had ploughed their way down the Volga into Russia. At the restaurant I see why Edna has asked me to wear the turquoise T-shirt with the short sleeves. She likes to play a sort of little game with the waiter. She does all the ordering and says things like: 'He'd [meaning me] like a steak, I think. He needs it to keep his strength up . . . What have we got for pudding? I think he deserves a meringue glacé, don't you?'

Almost like a pretty, youngish mother with a rather mature son, or perhaps she means to suggest that I'm someone she wants to play a game with. Anyway, this goes on through the meal. A lively conversation. Politics, religion, art, she has a view on, but not dogmatic. Flexible when you argue from a different standpoint. At the end, with a slightly arch smile to the waiter (I've had two meringues glacés), we leave and I drop her at her hotel and arrange to meet her tomorrow.

12 October

When I awake this morning I remember I have to ring Olof Lagercrantz at *Dagens Nyheter* on Edna's behalf. I phone through as early as I can, but don't catch him. I then have the idea of playing a joke on Edna. I phone the hotel she is staying in and ask to be put through to her room. When she takes up the phone I speak in Swedish:

Olof/Ulick: 'Jag vill talar med Fröken O'Brien.'
Edna: 'I don't speak Swedish.'
Olof/Ulick: 'Could I speak to Miss Edna O'Brien please?'
Edna: 'This is me speaking.'
Olof/Ulick: (in a Swedish accent) 'I am the Literary Editor of *Dagens Nyheter*. My name is Olof Lagercrantz. I would very much like to do an interview with you about your novel for my page in the newspaper.'
Edna: 'Oh, that would be nice.'
Olof/Ulick: 'Shall I come to your hotel?'
Edna: 'Yes, of course. Where shall we meet?'
Olof/Ulick: 'I will bring my photographer with me. Could we get a picture of you in the swimming pool?'
Edna: (startled) 'But I can't swim.'
Olof/Ulick: 'That doesn't matter. We have available for the photograph the world famous Swedish heavyweight boxer, Ingmar Johansson. He will hold you up in the pool.'
Edna: (startled) 'What *do* you mean? Anyway, I haven't got swimming togs.'

Olof/Ulick: 'That does not matter at all. In Sweden we don't wear swimming togs.'
Edna: 'Christ, I don't believe this.'

I burst out laughing. Ominous silence on the other end of the phone. I say in my normal voice:

'Edna, are you there?'

No reply. I say it again. Then a voice with the metallic sound of a plucked guitar string:

Edna: 'I am still here.'
Me: 'It was only a joke. I thought it would be fun, especially as I had mentioned Olof Lagercrantz to you at dinner.'
Edna: 'It's not funny.'
Me: 'Well, I know women can have a different sense of humour.'
Edna: 'Of course, men know everything.'
Me: 'Well, I know I could play this sort of joke on somebody, some guy I know.'
Edna: 'I am not some guy.'
Me: 'Don't put down the phone, Edna.'

I tried her a few times during the day. No reply. I was puzzled, though. She has a good sense of humour, can be funny herself. Maybe she thought I was out to cause trouble. Later, I go to Alexandra's night-club. I am sitting in a corner watching young upper-class Swedes spin-ning around to rock music. Then I see two people coming off the floor. One of them is Edna. The other is Thor Heyerdahl, the Norwegian explorer who crossed the Pacific on a raft in the Kon-Tiki expedition. He looks in good shape but he is considerably older than I am and indeed has a few years to spare on Edna. I greet her with a friendly look. No dice.

13 October

Meet Wili Sandberg. We drive to lunch out of the city. Wili has to stop at three news-stands before he can find the socialist daily he is looking for. His ardour for ballet dancing has diminished.

'In two years I am finished. I go out in pension (45). It is import-ant not to strive beyond what you can do.'

My reply is that you are never happy when you get what you want.

He says that for a while he didn't want Margot, his wife, he only wanted Gerd Andersson, the Prima Ballerina at the Royal Ballet. Then after that he wanted Margot. He has two children. He feels they are dependent on him. I look around at his books. An interesting library, Nijinsky, Thomas Mann. This last is his exemplar and role model who he says lives on another planet. He remarked to me that I am in a good position because I don't have responsibility. Then he says:

'You have to have a cat's patience for women. You have to wait and pounce.'

He tells me his brother is a schizophrenic. Yet that fine sculpture of Icarus which is in the corner was sculpted by him. Wili is chuckling away about the visit of the French writer Jean Genet to Sweden. Genet, a sort of Paris sewer rat, has written some of the finest novels and plays of the twentieth century. He lives out in real life attitudes advocated in the existentialist feuilletons of Sartre and Camus. He has come over for the Swedish première of one of his best plays, *Le Balcon*. The Swedes with their hygienic sense of propriety have provided the homosexual Genet with a very beautiful young male ballet dancer for his stay here. What amused Wili was that when Genet saw this exquisite creature he rejected him immediately and asked them could they not find some greasy petrol pump attendant for him instead.

In the afternoon, I go to the ballet *Romeo and Juliet*. Choreography by a Russian, not Frederick Ashton's marvellous fling which was the first ballet I ever saw at Edinburgh in 1956. Prokofiev's music is divine with a sense of movement running through it which makes it suitable only for ballet and not for song. I didn't think the choreography was as good as Ashton's and indeed the dancing wasn't as good as the Royal Danish Ballet at Edinburgh, but it was still an enchanting afternoon. On the way out, I saw some children from the Royal Ballet School running down the stairs. They start training here at about nine years of age. From then on they will have nothing in their life till forty-five except ballet. They rushed away chirruping like flocks of birds leaving their trees. Very beautiful.

15 October

Haven't been able to get a typist up to now for my *Sunday Mirror* article. Finally one turns up but without a typewriter. She expects me to have one. This is crisis time. Unless I get a typist soon, I won't be able to get my piece in for the week.

Lunch with old friend, Gordon Elliot, at the Hungarian Palace restaurant. He tells me everyone in Sweden is now afraid of giving their
secrets to the computer. I go for a walk afterwards in the park. I see a
man pushing a pram alone. The women are out with their dogs. This
is the reverse of what happens in England or Ireland today. Then
notice once again that the voices are quiet.

Go to the Irish Embassy for lunch. Chatty chatelaine originally from
South Circular Road, Dublin. The Ambassador is a splendid
Kerryman who used to drink in O'Neill's in Suffolk Street. I give
them all the scandal of Dublin, Sean MacBride, Jack Lynch etc. In the
morning, had gone to see Vilgot Sjöman, the film director, whose
work I admire. His most famous feature film is *I am Curious Blue*,
which was followed by *I am Curious Yellow*. These involve a new
approach to feature films. We see a young girl reporter going round
Stockholm examining the various events that occur during a day.
Realism, but like Andrew Wyeth's paintings, *magic* realism. There has
been a tremendous battle in America to get Sjöman's films in. Barney
Rosset, of Grove Press, has been behind this. The films are alleged to
be pornographic and obscene. But of course they are nothing of the
kind. One of Sjöman's finest feature films is about an incestuous relationship among royalty during the reign of Gustav III. It is beautifully
made and superbly costumed and is much more about love than incest.
It is called *Syskonbädd 1782* (My Sister My Love).

Sjöman talks very slowly, rather like a Jesuit or a monk. There is no
trace of sensitivity about him, as if he had disdained the world to look
into his own soul. He says to me that I should begin now at forty-one
to work in film. He did so at thirty-seven. He couldn't work
machines, but somehow he managed to do it with a camera. His office
is bare like a cell. He sits away from me, crouched like a gnome. I feel
uncomfortable. Note again the balance of his voice. He says that like
Orson Welles, he learned everything from the cameraman. He wanted
to be a novelist. He works on his screenplays by talking to young actors
bursting with ideas. They fuel the fire that he wants to ignite. His next
film, he tells me, will be about a ship. After that, one that takes place
entirely in one room. When he learns that I have been a lawyer, he

asks me about criminals. How do they find living when they cease having to conform to the routine of prison.

22 October

I did my *Mirror* article this afternoon. Had photograph taken with young film star. She insisted on going to the open spaces along the quays. Lunch with Wili and Margot, she throwing meaningful glances. Wili won't let her drive me. She looks like a trapped fawn. Will he be glad to give up dancing, I wonder?

23 October

Going home tomorrow. Meet extraordinary fellow in Alexandra's night-club. He is expensively dressed, tall and fair, and looks like a successful film star. Turns out he is rich and an ex-judo champ. He makes a living out of making love to oldish Swedish and Italian women. If ten women give him £500 he can make £5,000 per week. When I ask him does he get that, he says he certainly gets over £300 a time. He is well versed in W.B. Yeats. He even quotes Oscar Wilde about the Irish – 'A race of brilliant failures.' He comes from a good family and tells me he has just come back from his father's country house where he has been taking a rest. Well he might. He tells me one fifty-four-year-old lady is paying him £700 a week. He is not in the least ashamed of what he is doing, and tells me all this with frank blue eyes and without a wince. He has an apartment in Rome. He says he will go back to university. When I ask him what he intends to study, he says he can graduate as 'a sex instructor'. This can be done in Sweden. He looks on his career as fulfilling, as a good orator might look to the law or a man with nimble fingers to the surgeon's art. He admits that he services men for even greater sums of money, and figures that this dual experience should help him in his ambition to excel as a sex instructor.

24 October

On the plane home meet Max Abrahamson. He is the son of a colleague of my father's, Professor Leonard Abrahamson. His brother Muff has already emigrated to Israel. Max says he will emigrate himself if Charles Haughey becomes Taoiseach. He heard from Dublin before

he took off at Stockholm that the defendants in the Arms Trial* have
been acquitted.

8 November, London

Dinner at Antonia Fraser's in Notting Hill. Antonia interesting on the
subject of incest.

'I wonder it doesn't happen more often. Tom used to pretend to
our class at the Dragon School in Oxford that we'd actually had it off
together. They said "you couldn't have done so because you'd be
locked up".'

I am quizzed: 'Are you fond of girls? Are you hiding something?'

At dinner, there is talk about the economy. A civil servant says
he is nervous about the future but 'our psychology will win.'
Antonia, who has written a bestselling life of Mary, Queen of
Scots, says the aristocratic Scots gentry spoke French but not
Gaelic. They liked Mary Stuart for her style. I think she's wrong
about them not speaking Gaelic. What I found extraordinary was
that the whole night, although Ulster was in an uproar and civil war
on the doorstep, no one made a single reference to Northern
Ireland. After all, I'd come over from Dublin and might have been
a source of information or at least comment from the higher civil
servant and the two MPs present (one of whom was Antonia's
husband, Hugh Fraser). Even, I thought, Antonia might have
expressed more interest in a country where her family have lived
for three centuries.

6 December, Leixlip Castle

Driving back to Leixlip Castle today, Desmond talks about his father,
Lord Moyne,† who has sent me a new play to put into the hands of
the Artistic Director of the Abbey. When Desmond's grandfather, the
British Minister of State in the Middle East, was assassinated in Cairo,
Bryan Guinness became 2nd Baron and vice-chairman of the family
firm. His new responsibility would limit his literary output and

---

* At which Cabinet ministers had been charged with importing arms in order to trans-
port them to Northern Ireland for the defence of the Nationalist community there.
† Bryan Walter Guinness, 2nd Lord Moyne (1905–92), a leading member of Evelyn
Waugh's group in Oxford and London in the early 1930s.

though overall he has published over twenty novels, plays, collections of poetry and two volumes of autobiography, his creative work has diminished considerably since.

'An unwilling Atlas,' comments Desmond with a sigh.

My view is that it was damn decent of the old man in the circumstances to have encouraged Desmond to become a leading conservationist and to let him opt out of involvement in the family firm. Particularly as he (Moyne) had refused to extend that licence to himself when he was faced with a family crisis.

Fortune found Desmond the ideal companion to undertake his chosen task with. Mariga's gift with people, her German flair for organization, her impeccable taste in design and furniture (she is consulted by Sotheby's agents) fit in with Desmond's passionate mission to preserve. Both have a genuine love of beauty and sense of taste.*

15 December, Dublin

Letter to Micheál MacLiammóir who has recently had eye surgery.

Micheál a Chara,

I have tried to find out news of you since your operation, but every time I ring there is either no reply or I miss you. I saw you looking very splendid indeed two days ago coming in full fig down toward Harcourt Terrace. I hope the operation has been a success. You looked marvellous the last time we had lunch in the Old Dublin, and the specs give you a distinct resemblance to Perry Mason. I hope I shall see you soon.

I will give you a ring next week in hopes that we can have lunch. Please don't reply to this as I shall be phoning you anyway.

---

* 'For Leixlip [Castle], Desmond and Mariga found many important Irish objects and it was their sense of scale, use of colour and feeling for arrangement, combined with an impressionistic approach to detail, that made those rooms so stimulating and so influential on both sides of the Atlantic. Amateurs, dealers and decorators all learned from Mariga, often much more than they would care to admit. Leixlip was the key house in the British Isles in the late 1950s and 1960s.' – John Cornforth, *The Inspiration of the Past* (1985).

Micheál writes back to say that as he doesn't watch television ('even when you're there'), he doesn't know who Perry Mason could be. Is he a relation of James Mason, he asks, who played for some time as a member of the Gate Theatre Company with Micheál and Hilton?

He's off to America at the 'shriek of dawn' on Saturday to do his Oscar Wilde one-man show.

22 December

Met Archie O'Sullivan, the Radio Éireann repertory actor, going into the Abbey Theatre. He vacillates between the Abbey and RTÉ for personal reasons mostly connected with the gargle. He doesn't look well and he tells me that it is his dread of Christmas. That day and Good Friday he finds almost impossible to handle. The pubs are closed and the very idea of what to him are these emporiums of light and cheer being unavailable, gives him the shudders. What makes it worse this time apparently is that last Good Friday he'd had to play the part of Judas in a radio play, and thinking of the Last Supper had him dreadfully thirsty during the broadcast, especially with the knowledge that the pub in Henry Street, *The Tower Bar* opposite Radio Éireann, would not be functioning when he came out. By some miracle as he emerged into Henry Street he saw a ladder leading into the first floor of the pub. The thrifty owner, George Brady, had decided to use the holiday to repaint the lounge. Up the ladder like a goat went Archie and stuck his head in the window.

Archie: 'George, for Christ's sake will you give me a drink?'
Brady: 'Do you know what day it is?'
Archie: 'Yes, it's Good Friday, but I'm dying – I need a glass of whiskey.'
Brady: 'All right here's a large one.'

Archie grabbed it and was about to empty the glass when Brady said 'That will be seven shillings and sixpence' (double the price in those days).

Brady: 'You know what Our Saviour had to drink on Good Friday, Archie? (*Pause*) Vinegar.'

Archie: 'Yes, but he didn't have to pay shaggin' seven shillings and six pence for it.'

Archie told me this with some relish as a good deal of his salary goes into the Tower Bar till. He went off cackling, an actor whom a lot of people think might have been another F.J. McCormick, by general consent held to be the finest actor the Abbey has produced.

27 December, Co. Kildare

Down for lunch at Furness – Pierce Synnott's place, Co. Kildare – Jacobean. No one staying except Elizabeth Longford. After lunch Lady Rosse comes in. Fantastically pretty. A coquette. Lovely eyes.

We then set out for Tullynally Hall which is the Pakenhams' country seat in Co. Longford. It is a splendid late Georgian building with a slight touch of merchant flash emanating from under a stern façade. After I've found my room I come down to a sitting room where there is an animated conversation going on. Pansy Lamb (the painter Henry Lamb's wife) is laying down the law in a strident Bloomsbury way. Everyone who doesn't fit into her pantheon is it seems a fascist. Hackles rise, especially mine. I end by calling her a fascist of the left, quoting a famous slogan of the far left in Ireland in the 1930s: 'No free speech for Fascists.' Needless to say I am put out like a bold boy and sent if not to bed at least to Coventry.

Later that evening when I come down to dinner, Frank Longford comes up. I brought to his attention some time ago that in his biography of Eamon de Valera, he placed Michael Collins very much in the background. As Collins and de Valera fought a civil war over their different interpretations of the Irish Treaty with England, and it was Collins who single-handedly guided the country through three years of intense guerrilla warfare, I felt he should have been given more space than he got in the book. Frank now says that I was right and he did not give Collins' character the emphasis it should have had. This is the decent side of old Lord Porn. He actually does listen to criticism even if he seems to bristle and then if he feels he is wrong he has an entirely admirable compulsive instinct to redress the wrong. Nine years ago, I wrote the obituary of Frank's brother Edward Longford (a founder with Micheál MacLiammóir and Hilton Edwards of the Dublin Gate Theatre) for *The Times* and he speaks about it with fulsome gratitude every time he meets me. I was asked to do the obit-

uary around midnight but because of Edward's enormous contribution to Irish life (the Gate Theatre could never have existed without
his input) I thought it worth sitting up till three in the morning and
then telephoning the copy over for the first editions. I think it wasn't
a bad obituary, because I knew the scene I was writing about well.
One thing I didn't put in was that after the removal I had walked with
Micheál MacLiammóir to Grafton Street. Before he left me outside
Switzers he had turned round and said quite seriously:

'That's the second of my three enemies gone.'

I said: 'Who were the other two?'

Micheál replied: 'Frank Dermody [Abbey Director] and Denis
Franks.'

I had an inkling of Dermody's clash with Micheál as I knew he had
played, when he was a young Corporal stationed in Galway, the part
of Cupid in *Diarmuid and Grainne* directed in Irish by Micheál. A
soldier scorned, he had later conspired with a singer (female) who was
also in love with Micheál to have the police search his house for signs
of illicit love. But the name Denis Franks surprised me. In fact, he and
I had been part of a television sensation in the Sixties. Because of his
camp irascibility I was able to make him hop up and down on the *Late
Late Show* week after week to the great delight of the viewers. Round
the country cats and dogs were named after us. But apart from his
ability to lose his temper in public, there was nothing much else to
him. He was an actor of a calibre just a little above the fit-ups. Hardly
worthy to enter Micheál's slender list of enemies.

Frank Longford tells me he is writing a book on suffering. There
is something strangely naïve, almost schoolgirlish about him. Yet he
was out hunting yesterday. He prefers it for exercise and says that
walking takes too much time.

Marina, Desmond's daughter, was crying a little in the car coming
down here. Think of the happy days three years ago going to the
North with them and Desmond and Mariga. I used to spend
Christmas Day in Leixlip with the parents and the two children. Just
five of us. The children are of exceptional beauty. A Reynolds painting. Ah me!

1971

Letter today from Gerald Brenan* which has been following me around. I missed him in December when I was in the vicinity of Churriana, near Malaga and left a letter at his house which he replied to, not knowing I had gone back. Gerald† is a fascinating conversationalist and storyteller; I am helping him trace his Irish ancestry from whom he may have got his gift of the gab.

He writes:

I was interested to hear that Lafcadio Hearn's‡ mother was a Brenan. He must be the only distinguished person my family have produced since St Brendan who discovered America to reveal the way. The Brenans are of Firbolg [Irish tribe of strong

---

* Gerald Brenan (1894–1987) was a traveller and member of the Bloomsbury Group. His books on Spain are generally considered to be the finest in English of the twentieth century. As a young man Brenan was very much a man of action, serving in the trenches throughout World War One and finishing up as Captain Brenan MC. I met him in 1969 at his villa in Churriana and we became friends.

† Here is one of Gerald's stories which I heard from him in January 1968 at his Churriana house and afterwards made a note of. 'Once walking in Almería, I became aware of a pair of eyes fixed on me through a grille in a window at street level. I stopped to speak to the señorita. Beautiful black eyes and oval face. Entranced, after another visit I became her *novio* (boyfriend). As the Spanish custom was, in certain parts, this meant that my only communication with her could be through the grille on the window. For some months I talked to her in this way, infatuated but frustrated too. One night I put my face against the grille and kissed her. She recoiled in horror; no man had ever touched her, nor would they, she cried, until her bridal night. I must meet her in the market square tomorrow to discuss the future. Next day I went along, heart beating, for she was exceptionally beautiful, to the meeting place. I was early but she was earlier and I glimpsed her in the distance waiting with her sister. She was a dwarf, barely three feet in height. The trick was, her sister would slide an orange box under her feet so that she could stand on it to survey the passing scene. I didn't keep that appointment but the next night I felt I had to go to say goodbye. But the sound of the orange box being slid into place was too much and I fled.'

‡ The writer Lafcadio Hearn (1850–1904) was the first person to interpret Japanese culture comprehensively for the West. See also 10 March 1973, note on Hearn.

men] descent but keep it dark and since the time of Strongbow [11th century Norse invader of Ireland] have lived under the protection of the Earls of Kildare . . .

We are both into mysticism, in particular the writings of Saint Teresa of Ávila and St John of the Cross. I have just published some translations of the latter's poems while Gerald is engaged in writing a life of the Saint himself. He, as I am, is a dedicated walker (in his thirties he would walk distances of up to eighty miles) and admits to a strong sexual attraction to women as creatures capable of conferring on us, if so persuaded, ecstasies beyond the expectation of our mortal state. When Gerald first told me that St Teresa, bothered by mosquitoes, refused to swat them but instead taught them to zizz in plainsong, I knew we would get on. On the debit side we share dislikes such as the writer Honor Tracy who defamed Gerald, persecuted him in his home and traduced other mutual friends such as Billy Wicklow.

15 April

Handwritten letter from Gerald Brenan thanking me for the Behan biography. He agrees with my stand in disclosing Brendan's sexual preferences.

Of course you are right, speaking of his passion for young men. I had always supposed that drink and violence were the substitutes for sex in Ireland and that sodomy was quite unknown. Not that I approve it. I agree with Clive Bell when he said that if you were on a desert island with ten beautiful youths and a female gorilla you would choose the gorilla to have sex with.

He has enjoyed meeting a girlfriend of mine who dropped in on me in Spain on her way back to Ireland from New Orleans.

I am sorry that she has gone underground like the river on her family estate (which I remember), but still it's something to have had a nobleman's daughter as a girlfriend, all the more since she came from enemy territory. It makes you a figure from a ballad.

Now about Linda,[*] his girl.

> The house, land and car are in Linda's name so I am a kept man
> and she can throw me out at any time. So far she hasn't even
> hinted at this which I find very flattering. For after all on the 7th
> of April 1971 I was 77. Three sevens is a biblical number bring-
> ing, I hope, every thought of blissfulness – but not an age when
> one is up to being kept by a lovely girl. We lead an unsocial life,
> never going anywhere separately but live like Siamese twins.
>
> All girls of her age like to have their own way so as young men
> won't give it to them they widely prefer the old who are at their
> feet all the time. So I have got into a permanently bewitched
> state, cast away on a desert Tir na nOg[†], without any need for
> the stimulus of jealousy. It is a great miracle of old age and
> someone ought to write a play about us – a Beckett-like play, in
> which nothing ever happens but couleur de rose.
>
> I see the Irishman whom I try to keep down in ordinary life
> breaking out of me, I shall soon be saying begorrah. Linda is
> now writing a play, I wish you success with your new one.[‡]
> Incest is a good theme, it's one of the few themes left which is
> more-or-less forbidden.
>
> PS. We've called our new home Santa Filomena to annoy the
> Pope.[§]

---

[*] Linda Price was twenty-five at this time, which made her fifty-two years younger than
Gerald. She was an art school graduate who had developed an interest in Saint John of the
Cross and philosophy which Gerald found agreeable. Perhaps as an inducement to Linda
to stay with him, he agreed to let her do the translations of the poems in the book he was
writing on the Spanish mystic. I was a little surprised at Gerald's enthusiasm for her work,
which may have been enhanced by his affection for her. Linda was a nice-looking girl,
with long brown hair and good eyes. Gerald used to send me out with her to the dance
clubs in Torremolinos to show her the town, but she had I think some knee trouble that
made spinning and jiving difficult. She remained with Gerald until he died aged 93 in
1987. By this time she had married a Swedish artist and had had two children by him.
[†] The mythical Irish Land of Youth.
[‡] *The Dream Box*, produced at the Project Theatre, Dublin in 1972, dealt with a mother
and son who owned a theatre and were lovers. David McSweeny, the Cambridge rugby
captain, back in Dublin for the summer, commented after seeing it, 'Things are changing here. I find that Brendan Behan's a bugger and Ulick O'Connor is a lesbian.'
[§] Pope Paul VI had recently declared St Filomena was a non-saint, and had been wrongly
canonized because of a printer's error.

19 April

Defended my public image on the *Late Late* tonight when Gay Byrne[*]
quizzed me.

> *GB:* 'We had some girls on the programme, Ulick, last week,
> from Bray – members of the Irish Countrywomen's Association.
> You had just given them an award for their play and they said you
> were absolutely gorgeous when you were on your own among a
> handful of women.'
> *UO'C:* 'Perhaps you are implying that you bring out the worst
> in me. Is that what it was?'
> *GB:* 'Well, I don't know, do I, Ulick, do you think?'
> *UO'C:* 'Well, I don't know. People often say to me that I'm not
> a bit like the louser they see on television. They say "You're actu-
> ally quite nice." I can't figure this out. What sort of image do I
> project? Is it because I say what I think that people take offence?
> In Ireland this can happen. We're so cute here that they regard
> somebody who speaks their mind as a kind of hero. Maybe it's
> the seven hundred years of oppression we've had. It doesn't
> matter how nice I am to some people, the sheer fact that I speak
> my mind actually terrifies them. What about all the people I have
> helped through the evening on the programme? The ballad
> singer, for instance, who was with Pete Seeger last month? He
> said I made his evening for him.'
> *GB:* 'I can't remember his name.'
> *UO'C:* 'Remember Sai Chin last year?'[†]
> *GB:* 'We all remember her. We all remember Sai Chin.'
> *UO'C:* 'Well, when we were at it in an argument she hit me for
> six right out of the studio. It was fabulous and I clapped with
> everyone else. When I asked her what her age was – I was trying

---

[*] Talk show presenter and broadcaster. His *Late Late Show* began in 1962, and became the
most-watched show ever on Irish television. This gifted presenter knew how to get the
best out of those he interviewed and create an interesting ambience which would attract
viewers from all backgrounds, young and old. In the first ten years of his programme he
acquired a reputation for bringing before viewers problems that up to then had not been
openly aired in the Irish media. In his later years he became something of a panjandrum
and involved himself in political and social confrontation in which he was out of his depth.
To some extent this was due to the paucity of talent in RTE at the time in handling public
affairs, so that this task devolved on Gay Byrne's entertainment programme.
[†] Sai Chin, stage and film actress, had just been the subject of a book.

to make her admit she grew up in Peking where her father was a famous opera director – she fixed me with the most inscrutable of oriental smiles and chirruped "I am four thousand years old." It brought the house down. I was prepared to stick my chin out for a good night's gas, but I never get any credit for it.

'I even defended a girl who was attacked by Denis Franks.* She was a ballet dancer and he said she was unbalanced. Afterwards, she sent me a very beautiful history of Russian ballet – illustrated.'
GB: 'Yes, but remember what you did to Denis Franks.'
UO'C: 'Well, Denis Franks was a godsend to me and to television. A natural balloon who just wouldn't burst. You said yourself the time we were on together the sales of new televisions broke all records.'
GB: 'Well, nice to meet the new Saint Ulick!'
UO'C: 'My halo is negotiable.'

This month I went to the United States for the American publication of the Brendan Behan biography. My publishers, Prentice Hall, had decided to make it their book of the year and had set up an extended promotional tour. This involved a number of television appearances, radio and press interviews in fifteen states and was frenetic and exhausting. In Seattle in one day I gave thirteen interviews of one kind or another, television, radio, press, before midday.

21 April, New York

To 45th and Park to tape the Dick Cavett Show on ABC television. There's a big crowd outside the door as I go in with the producers (both of them women). We have to shove our way through past this very heavy guy with a book in his hand which he claims he wrote. He says to one of the producers, who is puffed up with self-importance:

---

* An actor who arrived in Ireland via Poland, Scotland, and a whiff of Palestine. His talent for indignation was gigantic and I gave him every chance to express it. In fact, though we had only five shows together, many people to this day believe we were on television for years. But the chemistry was cumulative. Our last appearance together established a new viewing record. I suspected that night he was going to be shirty. He was always having acquaintances send in chocolates and flowers to be presented to him on the next programme. This night after he got a beautiful bouquet from 'an admirer in Rathgar,' I pointed out: 'I live in Rathgar'. When he shouted 'Are you suggesting that this gift is spurious,' I said 'I know it's not. I sent it, I'm your biggest admirer' and then produced the receipt from Jeanne, a well-known florist in Dawson Street. Pandemonium!

'I've written my life story and I want to get on Cavett's show.'

He pushes the book towards her and indeed, his picture is on the cover. The producer says contemptuously:

'I don't know you.'

'I'm Jake LaMotta* lady, you ought to know me.'

'Get rid of this animal.'

The door slammed as we slipped through. I tried to tell the producer who the man was, but it meant nothing to her.

In the makeup room this little guy comes in, and I ask him who is he looking for. It turns out it's Dick Cavett.

On camera he badgers me about alcohol, which I never touch. This surprises him coming from an Irishman and he fastens onto it like an FBI man in a speakeasy. Finally I ask him has *he* a drink problem which defuses the situation. We talk about Brendan Behan as a TV sensation in the United States – his habit of breaking up his own plays on Broadway to get publicity. Then the question.

'Was Brendan gay?'

'He did have sex with men.'

'Was he gay?'

'No, he preferred women.'

Make my point with a story of Brendan and Benedict Kiely† walking one day in Rathgar while Brendan defended his range of sexual choices by saying that in prison or in the navy you had no alternative. Kiely didn't agree and Brendan pointed to a young soldier on the other side of the road:

'Listen Ben, you'd take him before you'd take Eleanor Roosevelt.'

(I had put this remark to Cavett beforehand, as I thought it might be offensive to a listening public in the United States but he said to go ahead). Have to leave the studio almost immediately. Due in Deerfield School, Massachusetts at 9.00 pm. Car to Newark airport. After a pleasant dinner on campus at the house of one of the teachers (John Sutor), we watch the Cavett show. I'm curious to know just how the 'Eleanor Roosevelt' quip has gone down. I don't get the chance, however, as her name is bleeped in transmission. The result is the

---

* In a legendary fight in 1946 Lamotta beat Rocky Graziano to become middleweight champion of the world. Robert De Niro plays him in the film *Raging Bull*.

† Novelist and biographer. Along with Francis Stuart, Seamus Heaney and others he has been named a Saoi (wise man) by Aosdana, the body of Irish artists and writers which honours those whose work has made an outstanding contribution to the arts.

studio audience are seen laughing loudly while my remark without the 'Eleanor Roosevelt' reference is rendered meaningless to the viewers.

24 April

Visit Padraic Colum* in hospital this morning. The place is about ten miles from Deerfield, Massachusetts and I go by taxi. Emaciated. He says I look different. He always has a slightly bird-like quality, rather like a cheerful robin. He talks about George Moore the novelist who, when he returned to Dublin at the turn of the century, adopted him as his literary protégé. One day they were walking through Stephen's Green and Colum remarked that Saint Gaudens, the American sculptor, had been commissioned to do a statue of the recently dead Parnell on O'Connell Street; the work was only partially completed and there was speculation as to what form it would take. Moore suggested immediately that they could add a fire-escape. (This was a reference to the fact that in 1888 Parnell had escaped down the fire-escape of the house of his mistress Kitty O'Shea). Colum, who must have been a perky young chap, said:

'That is not a worthy remark Moore, Parnell was a great man.'

Moore unexpectedly replied: 'Yes, you are right, Parnell was a great man and I shouldn't have made it.'

A few minutes later he said to Colum: 'You think you're a great poet?'

Colum: 'Yes, Moore.'

'I've read your little book. I didn't like your little book.'

Here Padraic calls the nurse in to shift him to a more comfortable position. He asks about Mariga Guinness. A Swedish friend of hers has given him a poem about Abyssinia. He recalls my appearing as a barrister in the Singer Stamp Fraud case (1961–64).

'What happened eventually?'

'He got off.'

---

* Padraic Colum (1881–1972) was a leading poet and playwright of the Irish Literary Renaissance. Yeats thought highly of him. His plays *The Fiddler's House*, *The Land* and *Thomas Muskerry* were the first realist plays to be performed at The Abbey. Some of his poems are in every important anthology: *The Old Woman of the Roads*, *The Drover* and a *Cradle Song*. He wrote the words of the song *She Moves Through the Fair*, which has become popular again today after it was used in the film *Michael Collins*. He was described in 1904 by Yeats as 'Young for his age. A man of genius in the first dark gropings of his thought.'

'Your eloquence?'

'No. My persuading one of the accused to plead not guilty.'

25 April

After five days of Manhattan frenzy, the Racquet Club on Sunday becomes my blessed plot. I can leave the Chelsea Hotel on 23rd Street and, after a four-minute subway journey, rise Antaeus-like at its temple-like entrance.* It occupies a whole block on Park Avenue where it is dwarfed by the surrounding skyscrapers. When you go in under the carved doorway it's like entering a fortified Florentine palazzo. The windows are Romanesque except for those on the second floor which have classical pediments. At fourth floor level the crescent openings are bricked. Behind them, most days of the week, real tennis is played, the Henry VIII sort, by men clad in long white flannels in which the ball is hit back and forward over a distance of 30 yards or so, often sent skidding along the buttresses to confuse an opponent.

As I go in Tim, the porter, tells me there are only a few in this Sunday. Manhattan empties out at weekends. As I go up the beautiful staircase, I reflect how much the place does suggest a Renaissance palace. Arriving on the second floor during the week, from the staircase, you feel like a Roman senator arriving at the Forum. Members stand at the pillared columns or are seated in exquisitely comfortable armchairs, custom-designed for members who want a quick nap after a furious bout on court or in the gym. In the Oak bar on the back wall there is an enormous mural running the full length depicting the Dutch settlers of New Amsterdam playing bowls. A reminder of where the real rulers of the city come from. You can find the names in the members' book – Van Alen, De Gersdorff, Auchincloss, Van Rennselaer and a lot of Vons who may have swapped vowels over the years.

I smash a few balls down the sidewall of the squash court on my own, do a mild workout in the excellent gym and then head for the showers where I conclude that the lean, rangy, very tall figures one sees here during the week have the musculo-skeletal frame of the Northern Hollander.

---

* The Racquet and Tennis Club building, 370 Park Avenue, was designed by Stanford White (1853–1906), as a gathering-place for 'gentlemen athletes'. White, one of the boldest and most brilliant of American architects, also designed the Washington Triumphal Arch and Madison Square Garden.

A sandwich will be brought to me in the Library, a chamber which if it wasn't so well proportioned would seem as big as Grand Central Station. There is no sound from the thick carpets as I walk there. Most papers are unread as I make my selection and then peace. Perfect peace.

10 May

Cleveland. At a radio show I meet Abbie Hoffman who is on a book tour. He's a current high-profile anarchist who believes that cracking the system is a full-time job. Nice guy, twinkling eyes. We are on the same programme and I think what triggered his interest in me was my reciting Dylan Thomas's *Poem On His Birthday*. Also the Irish are regarded outside their own country as inherently anti-establishment (which is not always the case but often is), which helps.

I play casual soccer in the afternoon in a mean little park which backs onto a rather horrible city zoo. Most of the players are black and nearly all of them kick in the American (wrong) way, with the toe instead of the instep. Later meet Abbie Hoffman for coffee and he explains to me two methods he uses to buck the system. He cuts out the free postage slips from magazines, gets the heaviest brick available, puts it in an envelope and sticks the address slip onto it. By the time it reaches the addressee (hopefully a multinational), the parcel can have cost the recipient hundreds of dollars. When Abbie wants to dispatch books and doesn't wish to pay freight, he addresses the package to himself and doesn't put a stamp on it: this will ensure that it is returned to the person whose name is written at the left top of the envelope, the one he wanted to send it to in the first place.

15 May, Chicago

Arrange to meet Nelson Algren.* Chicago writer who before the Beats ever came on the scene wrote from an existential stance.

---

* Nelson Algren (1909–81) came to the fore in the 1930s with uncompromising novels about Chicago. He was one of the Chicago 'realists', with James T. Farrell, Theodore Dreiser and the poet Carl Sandburg, who had much influence at the time. His best known novel is *The Man with the Golden Arm* about a morphine addict which was made into an Academy Award-winning movie. In the 1950s he met Simone de Beauvoir and they had a much publicized affair which she has written about extensively in her memoirs and in her novel *The Mandarins* in which Algren appears as Lewis Brogan. He did not however himself write about his side of the relationship which he regarded as a private matter.

Lifestyle more ascetic than the Beats, however. He does five miles on a stationary bicycle every day and still punches the bag. Tallish and slim with something of the ascetic look of a civil servant. He has blond hair, white complexion, bright blue eyes and well-cut features. A Mid-Western Swede with some Jewish blood.

Nelson is easygoing. We just slip from one bar to another walking all the time, assured that he will know the barman (and many of the clientele) when we enter a pub. Much Chicago life is wrapped up in boxing. Some of the great heavyweight world championships in history took place here on Marshall Field. The three epic fights of Tony Zale (from Chicago) and Rocky Graziano (New York) are remembered blow by blow. Nelson makes sure that first thing when we enter a bar they know I am an aficionado of the ring.

It was to Chicago that Simone de Beauvoir* came in search of Algren in 1947. She had read an article by him in *Partisan Review* and may have also seen his photograph. Anyway, she fell for him like an anchor falling to the seabed. The story was *world* famous at the time. She doted on this big handsome Swede as 'existential man incarnate'. She and Sartre admired Algren's writing and both of them did their best to make his name known in Paris. As Sartre has also been de Beauvoir's lover, I asked Nelson wasn't the old boy jealous at seeing her appear on the Boulevards with a handsome GI. Algren shook his head.

'No. The French aren't made that way. We got on swell. I admired Sartre, liked his work but there was one real mix-up. De Beauvoir had other lovers and one of them translated my junkie book *The Man With the Golden Arm* into *plume de ma tante* French. It really was a corny presentation so Sartre rewrote it. The young guy was going around scared because there was a chance now that his translation might win the Goncourt Prize. Actually he did win it, a lot of money, and he could have ended up in the Bastille if it was found out that the translation was mostly Jean-Paul.'

But what about de Beauvoir? Did she chase him?

'Yeah, I guess she did. She'd decided she wanted to meet the guy who had written *The Man With the Golden Arm*. I didn't speak French and she didn't speak English very well so we didn't understand much. It didn't stop her however because she talked all the time. In fact I

---

* 1908–86; French novelist and feminist, author of *The Second Sex* (1952) and *The Mandarins* (1954). As a philosopher she was associated with Jean-Paul Sartre in the existentialist controversies of the 1940s and '50s.

thought she was peremptory. After we met in Chicago she stayed with
me for three whole days and then to break the monotony I took her
down the river to Mississippi on a boat. We didn't talk much there
either. She left eventually and asked me to come to Paris which is what
I did – for a while.'

We talk about the writer's function. Nelson says:

'I'm a Chicago poet.'

'What does that mean?'

'I have no security.'

He could have had security if he had married de Beauvoir (she
wanted him to) and lived in Paris.

'If she wanted it that bad then she could have come and lived in
Chicago.'

Parisians love Paris, New Yorkers love New York, Dubliners love
Dublin, with Chicagoans it's the same. However, Nelson's home town
is not showing too much friendliness towards a native son at present.
The City currently has him in court on a telephone rap alleging that
he used the public phone in his frugal apartment over a period of a
few years without inserting coins.

'What else could I do? I have to make a lot of long-distance calls.'

18 May

At the movies tonight the newly released *The Exorcist* gives me a real
scare . . . a primitive thrill that makes the hair stand on my head. I
walk back to the hotel under Chicago's loop line bridge, looking over
my shoulder everywhere. Even when I've gone to bed that image I
have seen on the screen of the little girl looking at the priest, vomit-
ing and then turning her head right round so that it does a full circle,
keeps coming in front of my eyes. Most horror films leave me cold,
but (as with *Rosemary's Baby*) it was the presentation here of evil taking
root in the mind of a very ordinary person that put the frighteners on
me. After the movie I went to visit the mother of Barney Rosset* who

---

* Arguably one of the great publishers of the twentieth century, certainly one of the most
courageous. Barney has seen his role as making great literature available to all, and removing censorship from the works of writers like the Marquis de Sade, D.H. Lawrence and
Henry Miller. In 1952 he published Samuel Beckett's *Waiting for Godot* which in its first
year sold four copies in the USA. In 2000 it sold its five millionth. He was also the founder
of the influential radical magazine of the Sixties, *Evergreen Review*. Died in January 2001.

lives in a penthouse at the top of the Hancock building (Barney has just bought the paperback rights of my Brendan Behan book). Because of his publishing record and his association with sexual politics Barney is sometimes regarded as a licentious satyr, so I wonder how his Mum will seem. Mary Rosset turns out to be a sweet old Irish mother, big blue eyes, white hair and porcelain skin.

She's ensconced with a female pal with whom she has been having a few snifters. Greets me with eyes dancing. I detect an Irish flavour in her accent so I ask her what part she's from.

'Connemara. Tansey was the name before I married Mr Rosset.'

Sara Tansey is the name of one of the girls in Synge's *The Playboy of the Western World*, so I quote a line from the play: 'Sara Tansey, Susan Brady, Honor Blake! What in glory has you here at this hour of day?'

Mary and her pal break into an avalanche of laughter and do everything except slap me on the back. Unbelievable for 79. It's easy to see where Barney gets the flair. Her Jewish husband, Bernard Rosset was one of the richest men in the United States. Mary tells me she baptized him after he had a heart attack and was lying at her feet on the floor.

'Mary, that was a horrible thing to do. You didn't give the poor man a chance to make up his mind.'

'Oh no, he had it made up. I knew he wanted it. I was doing him a favour.'[*]

The phone rings and Mary takes it.

'Oh, hello Barney.'

After she has put the phone down she says:

'Barney was wondering why I hadn't been on. We talk at ten o'clock every night.'

Mystery solved. When Barney's in the Lion's Head bar[†] he will usually take a call at 10.00 pm. Everyone assumes it's a girlfriend. When he comes back he usually mutters:

'That was my mother.'

'Come on, Barney. Is she good in the hay?'

---

[*] I was sceptical of Mary's claim over her husband's disposition at his death. But Barney assures me that this was so: his father had spent a lot of time drinking and negotiating with the cardinal and the bishops in what is a predominantly Catholic city and had decided that at a convenient moment he would join the club.

[†] A bar in Christopher Square, New York where writers, actors and musicians hang out.

5 June, New York

Arrange to meet Milton Macklin, an old friend, in the Lion's Head. He is the editor of *Argosy* magazine and has written some notable biographies. Milton knew Brendan Behan in Paris in the late Forties when there was quite a group of aspiring American writers there. The GI Bill of Rights provided a decent income for war veterans who wanted some breathing space to decide whether they could stick it out in the writing game or not. As well as Brendan Behan (who of course was over in Paris on his own steam), Norman Mailer, Terry Southern, James Baldwin and James Jones, all bankrolled by Uncle Sam, were in town at the time.

Milton who is glad to be out of one war now rails against another, the Vietnam engagement which has been running for nine years. I mention Father Dan Berrigan the Jesuit whom I admire greatly and who is at present serving a stiff sentence for anti-war activity up in Danbury prison, Connecticut. I seem to have touched a spark because Milton's face lights up and it turns out he also carries a torch for Berrigan. I recite a part of Berrigan's speech from the dock delivered before he was sentenced by a Federal judge two years ago.* When someone asks how in hell can I remember it I tell them that in Ireland you learn speeches from the dock with your prayers, and they'd want to watch out or I'd unleash Robert Emmet's dock speech on them, Thomas Francis Meagher's sword speech, and for good measure Patrick Pearse's speech over the grave of O'Donovan Rossa.

6 June

Albany to deliver a talk to St Rose's College. I have just read the horrendous *Adventure*, James Dickey's novel about hunters who are

---

*Father Berrigan's address to the jury dealt with the prosecution's allegation that he and his brother Phillip (also a priest) along with seven others had burnt military files (378 of them) which would have been used to draft young Americans into the army – also that they poured bottles containing their own blood on Pentagon papers.

'Our apologies good friends for the fracture of good order, the burning of paper instead of children, the angering of the orderlies in the front parlour of the charnel house. We could not, so help us God, do otherwise. For we are sick at heart, our hearts give us no rest for thinking of the Land of Burning Children. And for thinking of that other child of whom the poet Luke speaks. A child born to make trouble and to die for it, the first Jew, not the last, to be the subject of a "definitive solution".'

murdered by hillbillies in Arkansas and I feel nervous walking through this countryside even though it is a thousand miles away from the scene of the novel. I come across two men at a quarry. One is lying down at the feet of the other man who says, 'When you speak to me, open your fucking mouth and no basketball.'

Dogs are barking in the background. I hasten through the twilight.

7 June

Milton rings with an idea to raise money for the Berrigan Support Fund. My new one-man play on Brendan Behan is scheduled at the Abbey Theatre for the Dublin Theatre Festival in September. Would I consider doing a preview of it at the Chelsea Hotel, perhaps in the room that Brendan lived in during his last year. Great idea but I have no contacts. Milt says he knows the director Shirley Clarke who is currently riding high with her film *The Connection*[*] which has won awards. She has a penthouse on the roof of the Chelsea which she might lend us or else help us find another room to present the show. It would be a good tryout for the play I have been rehearsing since Christmas with Tomás MacAnna, Artistic Director at the Abbey. We could charge $40 at the door and make bucks for the Berrigans.

8 June

Look over the Chelsea Hotel today with Stanley Bard, the manager, to find a room for the Behan project. Arthur Miller, Dylan Thomas, Thomas Wolfe, Edgar Lee Masters have all stayed here as well as Brendan Behan. One of Brendan's quotes is on a plaque in his memory which is outside the hotel:

'New York, the man that hates you hates the world.'

We try a few apartments including the room from which Dylan went 'out to die' but they are all too small. Shirley Clarke meets us on the roof where she has created fertile patches of grass with flowers and small trees on them to create the effect of a garden. But her penthouse is too small and if I did this show in the open there could be safety problems as well as acoustic ones.

However, Stanley Bard seems determined that we shall stage the

---

[*] Much praised for its realistic portrayal of the drug culture, this film won first prize at the Spoleto Festival.

show at the Chelsea. After a few more inspections he brings us into a spacious artist's studio owned by a good-looking painter who doesn't seem to mind Stanley turning his living space into a theatre for a hundred people. Perhaps he owes one to the boss.

10 June

In the Lion's Head tonight. Somebody produces a piece from Wilfred Sheed's *New York Times* column on the Behan biography, and starts an argument. Can a teetotaller write a book about an alcoholic. Sheed has argued that there is no reason he shouldn't as you don't have to be deaf to write about Beethoven or blind to write John Milton's life. Hackles are raised and a chap sticks his face into mine saying with manic fury in his voice: 'You tell me how can a pussyfoot* write a book about a drunk.'†

I am about to reply when I see his left fist rising in an arc. A sharp left to his snout followed by a swift departure seemed the best of my play at the time of night that is in it.

12 June

Leave for Los Angeles to talk at Brentwood Women's Club. Am travelling first class as the Virginia Graham TV chat show is picking up the tab. Looking forward to three and a half hours of bliss on the plane, pleasant food, a comfortable seat to sleep in and peace perfect peace. Oh, the luxury of first-class travel. One is spared the anxiety that the trip will be ruined by drunks or screaming kids. Carefully select a window-seat for maximum privacy, and settle down to find myself looking straight into the eyes of an infant whose head has popped up over the seat in front of me. I summon the stewardess to find out has Mortimer paid a first-class fare (children under seven travel free in tourist class but not in first). Mum who is wearing a medium-sized handkerchief as a skirt and has her hair in spikes turns round and waves a ticket in my face.

'Leonard always travels first class.'

---

* American slang for someone who doesn't drink alcohol.
† Though I did not drink alcohol until my mid-forties, the *Times Literary Supplement* had described my Behan biography as a 'classic exposition of the psycho-pathology of alcoholism'.

Leonard scowls, waving his tiny fists in the air, and is clearly on the edge of a massive outburst when Mum introduces herself.

The name is an icon in the protest movement.

'Don't worry. I dope Leonard on flights. I'm allergic to yelling myself.'

I did notice that the child's eyes were beginning to droop, and a minute or so later they are putting a cosy blanket over him as he slips into the arms of Morpheus. His mother tells me she is making a picture in South America and is hoping to sell world rights in Hollywood. Seems impressed by my knowledge of the American protest movement which has spread a wider net than any other of its kind in history.

Dinner at my cousin Carroll's tonight in Los Angeles. Carroll came to Ireland first from America to see if my father of the Royal College of Surgeons could help get Carroll's younger brother Hugh into medical school. Carroll himself had been a schoolteacher but he stayed on for a while in Dublin and joined the MacLiammóir–Edwards Company at the Gate Theatre. Back in the United States he has since had a successful stage and screen career and has now become one of the most famous faces in America as Archie Bunker in *All in the Family*,* one of the longest-running soaps ever.

'This is great,' I say to Carroll, 'but you can't stay in a soap all your life.'

He looks at me with slightly popping, self-assured eyes.

'I know when to get out.'†

At dinner is John McGiver, actor. He has won an Academy Award for his supporting role to Jon Voight in *Midnight Cowboy*.

'When I got the script of *Midnight Cowboy* I said "it's filthy". I wanted to wash myself.'

'Jon Voight said, "It's about loneliness."'

'It was.'

13 June

Lunch today with Edgar Bergen the ventriloquist. He was the first great modern proponent of the art who created real characters with

---

* An American version of *Till Death Us Do Part*.
† In the event he didn't. Years later he was still in *All in the Family*, and when he got out of this soap he went into another series which he wrote, directed and acted in – *The Heat of the Night*, building his own studios in Atlanta to do so.

his voice, like Charlie McCarthy and Mortimer Snerd. He didn't
mind too much if his lips moved a bit, because people couldn't take
their eyes off his puppets anyway. I didn't dare tell him that I'd been a
boy ventriloquist myself but I knew enough about the trade to cause
him a little surprise. I talked about 'head voice' and the trick for saying
'W' without moving your lips.

A genius who endowed wood with life.

14 June, San Francisco

Lunch here with a Mrs Albert who claims to be related to Oliver
Gogarty. She lives in Nob Hill where the San Francisco gentry hang
out. The original Irish who came here, unlike those on the East coast,
were from professional backgrounds, doctors, lawyers. Some of them
arrived via Australia where they had been deported after the uprising
of 1848. Dress reception for the book ghastly. Lots of hula girls
swaying. Stares from women. Apparently, many come here after
divorce. Live on alimony until the next jump.

Meet Charlie McCabe. He and Herb Cain are the two best known
columnists in San Francisco. Cain writes for the *Examiner*, McCabe
for the *Chronicle*. McCabe full of chat and seems to know everybody.
In England as well as here. He is married to Lady Mary Dunn and
mixed among the Bloomsbury set* in London. I met him in New
York in the Sixties through Ned Gerrity, Vice-President of
International Telephone & Telegraph, who had bagged many of the
best journalists in the country. After we'd met Charlie said: 'I wonder
why Ned Gerrity always seems to know what's going to happen in
Chile before the Chilean Government do?' This remark impressed me
when the democratically elected Chilean President, Salvador Allende,
was brought down by a junta not unconnected with IT&T whose
stake in Chile was substantial.

Charlie takes me to Perry's bar/restaurant. Full of young socialites.
Two women grab me. One black the other white. One of them says

---

* Frances Partridge, writing in her diary for 1964, observed, 'Yes, McCabe has quite a
good head and uses it to think for himself.' Later she recorded her friend Mary Dunn's
view. 'Charlie was like a timebomb whose charge was very near explosion point. He
would rush in at the door like a bull and ask who had left the bathroom tap running or
merely fulminate against the Christmas preparations, shouting ironically and rather com-
ically of the tree, 'ISN'T it delicious? I could eat it and I shall!'

'I'm going to fuck you.' There is almost a wrestling match. As I'd only just come in I thought this was pretty frank. The white girl is a nurse and has soulful eyes. She says her name is Ellen, then nearly sucks the tongue out of my head. Charlie seems a bit put out by all the attention I am getting.

'That's all froth,' he says. 'It doesn't mean a thing.'

Whatever it meant, I ended up in the black girl's apartment. I would have stayed till morning but the San Francisco night became frightfully cold. I caught a cab back to the St Francis Hotel to thaw out and told the operator I wouldn't take any calls.

Next morning I realized I'd left my sweater in the black girl's apartment so I decided to call a cab and go and get it. I then called Charlie to have him collect me there. When I came out and he saw the girl at the door, his face fell.

15 June

Charlie has arranged to take me out to have lunch with David Bouverie, whom I met yesterday in Saucelito. David's a cousin of Lord Drogheda* whose niece Maureen was my girlfriend. His ranch is divine. Courtyard with rich, deep grass at the edge, which is woven against the hazy blue of the sky. Cows everywhere in the long grasslands. After lunch, a long walk with McCabe. He often locks himself up for two weeks to write batches of his columns. He's a fanatic for style and has modelled himself on G.K. Chesterton. He sees his column as an essay – beginning, middle, end. Chesterton's essay on a piece of chalk is his model.

'Maurice Baring could write about Pushkin in two lines and say more than anyone else could in a thousand.' He sees writing in a San Francisco newspaper as a continuation of a tradition of writer-journalists like Lamb, Goldsmith and Andrew Lang. I ask him why is he separated from Lady Mary Dunn.

'I married for power, position. Whatever a man marries for. Now my nerves are so fucked up, when I get into an elevator I have to sit on the floor and phone my analyst on Fire Island.'

We catch a taxi into town. The driver complains: 'Blacks spill their trouble out. Want me to be their sponge.'

---

* Charles Garrett Ponsonby Moore, 11th Earl of Drogheda; Managing Director of the *Financial Times*, 1946–72; died in 1985.

17 June

Francine Grey gives a party in her apartment on Third Avenue in Sixtieth Street to promote the show at the Chelsea for the Berrigan Brothers Defence Fund. Very much a 'radical chic' affair. Shirley MacLaine, Pete Hamill and Jean Kennedy Smith et al. A beautiful girl in a short cocktail skirt and sculptured hair-do introduces herself as Sister Liz McAllister of the Sacred Heart nuns at Marymount, New York; she is helping with ticket sales and has been involved in the anti-Vietnam protest movement. Another colleague, Sister Jogues Egan, is collecting money across the room. Father Joe O'Rourke, a civil rights activist, is handsome but boring.

In the Lion's Head later on I get into an argument in which some guy comes at me from behind, puts his arms around me and squeezes my chest. Strong as a gorilla. I had to ram my heels into his shins in order to get out of the grip and into a position where I could manoeuvre with relative freedom.

18 June

Chelsea Studio full for Brendan Behan One-Man Show. The Behan legend is still alive here. Audience close up, but I look over their heads to the back and then occasionally direct my gaze to the front row in a sort of tete-à-tete which I hope will be picked up by those behind. According to Norman Mailer it was Behan who first made the Beats (Ginsberg, Corso, Kerouac, etc) socially acceptable uptown, with his success on television talk shows. Hostesses vied to have him at parties. At this point the Beats were still looked on as talentless, incoherent, oversexed and probably not smelling too good either.

Irish Distillers have sponsored a reception in Shirley Clarke's roof garden after the show. The guests walk in between gardens and trees and in and out of the rooms of Shirley's penthouse which are hung with smart paintings.

Across the street the lights of the skyscrapers twinkle. The best whiskey is available, Jameson's and Power's. Very much a New York mélange: writers, musicians, nuns, priests, Senators, people from City Hall. Sister Jogues Egan (not wearing her nun's habit) is there. She too has done time for her principles. She inquires for Viva[*], a

---

[*] Viva Superstar; she was given this name by Andy Warhol who directed the notorious film *Blue Movie* in which Viva played the lead opposite Louie Walden.

former pupil of hers at the Sacred Heart Academy in Buffalo who is living at the Chelsea. Across the roof we see Viva breastfeeding her baby.

'Some motherfucker wouldn't let me into your show,' Viva shouts as we approach. She and Jogues embrace. Viva was a prize pupil at Sacred Heart Buffalo where she was known as Susan Hoffman.

Now someone has started to play a guitar. Malachy McCourt, actor and radio star, starts to sing *Johnny I hardly knew you*. There is a hush under the stars as his voice folds itself round the chimneys over the moving and glittering lights below. Milton Macklin tells me that people have been turned away and they have a nice packet for the Berrigans.

19 June

In the Lion's Head one of the barmen, Mike Reardon, has a go at me:

'That's enough, Irishman.'

This is getting worse than Dublin, where I get attacked on average once a month. Mike gets so angry that he tries to leap over the bar to punch me. This is too much and I threaten to call the police. I also call the head barman, Nick Brown, who is a friend of mine. Nick is mystified.

'He's so gentle.'

'Nick, I've met three of your "gentle" guys this year, and I'm not impressed.'

Nick tells me that Mike had spent the summer in Italy playing the lead in a cowboy film and has just found out that it's not going to be released, which is one reason why he is so shirty.

Do I trigger off violence? Is it the way I look or is it some tone in my voice? Anyway, I go back and make it up with Mike who is really a right on guy.

20 June

Stanley Bard has suggested that I stay at the Chelsea for the rest of my visit. He says he will give me a rate. Moving out today from the Algonquin.

Meet George Kleinsinger* in the Chelsea lift, he says he enjoyed the Behan gig and invites me to Room 1012 in the Chelsea to hear a requiem he's composed for Brendan Behan.

No. 1012 is a special room even by Chelsea standards. I hear a nightingale's song as we approach. Inside I find it is a real one (Chinese). Around the four walls of the room there are glass cases full of water in which a long-necked Amazonian turtle and a blind white catfish are swimming. At the back a real waterfall nourishes a large tree in which what look like an iguana and a lizard frolic. As George leads me in a monkey whizzes by my face and lands on his shoulder.

> *George:* 'Brendan came to this room to recover from the booze.'
> *Me:* 'That I know. What I didn't know was that this was an annexe of Central Park Zoo.'

George puts the tape on of the North Dakota Symphony Orchestra playing his composition *Lament for Brendan Behan*. It begins with a crash, followed by a few oaths from Brendan and then takes off. George accompanies the music on his piano, the sheets sticking out so far from the top of the piano that they almost touch his nose. Doesn't bother him as he swings his shoulders in time with a cigarette hanging from his lips. A large toucan with a beautifully coloured beak is tapping against the bars of his cage in counterpoint. The *Lament* finishes with a clearly drunk Brendan singing the Irish National Anthem.

George is dressed in what is thought of as Chelsea Hotel attire. A shining clean denim shirt, white trousers with a crease and loafers. The room is spotlessly clean as it must be in order to ensure that his 'family' as he calls them don't turn it into a sty. I notice a lot of framed pictures and letters in the porch on the way out; one photo is of a beautiful girl who was George's girlfriend and who was raped and killed nearby. Touching verse by George underneath.

A sweet guy. The Chelsea – organized anarchy?

---

* American composer best known for *Archy and Mehitabel*, one of the first American operas. His *Tubby the Tuba* with Danny Kaye (vocal) is nationally known.

23 June

Find myself encased in Room 747, with some writers and painters. Everyone is sitting on the floor. Much smoking of grass. Gregory Corso* is reciting Yeats. When he is finished, he talks about the yew tree which Yeats saw as a symbol of death. An English poet recites from *Kubla Khan*. He says if you take opium before you read it, you will realize that the poem is about a woman's body.

Greg says he makes notes for poems over a period and then composes verse for a few days all out without stopping. This gives him a series of poems that are related, otherwise his mind jumps like a frog. One of the guys quotes Andrew Marvell's *The Definition of Love*:

> 'Therefore the Love which us doth bind,
> But Fate so enviously debars,
> Is the Conjunction of the Mind,
> And Opposition of the Stars.'

Greg (a little vaguely): 'That's the shot.'
I quote Marvell:

'I saw Eternity the other night
Like a great Ring of pure and endless light . . .'

Greg: 'That's not Marvell, it's Vaughan.'

He's right. Metaphysics in the Chelsea. Someone wants to know how the name Cuchulain is pronounced. The air is getting sweeter.

Greg: 'Why are people so down on money. Money is all right if you have enough of it.'

To a Tibetan poet lying next to him:

'Why is Alan going to India? Burroughs came back looking very fit. I stayed in a monastery there. I sat in a court for two days before I was fed by a spooky monk showing off his coat.'

(Long pause.) 'Yeah! Yeats *is* the shot.'

---

* 1930–2001; the best known, along with Allen Ginsberg and Jack Kerouac, of the writers of the Beat Generation.

He asks me to do a conjuring trick that he likes, then drowsily:

'See you next time round.'

In P.J. Clarke's later I meet Malachy McCourt.[*] He tells me that when I recited the Behan poem about Oscar Wilde, for a second or two he got a distinct smell of roses. I scoff. There are no roses in the house-yards beneath Chelsea Hotel basement room windows where you would more likely smell a dead cat.

Malachy: 'You know the reason I really liked Brendan.'
Me: 'No.'
Malachy: 'He told me once he couldn't hurt even a jackal.'

24 June

Today when I come down to the lobby I find a group there entranced by the goings-on at the hotel desk. An owlish-looking resident with glasses and an English public school accent is making a complaint to the desk clerk:

'I've just had a ghastly experience. I've been ripped off.' *(Pause.)* 'First they stole my wireless.'

'Wireless' brings screams of delight from the transvestite section of the lobby for such a word has not yet reached New York.

'Then they took my gramophone apart.'

This really blows the audience's mind. Gramophones went out with Mary Pickford's eyelashes.

'Then they defecated on my floor. Can't think why. Freudian perhaps?'

Holding my hands on my ears to drown the shrieks I ask Gregory:

'Who is this guy?'

'Dracula's cousin.'

Many Chelsea throwaways contain a soupçon of truth. In fact the guy, whose name is Roderick Ghuika, turns out to be a son of the Crown Prince of Romania who is descended from Vlad the Impaler, on whom Bram Stoker based his Count Dracula.

---

[*] Limerick-born writer, actor and very talented broadcaster; brother of the author Frank McCourt. Host of a popular New York radio chat show and author of an excellent autobiography, *A Monk Swimming*.

Later I discover Roderick may be related to me. His mother was Maureen O'Connor, the daughter of Sir Nicholas O'Connor, British Ambassador to St Petersburg, in which city she met and married the Crown Prince of Romania and to whom she bore a son who was christened Roderick, the O'Connor family name. After I hear this, when I meet Gregory on 23rd Street I comment:

'The Chelsea must be the only place in the world where you can meet Dracula's cousin and find out he's also *your* cousin.'

26 June

Lunch with my agent Max Wilkinson at the Century Club. Max one of the old school, University of Kentucky, well cut tweed suit and hand-made shoes. He began his career with the crown prince of agents, Max Perkins.

The Century Club is enormous. After negotiating a formidable oak staircase you encounter a series of rooms as big as a law court. Books all round the walls and really high ceilings. Around a long table stock-brokers, lawyers, company directors and literary agents gather for lunch. Max's ear is constantly sought. An author is doing well. They've read the reviews. Paul Reynolds, six foot three and looking like an American version of Charles de Gaulle, towers over us and reminds Max that he prophesied good things for me last year. My cousin John, a director of the publishing firm Grosset & Dunlap, stops for a second to raise his hand in greeting.

'Hail, and farewell.'

It was the luckiest thing in the world for me to find Max. He has all sorts of literary celebrities and bestsellers such as Kurt Vonnegut on his list. But he has a weakness for books written with style, even if they're not bestsellers and that's why he says he favours me, though I won't bring him much money. He knows the business like no one else. Also a good middleweight boxer at university. The lunch went well, with people coming up to talk. Then disaster.

Me: 'I've just come back from Chicago. Greatest fun. Guess who I met there. Nelson Algren.'
Max: (*with a look of well-bred distaste*) 'Algren is dead as a writer. He's just another Beatnik.'
Me: 'He writes *better* than them. Besides, I like the Beats.'
Max: 'Bunch of phonies. Fags. Junkies. Algren's washed up.'

Me: 'That's what comes from living on Shelter Island.'
Max: 'Some of your jokes aren't funny.'
Me: 'Maybe living on Shelter Island makes you unreceptive.'
Max: (furious) 'I'll end this whole unhappy relationship.'
Prim guy (opposite): 'I'm one of the defendants.' *(Shrugs.)*

10 August, Dublin

Tea with Billy Wicklow[*] at the Royal Marine Hotel, Dun Laoghaire. We have made the appointment by letter as I daren't call the house since he got married. Dun Laoghaire is about seven miles from where I live in the city, and looks down on a beautiful bay flecked with yachts.

I glimpse Billy's George III profile across the lounge looking steadfastly out to sea. 'Hello Rudge,'[†] he says, tilting his head backwards. I give him some scandal. Hugely amused with a story about the Pro-Cathedral where a TV interviewer asked an old woman who was saying her prayers there what she thought of the new liturgy in English which had replaced the Latin one. 'It interferes with me prayers,' she said.

We have always been fans of the Pro-Cathedral, where on Sunday we can hear masses by Palestrina, Gabrieli and Vittoria. The choir (endowed by Edward Martyn, Lady Gregory's friend) are very fine and sing up as far as the Offertory, when there is a pause for the Archbishop's sermon during which Billy normally goes to sleep and occasionally snores. I have to nudge him to wake up as I've had to do in the theatre and on one occasion he thought he was at the latter and applauded vigorously with a loud laugh. Lionel Perry tells me he did the same with him at *The Ring* at Covent Garden, asking on being woken up, 'Am I at Willesden Junction?'[‡]

---

[*] See introduction and note to 2 July 1970.

[†] Billy Wicklow would call me by this name because with my barrister's bag slung on my back, I reminded him of Barnaby Rudge and his basket.

[‡] The Dublin that Billy Wicklow returned to after the war was probably closer to a medieval city than almost any in Europe, which was part of its attraction for him. In the heart of the town there were churches run by religious orders, the Franciscans at Merchants Quay, the Augustinians of Thomas Street, the Dominicans of Dominick Street, the Jesuits of Gardiner Street, the Carmelites of Clarendon Street, as well as the secular churches. Mass, Benediction, Evening Devotions were built into the pattern of life of the working people and on Sunday the bells could be heard pealing from early morning till noon. Holy

While we chat, in the lounge, I begin to realize he is clearly bored with the sedate existence of a seaside suburb and the sort of company that the wife provides for him. His talk is about the 'street characters', Bang Bang, Johnny Forty Coats, the Genockey brothers. But when I want to tell him of newcomers to the scene, he's reluctant to listen, perhaps realizing he has little chance of ever meeting them. Eleanor, his wife, has put her foot down. 'Rudge' is in her view not suited for Dun Laoghaire drawing rooms. Just as well as I wouldn't relish the sight of Billy, like the dormouse in *Alice in Wonderland*, stuffed into an imaginary teapot, nodding away as the chatter passes over his head.

Reminds me, as he sips his tea, that today is the feast of the Holy Rosary, and adds chirpily that he has found out that the 7th of next month is also the feast of St Bacchus, martyr.

'I wish I'd taken that name at my confirmation. Imagine the look on the Bishop's face as he would have had to say, "I confirm thee William Bacchus Cecil", etc.'

As I walk him to the taxi, I let him know that I will be in Gibraltar next week on my way to write in Spain.

'Mind you get Ryan of the Garrison Library there to make you a member. You don't have to be in the Forces. A very good collection of books up to 1900 and not bad after. Ten shillings a year and an excellent afternoon tea.'

He tears a page from his diary and writes an introduction for me. A dear friend, three decades older than I, who never stops thinking of how he can help.

28 September

Tonight my one man play on Brendan Behan, directed by Tomás MacAnna, opens at the Abbey Theatre (the Peacock) as part of the Dublin International Theatre Festival. Nervous in the dressing room. Onstage when the lights come up the first thing I see is an Alsatian in the front row. I almost scream out loud. The animal could wreck the

---

Week at Easter provided a sort of Celtic Bayreuth with elaborate ceremonies designed each day to represent the different stages of the passion and death of the Redeemer. This high Liturgy with its incense, candles, Gregorian chant and symbolism had been part of the tapestry of life for the ordinary people for generations. It was much to Billy's taste and he remarked once, as we arrived for mass one Sunday at the Pro-Cathedral, that Abelard's Paris may have been like this.

show as I will never know when it might bark, and even if it never does my timing will go to bits waiting for it to happen.

'Will whoever owns that dog please remove it?'

A man puts up his hand. 'It's a guide dog, I'm blind.'

'Oh my God,' I say. 'Please forgive me.'

I begged him to stay, saying I'd be shattered and would have to cancel the performance if he left. He very decently sat down and though temporarily shocked I got through the first act reasonably well and even received what might have been a woof of approval from the front row.

By the second half I was on my bicycle and think, with a bit of luck, the play could have legs.* When I got back to my dressing room the blind gentleman was there complete with his huge Alsatian who was wagging his tail vigorously. I was introduced to Seamus as the dog was called, who did everything except stand up and ask for my autograph. The man talked about how much he'd enjoyed it, adding that a one man show is a perfect vehicle for the blind. All the characters an actor has to conjure up for his audience are actually more vivid for the blind, as their imaginative faculty is developed so well. I told this nice man that a guide dog posed no problem for actors in a theatre, as they were trained to bark only when necessary. I had definitely made a hit with Seamus, so I made a point of informing his owner that he could tell any of his friends to come along with their dogs and I would make sure that they got complimentary tickets. Seamus had to be almost dragged out, looking over his shoulder at me with yearning eyes.†

29 September

Saturday morning. Today I am the map-maker, the seeker of streams. A game plan for a walk is required. Gerry O'Flaherty (friend of twenty years) will arrive at midday. The question is, where to? Setting off from my house, I can be at the sea in ten minutes if I take a left or at the mountain foothills in the same time if I take a right. But the mountains today look almost as if they are at the end of my garden, which could mean rain.

So what about Sandymount Strand flanked on one side by Howth Head and Killiney Hill on the other? I open the door to sniff the air

---

* It went on to beat the Abbey record for the run of a one man play.

† Two weeks later as the lights went up I peeped out into the auditorium to see an Alsatian *and* a Labrador in the front row.

and am hit by a blast. Will I walk into eternity on Sandymount Strand? Not today, Stephen.

No, I think it will be the dear little dancing Dodder for us today, meandering its way to the sea, whose banks I can reach in five minutes from here. It was George Moore's favourite walk when he lived in Dublin. Maybe I'll meet my favourite heron there, still and silent as the swans float by.

There is a knock downstairs now. Gerry is there.

'Dodder.'

Off we go.

3 October

Afternoon tea at Tara Hall, Sandycove with Monk Gibbon and Winifred. The large drawing room is full of light. One whole side of it, fronting the garden, is all glass with a big open door. The walls are quite extraordinary – almost art deco as if it were a cinema. One shade is a sort of light chocolate brown. Monk is laying down the law about modern poetry – Auden, Donald Davie and others he is not a fan of. As he is eliminating them, he pulls in Dylan Thomas's name as a potential victim for his poetic guillotine.

I give him *Fern Hill* off the cuff before he does his Madame Defarge bit. Fair play to him, he listens intently, turning his head in profile to concentrate and at the poem's sea-shattering end, he turns with some wonder and says:

'But that is beautiful.'

Ten years ago he read Patrick Kavanagh's *Soul for Sale* to me to bring out its texture, and I was entranced. Quits!

Monk has recently sent me a fine essay on Proust which he published some time ago in *Hermathena* [a Trinity College Dublin Quarterly]. Proust appeals to him as George Moore and Walter Pater do because of his matchless prose style. We agree that the attribute which most makes a writer great is his use of language, his balance and choice of words. Monk carefully avoids, however, the question of Proust's sexual habits in the essay. When I ask him about this a shadow comes on his face.

'What is the evidence that Proust was promiscuous?'

'Evidence Monk!' I scream. 'You have read Painter's biography, Proust was up to his neck in catamites.'

Monk keeps himself under control with some difficulty.

Monk: 'I made a special visit to London to see Painter when the biography came out.'
Me: 'You mean to say he is going back on what he says in the biography?'
Monk: 'He just implies that the evidence is thin. It may or may not be.'
Me: 'That gives you a funk hole to retreat into so that you can close your eyes against glaring facts. Anyway Monk, what does it matter if Proust was promiscuous? It's his writing that counts.'

He says nothing, just concentrates on the tree outside the window. He's the same about A.E. Housman whose poetry he loves; but who he won't admit went to Paris each summer for romps with the lads. Monk has a Jansenist streak where sex is concerned which prevents him giving wholehearted admiration to any writer whose lifestyle does not conform to his own rigid principles. Since Proust is his idol, his life must conform to Monk's rigid code. Where he got it from I don't know, as this attitude is more a Catholic than a Protestant one in Ireland. Yet here is the son of the Church of Ireland Rector of Dundrum spouting away like any scapulared Confraternity man.[*]

Anyway, this sort of thing drives me frantic. If an artist can't accept the human condition as it is then who the hell will.

4 October

Frantic call from Mariga at 2 am.
   'Mosebags is pouncing.'
   It seems Sir Oswald Mosley[†] who is staying at Leixlip Castle is

---

[*] In a letter written to Monk later, I touched on this repression: 'When I was growing up there was a predominant element in Irish society which would refuse to admit that Wolfe Tone, Daniel O'Connell or anybody connected with the national hierarchy could possibly ever have sinned against the flesh. It seems to me that your attempt to put people into the category that you want in defiance of facts is a similar approach, which is why I find it hard to accept.'

[†] Sir Oswald Mosley, 6th Baronet. After a distinguished war career in the Royal Flying Corps he was invalided out in 1918. Minister of State for Labour in MacDonald's 1929 government. Resigned in frustration and influenced by the current achievements of Mussolini's regime, launched the British Union of Fascists with Harold Nicolson, MP in 1932. Married twice, first to Cynthia Curzon and after her death to Diana Mitford, and thus became Desmond Guinness's stepfather.

knocking on her bedroom door. This has happened before when Desmond is away from home, so I zoom down the country by taxi to Leixlip (it takes 25 minutes on empty roads) through the fields and open countryside. When I get there Mosebags is sleeping peacefully in his own bed, having been told by Mariga that my arrival is imminent.

This same Mosley is a strange man. Often evenings, in front of the enormous fire in the sitting room I have talked with him, or rather he has talked to me, since listening is not his strong point. You sense the energy, power of a gifted talker. Where did he go off the tracks? I suspect English politics in the late Twenties and Thirties would have put a strain on an original mind. Stanley Baldwin and Ramsay MacDonald were so unattractive that able men such as Harold Nicolson were often driven into false positions.

Mosley was one of the first victims of the age of Narcissus. The advent of the loudspeaker and moving pictures paved the way for mass communication on a new level. As little boys envy film stars, so too the Mosleys of the day found it impossible to resist the drug of public adoration. Demagoguery was sweeping Europe. Mosley rallying an exhausted England under the canopy of Earls Court exhibition hall, with thousands of supporters screaming below, was a trip as seductive as any LSD-inspired experience that could be enjoyed in the Sixties. This was a far cry from the message of his powerful social programme, written as junior minister in the Labour Government of 1929, of which R.H.S. Crossman said that it 'revealed him to be an outstanding politician of his generation . . . spurned by every party leader at Westminster, simply and solely because he was right.'

A friend whom I had met in unusual circumstances was Olive Reid, who became an executive with the cosmetic company L'Oréal of Paris in Salisbury, Rhodesia. She had had quite a spectacular career in Dublin before having to leave at the age of twenty-four. A good-looking girl from a middle-class Protestant Dublin family, she'd served a sentence in Mountjoy Prison for blackmail. After her release she went to London and embarked on a successful career as a high-class call girl. Her personality, looks and conversational gifts ensured that she was soon at the top of her profession there and financially secure. An extraordinary meeting in a pea-soup fog with Sir Edward Marsh, one-time private secretary to Herbert Asquith and Winston Churchill and editor of the Georgian poets Rupert Brooke, Julian Grenfell and Robert Graves, resulted in his taking her to his flat in Grosvenor Square where, captivated by her bright *conversation and sense of fun, he offered her a room of her own in exchange for light housekeeping duties.* * *Sensing a mind hungry for imaginative expression, he guided her in her choice of reading and took her with him to galleries and exhibitions. After his death in the 1950s, she drifted on to hard drugs for a short while and came back to Dublin to kick the habit. It was then I met her and we became fast friends. I was in my twenties and though practising at the Bar, training on average two hours daily for my various sports had fuelled my energy to an extent that Olive assured me I compensated her for the cravings of drug withdrawal. I would come to dinner twice a week, which was cooked and served by an Old Etonian butler she had brought over from England with her, Thomas Torey, a gay ex-Guards Officer, in his middle thirties, six feet two, slim and well built. A gourmet cook, he served delicious meals. She had christened him Thomas Aquinas after the Dominican philosopher/saint and if 'clients' were giving her grief she would simply cry 'Aquinas' and Tom would immediately metamorphose to collect what he referred to as 'Madam's modest stipend'. I continued Sir Edward Marsh's good work and introduced her to the works of Yeats, Sean O'Casey and Lady Gregory, who had not figured on Sir Edward's reading list. I even persuaded her to call her recently acquired sealyham 'Christy Mahon', after the hero in John Millington Synge's play* The Playboy of the Western World.

After a decade or so in Dublin Olive decided on a career change and headed off to Salisbury, Rhodesia where she became an executive at the unsuspecting L'Oréal of Paris. Living in a cottage rented to her by Lord Acton's granddaughter, she would write to me regularly to describe her congenial lifestyle in what later would become Zimbabwe.

5 October

Letter this morning from Salisbury, Rhodesia from Olive Reid.

My dear Ulick

Just a short note to say that I found in the Library here 'Inglorious Soldier' and would have passed it by but for the name Monk Gibbon on the dust jacket, and when I got it home, lo

---

* In the course of arranging for James Joyce to get a Civil List grant in 1917, Marsh had read his work before passing it on to the Prime Minister, Asquith. Thus, he would have an awareness of the character of Dublin life, unusual at the time, and one which would make his affection and kindness to Olive more easily comprehensible.

and behold, I see 'Yourself' on the dedication page.* I remember your talking a great deal about him but cannot recall in what context, so am enjoying the book and shall wait and see. I like his rather old world description of his early days in Dublin, and to recognize old friends i.e. Easter Week etc, it always seems different somehow. Second piece of news, had a belated Xmas Card from Thomas Aquinas and he says he saw you in London, at least I suppose it was you as his writing has got worse but I think it said 'madam's young man' . . .

I am cured from whatever ailed me and am in high spirits again, especially as I have had a winning streak at bridge . . .

N.B. Did I tell you that your 'Gogarty' is in the library (2 copies).

Hope this finds you at home,

Best love,
Olive

My reply:

Dear Ollie R

Thanks for your letter. Wasn't it funny you coming across my name in a Rhodesian library in Monk Gibbon's book. Actually

---

* *Inglorious Soldier* (Hutchinson, 1968) is an autobiographical account by Monk Gibbon of his service in World War One as a Lieutenant. Back on leave in Dublin at Easter 1916, he was ordered to Portobello barracks in Rathmines during the Rebellion that began that week. While there he witnessed the murder of a Dublin writer (Francis Sheehy Skeffington) by an officer in the Royal Irish Rifles, Captain Bowen Colthurst. Skeffington had been distributing pacifist pamphlets.

An attempt was made to hush the affair up. Monk courageously allied himself with Major Sir Francis Vane who had Colthurst brought before a court-martial and sentenced. Monk was so affected by the affair, however, that having returned to the trenches he asked to be transferred to the Royal Army Medical Corps as an ambulance driver. He had now become a target for the establishment and it was only by the greatest luck that he avoided a court-martial and possible execution by firing squad.

Subsequently he had a nervous breakdown as a result of which he resolved never to read the substantial archive of letters and memoirs he had kept relating to the event. Meeting him one evening on the lawn of Monkstown Church, where his father had once been Rector, I persuaded him to take the plunge, rediscover the past and place before posterity a remarkable story of moral courage; hence the book he dedicated to me.

there was a hilarious incident about a year before the book
came out, in which I impersonated Terence de Vere White's
voice to Monk on the telephone and Gibbon didn't take it as a
joke at all. He then took my name out of the dedication
although he claims that I made him write the book. But by
mistake the proof reader left it in, so Monk didn't like to interfere with fate and left it as it was, which is how you came across
it in the Salisbury library. Anyway, he and I have made it up and
we are pals again now. I think it is a worthwhile book, don't
you?

I did meet Aquinas in London and he was in fantastic form,
flying as usual. He has a friend called Waldo who decorates his
walls for him and of course he's got Waldo on 'speed' as he thinks
it improves his temperament. Waldo's girlfriend is Chinese so
you can see that Tom is in his element. He told me a lot about
his mother and showed me her photograph. She's still alive and
I spoke to her on the telephone.

Tom now has some money and really behaves with great elegance of manner. I mean this truly. He has style and has succeeded despite misfortune in living his life in a curiously
dignified way, preserving his own personality. He talked a lot
about Pembroke Road where you lived. He even remembered
some of the jargon we used.

'I seem to remember you were always on the point of com-
pleting what you called your *magnum opus* [Gogarty] and when
it was finished . . . Whenever you came in your first words
were usually "What news on the Rialto, Olivia?" because your
Rialto was just round the corner on the Grand Canal, like
Bassanio's in Venice. Another Latin tag which gave Olive the
giggles was *ignis caput – fire ahead.'*

Tom seemed in remarkably good health considering what he
has been doing to himself for 20 years. He said those four years
in Dublin were delicious. He even talked a lot about John
Charles [the Catholic Archbishop of Dublin] who he knows in
some remote way, because believe it or not, the Arch writes to
help one of Tom's friends who has been deported and is living
in England.

My biography of Brendan has been published in the U.S. I

have used your quote and it has been commented on more than once as being very perceptive.[*]

If you come over let me know well in advance. I want to set a week aside. The last week in July will probably be best if you can make it around that time. I have to write a TV script on Gogarty this summer, and I am meant to have two plays coming off in the autumn which I have to rewrite.

Do let me know as near as possible the weeks you will be in Ireland and we can revisit old haunts. I am looking forward to seeing you.

Yours
Ulick

21 October

Ulick O'Connor's selected XV against Suttonians Rugby Club President's XV on the occasion of the opening of their new pavilion. Ronnie Kavanagh, Tony Ensor and Gerry Culliton (Irish caps) are in my team while International fly-half Mick English captains the President's XV. I give the lads a bollocking in the pavilion beforehand and stress no kicking for touch, a rule borrowed from Don Hingerty's team, the Fir Bolgs.[†] Good crowd. Absolutely beautiful day. In the first half I am handed a try as I nip in from the wing between the fly-half and the scrum and take the ball on the trot. Furious in the second half though. Ensor from full-back came through the centre at halfway. I stuck to him and forty yards from the line there was no one between

---

[*] Olive had given me a perceptive account of her memories of Brendan, which is quoted in full in the biography where I had given her the name Edith.

[†] Professor Don Hingerty, School of Science, University College Dublin, got four caps for Ireland and was the hero of a famous match in 1947 when Ireland beat England by 22 points, the highest ever margin up to that time. Though a fearless tackler Don believed in the importance of handling and passing the ball, and becoming depressed with the rash of kicking, fashionable then in Irish rugby, he retired from the game to found his own team, the Fir Bolgs (this means in English the Bag Men, a race who were the precursors in Ireland of the Celts). Don's strict rule was that the ball should never be kicked to touch. If a Fir Bolg put the ball in touch (even accidentally) he was sent off. The idea was an instant success and Fir Bolgs sides, which included a number of International players, regularly toured Ireland under the Professor's guidance. He himself played first-class rugby until he was over fifty.

me and it, if he had passed I was in the clear. He didn't and of course was tackled in possession by the full-back. Tony was at Gonzaga College (Jesuit), while I was at St Mary's (Holy Ghost Fathers). At Mary's in no circumstances would you hold onto the ball coming up to the full-back with a man outside you, as if you did you wouldn't be on the team for the next match and for maybe longer. The Jesuit (Spanish) system tends to cultivate the entrepreneur approach, as against the ordered Cartesian one of the Holy Ghost Fathers (French). It may be said therefore that Tony's failure to hand me a try on a plate stemmed from his parents' choice of schooling, which whether it did or not seems to me as I write pretentious nonsense, so I'd better stop.

As I came off the pitch Charlie Haughey* came up genially to say I'd played well. His tone of voice implied that he was somewhat surprised. Furious I was. What does he know about rugby and if it's as little as I think it is, what right has he to be *surprised*. In the pavilion I confirm with Mick English that a famous remark did originate with him. He was playing on an Irish side who got a hiding from the English at Twickenham. Explaining afterwards why he missed the slippery English out-half, Horrocks-Taylor, so often, Mick had told a reporter in the bar of the mailboat on the way back:

'Horrocks went one way and Taylor went the other, and all I was left with was the bloody hyphen.'

---

* Taoiseach 1979–81, March–December 1982 and 1987–92.

1972

In late 1968 at the height of the Civil Rights disturbances in Northern Ireland and aware of the necessity of promoting an Irish point of view in world media, I arranged to see the Taoiseach, Jack Lynch, on the introduction of George Colley (Minister for Finance). Lynch agreed that the present situation was worse than useless and thought the solution was to form a Taoiseach's Steering Committee which would look at the presentation of the Irish Government's point of view in Great Britain and elsewhere. For the next few years this committee would handle much of the Irish news in the foreign media and on a small scale manage to achieve a few notable coups. The committee was composed of Padraic O Hanrachain, the Taoiseach's private secretary (who had also served under Taoisigh de Valera and Lemass), John O'Sullivan, head of the Taoiseach's Office, Sean White, an outstanding journalist and publicist with Bord Failte (Irish Tourist Board), Noel Dorr, a Counsellor from the Department of Foreign Affairs, Bart Cronin, press officer for George Colley, Tim Dennehy, another senior civil servant, and myself. I had been asked to chair the committee and rule it with a firm hand. Foreign Affairs people in particular had to be kept on a tight reign because their performance in this area so far had been less than adequate. However, the nominees from the Taoiseach's Department offset any difficulties one might have had in relation to Foreign Affairs. Lynch was aware of mandarins in that department who guarded their turf jealously. But he didn't cross them; he simply set up an alternative programme.

In 1971 and at the beginning of 1972 the Northern Ireland situation was beginning to settle down. Since 1968, with the Civil Rights Marches and the creation of a mini-state within a state in the Bogside in Derry, the disturbances there had become familiar on the world scene. The British Army had been welcomed into Northern Ireland by most Nationalists, as it was seen as coming to protect them against the violent elements in the Protestant Loyalist section of the community.

In January 1972 there were many who believed that a resolution of the Northern Ireland problem was possible within a few years, five at the most. Single-party government by the Unionists who had been in power since the beginning of the State would now be challenged by an energetic young and politically gifted group, who in 1970 had formed the Social Democratic and Labour Party. John Hume was its outstanding figure, and with Austin Currie, Ivan Cooper, Gerry Fitt and others to support him, it seemed clear that parliamentary democracy could work in Northern Ireland if the Unionists would accept the democratic process.

28 January, Paris

Off to Paris for the rugby international – Ireland against France. Have my togs with me as on the second pitch at Stade Colombe Old Ireland are to play Old France. Old Ireland consists of former rugby internationals with a few mavericks included, and we are to play at 11 am on Saturday morning before the afternoon match. In the plane on the way over I feel quite ghastly. I've had a gingivectomy (an operation to cut back inflamed gums) and I am fairly well recovered but still exhausted from the operation. It turns out to be the coldest day in the history of France and the cold in Paris is worse than anything I have ever experienced in London or Dublin. I glide through the football match accepting any passes that I get, but not devoting any special energy to tasks which involve coarse contact such as tackling or going down on the ball. Afterwards, I manage to warm up in the shower after being colder than I ever have been before. I am apprehensive about the international match which commences very soon on the next field of the Stade Colombe. How am I going to sit in the stand with the temperature as it is and survive, with my constitution weakened by the after-effects of an operation? All my hypochondriacal instincts surface. Then an idea. Seeing free bottles of Jameson whiskey handed out by the sponsors I recall reading about how the Aran fishermen in their currachs never suffered from cold because they drank *poitin* (home-made whiskey) to keep their circulation going.

'Whiskey's my man', I said to myself and asked for a bottle, filled half a glass and drank it neat. I had to let it down the hatch fast as it burned my tonsils. Clutching my bottle under a heavy coat and wrapped in scarves I set out with the team to locate the fine seats that had been reserved for us in the nearby stand. Thinking I was going to have to be carried out on a stretcher with lungs shattered from the cold, I decided to try another swig from the bottle. The match was excellent – what I saw of it. By half-time I was certainly gone. The rest of the lads were enjoying not only the football but the spectacle of me and my first ever experience of whiskey, replenishing myself frequently from the bottle in my hand, explaining as I did so that it was the only way to avoid hypothermia.* I kept assuring myself that I was quite sober and that the whiskey was not affecting me. Suddenly,

---

* I did not drink until I was forty.

about half an hour from the end, I realized that I had to make a move. I scudded off the stand into the street hoping I would find a taxi. I asked somebody where I was, seeming for some reason to speak better French than I normally do. He told me I was fifteen miles from Paris and that there were no taxis in the neighbourhood. Usually such information would have put me into a panic. Now I didn't give a tinker's damn; nerves were asleep, thank God. I wished I had a green hat on in the hope that some driver who was on his way to the centre of Paris might take pity on me.

Miraculously a car did stop; the chap inside spoke English and drove me right back to the hotel where the Irish team were staying. I went straight up to bed at five o'clock and lay down. I woke up at 7.30 feeling superb – no headache – nothing, mind as clear as a bell. I went downstairs to the banquet at which the English and Irish rugby teams as well as the Oldies were present. Andy Mulligan kept after me, anxious to know what was happening in Dublin on the political side. Andy works for the *Observer* in Paris.

After midnight I was lying on my bed upstairs when Brian O'Halloran, the number 8 on the side, broke into the room.

'Did you hear what's happened?'

'No.'

'They've shot thirteen people in Derry.'

'Who shot them?'

'The Army, the British Army.'

We convene a meeting of the team in O'Halloran's room. Ronnie Kavanagh and Brian O'Halloran are there. Someone wants us to march in protest to the British Embassy. I say no, having learned on the ground over the years that the French gendarmerie are not particularly partial to protesters and not at all averse to resorting to their hardware if things get nasty. There is real indignation but in the end we decide to wait until we get home and find out all the facts. (We are leaving early tomorrow for Dublin.) I immediately get on the phone to my Committee, Sean White, Padraic O Hanrachain, Bart Cronin, and arrange a meeting for the next day in Dublin.

31 January, Dublin

Was up all of last night. Have rung Bart Cronin of the Steering Committee and asked him to talk to his boss, George Colley, about letting us do an all-out public relations job to present the facts behind yesterday's shootings before the British propaganda machine gets to work. Colley has agreed and has mentioned it to the Taoiseach. When I contact Lynch he says we'll have a full talk about it on the way up to the funeral in St Eugene's Cathedral, Derry, which is on Wednesday. In the meantime, I am to contact Brian Lenihan, the Minister for Transport, in order to set travel arrangements in motion.

My proposal to Brian comes from a clip that was shown on television. A Derry priest, Father Ed Daly, is in the middle of an armed attack in front of those carrying a dying boy and waving a blood-stained handkerchief to try and put an end to the gunfire directed at them. He will be the right man to tell on television what actually happened – if we can get hold of him and if he will agree to go. I say to Brian that we could airlift Ed Daly out of Derry after the mass for the thirteen dead on Wednesday and get him to London by that evening for a New York flight. Once in the US he will be in a position to counteract any false propaganda which might be in the papers or on television.* I have contacts with some major American TV shows and if I can telephone right through the night I will be certain of landing Father Daly a few choice appearances. Brian, an old Law Library pal of mine, offers the use of one of his CIE† offices for three days after 5 o'clock to make phone calls to the USA. He says that an Assistant General Manager of CIE, James McMahon, a young Turk with a lot of vim, will work with us. Brian is to meet me at 12 o'clock in the Shelbourne Hotel. I wait for him in the hotel at midday, having coffee with Sean White who has worked in the USA and is one of the outstanding PR people around.

White: 'If Lenihan doesn't turn up I'm not going to New York with Father Daly.'

---

* In London on 30 January the BBC had announced that gunmen had attacked troops in Londonderry and the army had retaliated by shooting thirteen IRA members. The British had circulated in the USA a story that the return fire came when the army fired rubber bullets to clear the streets and that four of those shot dead were on the security forces wanted list. This was untrue. Not one of the dead men had a paramilitary connection or carried a weapon. A tribunal is currently investigating the events of Bloody Sunday.
† Coras Iompair Eireann (Irish Transport Company).

Me: 'Can't you speak to Brian on the telephone?'
White: 'No, I couldn't. I know Lenihan too well. I'd need to see his eyes to know if anything was going to be done.'
Me: (rather despairingly) 'Well, what are we going to do?'
White: 'Phone and tell him the scene.'

I go out and phone Brian.
'You're late. White is not going to work with us unless you come and see him in person.'

When he asks why White doesn't trust him, I reply tactfully that his title as the 'promising young Minister' is perhaps an indication of a certain tendency to rest on his oars when it comes to delivering the goods. Decently enough Brian doesn't choose to look on this as a threat (which it is) but comes along and authorizes Sean, to his satisfaction, to head the project in the USA. McMahon and Cronin now join us. Arrange to meet McMahon at 6 o'clock in the CIE building in the heart of the city near O'Connell Street. The offices are clear when we arrive.

I have five TV shows in the USA that I have useful contacts with. The leading Network talk show is Johnny Carson's on NBC where I know Shelly Schultz who was a producer on two occasions when I was on myself. I am certain we can get on the Dick Cavett Show. By 4 am we finish. We have three major TV shows in addition to a number of radio ones. When Sean gets to America he can extend this programme. In the meantime we have established a firm foothold.

2 February

Bleary-eyed, I stumble into a State car with Brian Lenihan to travel to Derry for the funerals of the thirteen deceased in St Eugene's Cathedral. (Lynch is attending a Requiem Mass in Dublin's Pro-Cathedral). Five of the Cabinet are coming up for the funeral. Our plan is to get Father Daly away before the security forces up North know what we are after (I hope our telephone lines haven't been tapped).

The thirteen coffins are a fearsome sight, arrayed on the altar, while in the front pew the Cabinet members sit as the Bishop of Derry says mass. I sit beside them (in an aisle seat for a quick getaway) hoping that the television camera won't spot me. After the Deo Gratias I go behind the altar to collect Father Daly. First of all, however, he has to attend at the burial of young Jackie Duddy, the Derry kid who died in his arms. We collect him afterwards at the presbytery.

On the way down we discuss plans in Brian's extremely spacious car. It is decided to fly via London to obtain the necessary US visa rather than approach the US Embassy in Dublin. There is a feeling that the Irish Foreign Affairs people might make it difficult to get a visa for Father Daly by putting pressure on the American Embassy in Dublin to refuse it, on the grounds that the situation is too delicate to allow him uninhibited access to the US media. (The Minister for Foreign Affairs is to address the United Nations this week and his officials are nervous that his show might be upstaged.) Father Daly and Sean White will operate under the umbrella of the Irish Tourist Board, which is Brian Lenihan's bailiwick as Minister for Transport and Power. We drop the pair of them at Dublin Airport to get the London plane.

Good luck! They have a big job, to turn around in two days the canard that the thirteen dead were armed gunmen.*

3 February

Tonight a massive crowd storms the British Embassy in Merrion Square. The police are guarding it armed with batons, and using Alsatian dogs on leash to keep the crowd back. The Square is packed. It is estimated 100,000 are present. There are baton charges. Some of those taking part in the protest are savaged by dogs. Finally a man breaks through the barriers and climbs up the side of the Embassy, setting it on fire. The crowd roar as the building begins to collapse in flames.

5 March, Tipperary

Down today in Clonmel, to play for the Firbolgs XV against a Munster selection. We dropped into a bar on the way down for coffee.

---

* Father Daly's TV appearances had a massive effect. As I had thought when I saw him on TV on 31 January, he was a natural for the box. He made it clear with each appearance that he knew all those who were shot dead that day personally, and that none of them had any connection with terrorism. Thus the official smear in circulation was wiped out and 'the priest with the bloodstained hankie' became overnight an envoy of truth.

As we came into the bar a man was shouting: 'Ulick. Ulick.' As he couldn't have seen me, I didn't know how this could happen. It turned out that his wife, a great *Late Late* fan, had named a cat after me. On the last occasion this happened to me it was a parrot who bore my name.

Whatever the reason for this response, it is useful when it comes to putting over ideas which need a public airing. It provides a sort of instant Letter to the Editor which one feels so often one ought to write but never gets down to doing so.

At the match, when I got the ball on the wing some of the crowd reached out over the touchline to get a touch of me as I flew past, one of them so obsessed that she accidentally handtripped me.

6 March

Today a waiter in the Shelbourne, Andrew O'Connor, who has the face of an American Indian chieftain, lent me a manuscript he has written, 'Dublin in the Twenties'. He asked me if I knew anyone who would publish it. After he left me with it, I opened it at a section in which Andy has described how in the Dominick Street slum he grew up in, instead of killing rats, they used to collect them. Oh the damnable ingenuity of the Celt. He describes how his father and some young companions went out to Co. Dublin where a farmer who kept pigs was plagued by rats and they offered to get rid of them for a substantial fee.

When we got there the first thing we unloaded was a cage full of rats. When the farmer saw this he rushed up to my father shouting,

'Jasus man I don't want more fuckin' rats, it's rid of the bastards I want.'

My father looked at him and laughed,

'And get rid of them you will and bloody quick at that.'

The father and his crew then proceeded to locate all the ratholes in the place. Then the boys with the dogs were placed in position and his father showed the dogs a male rat which was easy to pick out as it was darker in colour than the others. The cage it was in was placed opposite a large hole and then a can which contained a mixture of heavy oil and paraffin was given a good shake and the oil poured over the other rats.

Next my father dropped a lighted rag among them setting them alight and at the same time opening the cage door leaving the rats to bolt down the holes, squealing in terror and looking like living torches. The smell of their burning flesh was sickening. A few minutes elapsed and then rats came out of every hole, terrified of the fire, only to be met by the dogs and people intent on their destruction: the dogs silently working, the men, women and boys shouting with excitement as they killed the rats. Of course we didn't kill them all. Some made their escape which wasn't surprising as there were dozens of them.

In a short time they had killed a hundred and nine according to Andy's count. The dead rats were burned with the remainder of the oil.

The farmer invited my father and the men into the house, I don't know what they were given but they were soon spifflicated. They could hardly walk, but after a bit of messing about we got underway and made our own way home thanks to the ponies' instinct because the men fell asleep and we kids hadn't a clue where we were or how to get home.

I find this writing very fine. A whiff of Hieronymus Bosch about it. The scene comes so vividly before the mind that I have to go into a sort of artificial shudder to bring me back to the reality of the Shelbourne tea room. If the rest of the manuscript is as good as this, Andy won't be a mute inglorious Milton for long.

19 March

Coming home on the bus, I think how much I've forgotten the pleasure of travelling from Stephen's Green to Rathgar on the upstairs part. Really since the trams were taken off the streets in 1956, I've tended to use public transport less and less. The service has become quite hopeless whereas the old trams were impeccable. The Dublin United Tramways Company had some of the best trams in the world and by the Forties and Fifties going home in one of them was like travelling in a luxury carriage. You met everyone, judges, professors, company directors on the way from Rathgar to Grafton Street. The journey was delicious. Apart from the chat, the first burst after you boarded at Rathgar to go into town was down a mile-long boulevard on either side of which were variations of Georgian housing; as you got into Rathmines, with its clock tower and great green-domed Rathmines Church, it became less domestic but still Georgian. Once you got to the canal, of course, and crossed over and went around the gentle curve of Harcourt Street, you were in Stephen's Green. What a pleasant journey. Down through three little townships, built on a single idiom until you reached Stephen's Green and the glory of its square.

17 June

Call today from Monk Gibbon to tell me that Winifred has had a car crash and is being prosecuted for careless driving. Her car was coming out of Sandycove Avenue onto a main road when it was hit by a passing car. Her companion was Eileen Ganly, Gate Theatre actress of thirty years or so ago. Inclined to strike attitudes even when she is not on the stage. The two old girls are over seventy. I tell Monk to get his solicitor to brief me. I haven't had a seat in the Law Library in a couple of years but my hand is still in. Most important, I have the right of audience before a judge.

24 June

Horror of Horrors. I hear today that Monk has been up to the Dun Laoghaire Garda station trying to persuade the sergeant to drop the charges. Incredibly naïve. He can only succeed in handing over Winifred's defence lock, stock and barrel to the fuzz which will be of no benefit whatsoever when she comes to trial and in fact could blow it. I ring him as soon as I get home but he is not there. Later, I catch him at midnight. I tell him with some force that if he doesn't refrain from meddling in the case from now on, I will return the brief. He is acting as if it were the 'British' days before the First World War when if the Rector's son went to the police and chatted them up they could be expected to respond with winks and nods. Since Winifred has been charged and is due to appear in court in two weeks time the Gardai won't tell him a thing but instead might milk him of information that could help shore up their case. They might also resent him thinking that because of his class and his accent they would be susceptible to his approach.

The case is in the list at Justice Alfred Rochford's court, Dun Laoghaire, for 4 July.

4 July

Though barristers are not obliged to wear wig and gown in the district court, I arrive in full fig to put the Justice, Alfred Rochford, in good humour. The driver of the car told Justice Rochford that he was driving onto the Dalkey Road past Sandycove Avenue when suddenly a car shot across the road and he hit it. There was no way, he said, he could avoid this. I asked him did he recall a sharpish corner on the road about 150 yards away from Tara Hall, Gibbon's house. Then I called Eileen Ganly and Winifred to the box. Ganly with the face of a ruined diva was splendid as she described how there hadn't been a speck on the horizon as she moved onto the main road out of Sandycove Avenue.

Me: 'Where did the car come from then?'
Ganly: 'I don't know. From nowhere.'

She made it sound as if the car had materialized like the Angel Gabriel on his debut. Ganly had been renowned in her Gate Theatre days for her dramatic antics at MacLiammóir/Edward's parties, arriving in a sumptuous fur coat and then as she crossed the room shedding it to show herself completely naked except for her high-heeled shoes underneath. I almost hoped she would do something approximating this now as Justice Alfie Rochford was clearly smitten. He had been an actor himself (as many in the legal profession in Dublin were in their young days) and one hoped he would respond to Ganly's statuesque presence. Having had enough of her lofty disdain without making any impression, the disgruntled prosecutor sat down. (She had repeatedly turned to the judge with 'What is he saying, I can't make out', as if the poor man spoke some obscure aboriginal tongue.) The Justice now ventured discreet questions to her, not about her evidence, but to recall how he had admired her Ophelia in the Gate opposite MacLiammóir's Hamlet. Ganly did everything except offer her ring to be kissed in Papal fashion and presently the Justice announced that the defendant was discharged. Smiles all around. Winifred very relieved. She wasn't too keen to have her Dingwall and Spender relatives reading about the affair in *The Times* the next morning.

As we got into the car Monk very decently didn't go in for any of the 'what did I tell you' stuff. Back at Tara Hall Winifred had a storming lunch prepared for us and we'd got there in five minutes, including rounding the dangerous corner with Winifred driving.

6 July

Letter from Olive Reid.[*]

PO Box 1558
Salisbury
Rhodesia

Dear Ulick

Many thanks for your amusing letter and to note that Brendan Behan has taken over to boil the pot from our old friends Gogarty, Joyce etc. We have had some very good movies here, Waterloo, Nicholas and Alexandra. I got through the book of the latter. One wonders why they did not get out in time. Rather like the Jews in the thirties. Does anyone know when 'to get out'. Food for thought . . .

I did mention, I think, that my landlady was the granddaughter of 'Power corrupts, absolute power corrupts absolutely'.[†] So you know who that is. I really do not think I could take all the shi shi that goes on if I did not have her to talk to every day at teatime. Her eldest son got the Beit scholarship and is laden with honours and Marxism and reading for his doctorate at Oxford, the second son has just taken off for Exeter University on a small scholarship. Did you read in the Irish papers about her niece who unfortunately killed herself over that Judy Todd.

I wanted to read your Behan book again but had to get it from the library as someone gave my one to the drunken Irish clergy. There was a waiting list for your book so I put my name down

---

[*] See 5 October 1971.
[†] Lord Acton (1834–1902).

and laughed like hell. I'm reading Cocteau's life in French at the moment. He was just too camp. I wish it was in English as reading in French slows me up.

Yours,
Olive

20 July

Dear Olive

Great to get your letter and phone call. You sounded in great form. Your letter didn't arrive until well after Christmas which I'm sure had to do with the post.

You're writing a very good letter these days and I found the latest one most entertaining. When I saw the photographs you sent me of yourself, with the two labradors, I couldn't help thinking of the frightful Christy Mahon.* I never remember such a buff of a dog. I think though, after a while, he developed a healthy respect for me, though as soon as he recognized his master he became a rather hopeless toady. Your own beasts look marvellous. Can you imagine Aquinas sitting with either of them in the boot room in Pembroke Road trying to keep them quiet by taking out his false teeth and clicking them at him, as he used to do with Christy Mahon?† I'm sorry you had to go to the library to get my book. It is camp to think that they are queuing in Rhodesia to read my words of wisdom about the bold Brendan.

I heard a good crack yesterday about Bing Crosby who was down at the Curragh races recently. He was brought through the crowd there, surrounded by huge policemen. A tiny little Dubliner at the back of the crowd, who couldn't see for the heads, shouted:

'Hey Bing, leap up on your wallet and let's have a look at you.'

Yours,
Ulick

---

* Her sealyham.
† When Olive was entertaining a visitor, Tom, Christy Mahon and I would retreat to the boot room. The only thing that would stop his barking and putting the client off his stroke was Tom's legerdemain, which seemed to fascinate the little brute.

22 July

Postcard from Mariga today who is in Norway for her annual 'hut' fest. The picture on the postcard is of the inside of a small Lutheran Church in Fagernes.

> Open the door and there are the people – probably German tourists. Do come and stay. Glaciers, hot scented forests, fjords, and these pagan pagoda churches. One now flies from London to Oslo in one hour forty minutes, the train to Fagernes leaves Oslo at 4 pm arriving your time if you leave London am, to see the Viking ships on the way from the airport to Oslo. Do send telegram if this can be managed – please bring a leg of mutton.

> Love
> Mariga

8 August

Chair meeting of Government Steering Committee. They have approved the hiring of an international PR firm to publicize government policy on Northern Ireland. The firm chosen is Markpress who last year had an astonishingly successful record ensuring that the anti-government side in the Nigerian Civil War had maximum coverage from the world press. The Managing Director of Markpress is Bill Bernhardt, a suave Swiss German who bears a distinct resemblance to Charlie Chase, the film comedian. But a ruthless operator who is to be well paid by the Irish Government. But since he has taken over certain matters previously handled by Foreign Affairs, he won't be too popular up at Iveagh House.*

However, our Committee's remit is to do what we have to do and let the red tape strangle its own adherents. The Foreign Affairs representative Noel Dorr has Counsellor status and though able enough he is not quite up to making the running for his masters as they would want. At Committee meetings I usually go for him like a greyhound after a rabbit and shake him by the neck. Padraic O Hanrachain, the Taoiseach's representative on our committee, dislikes the Foreign Affairs crowd anyway and has given his full backing for whatever

---

* Headquarters of the Department of Foreign Affairs.

tactics we employ. I am able to read out a full list of events now, that old Slyboots Bernhardt has masterminded throughout the world. Sometimes he does exaggerate, using the names of a number of correspondents who can't all be working full-time for the Irish Government. But we have brought off a number of strokes recently, including the January Bloody Sunday presentation in America. Padraic O Hanrachain gives my arm a pinch as we leave:

'Well done yourself.'

13 August

Leprechauns Cricket XI at Mount Juliet, Kilkenny.* The pitch which lies behind Sir William Blunden's handsome Georgian house throws out a green glow, while a small forest on the far edge provides a dark backcloth, touched with green. Warm and drowsy. Bees lurch around lopsided with pollen, tipsy from the sun.

The Leprechauns field a useful side. Andrew Bonar Law is an excellent bat, especially when it comes to a slogging match. Our captain, Charles Lysaght, got his colours at Christ Church, Oxford and Lingard Goulding kept wicket for an outstanding school side at Winchester captained by Pataudi.

Contretemps. A condition precedent of UO'C playing with the Leprechauns is that he is allowed to keep wicket. Considers fielding a bore except at first slip. Behind the wicket on the other hand I can maintain a keen interest in every stroke, and leap round like an orangutan after catches and stumpings. In homage to my two cricket heroes – Godfrey Evans and Don Tallon – I insist on standing up to the wicket for every ball, whether the bowling is fast, medium or slow. This keeps me on the *qui vive* as if I make a mistake, I can get a hard cork ball going at sixty miles an hour straight in the puss, especially on dicey wickets.

Now I notice Lingard padding up and putting on the gloves to keep wicket and strike notice is issued. Lysaght adjudicates. Lingard will spend the first half of the innings behind the wicket and I the second.

Sir William Blunden comes out to bat. He is the tenth baronet, a splendid-looking figure – Gainsborough face with the brow of an

---

* The Leprechauns, founded in 1941, are an Irish touring cricket side, which came into existence to fill the gap when I. Zingari, the English side, ceased to tour Ireland in the Thirties.

Irish nobleman. Two daughters watch keenly, shy girls out of a Maria
Edgeworth novel.

By the time we come in to bat, the field is prone in haze and huge
bees drifting down the pitch take your eye off the ball. Not Andrew's,
however, who carts a large slice of the bowling into the nearby woods
before deciding to offer a catch to a grateful fielder. He is not all that
far from his hundred. But Bonar Law (whose grandfather as Prime
Minister was responsible for most of the mayhem here in 1922) thinks
making a century is *un peu de trop*. Almost a yawn. Slouches towards
the pavilion to be shorn.

19 August, Suffolk

Hintlesham Festival, Suffolk.* I'm first on the programme which
entails getting down to the nuts and bolts the day I arrive. A sound
system has to be set up which entails a certain amount of trouble and
irritation. David Broad who is in charge is very helpful. Later I go
down to Hintlesham parish church. It is very High and they have a
crucifix on the altar. The sexton shows me round with great courtesy
which goes well with his low-pitched East Anglian accent.

20 August

Show fine. Acoustic not as good as it had seemed in rehearsal and had
to raise the pitch. This morning went out for a huge walk, about eight
miles. On the way back, bumped into Francis Bacon whom I had met
in London with Dan Farson, the broadcaster.

Bacon has no means of making himself look friendly and seems to
carry a permanent look of outrage on his face. But civil. Muriel
Belcher, who runs the Colony Club in Dean Street, is barking away
beside him. She has become a 'character' simply by saying nothing
good about anyone. At the mention of a friend's name she lets out a
stream of oaths, finishing with a crack like a whiplash. Then says
confidentially in your ear:

'Scorched arse policy, my dear.'

---

* One man festival run by Robert Carrier, restaurant owner and gourmet, at his home
in Hintlesham Castle. This festival featured a one person show each night: this year
Siobhan McKenna, *Here are Ladies*, Georgia Brown, *Oliver*, and UO'C, *Brendan Behan*.

Photo taken of me with Angus Wilson and her. Later at lunch she offers me hash in a cake. David Broad tells me Frederick Ashton* was at the show last night. I adore his work and am anxious to know if Ashton liked the performance. Nothing doing, all I can extract is:

'Must have been pretty ten years ago.'

At coffee a beautiful girl with one arm. Courageously she sports short sleeves and brandishes her stump about. I ask her had it been bitten off by a tiger and she says yes with a sweet smile. (It hadn't.) With Paul Cusack who is prancing around. He's the spit of Cyril, plenty of brains but little of his father's sensitivity.

Organize a lift back to London with Francis Bacon. Dan Farson and Muriel Belcher also in car. The driver is a tall, blond young man. I have a lot of gear in the boot so when I get out in Leicester Square I ask him to help unload it. Bacon starts screaming from the front of the car. I hear him wrongly accusing the poor chap of trying to pick me up. God these married quarrels. I was tempted to say 'Goodbye Mrs Bacon' to Francis as the car shot off but I thought it would seem mean after scrounging a lift.

24 August, Dublin

Lunch with James McKenna.† James is an odd one. He has made a good deal of money recently out of his musical *The Scatterin'* which did well both in Dublin and in London, and has been termed the first Irish rock musical. This has enabled him to buy this fine eighteenth-century house in the Liberties in the heart of Dublin. Many echoing rooms and a blonde, slightly trampish but good-looking girlfriend. There is a life-sized wood carving of a horse in the yard. James says he carved it out of a single piece of wood. Round the house curious Aztec-like carvings.

Pleasant lunch. His girl, who is American, said little. James has brilliant blue eyes, is quite small but with a heroic head and the powerful

---

* Director of the Royal Ballet, 1963–70. The first ballet I ever saw was *Romeo and Juliet* at the première in the Edinburgh Festival in 1956, danced by the Royal Danish Ballet where Ashton was then Ballet Master. I didn't know what hit me. I had arrived in Edinburgh straight from pole vaulting at the Isle of Bute Highland Games, so the astounding leaps of the dancers amazed me. Watching Henning Kranstam and Mona Vangsaae float upwards impelled solely by leg power, feet fluttering like leaves in the wind, in time to Prokofiev's music, was incredibly exhilarating.

† 1933–2000; leading Irish sculptor.

upper body of a wrestler acquired not from sport, but from work as a sculptor. As he showed me to the gate, he remarked that the pretty American girl was leaving him.

'What's wrong?'

James remained silent.

'There must be something wrong James. She seems happy.'

James thought, then sighed.

'She breathes.'

'But James, what else *can* she do?'

'Well, it's what she does.'

Before I closed the gate, I reminded him of a story about the life-sized wooden horse he'd sculptured. It was first exhibited at the Independent Artists Exhibition in the Hugh Lane Gallery. The horse was so heavy it was going through the floor of the second storey of the Gallery, formerly the Georgian town house of Lord Charlemont. James was requested to take it away and came to collect it in a horse and cart. As he drove off with the sculpture on board, the porter shouted at him: 'Home James, and don't spare the horses'. I reminded him of the episode. He glowered.

12 September

Went today with Walter Curley, the US Ambassador, to take Kathleen Behan* out from Sybil Hill Home in Raheny for a drink. Taitsie his wife, who is a Mellon from Pittsburgh, with us. Walter is a genial chap, prep school and Yale. But he is not quite sure how to proceed as we drive along in the limousine. We have polite conversation with Kathleen who is seated in the front. In Bill Fuller's Old Sheiling on the main road, Kathleen smokes a cigarette while she conducts polite conversation. She is eighty-six years old. Her beautifully wrought features emerge from time to time from the smoke. I have never known her fail to put people at their ease and wonder how she will start here.

> *Kathleen: (casually)* 'Do you know the American National Anthem?'
> *Curley:* 'Yes.'
> *Kathleen:* 'Do you know the second verse?'
> *Curley: (startled)* 'No.'

---

* Brendan Behan's mother. See 12 July 1970, note.

Kathleen then sings the second verse of the national anthem which neither Walter nor Taitsie has ever heard of. She sings of course with her usual bravura and extraordinary true pitch. Another silence while she considers matters. Then to Walter, a little more forward this time.

'Do you know the Chinese National Anthem?'

Walter has to confess himself at a loss. Kathleen sings *Chu Chin Chinaman* and this time is joined in the chorus by Taitsie and Walter. This sort of thing continues for what Kathleen calls 'a lovely hour'.*
When we are going back in the Embassy car, Kathleen sits in the front with Walter, both of them well on with gargle.

> *Kathleen:* 'Did you ever hear tell, Walter, of an oul' song called *The Red Flag*?'
> *Walter: (cheerfully)* 'I have heard it mentioned.'

Kathleen took the United States Ambassador's hand and they both sang the Communist anthem with some fervour. We all joined in for the last line.

'We'll keep the red flag flying still.'

After we dropped Kathleen at Sybil Hill, Walter remarked that it was one of the best evenings he'd ever spent in his life, and Taitsie murmured from the sleep which seemed to have overtaken her at the back that she agreed. Later they told me that I had gone up in their estimation after Kathleen remarked that I was her 'seventh son'.

27 September

Today read Walter Benjamin† on Baudelaire, that arch-boulevardier. He makes a case for poets' absolute necessity to be among the crowd, in order to trigger off the correct responses for their work. Alone but alert. Lost in the crowd in order to feed his mind, Baudelaire saw himself as enjoying 'the incomparable privilege of being himself and someone else, as he sees fit . . . like a roving soul in search of a body, he can enter another person whenever he wishes'. Strolling, Baudelaire practises his 'fantastic fencing, striking against words as

---

* In Kathleen-speak this could mean anything from five minutes to five hours – the important thing is the quality of the minute.
† 1892–1940; German Marxist writer. One of the most original literary critics of the twentieth century. His study of Baudelaire is considered a classic.

against cobblestones'. He was the first to treat the crowd in this way
and his boulevard poems are a high moment of modernism, though
written half a century before the word began to have meaning for
verse. There always have been strollers, of course, who have used the
frisson of the street to excite the imagination. Yet Baudelaire went
further. He used the crowd as a narcotic, as a means of intoxication
by which he had surrendered to him secrets which an artist will seek
to unravel. His extraordinary poem *The Passer-by* describes a moment
of revelation which stands beyond the ravages of time and has a perfection that can never be assailed.

> A flash of lightning – night – beauty fled
> In whose glance I have been suddenly reborn
> Shall I see you in another world instead?
>
> Elsewhere; perhaps never; condemned to mourn
> I know not where you fled – or you not where I go
> You whom I could have loved – you who knew it so.*

Brussels, however, seems to have upset our strolling poet.

> The streets are unusable. There are no shop windows.†

Almost as if Toulouse-Lautrec complained that les girls used make-up
that didn't suit his palette.

11 October, London

Lunch in Fleet Street with Nick Tomalin‡ of the *Sunday Times* and
Don Edgar of the *Daily Express*. Both of these contacts were arranged
by Bernhardt. Tomalin asked me how I thought the Northern Ireland

---

* UO'C, *Poems of the Damned: Charles Baudelaire's Les Fleurs du Mal – The Flowers of Evil*,
Monarchline / Wolfhound Press, Dublin, 1995.
† Charles Dickens had felt similar withdrawal symptoms in Lausanne where he had gone
to write in 1846. 'I cannot express how much I miss these London streets. The toiled
labour of writing day after day without that magic lantern is immense. My figures seem
disposed to stagnate without crowds about them.'
‡ An outstanding journalist of the Seventies, and specialist in Northern Ireland. Later distinguished himself in the Middle East. Killed in the Yom Kippur War in 1973.

situation could right itself. I gave him my view but he shook his head:

'I'll tell you why the war will end. When people here realize how much their security forces have had to involve themselves in murder and torture in order to remain in Northern Ireland there'll be a call for withdrawal. The English people won't stand the army being corrupted.'

Later he tells Bernhardt to get his finger out about the recent assassinations and speak to the *Spiegel* correspondent whom they both know. Funny coincidence as somebody passes through the bar. It is Bob Edwards, the new, hated and bland editor of the *Sunday Mirror*. He has been editor of the *People* and the *Sunday Express* and was fired from both. While on the *Express* he sacked Don Edgar, on the *People* he sacked Nick Tomalin and on the *Sunday Mirror* he has just sacked me.

Dinner at La Popotte restaurant where there was a parade of drag queens.

6 November, Dublin

Private meeting with the Taoiseach. I tell him we are having trouble with the PR campaign because of the attitude of Foreign Affairs. Foreign Affairs officials have no idea what we are about. I maintain to the Taoiseach that diplomacy and PR are totally apart, otherwise it would be useless employing Markpress. Lynch is marvellous about taking this guff from me.

'Perhaps you could give us a formula,' he says mildly.

'I will.'

Later at Groome's Hotel a guy assaults John Hume. I catch him by the lapels and lift him off the ground, absolutely livid to see John assailed by a swine who isn't worth a drop of the saliva that is dripping from his drunken mouth.

7 November

John Behan* has a sculpture exhibition at the Dublin Foundry which he owns. James McKenna and Michael Kane are the other artists featured. John tells me he was at a recent lunch given by a rich American at which James was a guest, and James went on about sculpting in iron,

---

* Founder member of the Independent Artists, an organization which played an important role in modern Irish art.

which he regards as inferior to carving in wood or stone. Every time the American attempted to reply, James would start to whistle as he continued to devour the excellent meal paid for by his host.

21 November

This has been a terrible day. Sean Mac Stiofain, the IRA Chief of Staff, has been on hunger strike in the Mater Hospital, Dublin (where he is recovering from wounds) for a week – he has now gone on hunger and thirst strike so that the most he can last, if he continues to refuse food and water, will be about four days. The atmosphere is tense and anything could happen. I go to bed shortly after midnight with a sore throat and a hot drink. At 3 am I'm woken by the phone. It's John O'Connell, Labour TD and spokesman on Foreign Affairs in the Party. He believes I have influence with the Taoiseach and has a proposition to put about the hunger strike situation. An attempt was made to rescue Mac Stiofain early on in the week and there is now an armed guard round his bed. O'Connell has been in contact with the IRA and he says that if the armed guard is removed they will give their word not to attempt a rescue and Mac Stiofain will come off hunger strike.

It's very hard to conduct a conversation as my voice is no better than a croak. I ring Donal Barrington,* Senior Counsel, a close friend and the wisest of ones when it comes to advice. Dear Don gets to the point without delay. There can be no question of taking the guard away in view of the fact that an armed attempt was made to rescue Mac Stiofain earlier in the week when he was without surveillance. Barrington's view is that it would be gross negligence to accept the present offer when the chances of the IRA keeping their word are fragile. I ring John O'Connell back and tell him I am not prepared to contact the Taoiseach. He seems surprised, but while I know he is well-intentioned, a scatterbrained scheme like this is wasting time which of course I should have told him in the first place.

In the early morning there are crowds around the Taoiseach's house which is five minutes walk away from mine. Downtown the Dail is surrounded. The army are there.

---

* Later Judge of the European Court of First Instance in Luxembourg, and a member of the Irish Supreme Court (1991–2000).

23 November

To Dublin Airport to see Jack Lynch off. He's addressing the Oxford Union on the motion 'That this House would favour Irish Unity.' Hugh McCann, Secretary to the Department of Foreign Affairs, is on the tarmac when the Taoiseach gets on the steps to enter the plane. Lynch shakes my hand warmly and ignores McCann who is left with his paw 'all bright and glittering in the smokeless air'. This is authentic Jackspeak.

24 November

Lynch very good last night in Oxford. Motion passed with a large majority. Sit with him in the plane on the way home much to the discomfort of a Foreign Affairs flunkey. We drive to his house and just before he gets out of the car he has a call. When it's finished he says:

'I have just sacked the RTÉ Authority who supported Kevin O'Kelly.* I suppose you don't think much of that.'

'I certainly don't. It doesn't say much for your views on freedom of speech. You'll rue that.'

Lynch looks at me with a grin. 'Fuck them,' he says, and is gone into the night.

27 November, Derry City

Owens Pub, Derry.

'What are you doing up here? The UDA† will shoot you!'

Father Edward Daly (the brave priest who held the bloody handkerchief up last January as he helped one of his wounded parishioners from the slaughterfield) tells me that today he has had to tell a mother that her son has just been shot by the soldiers. This is the tenth time he has had to do this so far this year. In the city you notice the army at every street corner. Someone says the Provos should be in the new peace force because they know their own bad guys and would deal with them.

---

* Journalist who had refused to reveal the identity of a Republican interviewee.
† Ulster Defence Association. A Loyalist paramilitary group whose aim is to keep Northern Ireland in the Union with Great Britain.

I do my Brendan Behan show before a good audience in the Colmcille Theatre. John Hume is there. I think of the contrast in atmosphere between this performance and the last one at Hintlesham with its sultry haze and rolling Suffolk meadows. Ed Daly, who has brought the show up to raise money for the relatives of the dead, is pleased.

John Hume and Austin Currie* give me a lift back to Dublin in their car. They are going to meet the Taoiseach tomorrow. On the way down we are stopped at a road block. Currie shows the gun which he carries for his protection to the soldiers.

'We carry guns legally.' Very polite.

At the hotel we've left they have scares every night, and frequently have to evacuate the whole place.

30 November

Ed Daly has me back in Derry's Colmcille Theatre for a week. Tonight walk to St Eugene's Cathedral after it through the Bogside. As I go uphill I wonder will I get my head blown off from some passing car. A man and girl saunter along unconcernedly. Down by Glenfada Park (where the Paras opened up on 30 January) walk along an empty street. Stars in a clear sky. A figure approaches me. I feel with the light of the moon I must be silhouetted. Am I now the only person out in a deserted city? I'm at the heart of it near the Guildhall.

11 December

Letter from a girl in a nun's boarding school, Carrick-on-Suir, Tipperary, asking me will I escort her to the annual debutante's ball at Tower Hill on 27 December. She says the other girls have dared her. It could be a set-up. But I have checked and there is a Miss Ann M at the school.

---

* Austin Currie MP. Member for East Tyrone. A brilliant leader as a young student in the Civil Rights Movement, he was a key figure in the founding of the SDLP.

1973

Drink with Noel O'Brien, who is to direct a play I've written on Jonathan Swift.* Noel has that intensity which earnest Christians sometimes have and which when it goes with a good mind can throw up stimulating comments. Critical of the Catholic Church for retaining military symbols in its ceremonies. He won't allow his children, for instance, to attend Corpus Christi processions which are accompanied by military parades. He doesn't object to the military per se but the fact that they are carrying swords. He would approve of plastic pricks in place of lethal armoury. Life, not death.

Later, the taxi-driver says to me, 'I see you have a new play on the Dane coming up.' I was puzzled but then I realized he was referring to Dean Swift whose memory is still alive in the Dublin Liberties, where he was regarded as a patriot and friend of the people. The driver tells me he is himself a 'Huge-ennot'† from the Liberties and that his name is Dubedat which is the name that Shaw gave to his hero in *The Doctor's Dilemma*.

Ireland versus the All Blacks. Lansdowne Road. We lose but the visitors run some wonderful moves, reverse passes behind the back, one player running with his arms cupped as if he has the ball when it has actually been taken from behind him by another member of the team. In the middle of the match from the stand we hear a sudden thump. Was it a bomb, decide it wasn't. A lady in front looks round and says:

'I'm from Newry. It's a bomb.'

Johnny Moloney at scrum-half had a terrific game. A quick and elegant passer, he's like a ferret down a hole when he sprints through close to the scrum. Unstoppable.

---

* *The Dark Lovers.* Project Theatre Dublin, 5 March–3 June 1973.
† After the massacre of St Bartholomew in the seventeenth century, Huguenot refugees were received in Dublin. They prospered as weavers, and Huguenot names are scattered throughout the Dublin professional and commercial classes.

2 February

It's terrific that the English rugby side are coming after all to play Ireland on Saturday at Lansdowne Road. Wales and Scotland have funked it because of the political situation and the possibility of violence. But the President of the Rugby Football Union, Dickie Kingswell, says that England have agreed to come and come they will despite any side-effects from the Troubles. I drop a note to Kingswell into the Shelbourne Hotel where the team is staying to say 'thanks a lot'; also a copy of my biography of Brendan Behan, who used to play in the front row of the Hollesley Bay Borstal XV.

13 February

General Election in Ireland today. I can't see the Government losing. Lynch has done an extraordinary job keeping the Cabinet together after the Arms Trial. In other hands the Government could have split in smithereens. He has kept the country on an even keel during its most perilous period since our neutrality in World War Two. If the party wins this time he could be the leader who will preside over the end of the partition of the country. The October arrangement with Edward Heath has been satisfactory and forward-looking. The idea is that Northern Ireland is to have its own parliament again, but this time it will be democratically constituted with assurances that there will be some sort of coalition between Unionists and Nationalists which will lead to power-sharing. I do believe Heath knows what he is doing; he reinforces a popular belief in Ireland that the Conservatives can solve our troubles rather than Labour. It is not forgotten that it was Attlee's socialists who passed the Ireland Act in 1949, designed to copper-fasten Partition. Heath is a Tory radical when it comes to Irish affairs and from our point of view should be encouraged.

20 February

Horror. Fianna Fail has won a majority over any other party but if Fine Gael go into Coalition with Labour they will be just ahead and it looks as if this will happen. Liam Cosgrave (Fine Gael) could be Taoiseach and Brendan Corish (leader of the Labour Party) will be Tanaiste. That toad Conor Cruise O'Brien will be sniffing around

looking for a Cabinet post. He has been Foreign Affairs spokesman
for the Labour Party. If he gets this position in the Coalition government* it could split the country as in 1922. No man is more
entrenched in his opinions. Yet his prose remains lucid and serene
as long as he avoids matters unrelated to the furies that lie within
him.

5 March, New York

I have decided to stay in an apartment this year. Lynn Redgrave has
offered me her flat at the Osborne on 57th and 8th. This is one of the
oldest apartment blocks in New York and like the Dakotas (where
John Lennon lived) retains much of its nineteenth-century atmosphere and design.

'I'm Biff,' says a pleasant-looking girl who greets me in the lobby.
She monitors Lynn's flat when it's not in use. I get keys and instructions and settle in.

7 March, Dallas, Texas

Mornington Ladies' Club. After having given my talk, answered questions and had lunch, I scooted off to the Texas Book Depository. I was
here seven years ago and stood on the footpath opposite the Book
Depository on the exact spot where President Kennedy was assassinated. At the time I was surprised how near the window where the
killer had sat was to the President's car. I figured it could look much
further away when I got there today. Not a bit of it. The window and
the spot where the car was were so near that you could have thrown
a stone from it and if you were a good shot were bound to hit the
President or his wife.

9 March

After lectures in Dallas and Oklahoma drop in to New Orleans where
my brother Michael† lives. He drives me from the airport to his home

---

* Liam Cosgrave did become Taoiseach and Brendan Corish Deputy Taoiseach in a
Coalition government of Fine Gael and Labour, but Cruise O'Brien was given Posts and
Telegraphs, though from time to time he appeared to speak in a Foreign Affairs capacity.
† Michael was a well-known TV journalist with WDSU.

on the edge of Lake Pontchartrain where on acres of smooth lawn he lives surrounded by magnolia trees, oak, bougainvillea and bursting azalea. Twenty years ago I did postgraduate work in New Orleans and each visit is like a flower unfolding.

Tonight with Michael and his wife Marilyn to dinner at Antoine's in the French Quarter. We go in the back door instead of the front, which is posh. Marilyn is from the Quarter and has always come this way since she was a child. When I used to be taken to Antoine's in my student days I could never get anything I liked. I still can't. Cajun cooking slaughters tastebuds (mine).

10 March

Walk in the French Quarter. Images click into place. Royale Street with its overhanging balconies and intricate laced iron railings. Ordinary entrances which conceal magic casements behind. Secret gardens in a city's heart. Lafcadio Hearn,* ill with fever here in 1870, took succour from such secrecy and lines of his, learned two decades ago, never fail to evoke its atmosphere for me. 'But the gold born days died in golden fire and blue nights unnumbered filled the air with indigo shadows – and the days came and passed like a breath of incense.'

I'm at Canal and Royal now where Truman Capote changed trolleycars and set out across the French Quarter to visit Mrs Fergusson, the witch. He was aged nine and wanted her to change him into a girl. Voodoo is as indigenous to the Quarter as the rule of law on Capitol Hill. You sense it behind the annual masquerade of Mardi Gras and the fabulous prancing of the funeral bands.

Feel if I keep on any more, I may end up in a spin in some French courtyard confessing to a black priestess. Right turn. Jackson's Square brings you back to the New Orleans that thrived before Napoleon flogged it to the Americans in 1814 to stop the Limeys getting a foot-

---

* Born on the Isle of Leucadia to a Greek mother and an Irish father; see also 26 February, 1971, note. Brought up in Dublin, he went to live in New Orleans, where he wrote for the *Item* newspaper, having been hired by James O'Connor, a relative of mine. O'Connor was United States Congressman for Louisiana, who splendidly retained his seat unopposed for thirty years simply by delivering, once a year, an oration on the Battle of New Orleans (1814, at which the English were defeated) and calling for Louisiana's secession from the Union.

hold. En face, the cathedral to Louis, King of France with its three spires. In the same square are the Pont Alba buildings, the first apartment houses in the United States with their laced grills and French shutter windows: this, with the massive ships on the Mississippi below, making you think of a great Mediterranean port – Cannes, Nice, Marseilles.

To the Café du Monde in the French market to drink bitter-tasting chicory coffee. I had been put off coffee when I came here as a student by the tasteless sludge that passed for it in Dublin after World War Two. After a week here I was on five cups a day. Now, as I drink it with a special New Orleans sugar doughnut, I say '*Ça va?*' to a passer-by who, to my delight, replies '*Ça va bien!*'

12 March

Michael has arranged for me to meet Colonel Clay Shaw who was acquitted last year of conspiring to murder President Kennedy. Marilyn's people know Shaw, so I have an entrée. Shaw is a New Orleans gentleman who lives in a house with a courtyard in the French Quarter. When I meet him I notice the weary look on his face and sadness in his fine brown eyes. But he is clearly a citizen of no mean city. Well read, a few languages, knowledgeable about literature and art.

We talk about Cocteau, Proust, James Joyce, Dylan Thomas, Yeats and Lady Gregory. He was decorated during the war, but as his work was with the secret service, he can't say much about it. I ask him what was the motive behind the grotesque charade mounted by Attorney-General Jim Garrison against him, so that he has had to face a four-year trial before the judge threw out the case. He doesn't want to speculate and is too well-bred to show anger:

'The American judicial system presumes a sort of reasonableness on the part of the people who operate it. If anyone unreasonable gets into power like State Prosecutor Garrison, then this thing is going to happen. The bad thing is that it happened to me.'

Wasn't Garrison a presidential candidate maybe looking for publicity? Shaw is too polite to disagree, but doesn't say anything. He knows the trial has been shown up as a farce and that is enough. As we go to the door, I notice a fine drawing by Erni of Icarus with, in the background, Daedalus heading for the hills. This reminds him of Joyce, whom we have talked about, and triggers off a quotation from *The*

Dead he has been trying to remember and which he now trots out in a soft southern drawl.*

I take a streetcar out to the Lake. New Orleans ones are special and have their place in literature. Nowadays you can sit beside a black in them, which you couldn't when I was a student, when the streetcars were segregated. Whites in front, blacks at the back. I always made a point of sitting with the blacks and when the furious conductor came down to order me out would tell him 'Why don't you get your eyes tested. Can't you see I'm black – black Irish.'

The people I was sitting with would cheer and shout and start singing *Swing Low, Sweet Chariot.* I would have to wait until I got off the bus before shouting Swiftian abuse at the driver who, if he could have done so, would cheerfully have had me castrated.

Tonight at dinner a friend of Michael's who is an architect in the shipyards tells me that it's said that the real story behind Attorney-General Garrison's persecution of Clay Shaw is that Shaw had a lover who was a doctor and whom Garrison was jealous of. An internationally reported murder trial, concocted out of a gay tizzy? It could only happen in New Orleans. I remind Michael of another event that could only have happened in New Orleans – that he had photographed Lee Harvey Oswald, President Kennedy's murderer, distributing pamphlets in the streets of New Orleans, less than a month before the murder. Though the photo had been flashed all over the world, the Warren Commission† never questioned him about it. Mike puffs on his pipe:

'That's N'yawlins.'

24 March, New York

Beautifully mild day. Four mile-walk in Central Park. A kite climbs the sky, turning silver as it soars. The light wind makes the sky appear more blue than it may be. An Alsatian trots by with a frisbee in his mouth.

When I get back to the flat there's a message for me from Siobhan McKenna who is in New York. I call her and find that she has sad news, Jackie McGowran‡ is dead. He was undoubtedly the greatest

---

* 'His soul swooned slowly as he heard the snow falling faintly through the universe and faintly falling, like the descent of their last end upon all the living and the dead.'

† Set up in 1964 to investigate all aspects of matters relevant to the President's death.

‡ 1918–73; Abbey and West End actor. In 1971 he became the first non-American to receive the New York Critics Award for Actor of the Year.

Beckett actor of his time. Also a wonderful friend to me. I first met him when at the age of thirteen I had tried to get into a men's high jump competition at a big sports meeting at Glenmalure Park, Dublin, the headquarters of the Shamrock Rovers Football Club. Jackie was at that time Irish high jump champion and I boldly approached him and asked him if he could get the officials to relent. He did so, and I competed and was placed in the event, assisted by a generous handicap. Always afterwards I looked up to him for his kindness to a kid. Later when I was twenty I asked him another favour. I had been banned by a fascist-minded president of University College Dublin from attending a debate in the University after some high jinks, and had decided that the only way to get into the auditorium was to disguise myself as a woman. I asked Jackie to make me up in the Abbey Theatre where at the time he was a member of the company. He did a superb job, so good indeed that the disguise took in not only my parents when I had it on the night before, but subsequently the policemen at the door of the debating auditorium who had been called in by the President of the University to prevent me from getting in. Indeed, I took everyone in until after an hour I revealed who I was and handcuffed myself to the desk to prevent the police removing me.*

Later I would go to London for the first of Jackie's triumphs, *The Ice Man Cometh* at the Winter Gardens, and afterwards follow closely his extraordinary collaboration with Samuel Beckett who insisted on having Jackie play in his leading roles. It seems awfully bad luck that he should have died just now, because some time ago he'd given up drinking so that he could absorb himself completely in the art that he adored. He had just finished shooting an important supporting role in the film *The Exorcist* when he died.

It was Jackie who introduced me to Samuel Beckett in 1964 at the Closerie de Lilas after a performance of *Endgame* in Paris in which he played and which Beckett directed. He and Beckett shared Dublin accents and a passion for sport. (Beckett had been in the Trinity College First XI and is one of two Irish cricketers to have appeared

---

* 'He looked,' wrote Brian Inglis in his Quidnunc column for the *Irish Times*, 'as if he had stepped out of one of those pictures of suffragettes in old bound numbers of the *Illustrated London News*, yet with one leg chained to the bench and handicapped as he was by his tea gown, Mr O'Connor, who is college boxing champion, gave the impression he could look after himself.'

in Wisden.) Sport was not however on the agenda for the Beckett groupies who had gathered on the fringe of the conversation. They looked at each other with camp scorn when Beckett began to quiz Jackie about the centre of gravity and its relation to the high jump, and me about the potential of the new fibreglass vaulting pole.

What was remarkable was how Beckett's face changed as he listened to Jackie. Even his accent increased its Liffeyside content as he gently urged Jackie on with encouraging comments. This caused the groupies some unease. After all their Sam was High Priest of the Absurd. Was he about to defect to these barbarians, relinquishing his role at the Gate of Misfortune? It was all right to roll the stone up the hill but on no account get it over the top. Looking at Jackie's face side by side with Beckett's, I found both unmistakably Irish, but profoundly different in structure and expression. It's weird, I thought, if Jackie hadn't existed, he would have had to be invented by Samuel Beckett.

7 April

Tonight, party at Roberto Mattello's apartment at Third Avenue and 38th Street. He is an Argentinian (of Italian descent) painter who has done a lot of exploration of the mystical (including Yeats's Rosicrucian writing). His paintings glow on canvas. Actors, writers, musicians here, a fair mix of hip New York. Meet a pretty air hostess. Mexican. We hit it off. I have to go and talk to someone else, but I know that we'll meet later on. She has given me a time. I hear a familiar voice behind me: 'Älskling, Älskling.' *Älskling* is the Swedish word for darling and it's Brigitta, a girlfriend of two years ago. I had given her the name of 'Älskling' because its pale Scandinavian sound seemed in contrast to her outgoing Latin temperament (she is South American). Now she rushes up and literally jumps on me. I think she has been smoking dope. (At the country estate where we used to stay with her cousin who was married to a polo-playing Wasp, marijuana came up with the rations.) Brigitta talks now as if I had said goodnight to her the night before. It was she who taught me to dance rock and roll and took me around the New York clubs with the smart set five years ago. But she's been out of town for a while (did she say on the buzz line yacht)* and our paths haven't crossed this year. She talks

---

* What it turned out to be, when I unscrambled her South American accent: 'I was on the Bowes Lyon yacht.'

about going to a bar after the party. I tell her that I've arranged to meet my new Mexican friend. Later in the night I see her talking to Il Topo, which is the nickname of the Mexican lassie (it means mouse).

An hour and a half later, I am lying on the floor of Il Topo's elegant apartment with my head on a pillow which has been placed under it. The two girls, who are puffing away, open my mouth from time to time and blow in a sweet-tasting smoke. It doesn't do much for me as I find it difficult to inhale, never having been a smoker. However, it's a ritual. An hour later I'm between the pair of them in Il Topo's ample bed. As Johnny McArdle, the Dublin surgeon, said when he was asked in the Divorce Court:

'Did you sleep with this woman?'

'Not a wink.'

I didn't sleep much either. At seven o'clock however we three were fast in the arms of Morpheus, breathing heavily. I woke up as Brigitta was departing at 8.00 am.

'I have to take my mother to mass.'

She is a fabulously rich heiress and lives with her mum in an apartment in the same block as Jackie Onassis. The door clicks and I go back to sleep with Il Topo conked out nearby.

9 April

Bumped into Viva, Andy Warhol's Superstar, in the lobby of the Chelsea and asked her to lunch. She is lovely, a pale Pre-Raphaelite face. Looks as if it was painted by Burne-Jones. Very unlike the sex symbol she is portrayed as in *Blue Movie*, where with Louie Walden she played the lead, directed by Andy Warhol, in the first American soft porn movie to win distribution. She says that at school with the Sacred Heart nuns in Buffalo she thought of nothing else but infinity. How could it exist? How could we go on forever? Is there a consciousness? When she went on an LSD trip in the early Sixties she found herself getting furious.

'I feel each little particle knows more than me. We are just fools.'

I argue we can't be fools if we actually know this. She maintains that pot gives a heightened awareness and you can see things split into their various parts. However, she will concede that sometimes when she comes down she won't remember what she has supposedly learned. Viva comes from a well-off professional family in Upstate

New York and speaks in a languorous upper-class accent, which she has made into a sort of art form to enable her to constantly complain. As a child she used to be taken to the Iron Foundry in Buffalo to see the furnaces, so as to have an idea of what awaited her if she committed mortal sin. The Pre-Raphaelite face is explained perhaps by her mother's origins. She was an O'Shaughnessy and used to claim that her great uncle had been decorated by Queen Victoria for discovering chloroform and giving the Queen a painless childbirth.

Her parents' piety didn't have much effect on Viva, however:

'I love to be roused sexually. Men only. Though once I did fall for another girl. Apart from pot, I don't touch drugs or drink. The most awful thing is that sometimes I just lie down and do nothing. Depressed.'

I tell her about Brigitta and Il Topo. Viva's eyes light up. She wants to know everything, how many, etc. Her eyes shining, a distant look.

She wants me to write a letter for her to 'expose' Bernardo Bertolucci, the film director. She thinks that scenes in his *Last Tango in Paris* were influenced by *Blue Movie*.

'The only movie made solely by Andy and the actors – no script. Completely my idea, all those noises, animal sounds and the love scene, were mine.'

The Catholic benediction hymn in Latin, which she improvised in *Lonesome Cowboys*, was her idea too, she claims.

'I love Gregorian chant which I learnt from the nuns at my French finishing school. It's just like a mantra, which is why those male bastards in the Vatican took it away from us. Like I said in *Lonesome Cowboys*, I've been visited by angels. That's how I know.'

I say I'll write the letter for her but I'm not too sure about her sending it to the papers; it may be a hard claim to assert copyright on what is essentially a series of grunts and groans.

I notice a slight vein on her nose, transparent blue as she retails Chelsea gossip. She says Harry Smith[*] has tortured my 'cousin' Roderick Ghuika,[†] giving him food and taking it away again before he'd a chance to eat it, and that the poetess Isabella Gardner in Room 693 has taken a good-looking coke pusher for her lover.

---

[*] Admired film animator. His last film was *City of Mahogany*.
[†] See 24 June 1971.

Lecture on Joyce at the Gotham Book Mart at Fifth Avenue and 44th Street. This is very much a centre for literary talks in New York. The shop is owned by the amazing Frances Stellof, who has made it the leading one of its kind in the city. She runs monthly readings at which anyone important in literature has spoken. Frances is a beautiful-looking woman of over seventy with glowing white hair and perfect golden skin. Enormous blue eyes. One drawback, however, is the smug-looking white cat which perches on her shoulder. During talks it tends to flirt with blue rinse listeners and take attention off the speakers. This has happened before and I have warned Frances I won't put up with it this time. Hell's bells; halfway through pussy comes loping along the woodwork under the window-sill. Rather than lose my rag and perhaps the audience's sympathy, I address it sweetly as it sits in front of me, preening itself to gain attention.

'Now pussy. Go away.'

The vanity of cats is enormous; there is not a chance it will move itself. I let a roar out of me that could have been heard on Ellis Island and the cat who clearly has never been talked to like this before shoots out of the door in a white streak. One of the ladies remarks severely:

'That cat's psyche has been invaded.'

'Another part would have been invaded if it hadn't moved.'

Near the end of the talk a girl arrives at the back clothed in a long white gown, like the Lady of the Lake in mystic samite, and glides across the floor towards me. She has golden hair down to her hips. I recognize Rosie (daughter of the poetess Isabella Gardner) whom I'd spent some pleasant months with the year before. After the talk she tells me she has been six months in Haiti where she has studied witchcraft and is now qualified.

'Great, as long as you don't stick pins in *my* image.'

Not amused. Later she suggests dinner. We end up in bed in the Sheraton Hotel where I am staying for this week courtesy of IT&T Rosie tells me a lot about her craft and maintains she is well on the way to becoming a really top-class witch. About three in the morning she wakes me up to suck her toe. When I won't she gets shirty and takes off. In the morning what do I find under the pillow but a rabbit's foot. Gives me the shivers for a second or two. Is Rosie angry and putting the hex on me? I laugh it off but before I go out I measure my height on the wallpaper, using a pencil to mark it, just in case she does try a shrink job.

Everything goes wrong afterwards. The cab I am in crashes. No one is hurt but the cab is a write-off. Then the restaurant I am to go to for lunch has a food scare and is closed for the day. Walking up Fifth Avenue at 53rd Street I trip, fall off the footpath, sprain my ankle badly and limp home to bathe it, feeling it swell as I walk. I am feeling so wretched that I almost think of saying a prayer for help as I pass St Patrick's Cathedral, but decide it wouldn't be playing the game. Fair weather friend. In my room, I'm about to take my shoe off when the mark on the wall catches my eye. Should I? Yes, why not! I slide a book in over the top of my head and stand back to look. It is well over an inch short of the pencil mark which I marked on the wall before I left the room this morning.

Even if Rosie is a witch, it shouldn't have worked as quickly as this. After a few deep breaths I measure myself again. Still an inch under. I look a little feverishly to see if I've got the wrong pencil mark. No. It's in front of me indented on the wallpaper. Sweat. I lie down on the bed contemplating the ceiling. I simply cannot have dropped the best part of two inches in height because Rosie is sticking pins in my image. Now I think of all those people in Ireland who would never put a road through a fairy rath because they believe that if they did the Little People would get them.

Thunderous knocking on the door. I jump up like a scalded cat, nerves screwed to the sticking point. Two men outside.

'Can we put back the carpet.'

It is a wall-to-wall one which they took out before lunch for cleaning. It is the thickness of this which when it was removed resulted in my being over an inch below the pencil mark on the wall.

I ask the carpet men to share a bottle of champagne. 'Luck of the Irish,' one of them says, raising his glass.

5 May

Tonight went with Brigitta to Le Club. It's preposterous to think that it was here only five years ago that I first learned to dance. When rock music was at its peak, one night Brigitta pulled me onto the floor. I had never tried because I thought I'd have to learn it like the foxtrot and I hadn't the patience. However, I put my ear to the beat and was soon spinning like a top. One could hardly call them the finer points, but whatever polishing was to be done, Brigitta did it. I suppose ballet training helped and the whole scene was so flexible that no one bothered if you broke into entrechats or pirouettes in the middle of a session and in fact on occasion people would clap their hands in time to urge one to further effort.

7 May

To Washington to interview Teddy Kennedy. Arranged by John Hume through a Kennedy aide, Carey Parker. Washington in early summer is beautiful. Lush green trees lining the drives. Spectacular after New York, where in Central Park still the bare branches anatomize the sky.

Kennedy himself is well versed in Northern Ireland. He corrects me when I give the wrong number of internees in Long Kesh:

'Around 2,000, I think.'

(I checked, he was right.)

He is on top of his brief. Would that his English counterparts were the same. I tell him I was on the Kennedy election plane on Bobby's last jaunt, just before he died. He showed me a picture of Bobby in his Harvard football kit.*

'Great little guy, wasn't he.'

He looked wistful for a while. He has had two brothers cut down in their prime who, when he was a baby, used to affectionately toss him between them like a football, two handsome Micks with a dash and brightness that were specially theirs – all gone.

25 May, Dublin

When I get to Grogan's tonight Bob Bradshaw† is there. He asks me about Watergate and what I learned of it on my travels. He thinks the

---

* Bobby Kennedy had played for Harvard at only 152 lb. This was exceptional in American football, where even in those days you had to be over 190 lb to survive.

† In the top bracket of the great Dublin pub talkers. He was widely read and had an acute interest in politics and finance as well as literature but never wrote a book, belonged to a political party or was well off. He was a small builder by trade and walked everywhere. Partially paralysed by a stroke in 1980, he was confined to a wheelchair afterwards. His mind remained as acute as ever and his conversation as entertaining and informative as it had been. But he railed a good deal at his enforced immobility and the fact that his sight had been affected by the stroke. He died aged seventy in 1992.

inquiry demonstrates that the United States is the most open country in the world – fair enough for someone who was an unreconstructed Communist twenty years ago. Bob also admires the American willingness to accept the validity of another point of view, and sums up this agreeable characteristic in a phrase so fine that it is hard to believe it is spontaneous, though knowing Bob it most likely is:

'Ambivalence is a surrogate of intelligence.'

Bob nearly went out to Spain in 1937 when he was in the IRA. Tomas MacCurtain came up to him and Sean Keating* in a training tent on a farm in Swords, Co. Dublin to ask him to join the Republicans in Spain. Because of the decision of the Russians not to recruit for that war, Bob didn't go.

28 May

Out to see Christy Brown† in Rathcoole where he lives with his handsome wife, Mary, in a private extension to his brother's house. I have got to the stage where I can talk to him fairly well, despite his plundered speech. He is depressed today as Mary is away for the weekend.

'She's in London every month; pot and lesbian friends. Goes to Bayswater every second weekend. She wants me to live in the country. Only culchies‡ want houses in the country. I was lonely before I married her. But that was the loneliness of a writer. Now I feel a different sort of loneliness.'

Christy's face rends itself in an expression of anguish. He raises his eyes (appropriately) like El Greco's St Francis.

'If she leaves I'll write an incredible poem. That's all I've left. To make art out of anguish. You have suffered, you are gentle. Mary wonders how you and I can be friends? She forgets we're Dubliners.'

Christy has an idea for a poem which will tell how he gets his anger about Mary out of himself by working on the typewriter, tapping away till what he feels has left him and entered the page. He brings me into his working room and asks me to take off his sock so that he can write with his foot. There are blisters on the toes with which he pounds the typewriter.

---

* MacCurtain and Keating were prominent Irish revolutionaries.
† See 30 May 1970, note.
‡ Pejorative Dublin working-class term denoting people from the country.

2 July

An election today in Northern Ireland could lead to something new. Edward Heath has devoted a lot of energy in the last few months to putting in place a structure which looks impressive. A power-sharing Executive is to replace the Stormont Government which ended two years ago. The Executive will be formed from those members who have been elected to the Assembly today. The Nationalist parties have won 45 per cent of the vote.

10 July

Up today to Dungloe to address a meeting which John Hume has arranged. They have provided a chauffeur for me. He is a Dublin man named Bergin, who has an acute contempt for rural dwelling. Seeing the smallholdings of the Donegal farmers, the rock walls and the little cottages, he is constantly disparaging.

'No wonder they fucking emigrated. I don't know how they'd even enough strength to get out in the first place.'

Give talk at midday. As I talk I can see melancholy grey clouds through the window which reminds me of holidays in Donegal when I was a boy. An able group here. Some with the alert look of working-class politicians. After dinner I have a long walk. Then the limousine comes with Paddy O'Hanlon[*] and John Hume.[†] They both sing all the way down, Negro jazz, Bob Dylan, no 'National' songs. I know John is worried about the Irish Government's presentation of their human rights case at Strasbourg which complains of the torture of Nationalist prisoners in Northern Ireland. John thinks there will be a bad reaction among Northern Nationalists if the recently elected government under Liam Cosgrave and Cruise O'Brien don't prosecute.[‡] The latest he's heard is that they are going for a settlement. He has asked me to talk to Paddy O'Hanlon about it on the side.

We meet up with Austin Currie in Dublin and Gerry Fitt. We try the Gresham in O'Connell Street for a hotel room but it is full. Then

---

[*] SDLP Northern Ireland Assembly member.

[†] Founder member of the Social Democratic and Labour Party, MP for Derry and MEP. The outstanding political figure in Northern Ireland's Troubles who has devoted his life to bringing peace to the Province and establishing a just society for his community. In 1999 shared the Nobel Peace Prize with David Trimble.

[‡] They did fight the case, and won.

a melancholy pilgrimage begins around Dublin for sleeping space. On an impulse I bring them along to the Burlington and ask to see Vincent Doyle, who has built and owns the Doyle group of hotels. We are standing talking to a porter and suddenly Vincent materializes as if he's come up through the floor (he has this habit of suddenly being there which I think comes from a constant watch he keeps on the main lobby of the hotel). I put our problem to him and he takes the four Ulster politicians upstairs and puts them in penthouse suites. He instructs them that when members of the party (SDLP) are in Dublin in future they are to stay at the Burlington with his compliments.

12 July

By chance meet John Hume in Groome's Hotel at 1 am drinking at the bar. He has been in to see Cosgrave* with whom he says he has had a splendid meeting.

Hume is concerned that the SDLP should not break with Cosgrave's cabinet. The ogre that leans on everyone's shoulder in the Republic today is civil war. The termite created in 1922–23 still gnaws at the vitals of the nation.

14 July

George Reavey, the American critic and poet, is in town. We had a few good meetings in New York a year ago and I asked him to look me up in Dublin. George was born in Belfast but grew up in Russia where his father was a businessman. He was Beckett's first agent and published his poems as well as persuading Routledge to publish *Murphy*. George is not at all averse to hearing the sound of his own voice, and so after he meets Bob Bradshaw who is ensconced over a pint in McDaid's he rambles on somewhat on the subject of Russian literature. He is no match for Bob however, who is delighted to find a foreigner against whom he can enter into combat on literary matters. When Reavey insists, somewhat pedantically, that Pasternak is the precursor of modern Soviet literature, Bob pooh-poohs this and, in some detail, adduces an impressive argument to demonstrate that Pasternak is in a direct line of descent from Tolstoy, Dostoyevsky, Turgenev et al.

---

* See 20 February 1973, note.

Since George is a fluent Russian speaker and regards himself with
some justification as very much an old Russian hand, he makes a few
vain efforts to check Bob's torrent but falls aside like a skiff swallowed
up in a gale. In the end he cuts his losses (not very enthusiastically)
and subsides under Bob's flow, as I slip out to another bar.

15 July

Whee! By sheer luck, have landed a no-holds-barred meeting with
Dev.* It came through Colonel Matt Feehan, former editor of the *Irish
Press*, who has a leg of the old boy. Dev is ninety-one this year and is
in his second term as President. Of course, it's a moot point with many
whether to consider him a statesman or a devilishly clever politician.
I am rather on the first tack, while acknowledging some of what his
opponents say about him. One way or the other, he became a world
leader for the new countries which were emerging out of the web of
empire. Now, sitting in the pillared drawing room where Viceroys
once received royalty, he seems, if anything, very much at home. He
has an extraordinary voice, soft, persuasive, yet with a cautionary note
like the twang of a rubber band.

'Will you have a cup of tea?'

He sits sideways to me, as his sight is extremely poor and any vision
he has left is peripheral. My grandfather Tom Murphy (who was a
supporter of the Treaty, unlike Dev) had been a senior civil servant
when Dev came to power in 1932, trailing remnants of the wild men
he had tamed and a reputation for political deviousness.

'Tommy Murphy. I remember him very well. He used to pair with
James McMahon.'

As James McMahon was Under-Secretary in Dublin Castle from
1919 to 1921, I was puzzled until I remembered Grandfather and he
were at Blackrock College together and were both members of the
school St Vincent de Paul Conference. When they went out to visit

---

* Eamon de Valera (1882–1975). Sentenced to death as a leader of the 1916 Rising but
the sentence was commuted. Elected President of Sinn Fein in 1919, he quickly became
a figure on the world scene when he negotiated a truce with Lloyd George in the summer
of 1921, after an Anglo-Irish war of almost three years. Taoiseach of Ireland from 1932
to 1948, out of power between 1948 and 1952; his party were again elected in 1953. In
1959 he resigned from active politics and was elected President of Ireland, with a seven-
year term. Re-elected in 1966, he retired in October 1973 at the age of ninety-one.

the poor, they went in twos. Dev was in the same conference, though somewhat younger, and would have shared with them a love of rugby, which came a close second to religion in Blackrock, who had the best school side in Ireland. Dev showed me, on his forearm, the scars of smallpox which he caught on a visit to the slums.

I have prepared with care for the interview, as if I were examining the chief witness in an important law case. After all, this is the man who could sidestep a political opponent as well as Tony O'Reilly could beat a full-back on the rugby field. At thirty-seven, Dev had taken on Lloyd George and the British Empire after they had won the biggest war in history. The question that has divided Irishmen is why he didn't stand by the delegates who signed the Treaty which he sent them over to negotiate.*

'You see I wanted to convert the hard men to the idea of an association of States within the Commonwealth. I told Lloyd George when I met him in June that his proposition was no good. We were like an independent State going in. I extended the correspondence with him meticulously. You see, we got wonderful world press. Millions of pounds publicity. If we were going to reopen hostilities it would be better in the winter. Dark nights.' (*He has a slightly self-satisfied smile as he says this.*)

He has been criticized for not going over himself to negotiate the Treaty.

'I didn't want the idea to get around that I was nabbed in London. If Collins signed I felt I could bring the hard men with me.'

He turns round with a slight smile.

---

* Irish politics since 1922 – when the Free State came into being – had been largely divided between supporters of de Valera and supporters of Michael Collins, both pillars of the Revolution. De Valera had been the only one of the leaders in the 1916 Rebellion not executed (because of his American citizenship). He developed his talents as a political leader between 1919 and 1921. Collins also built up his reputation in that period, creating an urban guerrilla army whose success was imitated in the first half of the century in Egypt, Cyprus, Palestine and elsewhere in the continuing decolonization process. When Collins was shot dead in 1922 during the Civil War, de Valera was left with the field to himself, a situation which would continue to arouse bitterness amongst his opponents for decades to come.

'Cathal Brugha* thought all you had to do was to send them a postcard. "I'm a Republic." I sent Collins instead.'

This gives me an opening for the question which I have prepared with such care:

'And who would you consider, besides yourself, the Irishman who contributed most between 1918 and 1921?'

I deliberately choose this time frame. If I'd said between 1916 and 1921 it would have allowed de Valera to introduce the names of Patrick Pearse, Roger Casement, James Connolly or other patriots from the 1916 Rebellion. The time scale I put to him narrows his choice, and I am eager to find out where he would place his rival for the title of the 'greatest Irishman' of the period.

I watch his face and say nothing. I think he senses I have him in a corner. Finally, after a minute or two, he says:

'I wouldn't like to single out anyone.'

I make no response to this. I wait for a full minute. It is like a Japanese wrestling match, perfect courtesy on both sides.

UO'C (in a tiny voice): 'Where would you place Michael Collins?'

Immediate reply:

'Oh, I selected Mick Collins as Director of the Blue Cross in 1917 after he came home from prison in England. He was clearly cut out for that and later, as Director of Intelligence in the IRA, he did very well indeed.'

Thus, having established Collins as his nominee, Dev is satisfied. He changes the subject gently.

'I'm afraid your tea is getting cold.'

He has a lovely smile now. The concentrated look has gone.

---

* 1874–1922; born Charles William St John Burgess but took the Irish form of the name after he joined the Gaelic League in 1899. Second in Command of the South Dublin Union in the 1916 Rebellion where he fought with great bravery after being severely wounded. Member of Dail Eireann and Minister for Defence from 1918 until 1922. A man of irredentist beliefs, he was unable to comprehend Collins' pragmatic Republicanism and he took the anti-Treaty side in the Civil War. He died of his wounds after a protracted street battle in July 1922.

Perhaps he does not want to reveal himself. But does he realize that halfway through I had him a bit on the gallop?

Yet, after what I would consider to be a serious error of judgement on the question of the Anglo-Irish Treaty of December 1921, he nursed the new State with remarkable skill through the developing years after he was elected Taoiseach, and his contribution just before and during World War Two was magisterial.

18 July

Breeze out to Sandycove today in fine fettle. I have with me a manuscript of Monk's 'Notes on the Meditation of Love' which I have held onto for nearly a year. I took it with me to America to read there but unfortunately didn't do so. I then put off having a look at it for about three months, until Monk, I think, began to feel that I had lost it. He hadn't told me it was his only complete copy, so he was understandably nervous. Now, however, I have it under my arm, well considered and things to say about it.

Winifred answers the door. I go in and hand the manuscript to Monk, like a runner passing on the Olympic flame. He looks at it with some relief and then says almost apologetically 'I thought you'd lost it.' This is exactly what I have been feeling he thought, but for some reason when he says it to me now, I get on my high horse and snap 'What reason have you to think I was telling a lie?' Then taking my eye off the delicious afternoon tea prepared by Winifred, I turn on my heel and flounce out in high dudgeon. As I walk up the Sandycove Road towards town, just missing a bus, I try to see in perspective what has occurred. Maybe it is an older generation looking on a much younger one as not up to snuff. Or Anglo-Irish sniffiness of the kind 'Oh, you can't trust *them*'. There is, however, a nagging doubt in my mind that I may have acted the prima donna simply because I was long overdue in coming up with the goods and wanted to justify myself without admitting it.

As I stood at the bus stop a car drew up. It was Ronan Keane,[*] a friend and colleague at the Bar. He offered to give me a lift into town which was gratefully accepted. Then I discovered that I had left my wallet at Tara Hall. Drove back but rather than face a

---

[*] Now Mr Justice Ronan Keane. He became Chief Justice of Ireland in 1999.

possible onslaught I asked Ronan to go in and get it. He returned in a few minutes looking amused but a little taken aback. What had happened was that the door had been opened by Philly (Monk's daughter), who called in to her father 'Daddy, it's Ulick's friend at the door.' Then, according to Ronan, 'a somewhat peppery, military-looking gentleman came out and handed me the purse saying, "I'm not surprised he lost it, he left in a rage without having his tea".' When Ronan told him he was taking me home for tea, Monk said irritably 'Oh, leave it to him, he always falls on his feet.'

23 July

Meet Kevin Monaghan in Grogan's where he sits like a member of a royal court in exile. He has twirling waxed moustaches and a tilt to his head which suggests a Frans Hals painting. He had been decorated by the American army for bravery in battle before arriving here on a GI grant. In Dublin, where he runs an antique shop of sorts, Kevin has become a character. Sales are rare because he is often reluctant to let go his treasures for something as common as cash.

He always manages to look surprised no matter how you catch him off-guard. He will gather himself to full height to deliver a witticism, brace his shoulders, lighten lips and then with an almost feminine yelp out it will come. Vulnerable (as all wits are), he keeps a straight face, to assess the impact of a remark on his listeners. There is a slightly mocking look at the corner of his eyes and if he feels you are in on the joke he may allow a glimmer of collusion to creep into his expression. Diaghilev couldn't have choreographed an entrechat better than Kevin does when he makes one of his wisecracks.

'Cast in the same mould,' he said to me once when I had recalled that my father had worked on the development of penicillin with Alexander Fleming.

Recently in the Dawson Lounge (the smallest pub in Dublin) he excelled himself. We had held a seat for him in the corner from where he was accustomed to preside over a group of two or three. After he had arrived and settled in he perceived a good-looking woman, with a big bust and blonde hair, heading for a seat beside him. She picked her way through the minefield and finally slumped down. He regarded her with some distaste, his moustaches *en brosse*, face rigid with disapproval.

'Madam, I admire your parking technique, but haven't you forgotten to switch off your headlamps?'

28 July

Play for Shamrock Rovers* Touring Side today in Kildare town. Their left wing, Damien Richardson, is out for the summer. Luckily, I have the 'Rasher' Tuohy, the former Newcastle and Ireland forward, inside me who plies me with good balls which I accept gratefully and sally goalwards.

It was Rasher who asked me four years ago to play in his selected Irish XI against a group of English internationals which included the legendary Stanley Matthews. As luck would have it I was marking this remote, revered figure whom I regard as one of the great athletes of any sport in history. Not only did Rasher select me but as inside forward he fed me with the most exquisitely presented passes, with the result that my footballing stature was raised to an entirely artificial level in front of a 40,000 crowd at Dalymount Park.

24 August

Walked this evening through the city streets to the North Star Hotel at Amiens Street with Oliver Edwards. He is professor of English in Queen's University, Belfast and knew Yeats. He has a marvellous slow voice, like an organ warming up, which is ideal for impersonating Yeats's sonorous chant. He remembers Yeats on Gerald Manley Hopkins for instance:

'Hopkins is that inherent absurdity, a religious Englishman.'

We walk through Foley Street, Summerhill, part of the old brothel area of Joyce's Nighttown. Oliver tells me he can sleep standing up.

25 August

Letter today from a *Late Late* viewer.

Dear Ulick O'Connor

You are welcome back from your holidays. I saw you this morning – wearing your nice smile – outside Brown Thomas, in

---

* The leading Irish professional soccer club.

Grafton Street. Thought I would speak to you, but some lady in green pulled you by the arm as I was going in the door. She must have been saying all sorts of nice things because you were replying: 'Thank you very much!'

I would love to have a chat with you sometime. A writer's life is not easy . . . on the system!

By the way, I am a nurse but I have worked mostly abroad, America and England.

Say I will be outside Brown Thomas at 11 am, side door, Wednesday. If you are unable to be there, please phone 74074 on Tuesday evening.

Marie G

26 August

Somebody up there hates me. This in the post today.

Dear Uneuch [sic] (you must be)

It is sad to see a man with such an *Inferiority Complex* make such an idiot of himself on TV.

You must be very unsure of yourself and so childish.

I always thought you were supposed to be clever, why don't you catch on to yourself and not be such an ignorant lout.

By the way, your 'Crown Topper' does not suit you either.

Yours sincerely
Julie C

28 August

Rock concert in Blackrock Park, Dublin. I have been asked to do a gig. We are down in the bowl of the park, round a concert space. Feel drowned in blue, till I realize there is a lot of denim around. Tiny girl with fair hair approaches me as I am coming off the stage. About six years of age. She points a disapproving finger and says with an American accent:

'You used Jesus's name. You shouldn't say the name of the Lord Jesus in vain.'

I try to fob her off.

Me: 'It was in a joke. I used it because I like Him and I'm sure
He has a sense of humour.'
Little girl: (stamping her foot) 'Yes but it wasn't in a prayer.'
Me: 'But it would be worse if I ignored Him.'
Little girl: 'But the commandment says you mustn't say it.'

Fixes me once more with a gimlet eye.

5 September

Start of rehearsals today with Tomás MacAnna at the Abbey Theatre,
for my one man play on Oliver St John Gogarty,* *The Last of the Bucks.*
Tomás, who directed *Brendan*, is a gift to work with. He has inherited
much of the minimalist tradition of the Abbey, which Yeats imported
through Gordon Craig from Paris. When Tomás first came to the
Abbey in the Forties, the Craig screens were still in the prop room, on
wheels so they could be shifted around the stage and lit from behind
to suggest anything, from the burning of Troy to the interior of a
country house. While working with the Berliner Ensemble Tomás
recognized that the Craig-Yeats approach was still somewhat ahead of
its time and since he returned to the Abbey as Artistic Director he has
identified the Abbey tradition and advanced it further. For three weeks
I shall be like a marionette on a slack lead, while the director seeks to
merge word and movement to create a tale for the stage.

9 September

In to Moylan, a perky little tailor in Abbey Street, one of the very few
in the city who knows how to cut an Edwardian suit. No shoulder
padding, four buttons, lapels on the waistcoats and flaps on the lower
pockets of it. He was an apprentice tailor, he tells me, when there were

---

* 1878–1957; poet, athlete, Senator, surgeon, wit and conversationalist. Yeats called
Gogarty 'One of the great lyric poets of our age,' and included seventeen of his poems in
the *Oxford Book of Modern Verse*. Gogarty was regarded as continuing a Dublin conversational tradition out of which came Oscar Wilde. Their mutual tutor in the art of conversation was Dr John Pentland Mahaffy, Professor of Greek at Trinity College. Gogarty was
the original of 'stately, plump Buck Mulligan' in Joyce's *Ulysses*. He and Joyce were close
friends and stayed in the Martello tower in Sandycove, the mise-en-scène for the beginning of the novel. Padraic Colum once told me that Buck Mulligan's speech in *Ulysses* is
a perfect reproduction of Gogarty's talk even down to the cadence of the sentences.

still 'gintlemen' to be seen in Sackville Street, now O'Connell Street, in such suits.

15 September

Bad news. Tomás MacAnna is in hospital, seriously ill. By luck my friend Dr Pat Keelan is the consultant and can give me a straight read, however disappointing, on the situation. He tells me there is no chance of the patient being well enough to work in the next few weeks. Can't believe such bad luck. If a one man play goes up the river, there's only one guy in the front line who will take the barrage – and that's little me. I was convinced Tomás was the one who could keep me out of the mulligatawny.

18 September

Jim Fitzgerald is my new director for *The Last of the Bucks*; Noel Pearson thinks he's the right man for the job. OK, Pearson knows his stuff; he's had huge success both here and in the USA. But I remain a little apprehensive. In the past Fitzgerald has had a record of going on the tear just at the wrong time in a production. On the other hand, he is quite the most brilliant director of the last decade, having made a big impact on the London stage with his production of Hugh Leonard's adaptation of Joyce's *Stephen Hero*. At present he is on a regular salary at RTE but I don't know how much good that has done his tendency to overdo the hard stuff. He likes the idea himself, however, and that counts for a lot.

22 September

A Nigerian academic sent to me by Bishop Whelan (a teacher of mine at school who became Bishop of Owerri) is trying to get a flavour of literary Dublin. In McDaid's we bump into Bob Bradshaw who is immediately interested in somebody from the heart of the Dark Continent and the prospect of gathering new information from a remote source. After a few cursory remarks about the Nigerian Civil War Bob brought him around to the subject of art and sculpture in Africa.

'We don't have any Nigerian sculpture to compare with Europe.'
'But the Benin bronzes,' Bob protests, 'what about them?'
The unlucky fellow, caught off guard, mumbled something.

'They are,' said Bob, 'works of art equal to anything in medieval Europe.'

Your man knew he had made a gaffe (rather like an Irishman being caught out on not having heard of Yeats) but ploughed on regardless. But his argument was in vain. Soon the poor fellow slipped off his stool and suggested we go to the film *Mogambo* starring Grace Kelly, Ava Gardner and Clark Gable which was running round the corner at the Stephen's Green cinema.

24 September, London

Cecil Beaton in London.

> *CB:* 'Are you over here for a rest?'
> *Me:* 'What?'
> *CB:* 'To get away from the violence.'

Talks about Maud Gonne. Whether a photograph could evoke her real beauty or not. Tchelitchew for instance: thinks no photograph could capture this artist's painting of Serge Lifar *en grand jeté*. When Beaton's face lights up he takes on a slightly El Greco look. Knew Lady Lavery when she wasn't on top of the social world she once held sway over.

'She gave you scrambled eggs and gooseberry fool for lunch, but it was the best scrambled eggs and the best gooseberry fool ever made – that's why we all longed to be asked; she was the perfect hostess, though near the end she was very poor.'

30 September, Dublin

Letter today from a *Late Late* fan.

> My father arrived up last Sunday morning and threw *The Mirror* on the bed with your page uppermost and shouted, 'Read that', and there I was, me and me Convent Education and I practically using four-letter words in public – I was ecstatic – the best value I've had for years!!!
>
> Anyway, somebody will be glad to know that sales of that paper soared to heights hitherto unheard of last Sunday in Cork – as a matter of fact, they're still looking for it (is 'it' a preposition??).

All I said was 'I like Ulick',
A simple statement – nothing more.
From the scared expressions round me
I could've said I like abortion, rape and war!
One peered at me, she said 'He's queer',
A laugh went round the hall,
As me uncle in the country says,
'Barren Bitches all!'

All I'm saying is 'I like Ulick',
And I'm sure, without being told
That beneath that cold exterior
There dwells a sexy soul –
Ah Ulick, don't deny it
For I have got you tagged.
When you came back from Sweden,
How come you looked so shagged?

1 October

Sat in the wings of the Gate Theatre all morning frizzelized (to use
one of Nanny's Northern words) with the cold. NBC, the American
TV network, are filming selected short excerpts from some of the
events in this week's festival. To ask an actor to cut a performance is
like asking the priest not to give you absolution just after you have
spilt the beans in confession. Most of the 'excerpts' up to now have
been horribly long. Micheál MacLiammóir has just spent fifteen
minutes on Larry Doyle's speech from Shaw's *John Bull's Other Island*.
Mine, if I ever get to it, is devised to last only 3 minutes 50 seconds
(in fact it goes a little over), but at least I shall be out of this icebox.
Finally I'm through and on my way, in a taxi, down to Castletown in
Co. Kildare,* for a lighting rehearsal. When I get to the vast dining

---

* Castletown House, as it is nowadays called, is the earliest of the great Palladian houses
designed by Alessandro Galilei and Sir Edward Lovett Pearce. Its front is without orna-
mentation but, with thirteen-bay windows, is reminiscent of an urban Renaissance
palazzo. The decoration, as is the way with Irish Georgian, is on the inside. The dining
room where I performed the one man play has a cracked hearthstone – cracked, it is said,
by a hunting guest who turned out to be the Devil and vanished up the chimney after a
priest had hurled a bible at him.

room on the left of the entrance hall where the play is being staged, I find everybody looking up towards the ceiling with its beautiful geometrical Chambers plasterwork. What's going on? No, they are not starstruck 'architectural groupies' but concerned stage people who are gazing at Jim Fitzgerald, supported by God-knows-what, crawling round the cornices like Quasimodo among the steeples of Notre Dame. Under the pretence of hanging the lights which will convert this beautiful room into a theatre space, he is now, roaring drunk, having the time of his life terrifying those below who expect him any minute to fall fifty feet. His crazed face leers down at me:

'Now we're motoring old son.'

Wish that he was, out of bloody Castletown and back to Dublin. Noel Pearson, the producer, has phoned and has cancelled the rehearsal until tomorrow morning.

Nothing to do but order a cab back to Dublin and hope that Fitz will be dried out for the dress rehearsal tomorrow.

3 October

Opening night. Fitz has sobered up. Castletown is lit up in the autumn twilight. My dressing room is one of thirteen on the third floor. I have been told it was Lady Louisa Connolly's own room so when I walk into it to put my costume on and find a lady in a revealing long loose dress already there, I think this may be an eighteenth-century revenant. A snarl disillusions me. I am informed by the person that she is Lady Blackwood and is in residence at Castletown writing her next novel. Anxious not to burst my boiler before going on stage (it always shows), I explain my mistake as best I can, but her ladyship is not disposed to receive my apology. Well, what can you expect from a pig but grunts?*

The slow movement from Chopin's Sonata No. 3 carries me in through the audience to the stage. Two rowdies in the front row (who turn out to be journalists) won't stop chattering, but eventually I get silence. Gogarty was a poet, a wit, and led a life that to some extent could have come out of a novel, so that I have three basic elements available with which to charm an audience. It goes smoothly and I feel I now have a show that I could keep on the road for a few years to come.

---

* Later I would read Caroline Blackwood's novels, diaries and essays and realize that she had rare gifts and insight as a writer.

Afterwards I meet the Taoiseach and his wife Mary. Liam Cosgrave grew up with the Gogarty legend as the poet was a close friend of his father, W.T. Cosgrave, the first President of the Irish Free State. 'Boss' Cosgrave, a pious man, was somehow never shocked by Gogarty's bawdy humour or blasphemies, applying to him the Dublin licence for jest, no matter how extreme, if it is genuinely funny. I told Liam I hoped he hadn't been offended by escapades of his uncle, 'The Bird' Flanagan* which I had related onstage, but again it seems he sees them in the context of the fabric of Dublin life which anneals any scandal they may give. There is a touch of 'The Bird', I thought, in the little silver fox that Liam now sports in his button-hole. Last week in the Dail he had referred to the new left-wing element in his party as 'mongrel foxes', and declared his intention of pursuing them with the vigour of a huntsman, which as a master of the South Dublin Hunt he is well capable of exercising.

We had a photograph taken for the press. After it was taken the Taoiseach said, 'I hope this will be of use to you.'

5 November

In to see Jack Lynch. Looking very drawn. Two civil servants have told him they thought that extradition of IRA activists is unlikely. Says he will talk to Cosgrave. Heel badly hurt. Still in pain. I refer to him by his old title and he says wryly: 'Not Taoiseach any longer.'†

27 November, Belfast

Up to see Paddy Devlin,‡ he has just been appointed Minister for Health (in waiting) in the Northern Ireland Assembly initiated by Ted

---

* 'The Bird' got his nick-name after he had gone to a fancy-dress ball on roller-skates dressed as the Holy Ghost, and assisted by two disciples laid an egg (a painted rugby ball) on the floor in front of a large audience, who chased him out of the arena. He escaped however on his roller-skates, ably assisted by his disciples. 'The Bird' was not particularly well disposed towards the constabulary and on one occasion he approached a policeman who had a grudge against him, and opened up his coat revealing a sausage sewn onto the fly-buttons of his trousers. The policeman, thinking he had Flanagan for indecent exposure, arrested him whereupon 'The Bird' cut off the sausage with a razor and the horrified bobby fainted.

† Lynch's party, Fianna Fail, had been defeated in the recent general election.

‡ SDLP member and member of the power-sharing executive in Northern Ireland.

Heath's Sunningdale Agreement, which will be inaugurated in May. We go into a restaurant and Paddy takes a gun out from a holster under each armpit. He places them on the table. He looks at the door and then says: 'If any fucker, IRA or Loyalist, comes in here, I'll blow his head off.'

This underlines the tension underneath the settlement. However, the Assembly has been brought into being by an Act of Parliament. The Government cannot afford to back down on this one. The majority of Nationalists support it and obviously Faulkner has brought his Unionists onside as well. For the first time ever there will be an emphasis on justice for all in the decisions of a Northern Ireland parliament. Paddy is looking forward to his job as Minister for Health. He is a genuinely compassionate guy and I can well understand this. A chance to try and do all the things he felt ought to have been done when he was a kid in the poor part of Belfast. He takes out some quite illegible letters. These are a sample of ones coming to the Minister for Health's office every day. Often written by old people or the semi-literate. Up to now they have got tossed out of the window or into the rubbish basket when they arrive. Paddy has hired a handwriting expert from the Northern Ireland Office who will transcribe the letters in readable script so that the contents can be conveyed. Paddy looks like a cat who has just drunk the milk and is looking forward to more.

The Sunningdale Agreement is the biggest leap forward in addressing the problems of Northern Ireland since the 1914 Home Rule Bill.

29 November, Dublin

Talk to John Hume. He says not much will happen until the Council of Ireland* gets into shape. Hume said that in five years Jack Lynch's honour would be proved and what he had done for the country acknowledged. He thinks the best thing would be to open the jails. Hume also told us that Cruise O'Brien informed him that the Irish Association for bringing people together from North and South wouldn't have him to speak which rather shocked him. Anita Currie[†] is at present under siege. She is afraid to leave the house. I hardly dare to write this but it is very difficult to imagine how either John or

---

* This was provided for in the Sunningdale Agreement and effectively meant that nominated Southern politicians would have a say in the running of Northern Ireland affairs.
† Wife of Austin Currie.

1. Me (*left*) with Mariga and Desmond Guinness, Leixlip Castle, 1959
'But westward, look, the land is bright.'

2. Nanny, who came to Fairfield Park when I was five

'Yes, I was brought up well By Nanny Ann Bell.'

(See Appendix 2, 'Requiem for a Nanny')

3. Anne Brady, housekeeper and loyal family friend. She came to Fairfield Park when I was nine

4. Billy Wicklow, 8th Earl of Wicklow, a pal since my student days. According to his friend Evelyn Waugh, 'At Merton, Billy had early given evidence of reckless courage in climbing the roofs of Oxford and insulting Rugger Blues.' In the working-class pubs of Dublin he was greeted:

5. Bob Bradshaw, revolutionary, intellectual and one of the great conversationalists in a golden age of Dublin pub talk. Oil on board by Cossie

6. With Sarah Churchill before the first night of *Counterparts* at the Group Theatre in Cork, a two-person show I wrote and acted in with her. Telegram, 3 March 1970: 'Please call me. I am at home. Love Sarah.' Says she is 'dying to do the show again'

7. Judge at the Trinity College races, May 1970, College Park, Dublin (jaw still intact!)

8. Passing the ball for my Selected International XV vs the President's XV at the opening of the Suttonians' club's new pavilion, October 1971

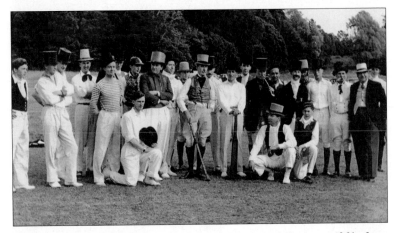

9. Georgian Society cricket match. UO'C in gondolier vest (fifth from left). At centre (with cricket bats) Pierce Synnott (in cloth-of-gold waistcoat) and the Hon. Desmond Guinness. Genial cove on extreme right with unbuttoned waistcoat – Lord Carew of Castletown

10. Rathgar *circa* 1900. Highfield Road on the right, leading to Fairfield Park. Virtually unchanged today except for the cab rank, now replaced by horseless carriages

11. Micheál MacLiammóir in the Gate Theatre production of Anouilh's *Ring Round the Moon* in which he played both Hugo and Frederick

12. With John Hume – future winner of the Nobel Peace Prize – in Derry, 1972

13. Viva Superstar – born Susan Hoffman. She was Andy Warhol's first Superstar. Knew her when we were both in residence at the Chelsea Hotel, New York

14. With Stephen Smith and Ambassador Jean Kennedy Smith, New York, April 1977, after acting in my one-man play on Brendan Behan

15. With Monk Gibbon, Christopher Sinclair-Stevenson of Hamish Hamilton and Jack Lynch (Taoiseach 1966–73 and 1977–79) at the launch of my book on the Irish Troubles, 1912–1922, *A Terrible Beauty is Born*, at the National Gallery of Ireland in 1975

16. With Mary Ure at the launch of *Irish Liberation*, published by Grove Press, at the Algonquin Hotel, New York, 1974

17. Playing the part of Oliver St John Gogarty, poet and surgeon, in the
RTE film *An Offering of Swans* (1977)

'Golden stockings you had on
In the meadows where you ran.'

See page 225

18. At the National Boxing Stadium, Dublin, in 1950, after knocking out an opponent from the Parnell Club within four seconds of the start of the welterweight bout

19. Thirty years on – having a spar with British lightweight champion Charlie Nash in Derry before Nash's world championship fight with Jimmy Watt, Glasgow, March 1980

Austin can avoid being shot and maybe killed before the Northern trouble is over.

23 December

Rang Sean MacBride.* He lives in his mother's house in Clonskeagh. As an Assistant Secretary-General of the United Nations, he has just resolved the South African problem in Namibia. Now he thinks that the new Assembly could be a real success in Belfast and the Sunningdale Agreement will flourish. I rang John Hume. He is interested to know how many in the Republic are behind the settlement. Don Barrington thinks we can't 'crow too much'.

30 December

Lunch with MacBride.

> *Me:* 'Hume is in a 1922 situation.'†
> *MacB:* 'He knows he has to contain the Army' (IRA).

---

* Born 1904, son of Major John MacBride and Maude Gonne. His godfather was Ezra Pound, who taught him Latin, and from Yeats he learned English when he was growing up in Normandy with his mother. MacBride served as a very young volunteer in the Anglo-Irish War, taking the anti-Treaty side in the Civil War; he was Chief of Staff of the IRA from 1935 to 1937, when he resigned to practise at the Bar and embark on a career in which he had outstanding success as a specialist in constitutional law. In 1946 he founded Clann na Poblachta (the People's Party), which was intended to bridge the gap between the two main parties of the Republic, Fianna Fail and Fine Gael, caused by the Civil War. He was Minister for External Affairs in the Inter-Party Government of 1948. In 1977 he won the Nobel Prize for Peace and the Lenin Peace Prize, the only person ever to be accorded both honours. He became an Assistant Secretary-General of the United Nations in 1980.

† This is a reference to the Irish Civil War of 1922–23 where the settlement with Britain, though agreed on by a majority at the ballot box, was rejected by an anti-Treaty group who waged war on the new government. The anti-Treatyites dumped their arms in 1923. In 1922 General Michael Collins, though aspiring to an all-Ireland solution, had accepted a settlement which partitioned Ireland, leaving the six Counties in the north-eastern part of the country under British rule. Collins believed that there was enough in the settlement to allow through peaceful negotiations for an all-Ireland solution, but this could only be if he brought the whole army (IRA) with him. Though many of the most able stayed with him, a substantial section revolted and a dreadful civil war broke out. What MacBride meant was that no settlement could be made in the North without the united support of the IRA.

I see the Provos as Treatyites and the renegade IRA as Anti-Treatyites. Later George Colley* agrees with me that Cruise O'Brien wants to be Taoiseach. His election could I think have no other effect but to sow the seeds for serious civil disturbance.

---

* A former Minister for Finance.

1974

Milton Goldman gives a party in his apartment on the East Side. He is a leading agent here so there are lots of stars present. One of them is a famous English film actor who lives in Ireland and comes over for a chat. He is a friend of Pierce Gill whom I play squash with in Fitzwilliam. Introduces me to his wife, whom I had first noticed as a stunning beauty in films ten years ago. She knows of me from seeing television and wants a chat. When we sit down it turns out she wants to join the IRA.

'I'm Scottish and don't like the English.'

After the party we go to the Lion's Head to eat. A note is pressed into my hand under the table.

'What hotel are you staying in?'

It's from herself; but with himself sitting next to me it seems a bit much. No go. Cute enough, however, she finds out what she wants on the way home when I share a taxi with them and ask to be left off at the Algonquin. An hour later there is a ring from the front desk.

'I'm coming up.'

When I open the door, she flies in.

'I'm so well known in this hotel. Stayed almost a year when himself was acting on Broadway.'

I make a weak protest. In a second she has her sweater off and then the rest, almost like an instantaneous striptease. Her skin is beautiful, like polished ivory. Maybe this is what she wanted to show off. She leaves some time later. I tell her I have another girl in New York.

11 April

Once I've had my launch party* at the Algonquin, I change hotels and head back to the Chelsea. Stanley Bard, the manager, welcomes me.

---

* For *Irish Liberation*, commissioned by Barney Rosset and published by Grove Press in 1974. A collection of essays I edited about the crisis in Northern Ireland which included contributions by John Hume, Senator Edward Kennedy and Andy Tyrie, amongst others.

Whenever I arrive he makes me look like a long lost son, arms round me: 'Great to see you.'

Things haven't changed. His brother Milton is still on the point of going out to get shrimp salad, but never actually making it past the lobby. A girl comes up behind Milt and puts her arms around him.

Milton: 'I hope it's a pretty girl.'
Girl: 'I hope it's Milton Bard.'

Stanley takes me to my apartment, which as usual he gives me at a generous rate. The place is splendid. An enormous sitting room, authentic fireplace, elegant bedroom and a kitchen you could play a football match in. As usual in a Chelsea apartment, the walls are virtually bare. The occupant puts up his own posters and decorations. You make your space as you make yourself in this twentieth-century version of Liberty Hall. It is also well heated.

The hotel itself is a beauty. Outside the windows are wrought-iron balconies crafted by the tradesmen who built the hotel in the 1880s and used to stay there. The Chelsea had the first Duplex studios, pent-houses and roof gardens in New York. The walls are of double brick with air space between and three feet thick. The fireplaces are the size of cinema screens with ornate Victorian mantelpieces. There are over 400 rooms.

Downstairs with Stanley in the lift, or should I say elevator. It has become for me the navel of the Chelsea. I have hardly ever been in it when I haven't heard something to brighten my day. Today, perhaps because Stanley's there, nothing happens on the way down.

The lobby is where Chelsea persons gather, like burghers in a medieval market place. Resident artists who have stayed here have donated works which are on the walls. They include paintings by Jackson Pollock, Larry Rivers and the renowned set *Puppets of Artists* by Eugenie Gershoy. Viva* is there today with a baby she is breast-feeding, and talking to Gregory Corso, who is nursing a cup of coffee. Greg greets me with 'Hey, whadda ya know?'

Viva seems glad to see me. Chelseaites splurge affection on each other. I am hailed as if I were a world figure who has suddenly decided to come back home. Arms are thrown around, eulogies exchanged.

---

* See 18 June 1971, note.

Viva even asks me to hold her baby for a second. I take it, make suitable sounds of approval and hand it back to her. Gregory seems relieved that I haven't passed it to him. Viva is determined not to let him escape however.

'Gregory, would you hold my baby a minute, I have to go upstairs.'

Gregory: (*startled*) 'No I won't Viva. The last time you handed me your baby, you didn't come back for two days.'

As he spoke he whipped his cup of coffee off the table. Viva had made a grab, with the speed of a rattlesnake's strike, to fling the hot liquid over him. Failing to do so, she delivered, as she headed for the elevator, a running commentary that would have received a round of applause in a Marseilles brothel.

12 April

My admirer's husband is playing the lead in a Strindberg play on Broadway, which is pulling in the crowds. She rings me to ask will I come along. I ask her for two tickets. Silence for a second at the end of the phone. Then:

'OK.'

The play is wonderful. One can almost see the pale golden northern light coming off the set, generated by the acting and text as much as by lighting and decor. Afterwards I go back stage with Martha whom I'm with. What else can I do. We all go to drinks in the Lion's Head. My admirer says she is upset because she is worrying about terrorists blowing up her children back in Ireland. Lip trembling. She goes out to the bathroom with Martha and I suspect perhaps they have a talk there about bold Little Boy Blue.

14 April

Flying back to New York from Chicago where I had gone to promote *Irish Liberation* on the Kupcinett Show, I pass a truly enormous black man in first class as I board. He is sitting with another black.

'Hi,' says Muhammad Ali, 'How's it going?'

I met Ali a number of times in the late Sixties and also covered his fight in Dublin in 1970 against Al Blue Lewis when we had become well acquainted over three weeks.

'Come down and see you later,' Ali said.

I have just finished my modest airline nosh when Ali plops down beside me. He has short sleeves and his enormous bicep rests near mine with the vein in it pulsing like a python.

'I'd like to show you some poems.'

This is the guy that put Sonny Liston away in round two so I listen. To my credit, I don't nod acquiescently but try to remain detached. Fortunately, two lines come up which I can approve:

> The same road that connects two souls together
> When stretched becomes a path to God.

I nod and he doesn't stop for half an hour. His face is unlined, miraculously free from the damage that boxers can acquire. Of course, in the ring he bobs like a bamboo and it is almost impossible to land a clean punch on him. His ears are close to his head, neat and well formed. When he straightens up you can see his trousers stretched tightly over gigantic thighs, each more than two feet in circumference. I asked him was he never afraid he'd get shot when he was a Vietnam protester and had his title taken away from him because he wouldn't join the army.

'A true Muslim doesn't fear, neither does he grieve. I was happier than I had ever been then in my little car, riding round the States. I never sold out. I was no Uncle Tom.'

He goes back to his chum. I don't see him again till I am getting off the plane. He introduces me to the man he is with.

'This is Kid Gavilan.'

I am impressed. Kid Gavilan is the inventor of the bolo punch and one of the great all-time world middleweight champions. Ali says he'll give me a ride into town in his chauffeur-driven limousine. He sits in front while he puts me in the back of the car with the Kid who starts to sing for me, in Spanish, bits of a musical he is composing about the boxing ring. He says he was down and out recently in Alabama when Ali saw him at a petrol station where he was working and took him on board for a month's holiday. As we roll into Manhattan, the Kid is singing away at his own songs, while Ali's well shaped head rolls from side to side in the front seat. Out for the count.

18 April

On the telephone today to Dublin. I hear that 300,000 Loyalists have signed a petition to demand that the new Assembly be abolished.

Doesn't look too hot for the Sunningdale Agreement. Heath has gone for his tea in the February general election and Patrick Mayhew, who is the best Secretary of State the North has had so far, acquired a new portfolio last September.

19 April

Going down in the Chelsea hotel elevator today, a pleasant-faced little guy in a porkpie hat.

'What are you into, strangling?'

'Not yet.'

'Ordinary homicide?'

'Brooklyn Bridge perhaps.'

'Not chic these days.'

A fair-haired girl is screaming in the lobby. A Beat with crinkly hair and huge glasses is addressing her.

Beat: 'Why if it isn't Mary Crowningshield.'

Mary Crowningshield: (for it is she) 'Are *you* allowed back?'

Beat: 'Are you?'

Mary Crowningshield: 'I live here.'

Beat: 'Well, whadda ya know. Did you see the story in *Time Magazine* I wrote about you.'

He rushes to the counter to grab a copy of *Time*. Mary Crowningshield turns to me:

'He's disgusting, he's a rapist. He got off on one rape charge but then was jailed on another.'

Later, Isabella Gardner* has me up for drinks. She has an amazing apartment even for the Chelsea, stocked with her rich Boston parents' antiques. Roddy† is prowling around looking at the paintings. He cocks his head.

(To Isabella): 'Allibesa,‡ would you care to acquire an early Ghuika?'

---

* Poetess much admired by Sylvia Plath. Received first Walt Whitman Citation of Merit in 1981. Daughter of Isabella Stewart Gardner, the art collector, who presented her collection including Rembrandts and Vermeers to the city of Boston; grandmother of Rosie Gardner (see 20 April 1973).

† Roderick Ghuika; see 24 June 1971.

‡ Anagram for Isabella.

Isabella has clearly had a similar hit before, so she replies firmly without a hint of irritation:

'Not now, Roderick.'

Isabella shows me a press under her bookshelves where she has some letters locked away. These are from Erskine Childers,* former President of Ireland, with whom she claims she had a torrid love affair when she was nineteen! She says the letters are so hot that sometimes she feels she should put them in the icebox in case they go on fire. Good old Erskine. He lived a few houses down the road from me and was often to be found in our drawing room discussing medical matters with my father, to whom he once confided that his ambition in life was to have been a surgeon. Outside afterwards I encounter something which is very much Manhattan, but which is impossible to explain unless you actually see it. Two little black children, a girl skipping along, the boy riding a bike. The little girl is patiently holding on, running behind. Though this is 23rd between Seventh and Eighth, a neighbourhood atmosphere predominates.

25 April

Arlene Francis's radio show. Jeannie Bach, her assistant, always fixes me up for this when I come to town. Almost two million listeners. Arlene is very indulgent to me, even to the point of being embarrassing. All my shirts are in the wash, so I had to come along in the one I wear for the Behan show, designed by Tomás MacAnna. I have always thought it would be much more suitable for John Barrymore in *Hamlet* than as an article of dress which would evoke memories of the barking Brendan. But Arlene hymns its praise and says she is going to forward the pattern to listeners. We talk about soldier poets and I pile in with Alan Seeger's *I have a rendezvous with death* and Rupert Brooke's *The Soldier*, both of which I know by heart. Seeger is barely known in America and Brooke is out of fashion in England, so it's a pleasure to intone the word melodies that they have left us. When I am going on about soldiers, I think I might allude to massacres by

---

* Son of a famous father who though he was a decorated hero in the Royal Flying Corps in World War One had run guns from Germany into Ireland for the Irish Volunteers in 1914 to resist Carson's Orangemen. Erskine Childers the younger was a professional politician in the Fianna Fail party. He became Minister for Transport in 1987 and Minister for Health in 1952. He was elected President of Ireland in 1973.

British forces that have taken place in Irish history. Cromwell's near-final solution at Drogheda, the Black and Tans' machine-gunning the crowd at Croke Park in November 1920, and recently the Bloody Sunday episode in Derry when soldiers killed thirteen civilians. At coffee after the show, the phone rings. Arlene takes the call herself and talks for about five minutes. When she puts the phone down she says:

'That was the British Consul in New York. They ring, if there's anything about Northern Ireland, to give their side of it.'

'Fair play to them,' I say. 'That's how the Empire works. A press office to churn out guff in every town from Baghdad to Berlin.'

What bugs me though is when Arlene tells me that Irish officials are usually on within half an hour backing up the British calls.

On the way out I notice Arlene has some flowers and cards pinned to the board.

'Your birthday?'

'No, it's Armenian Massacre Day. One and a quarter million slaughtered by the Turks in 1915.' She suddenly stops and turns on me in fury.

'You and your fucking Irish Famine made me forget that it's Armenian Day and my mailbox will be stuffed with abusive letters about it.'

If the blue rinse matrons who form a substantial part of her listenership could see their favourite broadcaster now, red as a turkey-cock and using the language of the Fulton Fishmarket, they'd be fit to be tied. Sweet Arlene: what kindness she's shown me.

26 April

In the Chelsea elevator today, a slightly tipsy fellow:

'It doesn't matter what floor you get off, you'll still be in the same dump.'

He quickly wraps his arms around himself as if to ward off a reply. As he gets off, he says resignedly: 'Back to reading Voltaire.'

About two in the morning I get a ring from Gregory Corso.

'I want $20 to take a Vassar girl to dinner.'

'I'll be down in half an hour, Greg, with $10.'

Greg: 'No good man.'
Me: 'Fuck off Greg.'

I do come down to the restaurant in half an hour and he's still waiting. The girl is a beaut. College intellectual. First thing she asks me is: 'How do you pronounce *Táin*?'* Then she wants to know what's the correct way to pronounce Ferdia and Cuchulain. Gregory thinks she is taking too much interest in me, and so he jumps into the ring.

'What were you doing upstairs for the last half-hour? Fucking that stupid-assed chick I introduced you to? I'm going off to spend this money on drugs. I'll pay you back later.'

The girl glares at him and he's off like a cat up an alley. Then she asks about Queen Maeve. Roddy Ghuika comes up and asks if he may join us. He bows to the girl as if he were being knighted at Buckingham Palace and, of course, she is charmed. Horror. Charlie Peters, a sailor friend of Brendan Behan's, comes by and before I can stop him is off on a favourite pastime which is to recount in detail how he has just beaten someone up, stuffing their head down a toilet bowl, trampling on them until he drew blood. Roddy, who knows Charlie's form, torpedoes this with:

'My father was devoted to blood sports. At the Palace outside Bucharest, he used to hunt boar with Paddy Leigh Fermor at three in the morning.'

This stops Charlie in his tracks all right and he removes himself without a word.

'I ask Roddy about Greg's girl:

Roddy: 'Hooked.'
Me: 'On what?'
Roddy: 'Extremely large collections of pills.'
Me: 'What about Greg?'
Roddy: 'Greg's on things of that kind.'

Waves his hand vaguely and then falls into an attitude in which he scrutinizes one with his head held to one side. I think of this as very much a donnish affectation used when they want to avoid having to look one straight in the eye. I slip out to go to bed at 5.30 am. In the lobby:

---

* The *Táin Bo Cualinge*, the Irish equivalent of the *Odyssey* or the *Nibelungenlied*; Cuchulain and Ferdia are two of the heroes in it.

She: 'I'm an artist, not a whore. I have too much integrity to take money.'
He: 'I would have liked your pussy so good.'
She: 'You know nothing about sex. You think you do.'
He: (mournfully) 'I would have liked your pussy.'

In the elevator a girl says:
'I know you're staying in 330. Would you like some coke or Quaalude?'
As the lift door closes, another guy gets in.
'I could use them.'

17 May, Philadelphia

On the Mike Douglas TV show with George Raft.* During a commercial break, Raft leans over and asks if I have heard of the bombings in Dublin and Monaghan. Apparently, a no-warning blast of high intensity has killed 33 people and wounded a total of over a hundred. I hope the Government keeps its head and doesn't agree to a postponement of the Assembly at the end of the month. The strength of the South's position has declined since last year. Heath losing the February election has been a disaster. He would not have condoned blatant breaches of the rule of law as a craven Labour Government (admittedly governing with a small majority) is doing at present.

22 May, Dublin

All-out strike in full swing in Northern Ireland. A Loyalist based, Ulster Workers' Council has closed most of the petrol stations in the province and has succeeded in paralysing public and private transport. The water supply and electricity have also been commandeered by the Workers' Council. The organization of the strike is impeccable and must have taken months of planning. The purpose is to prevent the Assembly meeting on the 28th of May, when Westminster will devolve power to the Northern Ireland executive.

---

* Film star famous for gangster roles.

23 May

Brian Faulkner, head of the Assembly, comes on television tonight. 'Unionists have nothing to fear,' he says. 'There will not be an all-Ireland Republic.' It is not, however, the Republic that Ulster Unionists fear, but the prospect of having to concede equal rights to Nationalists. Privilege has been theirs for so long that they fear any change in the system. It is the problem of the colonizer and the colonized. The middle-class Unionist is on his horse looking down. If he dismounts, he risks having to accept equal status with those below. What makes this attitude potentially dangerous in Northern Ireland is that it is built into the system. A working-class Unionist can look down on a working-class Nationalist, because he knows a job is his if he wants it, no matter what his rival's credentials may be. In Derry, though 70 per cent of the voters are Nationalist, there has never been a Nationalist Mayor elected. The real question is, will the British Government continue to bankroll bigots?

However, the Power-sharing Executive is still there, Faulkner, Bradford, Smith, Hume, Currie, Devlin and others have not resigned. The Nationalist members however are under considerable strain and some like Hume are in danger of being shot by either side. There are Loyalists crazy enough to shoot him and breakaway groups among the Republicans who would do the same.

It is clear that before the Northern problem is solved, there will be more bloodshed. The question is, can it be limited? If the Government gives in to the strikers now, it could be Armageddon. I keep hearing stories about last week's no-warning Loyalist bombings in Dublin and Monaghan. At Lord John's disco tonight a fellow remarks:

'They've loads of arms and legs in Jervis Street Hospital and they don't know who to put them onto.'

The explosives were planted, it seems, by Loyalists, in collusion with the security forces. Today's *Irish Times* carries a comment from Sammy Smyth, the press officer of the Ulster Defence Association: 'Am I happy about the bombing? Yes I am.'

Drop in a letter to Jack Lynch. He's no longer Taoiseach but I suggest to him that he should send a letter to the *New York Times* about the Dublin bombings in which more people have been killed than in any other urban terrorist attack in Western Europe.

28 May

Horrors on horror's head accumulate. Hear at four o'clock that the
Northern Ireland Assembly has been dissolved. Faulkner has resigned
as Chief Executive. It seems the bullies have won. I go down to the
Dail to see Jack Lynch. Meet Eugene Timmons TD in the hall. He
seems to accept the news with equanimity. Then I see David
Andrews.* He does not seem as downcast as he should be (I wonder
has he something up his sleeve?). Brian Lenihan passes us with a
cheery smile. Then I go into the Dail chamber. Afterwards I meet Jack
Lynch. Exhausted. He looks like an old man, shrunk. He puts off our
meeting until Thursday. I go to discuss what's happened with George
Colley (former Minister for Finance). He says we were closer to
trouble in 1969. I point out that then the British Army were regarded
as peacekeepers by the Nationalists, now this is not so. Therefore the
situation is significantly worse. Rory Brugha TD who is also with us
remarks that the British will always suit themselves. George Colley
says he thinks the real danger is unilateral declaration of independence
by the Unionists. I suggest that we should consider sending in the Irish
Army as a protective force with a view to getting the UN to come in
at a later stage. The general feeling is that the Irish Army should have
gone into Northern Ireland in 1969 after Lynch had said that the
South would not 'stand idly by' when the Nationalist population in
Northern Ireland were being attacked and burned out of their homes.
If they had gone across the border at Derry then to protect civilians
they could have remained *in situ* and refused to evacuate until the UN
came in with a peacekeeping force.

My thinking. The British will now get very tough with the
Unionists. They may cut Harland & Wolff's subsidy and that of other
industrial jewels in the British Crown.†

29 May

Listen to the news all day. Faulkner makes a sad speech on television
announcing the demise of the Executive. No one seems to see that

---

* Elected TD for the Fianna Fail Party in 1976. Barrister by profession; took Silk in 1992.
Appointed Minister for Foreign Affairs in 1997.
† In fact they did not get 'very tough' with the Unionists. Under Roy Mason as Secretary
of State for Northern Ireland (1976–79), the government increasingly made the
Nationalist situation so intolerable that further recourse to physical force became inevi-
table.

this is all the result of Orange blackmail and intimidation. These tactics have worked since the beginning of the century, so why shouldn't they work now. Later in the morning I talk to Paddy Devlin. He tells me he resigned from the post of Minister of Health in the Assembly last week in anticipation of what was going to happen today:

'My wife is going to her grave and my children are being attacked by Loyalist thugs.'

The *Irish Times* has this in today's editorial: 'In all the shame Britain has suffered at the hands of her departing colonialism, this lying down to the bigots of Belfast ranks high in infamy.'

This infamy has been perpetrated less than one hundred miles from the house I'm living in.

30 May

In to see Jack Lynch at 2.30. He believes that the present Coalition government are not sympathetic to Nationalists in the North. This may be due to the influence of Conor Cruise O'Brien* who has a dislike of Nationalist ideas probably inherited from a confused youth and upbringing. Although I would have expected better from Cosgrave. Nevertheless, he is in a difficult position because he is in coalition with Labour and he has to make many concessions. There is a potentially dangerous situation at present where Cruise O'Brien tends to speak on Foreign Affairs matters while he is Minister for Post and Telegraphs. In a bizarre claim, having been the opposition spokesman for Foreign Affairs, he now maintains that in government he still has authority to present himself wearing another hat. This of course is total balls. Lynch thinks that President Childers should make a statement asking the British to make a Statement of Intent that they will disengage from Northern Ireland at a given date. It could be as much

---

* Historian, biographer, playwright, political commentator and respected literary critic. Noted for his distinctive and vigorous prose style. His reputation was established in critical works such as *Maria Cross* and a biography of Charles Stewart Parnell (1957). In 1992 his *Life of Edmund Burke*, published after many years' gestation, received much praise. He has been less successful in a desultory political career which he has revived from time to time. In 1961 he was Representative of the UN Secretary General (Dag Hammarskjöld) in Katanga. He joined the Labour Party in 1969, and failed to be re-elected after his first foray into Irish politics in 1973. Nevertheless, it is on political matters that he speaks most often, frequently, in my view, with disastrous consequences. See further 28 January 1977, note.

as twenty years hence. But any such statement would help. He says he will write a letter to the *New York Times* on the matter.

In another room I work on a draft for Lynch's letter to the *New York Times* with Esmonde Smyth,* one of his backroom advisors. He has said he will work with me on it as long as I'm not asking him to play in a cricket match which I usually am. Meet Paddy Harte, Paddy Belton and Garry L'Estrange, all three Fine Gael TDs driving to Dun Laoghaire. Somewhat uncouth. They don't offer a lift.

31 May

Nanny cooks my lunch today as it's Annie's day off. Nanny is a staunch Tyrone Catholic from Cookstown but has Protestant relatives. Some of the virtues I acquired from her are specifically Ulster ones so I see her as a mirror of two cultures up there. Her view is that: 'The English are at fault and the Protestants won't give in.' That's the way she recalls it sixty years ago when she was a girl and worked in a Cookstown factory. Catholics were about one-tenth of the work force. At election time, mass would always be said for Nationalist candidates.

She remembers Shane Leslie going up for mid-Tyrone in 1905 (the convert son of a Monaghan baronet and first cousin of Winston Churchill who had adopted the Nationalist cause). 'If we didn't win at the elections then we would have had nothing. Protestants would do you a favour and be kind until election day.' Nanny was educated by the nuns in the same school as Bernadette Devlin.† Sister Benignus taught her in 'the ladies school'. Some of her school friends were Protestants, a girl called Maeve Brett she remembers well.

'The nuns were great teachers.'

Lunch is delicious. Roast beef and fruit salad. Afterwards I walk to Fitzwilliam Lawn Tennis Club with the intention of going to the Gate

* Now the Hon. Judge Esmonde Smyth. President of the Circuit Court.
† Bernadette Devlin McAliskey. The youngest woman ever to be elected to Westminster. Bernadette Devlin represented mid-Ulster in parliament from 1969 to 1974. She had gained a world-wide reputation as a Civil Rights activist when she was one of the leaders of the 'Free Derry' complex which came into being when the people of the Bogside created, to all intents and purposes, an independent mini-Republic in defiance of British rule. Her brilliantly conceived activism made her a hated figure in Loyalist circles and she was seriously injured when she was attacked by Loyalist gunmen and machine-gunned with her children under the bed in her own home.

Theatre later on to see Micheál MacLiammóir in Yeats's translation of
Oedipus in which he is playing the leading role as well as having
designed the sets.

2 June

Letter today a bit scary. Well-written. There is a name and address,
Slaney Street, Wexford but I don't know the writer. She writes that
she's in bed at 1.45 am and says she has been looking *into* me many
times on television.

> I sense trees nearby. Come on Ulick, touch them, feel their solid
> bark. Run your hands round her waist. Caress her, for if you love
> her, she's yours. Maybe she'll bend her leaves down to stroke you
> or she'll hit you if you hurt her. Then you spy cold hard rocks.
> Greenness abounds – they too are alive and listening. Overhead
> again the sky is hurrying, it breaks the spell, we are dying we
> two . . .

8 June

Ramble down the city Quays and almost memorize Dylan Thomas's
And death shall have no dominion. On the Quays a turquoise sun in the
evening sky. I drop into the Olympia Theatre to see who is in the bar
and on the way pass through an empty parterre. I stand there for a
second, looking up at the baroque boxes in this jewel of a theatre. One
night at this time I had brought an actor here who was in Dublin with
the Berliner Ensemble. He simply knelt down in the aisle and joined
his hands:

'A shrine,' he said.

13 June

Lunch with Austin* and Anita Currie in the Hibernian Hotel.

Austin: 'I'm becoming anti-British. Our main object now is to split
the Unionists. There are two alternatives, re-partition or power-
sharing.'

Anita Currie agrees that the British Army should leave. Troops out.

---

* See 27 November 1972, note.

They haven't afforded her much protection. A collection of Loyalist heroes recently broke into the Curries' home and carved Anita's name on her chest with a knife.

Later as I walk down by the Quays and pass the Four Courts* I recall that behind its beautiful Gandon portico in the summer of 1922 were Sean MacBride and Sean Lemass crouched over their guns as they replied to the shellfire of Michael Collins's new Free State army. Sean MacBride later won both the Nobel and the Lenin Peace prizes and Sean Lemass would become an effective Taoiseach. Do we have to go through another such cataclysm before we can get peace in the whole country? Poor old Four Courts, I hope they'll survive a second time.

6 August

Message at 5.30.

'John Hume wants to see you. In the Shelbourne.'

'Cruise O'Brien has to be stopped attacking us,' he says when I get there.

'It's the name of the game. We are putting candidates up in the election and the people here are saying we've become Unionists. Otherwise we will have no credibility as a unified party.'

9 September

As I go down this evening to Lord John's disco, in the city centre, a blonde girl with a cross around her neck kisses me in the street. In Lord John's discuss Yeats's (alleged) fascism.

One of the reasons I go to this disco is that I can get a steak there very late at night. A steak is part of my weight-reducing diet and I need a good one. Bob Bradshaw drives me down from Grogan's pub. As I am getting out of the car at Sir John Gray's statue in the middle of O'Connell Street I see across the road, outside Wynn's Hotel, a young man being knocked down by a gang. They kick him in the head and body with unrelenting ferocity. I tell Bob to stay where he is and run across the street yelling at them to stop. I shout at the porter

---

* The Four Courts house the Circuit Courts, the High Courts and Supreme Court, and the Law Library where barristers wait for attorneys to brief them. Occupied by extremist Republicans in June 1922 in a protest against the signing of the Anglo-Irish Treaty and the subsequent setting up of a 26-county Irish state.

standing outside Wynn's Hotel to get the police. The young man on the ground is not moving, bleeding heavily and looks a goner. I try to draw some of the thugs away by punching and then retreating. Then I see that Bob is lying on the ground with his head opened and blood turning his white hair red. One of the gang has hit him with a cosh. Not a policeman in sight. I yell at the porter again. He looks at me like a floundered jellyfish. None of the onlookers will help. I dance and prance with fists up. Suddenly the gang scarper. I'm so furious that I run after them in the hope that I might drive them into the arms of a policeman in O'Connell Street. Not a chance. Street patrols are out of fashion these days. I get as far as the GPO but there isn't a cop in sight. When I get back, Bob is being lifted into an ambulance. Ten minutes later the police arrive. I get into their car and ask them to drive me around various bars looking to see if I can identify the thugs. No go. Back to Store Street Station where Bob has come to be patched up temporarily. I take him out to my doctor brother-in-law, who sews his head wound up. In the station I learn there have been three murders in O'Connell Street since the beginning of September. Also on this particular night there were four assaults and a boy was thrown into the Liffey. Police, I ask you?

I sleep badly later on. A bit tortured. Had I mixed it enough with the gang? Had conscience made me a coward? I was thinking of my fragile jaw broken three years ago. By dawn I have convinced myself that if I had closed with them instead of boxing, I might have ended up like Bob. Then they could have continued their kicking and the young man might have* . . . Who knows?

15 September

An extraordinary afternoon at Tara Hall. A real row with Monk over Proust's sexual proclivities. It all started when he brandished at me a recently translated book of memoirs by Céleste Albaret, Proust's devoted servant.

> *Monk:* 'This book shows that Painter's biography has got the facts wrong. Céleste, his housekeeper, states unequivocally that Monsieur Marcel was attracted to girls, not men.'

---

* I discovered the next day that he was in Jervis Street hospital where he would remain on the critical list for three weeks.

Me: 'Does she say anything about the rats?'

Monk: 'What rats?'

Me: 'The ones he tortured in the male brothel, that he bought for his butler.'

Monk: (suppressing a slight scream) 'There's no evidence for that.'

Me: 'Monk, for Christ's sake, Proust has written the most beautiful prose this century. But he had eccentric tastes and habits. He used to hire soldiers home from the Front to run naked after rats and impale them with daggers, while he watched.'

Monk: 'Céleste is emphatic that that's a lie.'

Me: 'What the hell did she know about it? Listen Monk. James Harding, who is writing the life of the critic James Agate, has come up with real evidence that Marcel Proust was a fellow customer with Agate at a male brothel in Paris. Agate was back from the Front and using a brothel on the Rue Marigny when he noticed Proust walking in front of him, accompanied by a young soldier carrying a cage of rats. If you really want proof, that's it.'

Monk sat as if he hadn't heard what I had said. He was looking at the apple tree again.

Me: 'Monk, why does all this appal you? Are you sorry for the young soldier with the erection who chased the rats?'*

Monk: 'No, it's the rats I am sorry for.'

4 October

A judge, Stephen Kelly, shot dead by Loyalists in Belfast. He is a Catholic.

2 November

Meet Bart Cronin and Sean White of the former Markpress Committee at the Shelbourne Hotel. We agree situation is perilous. The present Government Information Service is dreadful. And predictably, Cruise O'Brien has sacked Markpress. I tell Sean and Bart

---

* André Gide wrote in his diary after an evening with Proust, 'The pursuit of rats among other devices was to be justified in Proust's intention to conjoin the most disparate sensations and emotions for the purpose of orgasm.'

that I wrote to the Taoiseach, Liam Cosgrave, and offered my services as I had done with Jack Lynch. Cosgrave said the matter is now in the hands of Conor Cruise O'Brien who, in addition to his Cabinet post (Post & Telegraphs), has also had a new one created for him, Minister for Information. What a travesty.

On *Late Late Show* later. Max Factor over a pimple on my cheek before the show. Mary Peters of Belfast, the Olympic gold medallist in the pentathlon, is a guest. I had intended to quiz her about the North, but she is so upset about what's happening there, it won't work. Mary is an all-English type of Irish girl, blonde, blue-eyed, with a soft Ulster accent. I was on Irish international teams with her when she was number two to Thelma Hopkins who held the world record at that time in the women's high jump. Mary makes a crack on the show about my pole-vaulting into the women's section of the Olympic Village. I tell her if she wants to learn the breast stroke, Gay Byrne* will be able to teach her. Byrne asks have I anything to say. For a lark, I go up to him and using a bit of conjuring produce a pear from under his armpit. I swallow it and then take it from behind my knee. I thought this was during a commercial break but we were actually on camera and when I discovered this I presented the pear to Byrne asking him to take a bite:

'The Dublin oul' ones will pay a fortune for the bit that's left.'

Mary discusses new sex tests for Olympic athletes. Some hairy women have been appearing in women's weight events recently. She says people sometimes quite honestly don't know what sex they are, and asks me if I am sure I am a man. I say I'll prove it later and Mary gives me a kiss and cuddle. Kenneth Griffith, the film maker, is on too whose work I admire. He has taken a melodramatic style out of the last century and transferred it to this one. He plays many parts in his latest film, which deals with Napoleon's last years.

* See 19 April 1971, note.

1975

Tonight do my one man show on Oliver St John Gogarty* at the Irish Club in Eaton Square. The special stage they have built for me in the Club works wonderfully and everything goes well. Peter Watt of A.P. Watt, my new literary agent, came backstage after the performance to tell me that the show had 'transported' him. Goodie. I have been trying for years to get a first-class agent and having landed Peter recently I am delighted that the boat is so soon on an even keel. My editor, Christopher Sinclair-Stevenson, from Hamish Hamilton, is also there with his wife Deborah. He too is glowing when he comes up. He says Deborah has given him an idea which he would like to discuss with me the following morning if I can come up to Great Russell Street. I feel like the Bard coming off the stage after playing in *Hamlet* and finding the Lord Chamberlain waiting to commission a play. The Irish Club representative gives me dinner. He is a Northerner, an SDLP man and an admirer of John Hume and, like myself, a bit in despair about the way things are going in the Six Counties.

Am just in bed when the phone rings. It's Peter Watt to tell me that he's just opened a bottle of Dom Pérignon.

'I'm so exhilarated.'

The A.P. Watt agency is best in the business so I'm so exhilarated too.†

Over to Great Russell Street to Hamish Hamilton offices. Christopher is still beaming like a headmaster about to present a medal to head boy on prize day. What he wants me to do is to write a book on the whole Irish Renaissance, Yeats, Synge, Lady Gregory,

---

* See 5 September 1973, note.

† Alas, a few weeks later Peter died. He was only in his forties and had been in good health.

James Joyce, George Moore et al. (most of the people I dealt with in last night's performance). What he's looking for in fact is a biography of the Irish Literary Renaissance. While Cape published my first biography of Oliver St John Gogarty in 1964, Hamish Hamilton brought out the Brendan Behan biography in 1970. Christopher, therefore, knows my form. Hamish Hamilton will also publish *Lifestyles*, a new book of poems I have offered them. As grist to the mill they want to see the manuscript of 'The Troubles: Ireland 1912–1922' which will be published in the late spring in New York with Bobbs-Merrill. All this is gratifying.* But I have to point out that while I am pleased with this proposal I had hoped that he would have accepted one which I made to the firm some time ago. Feeling that Richard Ellman's life of James Joyce left room for another biography which might bring the Irish writer alive in a way that Ellman had not attempted to do, I had put this idea to Hamish Hamilton. Christopher explains that Ellman is now writing a life of Oscar Wilde for them and the firm feels that at present it doesn't have room for another book about Joyce.

Off to lunch at El Vino's with John Lovesey, my *Sunday Times* editor. Talk about possible interviewees for my pieces from America.

29 January

Yesterday crossing Eaton Square I bumped into Philip Corley, a painter, whose brother Tom, a hefty former US marine, attacked me in a Dublin coffee bar twenty years ago, but luckily for me came off worse, ending up in a hospital bed having necessary repairs. Philip clearly wanted to let bygones be bygones, so I asked him if he'd like to come to the one man show later on. He said he couldn't but would I come to dinner the following night at his place. He assured me his flat-mate, Christine Keeler,† was a splendid cook.

Tonight a taxi brings me to a flat off Sloane Square. Philip opens the door and I am led into a pleasant sitting room, where La Keeler is reclining in front of a blazing fire. She's still attractive in the way that people with high cheekbones can be, unless they run to fat which she hasn't. The difficulty throughout the evening was that one constantly

---

* See 21 August 1970, last note.
† Model at the centre of the Profumo case in 1964 which helped to put the Macmillan Government out of office.

thought about what not to say rather than what one might say, and as a result the conversation tended to remain unadventurous. I got the impression of a pleasant lass who has managed to hang on somehow to the nicer side of her character even though she has been through the maelstrom. Philip's work, displayed here and in the hall, is good enough to show that he is serious about what he is trying to do. As neither of them told me how they had met I didn't like to ask. We talked about Dublin and Philip's friendship with Brendan Behan (there is a well-known photograph of the two of them out of their minds taken in a photo-booth). Later, after smoking a couple of joints, Christine went to bed, and I remained with Philip. When the time came to leave he said that I should go in to say good-bye to her. I found her sitting up in a Queen Anne four-poster bed looking the image of Nell Gwyn – quite beautiful. I thanked her for the evening and waved good-bye. I would willingly have lain under the Queen Anne canopy with its beautiful occupant . . .

29 February, Dublin

Lunch with Micheál MacLiammóir. We meet in our unfashionable restaurant with the marvellous food on the north side near Mountjoy Square, Crowley's. Very amusing on 'Pauline' Smith who is in charge of wardrobe at the Gate Theatre.

'Pauline' (real name Paul) is gaining a reputation as a novelist. Micheál has read a short story by him in a literary magazine about a beautiful girl with blue eyes and golden hair who lives in a tenement – since Paul grew up in a tenement I suggest that the piece may be autobiographical. But the girl with the blue eyes and golden hair? Who can she be?

Micheál (eyes sparkling): 'Himself, of course, that's why it's so good.'

Paul Smith calls Hilton Edwards* 'Hillie'. In Paris where he studied costume, he used to do a shimmy dance on the side to make extra bread, as Mabel Beardsley did. Micheál mentions Mrs McEntee, wife of a Fianna Fail Cabinet Minister, who abused him recently for using the word 'whore' in his play *Ill met by Moonlight*. She said it was letting down Ireland and assured him that there was

---

* See 20 March 1970, note.

no word for whore in the Gaelic language before the Norman
Invasion. I remember her as an unpleasant professor of Irish who
used to play bridge with my mother and, I suspect, plucked me in an
exam when I was at college.

21 March, New York

Lunch today with James T. Farrell,[*] Jimmy Breslin[†] and Malachy
McCourt.[‡] Also Patricia Blake from *Time-Life*. Tell Farrell I've been
to see Nelson Algren in Chicago. He says Algren's work is good but
no more, remembering perhaps an Algren snub. I also mention my
regard for Studs Terkel and his marvellous broadcasts. Farrell's reply is:
   'One weakness – shortness of brains.'
   It's getting like Dublin here.

5 April

George Kleinsinger in the elevator of the Chelsea Hotel. 'Glad to see
you back.' Perpetual smile. Marcel Ophuls the film director (*The
Sorrow and the Pity*) with him.

11 April

Today, at the Chelsea, Roderick Ghuika tells me he's playing a film
director in a porno movie. He's like a naughty little boy who has
found a toy.

17 April

To the McMillin Theatre at Columbia University for Beatniks'
'goodbye'. Allen Ginsberg, Gregory Corso, Peter Orlofsky and
William Burroughs read from their work. I find I am in a back seat. I
have asked Gregory to find me a better one but he hasn't. Instead
when the auditorium gets overcrowded, Gregory just asks the audience to come onstage. This narks Ginsberg, who clearly has an

---

[*] A novelist of the Chicago realist school, best known for his Studs Lonigan trilogy.
[†] New York columnist whose robust style and social insight have made him one of the
most influential journalists in the USA.
[‡] See 23 June 1971, note.

authoritative view of crowd control (like myself). Gregory stands up and says 'I am not a product of the generation which raised rich kids for the funny farms. I was fortunate. I went to prison. There my brains were fried – I used to wake up and hear myself say "I can't remember where I lost them."'

Orlofsky looks muscular. He talks about recycling sewage, and then goes on about growing sunflowers as if he'd never stop. He gives us a poem about how he made love to Allen Ginsberg. The crowd not entirely at ease. Orlofsky says he became gay because of Allen. The poem contains lines like: 'Come on Allen, faster and faster'. It ends up on the bed sheets with presumably the two of them underneath. Burroughs quite boring. He talks about his heart operation. Ginsberg is now becoming bossy. He tells the crowd 'Don't interrupt'. Of course he is right and I would do the same, but I can see that we would both be outcasts in this generation. He recites a fine poem from his collection *King of the May*. Middle-class tone of his voice. Strangely persuasive, an odd dissenter. He finishes with a boring song. At reception chat with him. Strong face of the professional classes. Good features. He tells me that Brendan Behan used to talk to him about 'ammunition' meaning marijuana. I talk also to Burroughs. He's dressed in a well cut three-piece suit. Look of a severe professor. 'Do you live in Dublin?' Surprised that his books are on sale there. I explain to him that the banning of books is a mysterious procedure in Dublin. Joyce's *Ulysses* wasn't banned but most of Graham Greene once was. Michael J. Pollard of *Bonnie and Clyde* fame comes over. Half-witted grin exactly like the character he plays in the film.

29 April, Dublin

Get a ring from Susie Chaffee. Susie is the captain of the American ski team and a model. She is also known for having been the first Olympic skier to ski naked, and was photographed in the nip for *Vogue* magazine. I met her in New York and she said she was coming to Ireland – 'so here I am.'

30 April

Went to National Gallery with Susie. Then to the Pot Pourri for lunch. A bit boring today. Certainly not as exciting as when she was in New York. She is in love with Ireland, in a sort of *Ryan's Daughter* way. She liked the Abbey too when we went there last night to see *The Plough and the Stars*.

1 May

Lunch at the Unicorn restaurant with Susie. Then down to John Behan's* foundry where we have a look at an array of portraits and sculptures. Sunny, wind-filled day. Then out by taxi to Ernie Gebler in Killiney Bay. He used to be married to Edna O'Brien and is much taken with Susie. Tells her all about his novels. I think the best one is *He Had My Heart Scalded*. But the one that made him the most money was made into a film with Goldie Hawn who looks a little like Susie but not as robust or as tall. Ernie regales us with the story of how when he first met Edna O'Brien he took her to the Isle of Man where they stayed in a rather posh house owned by the family of J.P. Donleavy's wife. There was a knock at the door one morning and Ernie went out to answer it. Outside stood the O'Brien relations, over to rescue Edna from a life of sin. According to Ernie, he and Donleavy took them all on and sent them scampering back to the boat for Dublin. I wonder.

Later Susie and I go into town and have a meal at about 10.00 pm in the Trocadero. Susie and I sit opposite each other. She asks me did I ever play the knee game. When I say no, she explains it. She prides herself on the iron muscles in her thighs which she has acquired from skiing. The idea is that under the table I put my knees between hers. She will keep her knees closed and I shall try to force them open. We start off. She seems a little surprised at the strength of my legs which after all have been hardened by active participation in three sports while she has only been at one. I brace my legs and begin to push out with both knees. A look of slight surprise on Susie's face. I keep on pushing. She keeps on closing. We look at each other across the table. She tries to maintain a seraphic look with her large blue eyes and fair hair. But I notice a tinge of colour begin to invade the golden cheeks. Presently she begins to pant a little. I think the game goes on for about eight minutes. Finally she surrenders, intimating her surrender with a gasp. 'Never lost before.' Out of the corner of my eye, I notice some people at a nearby table. They are mesmerized. How could they have

---

* See 7 November 1972, note.

known what we were both engaged in? I am sure with the natural tendency of folk to let their minds run on, they have probably created in their imagination something rather frothy.

3 May

Susie heading off today. The sun was riding high, so we took a walk in Stephen's Green near the city centre. She lay on the grass and did her exercises. Those long golden legs twirling in the sky sent up the pulses of early morning strollers. As she shook the grass out of her hair Susie said:

'Watching the trees grow takes me back to living. You've got to let yourself bloom and follow your gut.'

Took her in a cab to the airport. She recited one of her poems on the way and rambled on about how enraptured she was with Ireland. The taxi man was mesmerized:

'Jesus, that one's like a mixture of Joan of Arc and Marilyn Monroe.'

10 May

Trinity Week. UO'C's XI against Trinity First XI in the College Park. Beautiful goal from a cross by Jimmy Conway (Fulham) which Ray Treacy smacks in after Don Givens' (Chelsea) is taken down. Young Liam Brady (Arsenal) magnificent. Early goal took the edge off. Home to sleep. (Drank noggin of brandy.)

Back to Luke Kelly's* flat for party in Dartmouth Square. A lot of singing including *A Nation Once Again*. Interesting faces. Ray Treacy sings *On the One Road*. Fellow says to me 'I see you got the shit beaten out of you in the New York papers for your last book.' Liam Brady comes over.

Me: 'Do you like London?'
Liam: 'Hate it.'
Me: (nodding, singing) 'This is it.'

He nods back. Johnny Giles† in command of the evening.

---

* Lead singer with The Dubliners, a world-famous group in the Seventies.
† A star player for Leeds United when they won the FA cup in 1972. Won 59 International Caps for Ireland.

30 July

Tony O'Reilly* to pick me up at 6.30 pm. His driver, Arthur, phones at 5.30 pm to say he will be delayed. Tony arrives at 7.30 pm, we start for Castlemartin, his country house in Kildare.

At drinks in Castlemartin, Andy Mulligan† is there. He and Tony used to do a soft shoe routine together on Lions rugby tours. Andy has become mellow and fat while Tony remains a lean giant. We decide that our own Jack Kyle was the greatest fly-half of all time, at the very least in the first three. Michael Lynagh (Australia), Cliff Morgan (Wales) other candidates. Kyle is incredibly relaxed or laid back as they say nowadays. Tony recalls how he once found him asleep in an empty room in the pavilion just before the Welsh match at Lansdowne Road. Cliff (Morgan) told him that coming out of the tunnel for his first international, Jack Kyle said to him: 'Hope you have a good match today.' Agreed this would not have happened today.

Lady (Valerie) Goulding heads towards me. Chuff chuff. I sense danger.

'When anyone attacks my man, I go for them.'

This 'attack' is a reference to something I recently wrote about her husband, Sir Basil, going somewhat over the top in his annual address to the shareholders of Goulding Fertilisers. Basil had read out his report in *Finnegans Wake* lingo which was not appreciated by the shareholders, some of whom expressed the view that he should have been shunted off to a funny farm without more ado. I brush off Valerie's attack by telling her (truthfully) that I am an admirer of Basil, who won three blues at Oxford for football, cricket and boxing and is very much his own man – as we can see just at this minute, for Basil is crossing the room in a velvet suit, with a stuffed frog on his shoulder and drinking gin through the teat of a baby's bottle.

Tony looks extremely fit. I advise him to stay that way. Karl Mullen‡ says he finally gave up soccer after Gerry Quinn, the Irish

---

* Sir Anthony O'Reilly, international rugby player; received knighthood in the New Year's Honours of 2001. Still holds the record for number of tries scored on South African tour with the British Lions. Picked to play for Ireland at eighteen years of age. In today's teams, comparable to Jonah Lomu. Later chairman of H.J. Heinz Company; currently chairman of Independent News and Media PLC.

† Lions and Ireland scrum-half (20 caps).

‡ Captain of the Triple Crown-winning Irish team of 1948–49 and 1947–48 and Captain of the successful Lions Tour of New Zealand in 1950. Well known Dublin gynaecologist.

International centre three-quarter, an old Belvederian like himself and Tony, died of a heart attack in his mid-forties.

1 August, Leixlip Castle

Tennis with Desmond in the morning, at Castletown House, Celbridge. Completely windless, everything still. The silence under these exquisite colonnades is supreme. The pock of the ball on the strings of the racket is the only sound. We play with studied precision like dancers under a ballet master. Nothing so common as rushing to the net. We lob the ball from the base line. Like the scene at the end of Antonioni's *Blow-Up* where the actors mime a game in Hyde Park at dawn. This of course enables Desmond to chat away as he plays, like Christabel Ampthill* across the drawing room at music recitals.

Later meet Eileen O'Casey at lunch in Leixlip. Her book *Sean* [about her husband Sean O'Casey] has sold so well that Macmillan are bringing out a second volume. She tells me how Abbey directors, scandalized by what they thought was blasphemy in Sean's *The Plough and the Stars* when it was first put on, begged him to take out the words 'Jesus, Mary and Joseph', which occurs in the third act. Sean did this for the first tour of the play outside Dublin. On the opening night in Limerick when a shot went off on the stage, most of the audience jumped up shouting: 'Jesus, Mary and Joseph.'

21 August, Dublin

Dreadful journey back to Dublin from Sligo. No first class carriage nor is there a restaurant on the train. Later go to my Swift play at the Project.† Theatre full. Phyllis Ryan‡ there. She thinks a lot of Martin Dempsey as Swift. The best she has seen. She is disappointed about

---

* Christabel Lady Ampthill, correspondent in a notorious ('the sponge') divorce case. Came to live outside Galway in Dun Guaire Castle (which she bought from Oliver St John Gogarty) and was seldom out of the saddle as she indulged her passion for hunting with the Galway Blazers. 'Vile harbingers of Spring,' she would refer to daffodils as, while galloping through the fields, seeing their arrival as a signal of the end of the hunting season.

† *The Dark Lovers*, a play by UO'C about Jonathan Swift, Dean of St Patrick's and his mistresses Stella and Vanessa, presented at the Project Theatre, October–December 1973.

‡ Managing Director, Gemini Players. Renowned Abbey actress of the 1940s. In 1941 she played the lead in Paul Vincent Carroll's *Shadow and Substance* on Broadway.

the whipping scene where Vanessa beats Swift in anger. It has become comic rather than savage. Things haven't stayed as they should since Noel O'Brien, the director, set the play loose from his care.

10 September

Girl in the Trocadero restaurant: 'Give me a kiss because you're so arrogant.'

27 September, London

A perk I have with the *Sunday Times* is that John Lovesey, my editor, rings me once in a while to come to London to cover a rugby match. I am paid an extra fee and generous expenses. I had a brief foray with English rugby in the Fifties, when I played with the London Irish first team. The glamour of it. In our dressing room, when we arrived, our togs were laid out, green jerseys and stockings and gleaming white shorts. (I actually think people washed football gear whiter then.) The game was still an upper class one and even the war had done little to dilute the standard English of dressing room and bar. Certainly soccer was not mentioned. Duffel-coated jolliness and good form summed up the atmosphere in the pavilions. No coach of course. That was left to Rugby League.

Now I arrive in on another moonbeam twenty years later and wonder how it will seem. The match is Rosslyn Park Club against Wasps, so I go out to the club early to have a look at the photographs from the Fifties on the walls of the Pavilion. Yes, this is how I remember the scene. All present and correct. Aware of the cut of their jib.

As the pavilion fills up I take a look at the arrivals. Alick-a-doos* you can always pick out. They ooze self-importance. By the nature of the job, top players don't usually push themselves for committee, so often mediocrities are left to run affairs. The wives are mostly dressed in short skirts that twenty-five years ago would have had the dogs set on them.

At the match, the President of the Gloucester Rugby Union has binoculars. He is watching the referee for form. Somewhere else in the stand a baby is crying from the cold. Someone says 'Good man

---

* Rugby word for a committee member. Etymology uncertain.

Andy.' Yes, my instinct is that the confident-looking chaps in the photographs would not have been at ease in this set-up.

12 October

Nanny comes in to wake me.

> *Nanny:* 'Do you know what day it is?'
> *Me:* 'Sunday?'
> *Nanny:* 'No.'
> *Me:* 'Blessed Oliver's* feast day?'
> *Nanny:* 'No.'
> *Me:* 'What is it then?'
> *Nanny:* 'Your birthday.' *Smiles.*

She reminds me that when she first arrived at Fairfield Park forty years ago to be interviewed for the job as Nanny to myself and my sister, she had been asked to come on the 13th and not the 12th of October so that I shouldn't be disturbed by a new nanny arriving in the middle of my birthday party. She could however only come on the 12th, and hence arrived the day festivities were at their height.†

Later we go for a walk. She is in a smart coat with fur on the collar. Also a little hat which makes her look like a petite Russian duchess. Perfect-looking, dignified. (Perhaps an oldish lady of the Court, not quite a duchess). Nanny saw a film on TV about Blessed Oliver Plunkett in Mrs Donnelly's house (her first employer) recently. A stern Presbyterian, Mrs Donnelly wasn't particularly interested and asked Nanny what the (future) Saint had done. Nannie said 'He died for the faith.' When she told me this she added, looking at me: 'Not

---

* Blessed Oliver Plunkett, Irish Martyr. Executed in 1672, canonized in March 1981.
† Previous nannies had left in a shell-shocked state. Usually with their shins in bits. Aged five, in the dining room, entertaining eloquently (I'm sure) my guests, I sensed that something was happening in the next room. I became suspicious and went in. 'Who is the lady in the blue coat' I demanded. On being told that it might be my new Nanny, I did what I had done to others and gave her a ferocious hack on the shin. She went into the hall, fetched her umbrella and came back and gave me a good hiding, whereupon Mummy said: 'That's exactly what we are looking for' and Nanny was hired on the spot. She would stay in the family home for 57 years, and for the last four years of her life lived with my sister until she died aged 92.

like some'. I hope she is referring to Garry, my apostate brother, who was back from the USA a month ago.

21 October

Nanny to lunch in the Zoo restaurant, Phoenix Park for her birthday. I haven't had a telephone call that I was expecting and can't give her the attention I should. It's infuriating how I'm distracted. As we go upstairs on the 14 bus,[*] I try to contain my dancing mind. Na sitting beside me who has been with me all my life is now 85 yet my attention is divided simply because of this accursed anxiety about a girl. That evening we have a party for Na's 85th birthday. Donagh, my brother, has some amusing memories of going with Na to the dentist. Aged ten, he told the dentist he'd sue him for causing pain. Nanny took him away mortified. 'He hadn't enough patience.'

26 October

Squash with Joe Hackett[†] at Fitzwilliam.[‡] My piece about Johnny Giles[§] was cut in today's *Sunday Times*. They took out a nice little paragraph I'd worked on to convey the loneliness of footballers. Hackett, with whom I have an agreeable match always (he's a lot better than me), says that he had a match earlier this week with an objectionable fellow who insisted on meeting him on the court and not in the dressing rooms so as to pressure him. Muttered beforehand: 'Haven't played for a fortnight' – as an excuse in case he lost. Hackett could have replied that he himself hadn't played for six months but refrained. The fellow retrieved well, tried all sorts of tricks and called for numerous lets. This annoyed Hackett so much that he went ahead and thrashed him. Both Hackett and Tony O'Reilly look enviously at my trim figure these days.

Dictate draft of *Submarine*, a Noh play I have written about Sir Roger Casement.

---

[*] She had refused to travel by taxi as she wished to avail herself of the free travel provided in the Republic for citizens over 65.

[†] First won Irish men's tennis championship as a schoolboy. Irish champion for 15 years. Final trial at rugby for Ireland.

[‡] Fitzwilliam Lawn Tennis Club. See 11 June 1977, note.

[§] See 10 May, note.

27 October

Tea at Monk Gibbon's. Mary Manning the playwright and Ninette de
Valois, Director of the Royal Ballet, here. Mary is a fabulous wag, full
of scandal and chat. I often wonder how she stands Boston where she
lives now with her husband, Professor Howe of Harvard. She claps
when Monk reads what he calls his prose poems and says it reminds
her of the old days at the Gate Theatre with Hilton and Micheál.

Ninette's a cold one. She grew up in the next county to Dublin at
Baltiboys Hall, but you wouldn't know it from her prim ballet mistress voice. She and Monk are related (all the Anglo-Irish seem to be)
and they talk about family as Mary and I conduct a conversation
around their backs. Ignoring the slight twitch in Monk's mouth as I
do so, I mention the name of Yeats to Ninette. In the Twenties and
Thirties she danced in his plays and he dedicated the last one, *The
Death of Cuchulain*, to her.

'For Ninette de Valois asking pardon for covering her expressive
face with a mask.'

She said Yeats had been very attentive and was as pleased as punch
that she had danced in *The King of the Great Clock Tower* to George
Antheil's music with a severed head in her hand even if it was in the
form of a triangle to suit the idiom he had written in. I longed to ask
her questions about Diaghilev and his ballet company in exile but her
prissy look put me off and I didn't know how to begin. I could see
her in my mind addressing her ballet class with that high-pitched
headmistress's voice only slightly softened by its Anglo-Irish nuance.
In fact I had a little ballet tale in my pocket, which I had written for
Hugo Alfvén, the Swedish composer, before he died and had hoped
to ask her to have a look at it. But I was afraid of getting sent to the
back of the class. So I asked Mary Manning to come into the Arts
Club with me instead and we left Monk and Madame exchanging
strangulated family chat.

30 October

Letter to Monk Gibbon.

Dear Monk

Thank you for a lovely tea last Sunday week. I enjoyed it very
much indeed. I liked Mary Manning and found her such nice

company. What you read for us was really fascinating. I don't like to call them prose poems because that's a term I hate. I think something is either poetry or prose and there's a good distinction between the two. What I think they were, were pieces of fine prose with the insight of a short story but without the tiresome twist that has to be introduced in order to give a short story 'significance'. They are a mixture of philosophy, poetry and prose, which I think is in some ways a new form. Anyway, I like them, especially the one about the sunset,* which some of the others didn't seem to like as much.

Give my love to Winifred and hope to see you soon.

Yours sincerely
Ulick

9 November

Take Na to see Edward McGuire† in Sandycove. He passes the test.

'Very sincere,' she says when he has gone out to make tea. 'Speaks nicely.' This is a reference to his Downside accent.

'You're from the North, Nanny, aren't you?' he says, 'my name is a Fermanagh one and that's near where you come from, isn't it?' Edward has a look of an ageing Aubrey Beardsley and I don't think Nanny is convinced that she and he share similar backgrounds.

She is, however, captivated by Edward's cat Wonky, who has taken a shine to her. She listens politely as Edward says: 'There is no good or bad colour in a painter's pallet Nanny, just as there are no good or bad people.' When the time comes to leave he gives Nanny one of his owl drawings from a calendar he has made for her.

'To Dear Nanny with love for a happy Christmas.'

---

* *Sky at sunset*: 'When I have seen that tideless sea, made only paler with the paler light of evening, and that great bay, flooded with crimson in one place, cloud-streaked and lost in many little pools and inlets, I have in mind a day when I will make its waters and come at evening up that silent coast, and moor my boat in some small quiet creek and go ashore into the eternal fields.'

† 1932–86; Irish painter, best known for his portraits of leading Irish writers such as Monk Gibbon, Patrick Kavanagh, Francis Stuart and Seamus Heaney.

11 November

In Grogan's I meet Bob Bradshaw. He has just got a substantial award from the Government as a result of a malicious injury claim (arising from the fracas in O'Connell Street on 9 September last).* He says if he got another award he would use it to read the whole of Tolstoy for the second time. Later in Barnardo's restaurant I meet John McCarthy and Isabel with Trevor West. John is rector (Church of Ireland) of Dundalk. He also plays on my soccer team along with Trevor, no mean performer. Confides that one of the UVF people involved in blowing up the Miami Showband in Armagh was in his parish and blew himself up as well. His name was Harris Boyle and he was on a team we played against last summer, in fact I marked him on the wing. At the funeral John McCarthy saw a guy, Jeff, whom he played rugby with. (Jeff shot up a Catholic disco.) 2,000 Loyalists in uniform at funeral.

27 November, London

Over to London for a *Sunday Times* lunch at the Gay Hussar. After which I read over a hundred sporting ballads submitted for a *Sunday Times* competition. Work all afternoon in the office. Plough through the entries which include one on pelota (Spanish handball) and another on Prince Obolensky, the England winger who got one of the most outstanding tries of all time, running across the field to beat fifteen players in 1935 against Wales at Twickenham. Only two poems on Rugby League.

Visit my publishers, Quartet, near Grosvenor Square. There has been bombing in one corner of it which is still noticeable. Lunch in Rugantino's in Soho. Back to the Park Lane cashier. After I have changed a cheque, the head porter leans over confidentially:

'You mightn't have heard yet. They've shot McWhirter.'

'Norris or Ross?'

It is Ross who has been taken out. He edited *Command*, a magazine which has called for draconian measures against the IRA. But it is an obscenity to shoot a man for his views, especially when he has had the courage to express them in public. My first thought is for Norris who will have to face the loss of a twin.

I first met the McWhirters at the St Enoch's hotel in Glasgow in

---

* See diary entry for 9 September 1974.

the Fifties when they were representing Scotland in the annual trian-
gular athletic tournament between Ireland, England and Scotland.
They were Oxford Blues and made a fine pair striding around in their
clan kilts. I was chasing the Irish pole vault record at the time and was
surprised to find that the twins knew exactly what height that was. I
then discovered they could fish up at will almost any sports statistic
you could think of. I tried them on everything, rugby, athletics,
cricket, boxing, even weightlifting, and the answers came back as if
supplied by a computer. I rather fancied myself in the area of sports
statistics at the time but I wasn't in it with these two geniuses, who
anyway were on a double whammy, as if one of them couldn't get the
exact figure or time right the other one would come in with it, the
way twins often do. When Norris came up with the world record for
pie-eating I finally knew I was on a hiding to nothing. They were both
grinning as they confessed that sports statistics were their bag. Later
they marketed their hobby in one of the most successful publications
of the century, *The Guinness Book of Records*. Twin millionaires.

I fear the conflict in the North has gone too far for any immediate
surgery. The IRA have been created by the situation – the lack of
justice for Nationalists in Northern Ireland. I can't see the violence
stopping in our lifetime. We could become a cockpit. Derry may
overspill again. I have never forgotten the wounded kids I saw there
three years ago.

3 December, Stuttgart

Long train journey from Frankfurt to Stuttgart for my one man Behan
show at the State Theatre. Met in station. Go to the Kammerteater
where I am to perform. It is one of the smaller areas in the State
Theatre complex and is over the Opera House. The house is almost
sold out. To get to the rehearsal room, it seems that we walk through
corridors for hours. Wolfgang is the stage manager. Relieved to find
the sound engineer can take on board cues in a foreign language. Big
heavy workmen on the stage are friendly. Always a bonus when you
start a rehearsal on a strange stage in an empty theatre. There is a ballet
room beside my dressing room. Down to canteen. Wolf gives me a
drink. Very friendly. I go upstairs to watch a rehearsal of *Drums in the
Night* by Brecht. Fall asleep in the middle. I am driven to the hotel by
a woman with rather thin features. She is Hungarian and sighs for the
old days when the Austro-Hungarian Emperor ruled Bulgaria,

Yugoslavia etc. Likes Russians in Hungary but doesn't like the Soviet system. I think I may have got a sore throat from waiting at the station before I set off for Stuttgart.

4 December

To the theatre in the morning for rehearsal. At lunch ballet girls come into the actors' restaurant. The unrelenting smile of the dancer. But then you look into their eyes and see that they are hooked on other sounds swirling inside them. Later I hear the ballet mistress in class bringing them through the opening movements of *Les Sylphides*.

'If I teach you this properly I should smell birch trees. See yourself landing. The bigger you are, the easier to land.'

Find my dressing room. Hear there is a good crowd outside. Five minutes warm-up, then the five minutes call. After that, alone on the stage. Speak very slowly at first because I feel the audience will be at best bi-lingual. Lighting cues perfect, also sound. There seem to be a lot of Americans and English in the audience as they get the jokes instantly. It turns out however there are no foreigners in the audience, only Germans. Many of them are Brendan Behan fans, members of a club which meets every week to sing his ballads and read the works of the master.

5 December, Paris

Philippe Jullian* in Paris. We met at Dublin at dinner. Thrilled I was. He writes biography the way I would aspire to. His Oscar Wilde biography is the first one to make the point that Wilde conquered not only London society with his gift of language and conversation but the Faubourg St Germain as well. It was Philippe who picked up this description of Oscar out of the *Gaulois* newspaper (1901):

> He scattered words about him, as Buckingham at the court of the French Sun King had scattered jewels which had been loosely sewn on his glittering doublet.

Philippe has also written a life of Count Robert de Montesquieu who has been a model for three great characters in literature; Huysmans'

---

* 1919–77; painter and writer, a specialist in Art Nouveau. Besides a biography of Oscar Wilde, he was also the author of a biography of Edward VII and the illustrator of Scott Moncrieff's translation of *A la Recherche du temps perdu*.

Des Esseintes, Proust's Baron de Charlus and Lord Henry Wootton in Wilde's *Picture of Dorian Gray*. He lives in an exquisite house on the Rue Jacob with a courtyard leading into it. He has small features. Very fine. Ancient régime. His drawings remind me of Ronald Searle.

'Of course I admire him very much.'

He is writing a biography of Violet Trefusis,* a splendid tramp of a woman, whom he knew well. He recalls: 'Violet was very witty if a little light, but she made you laugh. She was a fine line drawer. I have a number of her lesbian sketches. She always played the woman in that situation. As well though, she had men lovers even though Vita Sackville-West was the love of her life. She was very good at puns.'

Philippe has been in Russia with Mariga Guinness. Well organized tour. He thinks both the Guinness children are exceptionally good-looking. We talk about Sheridan Le Fanu. I tell him about Stoker and the Gothic novel. Oscar's uncle Maturin too. Has not read either. But Philippe is a good listener. It should be added that our conversation has been punctuated by the crashes of a huge dog who has hurled himself repeatedly against the door.

We talked about colonialism, English, Germans and French. The Germans in the Cameroons were, Philippe thought, the best. But it was Ireland in his view which began the rescue of the Third World and the downfall of imperialism. In Ecuador he saw a statue of O'Connell. Also in Chile the Irish have had much influence. Some people thought of the division in Northern Ireland as religious but of course it isn't. I explained that it is a classic colonial situation. He looked at me with as much surprise as he could muster on his tight well-bred face. 'Why has this not been told before?'

11 December, Dublin

Nanny getting very old. Repeats things that she wants to remind me of. Clinging to clarity. Hand trembling. Now that she is so tolerant it's almost harder to accept that the best side of her is still there.

---

* (Neé Keppel). Married to Major Denys Trefusis, she was involved in one of the more notorious society scandals between the wars when she ran away with Vita Sackville-West, the wife of Harold Nicolson, MP. Both husbands set off in pursuit of the errant pair and eventually Vita Sackville-West returned home to Sissinghurst Castle with her husband. Violet's marriage was never consummated and she lived out much of her life in Paris where her wit and sense of fun made her a popular figure in salon life.

Aengus Fanning* thinks I should do a piece on Sean O'Faolain.†
When I go out to Dun Laoghaire to see him the first thing he does is
to complain that people never 'stamp their feet' in the theatre or 'gasp'
any more. He still does both. Then grins. He thinks his novel *Bird
Alone* will only really be remembered as his first one. Talks about his
editors, David Garnett and William Plomer.‡ He is rereading Liam
O'Flaherty. He finds him sentimental 'like Colette' except for his
writing on animals. He talks about Maurice Craig. I say if ever there
was a one poem man it's Maurice with his 'Lord in your mercy look
down on Belfast' – a little masterpiece. Craig has written interesting
books on architecture, in fact one very well written book on Dublin,
but as far as the imagination goes he seems to have stopped there. I
mention my favourite 'one poem writers', that is, ones who have
written only one true poem, and the rest are blow-ins. William
Allingham's *Four Ducks on a Pond* for instance. Sean comes up with
Allingham's:

> Up the airy mountain,
>   Down the rushy glen,
> We daren't go a-hunting
>   For fear of little men . . .

My point though is that William Allingham in this category stands by
Four Ducks on a Pond. If he's to be remembered by one poem only,
then *Four Ducks on a Pond* with its seven lines is the one that passes
muster. I also mention William Cory's *Heraclitus* and Charles Wolfe's
The Burial of Sir John Moore at Corunna. Sean talks about his Cork rival,
Frank O'Connor. He says some of O'Connor's translations from the
Irish are not good, which I agree with, but I do quote one very fine
one – *Owen Rua* – to him. He seems a little put out with O'Connor's
fame.

---

* Editor of the *Sunday Independent*.
† 1900–91; novelist, short-story writer, editor of the leading Irish literary magazine *The
Bell*. One of the important literary figures in the generation that succeeded W.B. Yeats,
Lady Gregory and George Moore.
‡ Plomer rejected my Gogarty biography for Jonathan Cape, but old Jonathan, who had
commissioned it, told him to get his head examined.

'That fella on the *Sunday Independent*, Hector Legge, immortalized him.'

This refers to a period during World War Two when the editor of the *Sunday Independent*, Hector Legge, gave a weekly column to Frank O'Connor to write articles about his travels across Ireland which appeared on the leader page.

O'Faolain says Oliver St John Gogarty, whom he knew well, was obsessed with Joyce. 'He was annoyed at being Buck Mulligan in *Ulysses*.' The result, according to Sean, was that Gogarty became quite insane on the question of his former friend. You simply couldn't mention his name in front of him.

He doesn't like *At Swim-Two-Birds* by Flann O'Brien* or any work of Beckett at all. He thinks *Godot* means simply 'that there is no meaning in life'. I mention Jim Beckett, Sam's uncle and his wife Margot, who Beckett hinted to me were the originals of the two people in bins in *Endgame*. Both husband and wife, former champion swimmers (my mother learned the crawl from them), were confined to bed in their last years, after their legs, left and right, had been amputated because of poor circulation. But I've lost Sean on Beckett – simply not his bag.

22 December

Beautiful day for football match in Trinity. Pitch rolled. Mild sun. I am just over my cold. I play well enough, though worry about a slight strain in my groin which affects the accuracy of the pass. It is either a groin or an Achilles tendon injury. Then a red-haired guy shoulders me. I shoulder him back. He goes berserk. Tries to kick me on the ground. Ritchie Ryan (Trinity full-back) jumps on him. The chap fights madly. I throw a punch at him to halt him but he is held by Ryan at the time. My punch (blast it!) downs him. The goalie comes out and clocks me. I try and get back at him but only half-heartedly. I don't want any more. I am shocked at the sight of the fellow whom I've put on the ground. I crowned him because I feared he had gone out of his skull and would have belted me badly. But I shouldn't, no matter what, have hit him while he was being held. Not fair play. Trevor [West] shouts to play on and I am so upset that I decide to leave

---

* Real name Brian O'Nolan. He also wrote under the names Myles na Gopaleen.

the field partly to impress the others that what has happened was unin-
tentional. (Notice with relief the player concerned is back on the field
running up and down.) Also I have just let in a goal. My concentra-
tion is gone. Trevor furious. Instead of being friendly in the pavilion,
the others are cool.

1977

(and December 1977–January 1978, Tangier)

News clipping in the post from Charlie McCabe's* column in the *San Francisco Chronicle*. He has been writing in his Sunday column about a dispute he has been following in an Irish newspaper, regarding the Department of Posts and Telegraphs cutting off my telephone:

In late October Ulick in the course of his work for an English Sunday paper was calling a hotel in Barcelona. The operator told him the number he called was engaged; Ulick told her that this was unlikely as he was calling a large hotel with a switchboard. Ulick was aware that the phone people were keeping a close eye on him and so restrained himself from having a go, but said 'I think this is an appalling telephone system, the worst in the civilized world.'

His two phones were disconnected. His story was the banner yarn on the front page of the *Evening Press*.

A high court judge ordered his phones put back. Knowing Dublin and officialdom his honour explained that while it was an easy matter to disconnect a Dublin phone it was a hard thing to get it back to work. The inspectors in the Department, the judge explained, are 'a mysterious triumvirate with tremendous powers'. The three persons who could exercise these powers were not anywhere to be found, his honour went on, and no one could indicate when they might be available.

Conor Cruise O'Brien is Minister for Post and Telegraphs† and that is where the buck stops. So I have just written to the *Spectator* where he has been pontificating about free speech, asking how he can reconcile his 'principles' with taking my phone away. Not untypical of the 'liberal' ethos that he resorts to when he gets all hot and bothered about free speech.

---

* See 14 June 1971.
† He had become Minister for Posts and Telegraphs in the Coalition Government of 1973. See further on O'Brien 30 May 1974, note.

5 *February*

Dinner party for Monk Gibbon's eightieth birthday. Annie serves a delicious meal. The guests are American Ambassador Walter Curley,* Cearbhall O'Dalaigh, former Chief Justice and former President of Ireland, Ernest Wood, one of the leaders of the Irish Bar, and Sean White, academic and raconteur. I've chosen them to make sure that the ball is handed around in conversation.

Despite his flamboyant style of court oratory, Ernest Wood has a shy streak. After a while he thawed out. While we were talking about the proposal to remove Article Two in the Constitution (which deals with the Catholic Church) Ernest said:

'I don't have a view, I'm an Irish horse Protestant.'

'What's that?'

'Don't go to church, chapel or meeting house. On Sundays I go out to grass.'

Cearbhall gave us interesting gossip about his time in the Presidency (1974–76). He had only been in office two years when a new government, a coalition between Fine Gael (right wing) and Labour was formed. While the President is presumed to be above politics, the new government remained unconvinced that Cearbhall, because of his Nationalist views, would carry out his duties in an impartial fashion. The Taoiseach, Liam Cosgrave, had failed to meet with him on a regular basis as he should have done. Cearbhall became increasingly isolated until finally, after the pressure had reached an unacceptable level with an appalling attack on him by the Minister of Defence, he resigned.† (Incredibly, though the Minister did offer to apologise for what he had done, the Cabinet refused to allow him to do so.) The last incident in this sorry affair, as our friend James Joyce says, takes 'the solitary recherché biscuit'.

'After I had notified the Government,' Cearbhall continued, 'of my intention to resign, I was called that night to the telephone in Aras an Uachtarain. The Taoiseach asked me would I reconsider my resignation. I said it was too late. Suddenly the conversation stopped. I said,

---

* See 12 September 1972.

† The Minister, at an Army function, called the President, who is Commander-in-Chief of the Armed Forces, 'a thundering bollocks', in the context of his having referred the Emergency Powers Bill to the Supreme Court for a ruling as to its constitutionality. O'Dalaigh resigned as President of Ireland on 22 October 1976.

"Are you still there?" He replied, "Yes. But I'm looking for change to put in the phone." He was calling from a call-box. Later that night I notified the Cabinet of my resignation.'

— In addition, Cearbhall told us, during the Herrema kidnapping episode* the Government had withdrawn bodyguard facilities when he travelled by train. Cearbhall, during two-and-a-half years in office, had looked like being our best head of state since the office was created (1937). He had been recognized as a fine jurist and the best Chief Justice since the beginning of the State. He had made a very positive impact in his time as judge at the European Court of Justice and with his linguistic gifts and passionate love of individual freedom seemed set to exercise a beneficial influence on Irish society.

Walter Curley seemed gobsmacked at what he had heard and remarked that in the USA not only would a President of the United States be heavily guarded on a train, but he would almost certainly have a special one all to himself. Cearbhall smiled sweetly like the darling man that he is, but made no comment.

Monk looks splendid for his eighty years: his features retain an alert, slightly military look, and now and then a shadow flits across his face, evoking a resemblance to his cousin, the poet Yeats.

7 February

Extract from letter that arrived from Monk this morning:

> I enjoyed every minute and every mouthful of the evening. What civilized surroundings. (No one would ever suspect that you contained a dialectic tiger. And perhaps you don't really?) Whereas I do, but it is only allowed one roar a year.

In the afternoon post, this from Walter Curley:

> Dear Ulick:
>
> Your dinner party last Saturday was totally special. What fun: a perfect number, an extraordinarily nice house, and a super dinner. To blasphemously paraphrase Monk Gibbon's idea in his *Alphabet of Morality*:

---

* On 21 October 1975 the IRA kidnapped Dr Tiede Herrema, the managing director of Ferenka Limited, a subsidiary of a Dutch multi-national, and held him to ransom. The siege lasted for seventeen days, on the last of which, the leader of the group, Eddie Gallagher (married to Dr Rose Dugdale, the English heiress), surrendered.

U is for the Ultimate of evenings;

L is for the Lovely combination of personalities, the Learned minds at play and the genuine Laughs;

I is for the Introspection that everyone is allowed to show;

C is for the rather Courtly Conversation that flowed: and

K is for the basic sense of Kismet that we all shared.

A really memorable evening.

Yours ever

Walter Curley

18 February, New York

Tonight went down to Greenwich Village with my friend Bill Marx. He is a very rich businessman with an expense account at every good restaurant in New York, and after a delicious dinner in Cavanaugh's at 12th Street we sauntered down to the Lion's Head in the Village. I notice Bill always wears a hat and when he takes if off, fondles it with some care. But I didn't realize until we'd got into the pub how much the hat is part of the New York scene. I've never worn one myself but am intrigued by the conversation here. Nick Browne, the literary barman, has an intense exchange with Bill about whether his hat is in season or not. Another barman who is listening in but clearly a novice in such matters asks anxiously what is the right hat to wear just now as he is going up town tomorrow to buy a Spring Boater. By this time other people are taking off their hats to join the discussion, and exhausted by excessive chapeaugraphy, I slip out for a coffee.

13 March

An article of mine on the subject of Northern Ireland in the *Washington Post* today, on the editorial page. It gives an airing to some ideas that Trevor West* and I have been working on in between playing squash and running around the grass track in College Park. As well as being Professor of Mathematics at Trinity, Trevor is a member of the Irish Senate, representing the university, and has good contacts

---

* See 2 February 1970, note.

in Belfast. Using their sources as a sounding board, we have put together a scheme which could appeal to both sides in the Northern conflict.

Under the O'Connor/West 'plan', the Unionist community would give up the British connection. The Nationalists in a quid pro quo would put their all-Ireland claims behind them. A new independent Ulster State would come into being without any of the baggage which has previously divided the two communities.

'What is important at present' [I write in the *Post* article] 'is the growing grass roots acceptance of the idea of a shared community. The Protestant is becoming aware of how much closer he is in temperament to his Catholic fellow Ulstermen. The Catholic community is coming more and more to see that it has in common with the Protestants qualities of shrewdness, reliability and industry which are not as marked in the easygoing south.'

I remind the readers that almost 200 years ago the British moved out of America without any detriment to the inhabitants of that colony.

If Britain moves out and an Ulster State is formed it would mean two republics on the island of Ireland. But the curse of colonialism would have been laid. With Britain out, emerging new structures could lead to the establishment of a Federal system such as happened two hundred years ago in the first colony to break with the British connection.

I ring Trevor to say the piece has appeared and that I have asked the Irish Embassy in Washington to have it sent to him in the diplomatic bag.

25 April

Dinner at Jean Kennedy Smith's.* It is a party for her friend Alexandra Schlesinger's thirty-sixth birthday. Present are Lauren Bacall,† Irwin

---

* US Ambassador to Ireland, 1993–98. Sister of President J.F. Kennedy.
† Co-starred with Humphrey Bogart (whom she married in 1945) in such films as *The Big Sleep*, *Key Largo*, *Dark Passage* and *How to Marry a Millionaire*. Won Tony awards for stage work.

Shaw,* Sharman Douglas,† J.P. Donleavy,‡ George Plimpton,§ David Lord Harlech, Sam Spiegel,¶ Jean's husband Stephen Smith, and Arthur Schlesinger, Alexandra's husband.** I learn when I sit down that I am to propose the toast to the guest of honour, who is a descendant of the Irish patriot Robert Emmet, beheaded in 1803 by the English for treason.†† I've bits of Emmetiana in my head; speeches, ballads, Dublin lore, so it hasn't caught me as unawares as it might have.

(Now that I look at Alexandra, I realize that in profile she is a dead ringer for great grand-uncle Bob.)

Seated between Ms Bacall and George Plimpton. He is an aesthetic WASP who writes, among other things, personalized books about sport. His most recent one, *Paper Tiger*, describes how he trained with the Boston Tigers for three months and afterwards played with the team in a real football match. Plimpton was an excellent all-round athlete at Princeton, which enabled him to extend this formula and produce a series of *Paper* books about boxing, basketball, and even one about life as a trapeze artist in a circus. Knowing his athletic past, I wax enthusiastic about sportsmen I have known, but Plimpton turns the conversation to the *Paris Review*, of which he is co-editor. This is a quarterly publication, very much of the tape recorder era which specializes in interviews with the likes of André Gide, Jean Cocteau, Graham Greene, Samuel Beckett, Arthur Miller, Tennessee Williams, André Malraux, Albert Camus, Truman Capote. I beetle away about the Theatre of the Absurd in an effort to keep the ball in play but am not convinced that George P. has the same handle on modern literature as he has on sport.

On my feet to sing for my supper and having dealt with Robert Emmet and his kinship to our guest of honour, I give the peroration of his speech from the dock, pointing out that the last lines are among the most famous in oratory in the English language.‡‡

---

* Novelist.

† Socialite.

‡ Novelist, author of *The Ginger Man*.

§ Author, man-about-town and founder and co-editor of the *Paris Review*.

¶ Film director and Hollywood mogul.

** Former advisor in the Kennedy administration.

†† After an abortive rising against English rule in 1803. His speech from the dock has been translated into almost every language in the world.

‡‡ It would appear that Winston Churchill had read his Emmet. See Broadcast to the Nation of May 1940: *'We shall not flag or fail. We shall go on to the end . . . We shall fight on*

Let no man write my epitaph; for as no man who knows my motives dare vindicate them, let not prejudice or ignorance asperse them . . . When my country takes her place among the nations of the earth, then and not till then, let my epitaph be written.

Finish with a Dublin ballad I heard in a pub as a student in which Emmet's memory is celebrated by an old flower-seller along with two rebels of '98, Wolfe Tone and Michael Dwyer.

> She took and kissed the first flower twice
> And softly said to me:
> 'This flower I plucked in Thomas Street
> In Dublin City,' said she.
> 'Its name is Robert Emmet,
> It's the youngest flower of all,
> And I keep it pressed beside my breast
> Although this world may fall.'
> . . .
> She took and kissed the third flower thrice
> And softly said to me:
> 'This flower I picked in Wicklow Hills,
> Its name is Dwyer,' said she.
> 'And Emmet, Dwyer and Tone I'll keep,
> For I do love them all,
> And I keep it pressed beside my breast
> Although this world may fall.'

At the end of the dinner, Alexandra suggests tea next Thursday in the Plaza Oak Room on 58th Street. Just like one would make an afternoon tea appointment in Dublin's Shelbourne. Jean Smith's husband Stephen, hovering in the vicinity, not too pleased.

---

the beaches, we shall fight on the landing grounds, we shall fight in the fields and in the streets, we shall fight in the hills; we shall never surrender.' Compare with Emmet's dock speech: 'Yes, my countrymen, I should advise you to meet them upon the beach with a sword in one hand and a torch in the other. I would meet them with all the destructive fury of war. If they succeeded in landing, and if forced to retire before superior discipline, I would dispute every inch of ground, burn every blade of grass, and the last entrenchment of liberty should be my grave . . .'

26 April

Leave the Lion's Head pub tonight in a hired bus bound for Jersey city. Though New Jersey is a separate State, you can get to it from New York in less than half an hour by taking the Lincoln Tunnel. We're going to see Randy Newman, something of a writer and a regular at the Lion's Head, fight Sailor Arrington. Boxing is part of the grass roots culture in New York so there's nothing strange about a bunch of writers, actors and painters hiring a bus to go see one of their own, ranked sixth in the US heavyweight list after a win over Jimmy Young, who gave Muhammad Ali a fright last year at Washington Belt.

Atmosphere in the bus good. A lot of people are smoking something with a sweet smell that seems to generate a sense of well-being. Some of the Lion's Head girls are clutching copies of a woman's magazine which this week features pictures of Randy in the shower. We tumble off at Jersey City Stadium. An MC with the face of a well made-up corpse announces the fight. Sailor Arrington looks a tough customer. Angelo Dundee* is whispering things in his ear. Randy dances like Ali on the balls of his feet, while the Sailor tumbles clumsily in pursuit. Our boy looks as if he could win the fifty thousand dollar purse as his powerful left flicks out every other second like a cobra's tongue, knocking the Sailor's head back on his shoulders. But in the second round the Sailor does something to Randy's right eye which leaves it looking like a canvas by Francis Bacon. The Lion's Head hope has to bail out in the fifth round with double vision in his right eye. He looks cheerful enough afterwards, however, when I meet him in the dressing room with lots of sticking plaster over one eye.

This is the sort of fight scene that won't be around much longer. It has the atmosphere of a Thirties movie; large men chewing cigars and guys standing in their seats to yell. On the other side of the ring from us is this blind man with a seraphic smile fixed on his face, listening to a blow by blow account of the fight, described to him by an excited young man.

Back in the Lion's Head, I hear what sounds like a *cri de coeur*:

'Randy, Randy I love you. Why did you let yourself be photographed in the shower with that girl giving you a towel. I just tore you up, so I did.'

---

* Muhammad Ali's coach.

2 May

At two in the morning I'm taking a drink with Roderick Ghuika* in the Quixote (a Spanish restaurant attached to the Chelsea Hotel) when, up front, one or two roughs start a fight. Roddy seems more alarmed than he ought to be but he knows the terrain, and claims he's seen people 'bludgeoned to death' here. He raises his eyebrows and cocks his head anticipating any incredulity I may show.

'O yes' (pause), 'Oh Yeeess.'

We leave and go around the corner to the Angry Squire Pub. A guy called Hogan gives me a hard time: 'Go back to Ireland.' I shoulder him. Roddy flustered. Eventually, we eat a hot dog in a diner around the corner.

3 May

Squash with George Plimpton at the Racquet Club.

On court, Plimpton plays the role of the English sportsman to perfection.

'We'll play with whichever ball suits *you* old man, American or English.'

Quandary. Every year when I come here it takes me a couple of games to adapt to the bounce of the American ball. But I know that for an American, playing with an English ball is a different kettle of fish. While the American ball is solid rubber and has a predictable bounce, the English one is hollow and will bounce only about half as high. The result is that an American playing for the first time with the English ball can find himself swiping away as if he is in the middle of a swarm of bees.

Somewhat unsportingly, I accepted Plimpton's generous offer to play with the English ball. As I foresaw, the poor guy was at sea from the start. You could almost hear the wind in his racquet as he flailed away, often failing to make any contact whatsoever with the ball. Though he is a better squash player than I am, he lost. However, I had warned him about the limitations of the English ball and he, with his preppy past pressing on him, chose to give me the break.

---

* See 24 June 1971.

6 June, Dublin

One man Behan play starts another run at the Abbey. Siobhan McKenna* knocks at the dressing room door afterwards to know if she can come in. I say yes provided she hasn't Rory with her. Rory is an Irish terrier, a vile brute who has frequently sunk his fangs into my calf and is notorious among Dublin postmen. Siobhan, of course, dotes on the dog and tells me he would have loved the show. GRR GRR!

11 June

Get up late. Miscalculation. Dismal rain. Taximan from the rank won't come because I won't say where I am going. Can't find my comb. Apoplectic. Eventually arrive at Fitzwilliam Square in the centre of Dublin on edge. The Fitzwilliam Lawn Tennis Club is celebrating its centenary and a tennis party in period costume is being held in the square where the first championship was played in 1877.[†] I have put together a history of the club, and have to speak later on in the afternoon. This is a real pain in the neck as I must be at the Abbey by 6.00 pm for the last night of the revival of the Behan show. As soon as I finish my speech, I've got to leg it across the Liffey in time for a 7.45 pm curtain call. I'm nervous now about straining my voice gabbling away at the party as one is inevitably forced to do, and wondering will I have enough voice left later on to bring me through an hour and a half on the stage without lapsing into a continual croak.

Monk Gibbon, who is there, introduces me to Hilda Wallace, an old Fitzwilliam hand, four times Irish Ladies' Champion between 1924 and 1933. She was once engaged to Monk's brother. Great old gel, full of spirit. Twinkling eyes:

'I do think Gay Byrne[‡] is a stinker.'

---

* Member of the Abbey Theatre Company. Achieved international fame with her *Saint Joan* (Shaw) in London and New York. A grand dame of the Irish theatre.

† It has been claimed that the Fitzwilliam Club, founded in 1877, is the oldest tennis club in existence, but there is some evidence that the All England Club was founded a month or so earlier. The antiquity of the Fitzwilliam Club has not, in the year 2001, prevented children of five years of age from being encouraged to frolic, morning and afternoons, in the members' swimming pool.

‡ See 19 April 1971, note.

Hilda and her brother won the Feis Ceol Gold Medal* for duet before World War One.

Monk Gibbon remembers 'Rat' Hamilton, a solicitor and Fitzwilliam member, who won the All-England in 1894. Also 'Josh' Pim (winner of the doubles in 1896 with Frank Stoker), who took out his tonsils in Dundrum Rectory where Monk's father was Rector.

I later speak after the President of the Club, J.D. Hackett, has introduced the centenary book and find my throat already hoarse, which scares the bejasus out of me. The rain continues to come down at intervals. So the speech is not listened to with great enthusiasm. On the grass courts they are playing tennis with racquets of the period which look like lacrosse sticks. One of the waiters carrying the drinks round in the rain gets a belt of a ball from a lady, who as she struck it was holding the hem of her Victorian dress, with much decorum, just above the muddy surface.

Basil Goulding† (twice President of the Club) approaches. Puts a good side on things. Says the rain was fortunate because otherwise the afternoon might have gone on too long. Talks about the seven deadly virtues: 'Charity, poverty, etc.' Today he is dressed in a boiler-suit with a flower in his buttonhole. 'Zest is what you have,' he says.

I make a skilful exit and whiz down to the Abbey to snatch a nap on the dressing room couch. First I dry my socks, then sneak a half-hour nap before changing into costume. That eerie moment before you come onstage, the division between being a private person and suddenly confronting an anonymous audience beyond the footlights whose interest and enthusiasm you seek to engage. My voice cracks a bit for the passage when I speak in Micheál MacLiammóir's voice and have to go down deep for the pitch, but otherwise game ball. Colm O'Sullivan, my dentist, who is in the audience, kindly offers to drive me back to the Fitzwilliam Club in Appian Way where the Centenary Dinner is in progress. Seated next to Judge Cahir Davitt, President of the High Court. He was in the same year as my father at University College and played under his captaincy in the First XV rugby side.

We talk about Sean MacBride‡ who last week won both the Nobel Prize for Peace and the Lenin Peace Prize. Cahir agrees that MacBride was not popular in the Law Library, but says that he has

---

* Leading Irish competition for singers and musicians.
† Sir Basil Goulding; see 30 July 1975.
‡ See 23 December 1973, note.

always retained a personal admiration for him. Tells me the Shanahan case still rankles. I appeared in that case led by MacBride, in which Davitt ruled that a refusal of informations on a criminal charge by a Justice of the District Court could not be later overruled by the Attorney-General. This meant that once informations had been refused by the District Justice the defendant could not be brought to court again on the same charge. Davitt was rather proud of this judge-ment as it reinforced the judicial status of District Justices, established in 1922 by the new State of which he was one of the founding figures, and he is furious that it was overruled by the Supreme Court in 1964. I recall for Davitt how I worked on the appeal with MacBride until three in the morning in his library in Roebuck House the night before we went into the Supreme Court.* Ernest Wood who was second silk in that case had been taking it easy and drinking more than he should of MacBride's chilled Chablis as he assumed MacBride would be taking the main arguments next day. At about three in the morning, Sean said in his soft persuasive voice:

'Ernest, you will be taking this argument after lunch.'

'Will I?' said Ernest startled. 'Why?'

'Because I have to go away in the afternoon.'

'Where?' said Ernest, hoping it was somewhere near so that he could get an adjournment.

'Calcutta.'

'Oh Jaysus.'

Cahir tells me he advised Sean MacBride to found Clann Na Poblachta, which helped to remove de Valera's Fianna Fail party from power after sixteen years in office. It's strange talking to this man whose father, Michael Davitt, was one of the leading revolutionaries in nineteenth-century Europe. Davitt founded the Land League with my great-grandfather Matt Harris and both of them attended the meeting in the Hotel Odéon in Paris in 1878 at which the Supreme Council of the Irish Republican Brotherhood decided to adopt a con-stitutional approach and enter the House of Commons under Charles Stewart Parnell. Michael Davitt became MP for Mayo, and my great-grandfather MP for East Galway. Both Republicans good and true.

---

* In 1984 the Supreme Court overruled the 1964 decision, thus confirming Davitt's judgement.

12 June

Billy Wicklow* died yesterday aged seventy-five. The *Irish Times* ring for an appreciation which I have done. But many of the memories which filled the mind would have been out of place in an appreciation. My friendship with Billy wafted me into a world that I would never have known without him. Whenever I had an expenses paid cross-Channel rugby trip for Dublin Wanderers, after the muddied oafs side of the business had been taken care of, I would link up with Billy at a convenient station and continue by rail to Oxford to visit 'Colonel' George Kolkhorst† at Yarnton Manor. This was a splendid Jacobean house with numerous Oriental rugs hung on the wall and sometimes three deep on the floor as well, and masses of china and bronzes displayed throughout the oak panelled rooms. George Kolkhorst was noted for his Sunday mornings at his rooms in Beaumont Street, attended by 'galaxies of undergraduates'.‡ Those evenings at Yarnton Manor with Billy and the Colonel were memorable. Gossip about the Colonel's set, and what they were currently up to, Evelyn Waugh, Osbert Lancaster, Harold Acton, Alan Pryce-Jones, Lionel Perry, John Betjeman. I had met most of them at one time or another so the gossip took on its own life for me. Billy would see to it that I was given space in between for my Dublin bit which surprisingly seemed to go down well with the Colonel. I don't think he was much interested in sport, but he had been impressed when I informed him that a member of Vincent's (an

---

* See 2 July 1970 and note.
† Reader in Spanish at Oxford University. Known as 'The Colonel' because this was a title he was least likely to have had.

'I think of you two as Dublin's Quixote and Sancho Panza', he wrote to me in September 1954, 'and rejoice in your partnership. Don Quixote you can restrain from his tilting at windmills in the guise of giants. Beware of ingrown ego. I am an Egologist (as opposed to an Economist) and the ego must merge itself into the whole, what the Platonists call harmony. You are a charming, promising young person with a charming, promising young voice; so be extra careful never to develop into a discord! But, like the Cardinal or Prince of the Church in the Sistine Chapel, fit into your assigned and appointed chair. It will be a Throne all right, never fear.'

‡ These Sunday mornings would close with an anthem written by Betjeman beginning:

> D'ye ken Kolkhorst in his artful parlour
> Handing out the drinks at his Sunday morning gala;
> Some get sherry and some get marsala –
> With his arts and his crafts in the corner!

athletic Blue) had stopped me in the street and asked me to lunch at
the club.

In the mind's eye a vast dining room with a long oak dining table.
The Colonel sitting upright at one end, his cousin Ms Dolly Trelease
at the other intoning, in her Morningside accent, her mantra 'You
shouldn't annoy the Colonel'. Facing me Toby Strutt (the Colonel's
friend and whipping boy) sitting with head lowered in masochistic
resignation as the Colonel hurls abuse at him across the silver. To calm
the Colonel I am reciting Pater's *She is older than the rocks on which she
sits*, and he is reaching for his railway timetable to assure himself that
the time I have said I will leave the next day is a correct one. Flickering
flames and shadows. The Colonel's Flemish, almost doll-like face with
its fixed grin. Billy sitting at peace with the world, smiling occasionally at some remark that wafts into his consciousness.

Another memory. Billy among working-class Dubliners in a pub,
Lalor's of Camden Street. I had recited a ballad, the penultimate verse
of which contained the line 'To hell with the Pope', a sentiment I had
felt would be acceptable to the customers in the context of the one
that would follow it.* However, in the event the last verse was never
heard, as some grizzled characters at the back indicated their intention of knocking my teeth down my throat, with the result that I had

---

* *The Ballad of William Stoat*:

> In a mean abode on the Shankill Road
> There lived one William Stoat.
> The bane of his life was a nagging wife
> Who continually got his goat.
> Till one morn at dawn with her nightgown on,
> He cut her bloody throat.
>
> He settled her hash with a razor gash,
> There never was crime so slick,
> But the constant drip on the pillow slip
> Of her life's blood made him sick,
> And the awful gore as it rolled on the floor
> Grew clotted, cold and thick.
>
> He tore the sheet from his wife's cold feet
> And knotted it into a rope,
> Then hanged himself from the pantry shelf,
> 'Twas an easy end let's hope.
> In the jaws of death, with his final breath,
> He cried '*To hell with the Pope*.'

to make a hasty departure down the stairs with an infuriated mob in pursuit. I felt bad about leaving Billy in the lurch, but there wasn't much I could do. I needn't have worried. A quick glance behind at the mob, moving as one mass down the stairs, showed Billy's splendid head right in the middle carried in a sea of people, but well in command, as his ancestor Admiral Howe had been at the triumphant naval battle of the Glorious First of June.*

15 June

Sent Michael Davie [features editor of the *Observer*] the Fitzwilliam Lawn Tennis Club Centenary Book to see if he could have it reviewed. Michael is in some ways my 'onlie begetter' on Fleet Street. Twenty years ago he gave me my first journalist break in London when he suggested that I do a piece for the *Observer* about the difficulties I had experienced in trying to get my vaulting pole on buses, taxis and the underground. When published, the piece caught the public eye and brought me a brief notoriety in Fleet Street.

Now he has just edited a splendid edition of Evelyn Waugh's diaries which I am reviewing for the *Sunday Independent*, so I have a chance to return the favour. By a coincidence an entry for Thursday 9 June 1956 refers to a dinner given by Billy Wicklow at the Kildare Street Club, at which Daddy and I were guests.

Then came a father and son, surgeon–professor and pugilist-barrister. I [E.W.] sat between Terence de Vere White† and

---

But the queerest turn of the whole concern
Is only just beginning.
For Bill's in hell, but his wife got well
And is alive and sinnin',
For the razor blade was Dublin made
But the sheet was Belfast linen.

* After the *Irish Times* appreciation had appeared I received a letter from a Maurice Hogan telling me how Billy had endeared himself to ordinary Dublin people. A taximan had recalled to him that one of the compensations of his trade was to drive the Earl of Wicklow to Bray, where, parked on the edge of the railway line, a founder member of the Oxford Railway Club 'would wistfully watch the trains go by'.

† Novelist and man of letters. His memoir *A Fretful Midge* is a wonderfully written account of growing up in Dublin in the Twenties, and his life later on as a successful solicitor in the city. Married to Victoria Glendinning after his first marriage was dissolved.

Father D'Arcy.* White had read the reviews of every book published in English and many of the books themselves.

Terence had come primed for a literary tête-à-tête with Waugh and
was furious to find me on Martin D'Arcy's left which meant that if
Waugh talked to me over Fr D'Arcy, Terence was squeezed out. As
Waugh turned out to have a surprising interest in boxing, especially
Cockneys who'd won world titles such as Ted (Kid) Lewis and Freddy
Mills, I formed an *amitié* with him which didn't at all appeal to 'Severe
Blight' (my nickname for Terence). He complained afterwards to Billy
about my malign influence on the evening.

18 June

Strange day. Nip up to Rathgar at 10.30 am to buy the newspapers.
Landslide for Fianna Fail in the General Election, with a majority of
twenty seats, the biggest ever. Meet Douglas Gageby, editor of the
Irish Times, who has a small smile on his face. 'The Irish electorate
aren't too bad after all?' Patrick Cooney (Minister for Justice) has lost
his seat (rightly so) and the 'Cruiser' (Conor Cruise O'Brien) will now
have plenty of spare time out in Howth to 'fiddle and philosophize'.
By chance I meet my solicitor friend Jim Cawley, and both of us are
in a state of euphoria. Back for a nap. Then at 5.30 Cawley tells me
some tales of the campaign trails. He thinks Haughey† is not likely to
knuckle down to Lynch. When Marion Coyle's father approached
Lynch in Donegal and asked 'What are you going to do about my
daughter Marion?' (she was in jail for IRA activities), Lynch replied
'She broke the law.' Then as a sweetener, 'We have to get elected first.'
Cawley tells me that when he campaigned with Lynch in this unprec-
edented election, Lynch's slightly caustic sense of humour came to the
surface. When he saw a Frankenstein-like character canvassing for
Fine Gael down in Co. Clare, Lynch remarked, 'He won't get much
of the women's vote anyway.'

---

* The Very Reverend Martin D'Arcy SJ (1888–1977). Master of Campion Hall, Oxford,
1932–45. Provincial of the English Province of the Society of Jesus. Author of several
bestselling books on religion. It was D'Arcy who received Evelyn Waugh into the
Catholic Church in 1930.
† Minister for Agriculture, 1964. Minister for Finance, 1966–70. Minister for Health,
1977–79 when he became Taoiseach in succession to Jack Lynch.

18 July, Galway

Today shooting begins for TV film of my one man show on Oliver St John Gogarty, *The Last of the Bucks*,* that I have been asked by RTE to write and act in. The drive to Renvyle, Gogarty's old house in the West of Ireland, takes five hours. In 1917, when he bought Renvyle, Gogarty used to do it in four hours in his Rolls Royce on roads that were the next thing to dirt tracks.

Bad news. James Plunkett† our director, who has gone ahead of us to Renvyle, is ill. The doctor says the stomach is upset, but he should be better in a few days. RTE will send down a substitute to hold the fort.

Renvyle House is a delight. It was almost destroyed in the civil war by the anti-Treaty forces who burnt houses of Free State Senators, of which Gogarty was one. Restored by Sir Edwin Lutyens, designer of New Delhi. Exciting rooms. The sitting room for instance, where Yeats saw a ghost. The door had opened and there was nothing there. 'Don't move,' said the poet, 'it will close.' And it did. Augustus John,‡ J.P. Mahaffy (the Trinity Provost who taught Oscar Wilde), William Orpen, G.K. Chesterton, Lady Gregory and James Stephens were amongst those whom Gogarty had along as his guests. In the bar later on, I'm talking to a bright young chap who is, as it turns out, a doctor. I tell him the Renvyle GP (who is doing a locum) has diagnosed Jim Plunkett as suffering from dehydration as a result of a stomach upset. The youthful doctor looks slightly worried as I outline the symptoms, and says he will run over to Plunkett's cottage and have a look at him. He returns in a state of alarm. Jim is packed off to hospital immediately as he has a severe attack of salmonella which can be life-threatening. Indeed, it seems that if this decent doctor hadn't taken a look at him, our director could have snuffed it.

---

* See 5 September 1973. The TV film was entitled *An Offering of Swans*.

† Novelist, short-story writer and playwright. Plunkett has written a number of novels and plays, but his outstanding achievement is in the short story and some critics have claimed that his have the quality of James Joyce's *Dubliners*. His novel *Strumpet City*, about the Socialist leader Jim Larkin and the General Lockout of 1913, had a great success both in Ireland and England and was later made into a television series.

‡ This artist was a close friend of Oliver Gogarty, who introduced him to the delights of the West of Ireland. Gogarty wrote two poems to John and the painter did two portraits of his poet friend in return.

20 July

Laurie Bourne (RTE director), who is substituting for Jim Plunkett, arrives. A powerful wind is blowing but we get some scenes done. Go over to recce Ballinakill graveyard, where Oliver is buried. His grave is in a spot looking down on the lake below. On the gravestone is a verse from his *Non Dolet*:

> Then do not shudder at the knife
>   That Death's indifferent hand drives home,
> But with the Strivers leave the Strife,
>   Nor, after Caesar, skulk in Rome.

Certainly no strife here. Curiously, my memory of the terrain from the funeral here in 1957 is flawed. I had pictured the lake as set on the right of the grave when in fact it is directly beneath it. This is even more curious as an episode at the funeral had I thought graven the lake's image on my mind. I had found myself standing at the grave beside one of Gogarty's close friends, Monsignor Patrick Browne, classical scholar, a magnificent cut of a man, six foot three with massive shoulders and the profile of a Renaissance Cardinal.* The local parish priest sprinkled the holy water over the coffin out of a noggin bottle as he intoned the Latin chant:

'*De profundis clamavi ad te Domine. Fiant aures tua indendentes in vocem deprecationem meam.*'

The Monsignor had then leaned to my ear to whisper, 'Did you know that Oliver wrote some marvellous limericks?'

'Then out spoke the king of Siam,

For women I don't give a damn . . .'

The parish priest continued:

'*Qui apud te propitiatio est, sustinuit te Domine.*'

Monsignor Paddy purred on undeterred.

'You may think it odd of me,'

---

* Father Paddy Browne had been very much a part of the pre-World War One Dublin literary set and his elephantine memory for verse had enabled him to compete conversation-wise with talkers like Gogarty, Seumas O'Sullivan and James Stephens. He could memorize a new poem on a single hearing and was a walking encyclopedia of bawdy ballads and limericks including a number of Gogarty classics, which he very decently wrote out for me.

I prefer sodomy,
They say I'm a bugger, I am.'
He looked to see if I was appreciative.

'Oliver wrote some marvellous parodies too. He parodied Keats's 'Silent, upon a Peak in Darien' with 'Potent, behind a cart with Mary-Ann.'

Suddenly I had looked down on the lake and seen a swan there, tiny and silver in the distance. No one saw it leave the shore. It was almost as if it had come up through the surface of the lake. I thought of the Liffey and how Oliver had given it two swans thirty years before* and grabbed the Monsignor's arm, but he was off on some fine frenzy of his own. When he saw the swan he began to sing in his fine baritone from *Lohengrin*: 'Mein lieber Schwan! Ach diese letzte traurige Fahrt', 'My beloved swan, now for our last sad journey.' He saw Oliver's soul borne to Paradise by the swan as Lohengrin in German legend had been borne to Monsalvat.

Such is my image of what happened, yet it is a flawed one. For the lake is directly below the grave and the swan could not have appeared on our right as the lake doesn't stretch that far. Another puzzle is, why did other mourners who stood *en face* to the lake not see the swan as the Monsignor, I and a few others had done? Was it a case of nature's legerdemain vouchsafed only to a few?

7 August, Dublin

Today as I walked down Fenian Street with Senator Trevor West, a docker outside McGrath's pub roars across 'The King is dead. Long live Ulick.' I am puzzled for a second but then Trevor reminds me that Elvis Presley died this morning.

---

* During the Civil War, Gogarty as a Senator had been kidnapped by anti-Government forces. He was taken to a house near the Liffey and held hostage. He managed to escape by diving into the river and swimming to safety. Up to his neck in the freezing tide he vowed he would present two swans to the river if he survived. He did and presented the swans to the Liffey in 1924 in a ceremony conducted by Yeats. All the swans on the Liffey today are said to be descended from Gogarty's swans, and indeed those birds did seem to have a special affection for him. I once saw a swan come out of the canal at Wilton Place and nuzzle up to Gogarty like a pekinese.

15–16 August

Out to the Martello Tower* at Sandycove, Dublin, to film the opening passage of James Joyce's *Ulysses* for the Gogarty programme. In 1904 Joyce stayed in the tower with Oliver Gogarty who paid the rent. He used this sojourn to set the opening of his novel with himself as Stephen Dedalus and Gogarty as Malachy St Jesus Mulligan. I am to play the part of Mulligan (as well as doing Joyce's voice) and have to spend about an hour in make-up before I emerge. As they shape a young man's wig on my head, and work on my face, I read them the opening passage of *Ulysses* to evoke an image of what stately, plump Buck Mulligan should look like.†

After they're satisfied with the job, attired in silk dressing-gown with razor, shaving bowl and mirror and wig in place, I emerge on the embattled tower roof as the blasphemous Buck, hands raised in Episcopal blessing. *Introibo ad altare Dei.*

I put my mirror and razor on the parapet and begin to lather my face and call out 'Kinch', Mulligan's nickname for Dedalus. The scene ends with a reference to the cracked looking-glass of a servant as a symbol of Irish art. And the production team have it in the box after one take.

At lunch I have an interesting chat with Godfrey Graham, our cameraman, who played cricket for Ireland when he was seventeen and still a schoolboy in Blackrock. He was a leg-spinner, and in 1957 bowled out Denis Compton who was coaching a course at the MCC. Very much a sporting prodigy who these days spins the camera with just the same adept wrist he once used to turn a cricket ball.

Before we leave there is a loud cry, and in pops Monk Gibbon, who lives around the corner. Seeing me in make-up, he says 'Ulick Fairbanks'. It doesn't work though, because most people here have never heard of Douglas Fairbanks, Senior, who was all the rage when Monk was a young man about town.

---

* These towers were built in the early nineteenth century around the Irish coast as a protection against invasion by the French.

† A number of phrases surface here that have a flavour of Gogarty's letters written from the tower to an Oxford friend, G.K.A. Bell. 'Snotgreen sea' is one. And the two dactyls to which the Buck is compared may grow from a reply of George Moore's when Gogarty's mother complained that he had used her son's name in a novel, *The Lake*, which is about an adulterous priest, Father Oliver Gogarty: 'Madam, if you can supply me with two such joyous dactyls I'll gladly change the name.' Padraic Colum, who knew Joyce and Gogarty intimately, once told me that Buck Mulligan's dialogue in the opening pages of *Ulysses* seemed to him much in the style of Gogartian conversation – 'as right as could be – not only the words but the pace of the words.'

On my way back, I stopped in town as I was giving Nanny tea at the Shelbourne. I was early. When I got there I was still in my wig and with make-up on, so I decided to play a little joke on her. I told the waitress that when Nanny came in, to direct her to my table but not to say that I'd arrived. It was quite clear Nanny didn't recognize me when she sat down.

'Are you waiting for Ulick,' I asked her.

'Yes, I hope he isn't late, he always is,' she replied.

'He told me to tell you he'll be a quarter of an hour late.'

We chatted away, Nanny maintaining a demure but friendly attitude. After about ten minutes, I said:

'If he doesn't turn up, I'm afraid I'll have to leave.'

'Don't wait please, because of me,' Nanny replied.

'Oh, he's impossible,' I said.

Nanny looked a little alarmed. Then I broke into a laugh and said: 'It's me.'

She looked at me unbelievingly, until it seemed that I would have to take my wig off to prove I was me. However, she suddenly recognized me and was amused in her own inimitable way.

17 August

Up the Dublin Mountains today to film a scene as a background for *Golden Stockings*, a fine Gogarty poem though not one of those included by Yeats amongst the seventeen of Gogarty's he crammed into the *Oxford Book of Modern Verse*. The inspiration for this poem came to him when he was driving down the mountains before his afternoon surgery. He had taken his lunch sprawled in a meadow with his little daughter, Brenda, who complained that her stockings had been stained yellow by the buttercups. Before he got back to town in time for his surgery, Gogarty had the poem scribbled down on the inside of his prayer-book.*

---

* Golden stockings you had on   I have many a sight in mind
    In the meadow where you ran;   That would last if I were blind;
    And your little knees together   Many verses I could write
    Bobbed like pippins in the weather, That would bring me many a sight.
    When the breezes rush and fight   Now I only see but one,
    For those dimples of delight,   See you running in the sun,
    And they dance from the pursuit,   And the gold-dust coming up
    And the leaf looks like the fruit.   From the trampled buttercup.

Oliver St John Gogarty, *Collected Poems*, Devin Adair (1952).

The real problem for the take is that there are no buttercups around in early autumn. Someone suggests painting blackberries yellow but Jimmy Plunkett remarks: 'Anyone that'd do that would cheat his mother.' In the end, it is decided to shoot with yellow dandelions bobbing up through the green grass. An exquisite little girl, Aisling, is around to skip through the wild flowers. As a voice-over, Gogarty's lovely poem is used. When a roll of thunder comes, the little one leans backwards, looking up with the suppleness of a television aerial bent by the wind.

23 August

Butch Roche in Grogan's Bar. He is a local anarchist who set all England on alert last month when he threw a smoke-bomb from the balcony of the House of Commons as a protest against the imprisonment of Irish men in English jails. Butch now claims he is a pacifist and that's why he threw the smoke-bomb. I can't make out his reasoning on how he thought he would get away with it. He must have known that he was putting himself at risk of being shot by a marksman or brained by policemen who might reasonably have concluded he was going to blow the place up. I ask Butch 'How is Idi?' This draws a snarl from a black guy sitting nearby in the pub who thinks that I am referring to Idi Amin, the murderous President of Uganda. In fact, I'm enquiring about Butch's St Bernard dog, whom he has named Idi and who frequently drags him out of the sea when he's drunk.

15 October

Run into Mannix Flynn in Grafton Street. Mannix is a celebrity with his play *The Liberty Suit* about a reform school, produced and directed by Jim and Peter Sheridan in the Olympia, and which is a runaway success. How much Mannix, by appearing in the play as himself, bollock-naked, contributes to this success, is not easy to say. He has written another play and has an autobiography on the way. Mannix had a fearful time when he was a boy in Letterfrack Reformatory in Connemara. He was put inside for the usual nonsense; petty thieving, not attending school etc.

He tells me that when he was eleven years old, he and his little sister once approached me on O'Connell Bridge and asked for help. He was on the run from reform school, and the police were searching for him. The pair had recognized me from television and wanted me to smuggle them across O'Connell Street so they could get to a safe house on the northside. The place was packed with police at the time because of an IRA rally and the kids were terrified that the fuzz would nab them and send Mannix back to his horrible jail. He tells me now that I did smuggle them across the bridge and give them some small help.

What a reflection on our society – a little boy of eleven and his sweet, loyal sister on the run in a 'Free State'.

25 October

This afternoon at the Fitzwilliam Club, long-time member Dick Tunney tells me of a man he knew in the Club who was sub for Ireland in tennis on eight occasions and never got to play once. The Great War broke out in 1914 and he joined up. The man then nursed a grudge because he never got a cap. His life was ruined. I chat with Dick about some very hard rugby misses when it came to caps. My pal, Jack Sweetman, of Old Wesley, for instance, got six final trials but never got an International cap and Terry Coveney, of St Mary's, got one cap only, and yet was one of the finest wings I ever saw. There were numerous fly-halves during Jack Kyle's extraordinary rugby career who, because he almost never had to cry off, either through injury, sickness or work, were never capped.

26 October

Today I find myself in wig and gown (silk gown in fact) for the Gogarty film. I hadn't taken silk by the time I decided to shut down legal activities and woo the Muse. Now, however, I am accoutred in the finery of Senior Counsel, silk gown, striped trousers instead of dark suit and stuff gown. In this section of the film I'm playing the part of Jack Fitzgerald, Senior Counsel for Gogarty in a libel action which was taken against him in 1937. As I have to play three other roles in this scene, I'm wondering how we're going to resolve the costume changes. Jim Plunkett has a simple device in mind. When I'm playing the part of Samuel Beckett (who gave evidence against Gogarty in favour of the plaintiff who was a relative), I simply take off my glasses and go into profile. The voice should tell the rest. When I play the part of Jack Fitzgerald, SC, Gogarty's eloquent counsel, I will assume a Cork accent (which Fitzgerald had) in a severe cross-examination of Samuel Beckett.

Fitzgerald's cross-examination is a model. He was the leader of the bar, and used his rich accent for the jury to set off against Beckett's terse Trinity drawl.

> *Fitzgerald:* 'Are you the author of a blasphemous book called *Whoroscope* in which there is a description of a conversation between two Jesuits and a polar bear on top of the no. 15 tram?'
> *Beckett:* 'Yes.'
> *Fitzgerald:* 'Have you written a book about the immoral writer Marcel Prowst?'
> *Beckett: (in a pained voice)* '*Proust*, please.'

Fitzgerald apologized abjectly to the jury for his mispronunciation. In fact he had taken a first in French (Trinity College, Dublin) and he knew perfectly well how to pronounce the name but it wouldn't do to show too much familiarity with foreign fiddle-faddle.

Gogarty, in the heel of the hunt, lost the case and had to find the money to pay £700 damages (in today's money, £40,000 approximately) plus enormous costs. It disappointed him that a Dublin jury would have found against one of their own in such circumstances, and the incident played a part in inducing him later that year, at the age of fifty-seven, to leave Ireland to settle in London, and later in New York.

A slight faux pas. I begin my address in the TV production with 'Ladies and gentlemen of the Jury', forgetting there would have been no women on the jury in 1937, nor indeed were there during the period I practised at the bar.

14 December, Agadir

Have been in Agadir for three days. Hot sun. A vast beach, the biggest I have seen. When the tide is out it stretches for miles. Next stop South Africa. On the rim in the distance you can see liners, tankers and merchant ships chugging along in the South Atlantic. Idyllic but I can't find a bloody typist! My idea in coming here is to get going on my Irish Literary Renaissance book commissioned by Hamish Hamilton. I have made very little progress since the contract was signed. The Gogarty film has taken up a lot of this year, and last year I was around the States on a book promotion tour.

16 December

Have decided I won't get anything done in Agadir. Took a chance and rang the American Consul in Tangier. Name is Hal Eastman and seems a decent skin. Says if I come up to Tangier he can get a typist for me.

20 December, Tangier

Arrive in Tangier airport at midday. Haven't been here since the late Sixties. Same immediate impact. This is New Testament country. Camels, Arab men in djellabas looking like monks, women like nuns. The nice consul has arranged for a Ms Gervaise Hamilton to meet me. After a pleasant lunch in Guita's we agree terms. She will type for me from the dictaphone tapes which I will leave for her. She is Australian with an upper class accent showing no trace of a 'digger' inflection. Attractive but somewhat intense.

22 December

Am now set up in the Hotel Almohades about seven minutes from the city centre and overlooking the beach. I have unloaded all my books and laid out the manuscript I have brought with me. Never seem to learn from previous work. Perhaps I leave too much time in between. But now once more I must focus in my imagination on a vast swathe of material which I am thoroughly acquainted with but have no idea how to turn into a readable book.

The hotel is fine, design cosmetic Arab. Moroccan craftsmanship is of such a high standard that the beds and most of the furniture are handmade. So too with the curtains and quilts which are handwoven. Porters and waiters, of course, wear the fez, some of them pantaloon trousers. The beach below my window is packed with boys playing football. There are at least seven games going on and the colours of the various jerseys and the different shades of skin advancing and receding against the dark-blue sea seem like a painting emerging from under an artist's brush.

I make a few notes for my book but after a while set down the pen

– it is clear that I am going to have to do a lot of thinking in the next couple of days.

24 December

To dinner before midnight mass with Anthony Gilbey at his palace in the Casbah. He knows all the usual suspects, upper class Catholics such as Pierce Synnott, Grace Carroll, the Countess of Antrim, Fr Martin D'Arcy, SJ. Joe McPhillips, who teaches English at the American School in Tangier, is also there. He clearly enjoys the role he has created for himself among the Tangierines here as an *arbiter elegantiae*, though his reading list I have to say does not seem over-extended. He expounds at large on the subject of Evelyn Waugh's novels; but when I ask him which one he prefers, he avoids the question, implying that such pedantry is beneath him. He continues instead at some length about his production of Yeats's *The Only Jealousy of Emer* with his class in the American School and how he has persuaded Paul Bowles to do the music.

Ezra Pound's son, Omar, was headmaster at Andover Academy when Joe was there. One day Omar put a question to Joe asking when did the English language begin, and supplied the answer himself – 'With Chaucer.' Joe later found out this was the same question Ezra had once asked Omar. He told Joe that his father had left him nothing except Arabic which was one of the few languages Ezra hadn't taken up.

After dinner, we head for midnight mass in Tangier Cathedral, a bleak concrete edifice designed in mock-Spanish style. We are accompanied by one of Anthony Gilbey's house guests, Prince Freddie, a son of the Kabaka of Buganda, who is up at Cambridge and giggles and chats away in the back of the car in an incredible public school accent.

'I was, I regret to say, baptized a Methodist but became an Anglican when I went to school in Ghana. I do have a connection with the Roman Church however. Grandfather roasted a few Catholic martyrs' (giggle).

As we go into the church, there is a blast of ghastly music to let us know the Vatican II has reached Tangier. Joe, who shares my passion for the displaced Gregorian chant and the Latin rite, gives a slight shudder. Then he stalks up with Gilbey and Prince Freddie to the front pews. I remain at the back with the young Moroccans who crowd at the door chewing bubblegum, just as in an Irish country

church where the local lads group around the entrance, preferring to
kneel there rather than join the congregation.

At the altar, there are diminutive nuns in fancy dress singing something appalling in French backed by a raft of tiny tots. The priest
appears to be wearing an expensive bath robe. I'm glad I'm at the back
and wonder how long McPhillips will stick it. I haven't long to wait.
Suddenly there is a ferocious roar from near the altar and, looking like
Rasputin, Joe stalks down the church in protest while the congregation look at him in astonishment as if he were some mad mullah on
the rampage. This is a side of McPhillips that I find agreeable. But I
do wish he would not go on and on about the 'huge cocks' of the
Moroccans as if this were the highest achievement of a race who have
taught Western Europe architecture, engineering, and a significant
slice of philosophy.

27 December

Arrange to meet George Greaves in the Café de Paris on the
Boulevard Pasteur. I first met George in 1967 when I used to nip over
from the Torre Blanca on the Spanish coast to Gibraltar for a work
break and then on to Tangier. Billy Wicklow had given me some
Tangier introductions and one of them was to George, whom he had
met at Oxford. 'Very amusing but an extremely wicked man.'

George was decorated for bravery while serving with the Anzac
Division at Gallipoli. Though now in his seventies he retains his good
looks and commanding presence, which is assisted by his height of six
foot four inches. When he went to Oxford, he didn't attend university, but the Evelyn Waugh set took a shine to him and rather adopted
him as a character. In the Thirties he came out to Tangier as a stringer
for the *Daily Express*. Then during World War Two he became an MI6
super spy whose job it was to see that the enemy were kept under
control in what was then an International Zone.

When I arrive at the Café de Paris, I immediately spy George
holding court. He greets me effusively, introduces me and then
resumes his favourite pastime of sending out volleys of vituperation at
anyone who comes within firing range. He has spotted someone
going into Lloyd's Bank.

'There's that cunt Alec Waugh. I knew his brother, Evelyn, who
had a mistress called Pixie in Jermyn Street. He said to me one day,
"Pixie has a son aged sixteen who should be up your alley, I will

introduce you and push the boat out." I kept the appointment. The little ponce didn't turn up!'

George leaned back and surveyed his group with the most benevolent gaze one can imagine.

'Oh look at *him*.' (This was directed at a retired French consul who was walking past on the Boulevard.) 'That swine came to me yesterday sent by the Duchess asking for money for a taxi to Asilah. "I wouldn't give you the time if I had a watch on both hands" I said and "If you were dying I wouldn't give you a glass of water."'

The owner of the Parade Bar has just told George that he intends to leave his bar and business to the Arab boy with whom he lives and has let the lad know this. George lets a little scream out of him.

'Fatal. You know what they do, these boys? They go straight home and tell their mother. "My kind employer is going to leave me the business when he dies." The mother thinks about it. "Why wait till he dies?" Then she says to the boy, handing him some powder, "Put this in his soup – it will make him sleep." Of course, he never wakes up.'

George then draws his hand across his throat accompanying the gesture with a truly horrifying death rattle:

'Poisoned.'

1 January 1978

Read through all the previous drafts of my next book which I put together two years ago in Malta. The problem is how to write about a Literary Renaissance which produced some of the outstanding writers of the twentieth century and not fall into the trap of ending up with just a factual record. After some hard thinking, I have come up with a list of seven figures who I feel might anchor the project. Yeats, Synge, George Moore, James Joyce, Lady Gregory, Edward Martyn and George Russell (AE). I feel if I could do separate biographical studies of each of these and then set them against one another until they begin to react as real characters, I could produce a work that might capture something of the elation of the time. There were of course others whom I wish to have in, such as Oliver St John Gogarty, Padraic Colum, James Stephens, Seumas O'Sullivan and Sean O'Casey. But the first group will form the substructure on which I hope my 'seven pillared worthy mansion' will rest.

I take a taxi to the Old Mountain. Walking through a narrow, high-walled road, almost a lane, with great mansions on one side. This is where a foreign ruling class once lived with loads of servants and immense wealth. The air is beautifully cool. The Atlantic light, translucent blue. Smoky shadows drift like spiders' webs. Rich green foliage as in Ireland with the brilliant purple and reds that you see in West Cork and Bantry. I pass a little girl practising carrying objects on her head. When she grows up, she will be able to accommodate on her handsome poll weights heavier than any Irish navvy could carry on his back. Boys glancing with their eyes. Then suddenly, I hit the Atlantic. Deep rich blue with green underneath and flecks of white seagulls. On the right hand side, near the sea, vast green lawns with little villas. This is a Roman road, built out to the point which was the last piece of Europe over two thousand years ago. I see what seems a still figure down in the grass. Who could it be? A shepherd? It moves and is a little girl about six who passes me later in fashionable boots. Where is she going on this road to nowhere?

Halfway back, I start thinking about what I've promised to banish from my mind like bad thoughts, my book. The scene has filled me with such elation that I feel strong enough to let the old enemy in. Should I, I ponder, use the Lytton Strachey approach and suggest rather than recruit regiments of detail. I think of how Mahaffy, Oscar Wilde's tutor, could turn his scholarship into tinkling prose. Then I get worked up about James Stephens. Luckily I cop myself on. This morning I felt I had the book out of my system for a day or two at least. So stay away Peter, stay away Paul.

On the way back, an Atlantic breeze gives the slightest touch of cold. Down in the city it is mild again. I walk along through an Arab village street. Cobbles. Carpenters working at their doors. One shop has a wet floor where fish lie. Two wasteland fields are backed by mosques still uncompleted. Down a side road, boys playing football against a wall. I point to my foot, and with the *true* generosity of sportsmen they kick the ball towards me. I take three shots, two of them rotten because I hook the kick trying to keep the ball low so as not to put it over the wall. The third hits the wall with a satisfactory slap and draws a cheer from the boys. 'Bonjour Monsieur.' We raise hands to each other.

Lunch with David Herbert* at Larbis which is run by two brothers.
David has lots of connections with Dublin. His father owned a sub-
stantial slab of South Dublin and many people to this day pay rates to
the Pembroke estate. They were the first in Dublin to instal electric-
ity in the houses of their tenants and the power station's elegant tower
dating from the 1860s is still to be seen near the river in Ringsend.
David has resolved any difficulties he might have had as second son.
He lives like a lord out here with an enchanting mansion on the Old
Mountain were he cultivates his gardens and keeps rare singing birds.
The locals refer to him as 'Lord Herbert'.

Dublin has played a significant part in his life and he visits there regularly to see relatives. He is sad to hear the Russell Hotel is gone which
he remembers as an oasis of elegance and good cooking. I tell him
Dublin is at present undergoing a hysterectomy – vital parts ripped
out. Besides the destruction of public buildings by unscrupulous
developers, even hoteliers are also running scared and we have lost in
the last few years, as well, the Russell, the Hibernian, the Wicklow
and Jury's from the centre of the city. These were part of a Dublin tradition of hotel-keeping and cuisine mostly run by families who are
being wiped out in the general purge. David says it was because of that
sort of thing in England that he came out here in the Thirties. A lot
of painters had come before him, attracted by the dazzling light of the
town anchored on the edge of the Atlantic.

Sir John Lavery had a house nearby and came for a few months
every year. Lavery, who was born in and grew up in Belfast, has always
been a sort of hero of mine if for no other reason than that he has
been attacked by critics as being a photographer. He is not these days
regarded as a major painter, perhaps because of his numerous public
portraits, a reputation for which can often harm a good artist's career,
e.g. the one of Michael Collins laid out after his death in the City Hall,
the portrait of his wife Hazel which appeared on Irish banknotes, and
his well known picture of the trial of Sir Roger Casement. But his
Impressionist paintings of the 1890s remain in the first rank and he

* Second son of the 15th Earl of Pembroke. Though his friend Cecil Beaton chided
Herbert with wanting to be 'a big frog in a small pond', such a judgement ignores his
social talents and charm which enabled him to create an interesting circle from the bizarre
milieu of Tangier expatriates.

will come back some day with a bang. David adored Hazel, and remembers her 'almost translucent skin'. He was present once when she came into a banquet and the footman on the door directed her to the place he thought she had asked for when she gave her name at the entrance. She replied with perfect courtesy.

'I quite understand why you made that mistake, but my name is Lady Lavery, not Lady Lavatory.'

David is an absorbing gossip. He remembers Jane Bowles* when she first came to Tangier. Beautiful then, she later became bloated-looking as a series of illnesses overtook her, maybe brought on by a lesbian Arab maid who had put a spell on her. David also knew another famous lesbian, Violet Trefusis. Violet had run away with Victoria Sackville-West, the wife of Harold Nicolson, who became so fond of David when he met him in Berlin as a young man that he had a mask sculpted of his face. It hung in the hall of Sissinghurst Castle for a while, but later found its way upstairs to a pillow on Harold N's bed.

Though I am twenty-one years younger than David, our lives have criss-crossed in unlikely fashion. Here are some of the coincidences: David grew up with Garrett Drogheda who was an uncle of my girl-friend of seven years, Maureen Aherne. David almost married Patricia Moore who was Maureen's mother. His aunt Alice (Astor) married Prince Serge Obolensky, whose son Ivan published my first book in New York. Billy Wicklow, whose protégé I was, is David's cousin. Spinning tops in a whirlpool of coincidence.

David is not a fan of George Greaves. Recalls with some distaste how George arrived at a party dressed as a priest accompanied by two young Arabs dressed as altar boys, with a crucifix hanging down to his navel and a stole studded with bottle-tops.

Later I dictate last night's work to Gervaise in her apartment. It is a first draft of the section on Yeats. Back in the Almohades hotel and my writing den, I suspect that I am only partially on the way to finding a solution for my Literary Renaissance book but I will plough on with the 'seven key characters' and see what turns up.

---

* Novelist and playwright. Married to Paul Bowles (see 6 January 1978, note) who maintained she was a better writer than he was.

6 January

Tea with Alec Waugh* and his wife Victoria. Gervaise has arranged this. Though she no longer practises as a nurse, she comes along in the evenings to take Victoria's blood pressure. Alec is bald and has the cut of a regular officer about him. He is not at all reticent about his younger brother Evelyn for whom he has much affection. Unlike Evelyn, Alec was a dedicated sportsman and played good cricket well into his fifties as well as having been a rugby forward at Sherborne where he acquired the nickname 'the Tank'. He glides across the carpet to greet one with a strange mechanical gait like an electric doll. Later I think it may be because of arthritic hips which he tells me interfere with his daily walks.

Alec, as befits a dedicated clubman, is a great one for the chat. He can remember George Moore saying to him one day as he rose from his chair to greet him: ' I'm a dab at lovemaking.' He goes to the book-case and comes back with some quotes from *Avowals* by George Moore which is autographed to him. He seems besotted with Victoria. When she comes back with the tea he rises, raising up his hands in greeting, and says 'Hail Victoria'. Then bows. He is touch-ingly proud of brother Evelyn and has a framed letter from him on the wall congratulating him on making his first century at Sherborne. If Alec hadn't been expelled from Sherborne, Evelyn would have gone there instead of to Lancing, a firmly Anglo-Catholic institution as opposed to low church Sherborne. It could therefore be argued that if Alec hadn't been turfed out of Sherborne, Evelyn might not have become a Catholic.

Suddenly Alec rushes over to the radio. He has forgotten that the West Indies are playing England. But their batting has collapsed and England have won the test. Paul Bowles[†] was to have come to tea and just as I start to leave he arrives, apologizing for being late. He is fair-haired and young-looking, though (as I later found out) he is over

---

* Alec Waugh (1898–1981) achieved fame at nineteen with *The Loom of Youth*, a novel about Sherborne, from which school he had been expelled for alleged immoral conduct. He wrote many other novels and had a world success in 1956 with *Island in the Sun* which later became a record-breaking movie. Brother of Evelyn Waugh.

[†] 1910–98; American novelist and composer. Gore Vidal has said: 'Carson McCullers, Paul Bowles, Tennessee Williams are the three most interesting writers in the United States.' His novel *The Sheltering Sky* was made into a film by Bernardo Bertolucci. Author of many novels, including *Let it Come Down* and *The Spider's House*.

sixty. There is a soupçon of an American accent. Elegant. The air of a boulevardier. Well cut clothes, the only indication of the writer being in the large number of pockets on either side of his jacket presumably meant for jotters and books. Alec has now fallen asleep. The muscles of his face have relaxed and there is a hint of the cross old man there. He is so youthful and vibrant when he is moving round that one doesn't think of his real age. He wakes up however to show us courteously to the door. On the way out he tells me that *The Loom of Youth* was taken out of the Tangier Library after they found out it had been banned in England. I'm sorry I haven't had more talk with Bowles. But he seems slightly stand-offish apart from the fact that he arrived late.

7 January

Dropped into Madame Porte's at five. This is an elegant tea-room off the Boulevard Pasteur where the Tangier set meet. I sit down at a table and find I am looking straight into Alec Waugh's good eye. He is sitting directly opposite, with his cane in front of him and a flower in his buttonhole. I nod to him and sensing that he seems embarrassed, tip my hat. He has the expectant look of the *coureur*. A new girl in the offing perhaps? I slip off to the Café de Paris at the top of the street.

10 January

George Greaves has invited me to his flat in the Rue Goya. His arthritis is giving him trouble and when I get in, he is seated on what he calls his 'throne', an enormous chair into which he heaves himself from bed. I assist him. He says 'Thank you very much', with elaborate courtesy, and follows it with 'Oh my fucking back, I'm afraid I'm going to give birth.' His eyes beam with kindness and his great white beard is beautifully curled. Indeed he looks like a nineteenth-century saint (perhaps Edward Carpenter looked like this), almost as if a halo emanated from his white linen shirt. Yet he surely is a rogue if ever there was one. Alec Waugh looks on George as a satyr and says he once fancied girls but caught the clap and turned to lads. Alec however, out of collegiality and well-intentioned kindness, visits him once a week. George admits that Alec does have some good points but says that his visits only occur after 'being purified in church'.

As a general rule George despises the English upper class exiles who

come to Tangier for queer trade. There is a plastic surgeon who has
become besotted with a Moroccan lad here. He has his practice in
Germany and wants to bring the lad back with him but the author-
ities won't give permission. Desperate to hear the beloved's voice
again, he has asked George to have a cassette made and sent to him as
his protégé is unable to write. Chanting like a stream dancing over the
rocks, George puts on this cassette for me to hear. It starts with his
own voice – 'Say something Mohammed,' he says, 'any fucking thing.'
Mohammed hasn't an idea what to say so he takes out his spoons
which he plays on his knees with great dash. This brings into play his
limited vocabulary:

> 'I love you . . . (*bang bang with the spoons!*) 'Could you send me
> shoes?' (*bang bang!*) 'The ones I have are very old, I love you
> Angus, could you send me a new shirt? I need one.' (*Bang bang.*)

George is miming playing the spoons on his own knees in time to the
rhythm on the recorder when the phone rings. Takes it up and says in
a patient voice 'Yes, Arthur.' Then raises his eyes to heaven as he
listens. When he is finished George says in his best velvet voice 'Thank
you *very* much, Arthur.' He turns to me and lets go.

> *George:* 'That's the Reverend Arthur fucking Evans. It's amazing
> how these reverend gentlemen of the cloth always find their feet.
> Only seven months here and he marries a cow with a beautiful
> house. Now his reverence has a nice umbrella to shelter under.'
> *Me:* 'What does he want George?'
> *George:* 'What *does* he want?' (*volley of snorts*) 'He wants me to
> come to his house next week for another after-Christmas party.
> He gives a filthy fucking bash every year with condensed milk
> and whiskey.'

George then heaves himself up out of his chair and with a stick to
support his sciatic leg takes me upstairs to see a set of the *Encyclopaedia
Americana* which he has for sale. He chuckles away contemplating the
wealth he will get when he sells this. Just like an old peasant waiting
for the letter from America to come.* George also hopes that his war

---

* It turned out to be worth less than £300.

record at the Gallipoli landings may be of benefit to him now. Under an Australian Government scheme he can be taken back to his native land and given a house and allowance for the rest of his life. I can't see him going though. In Tangier he is accepted by a large number of people because of his style and outrageous personality. The white population here is bound together by a tolerance of and interest in diversity and in their disregard of what they see as repressive laws in their own country. Suits old George. Back in Sydney he would be bound to tread on somebody's toes and likely to end up in the slammer instead of a villa near the bay paid for by the Australian Government.

12 January

Up at 11.00 am. Walk eight miles. I notice the cold as I get warmed up. Paul Bowles has asked me to lunch. He greets me with much courtesy at his flat. Makes a delicious blackcurrant tea. He is an admirer of Cocteau,* remembers how good a mime Cocteau was.

He saw him once get down on the floor and imitate a bear. Longest fingers he'd ever seen. I say I thought Cocteau might have destroyed Raymond Radiguet. Bowles said that their relationship must have had some good points because Radiguet had written two fine novels before he died at twenty.

Despite his outward calm Bowles seems to bustle about, going in and out of different rooms to fetch things. His hearing is acute. When I hear sounds next door he says that a girl who sells sex and is married to a Basque lives there. They often play Moroccan drums which are varied in tone. Also the flute. As my own hearing is sensitive I remark that this must be hell. Paul says no because he likes the music but what does get to him is that they continually fight in bed.

William Burroughs† came here to stay with Paul. Paul says it was

---

* Jean Cocteau (1889–1963), playwright, poet, novelist, film-maker and critic, was a Renaissance man of postwar Europe. Everything he did was of artistic value, something that tended to be obscured by the wide range of his talents. His most famous work for the stage was *The Infernal Machine*, a variation of the Oedipus theme. In his films, where he created many famous roles for Jean Marais, he will be remembered for *La Belle et la Bête* and *Orphée*.
† 1914–1999; author of *Junkie*, *The Naked Lunch*, etc. With Kerouac, he had a major influence on the evolution of the novel in the Sixties.

Brion Gysin* who persuaded Burroughs to cut up newspapers with razors and stick them together. He remembers the two of them on the floor cutting away. 'That's how *The Naked Lunch* was compiled and why it doesn't work.' But there are more influences in *The Naked Lunch* than simply collage, I point out, such as scientology and forays into the unconscious which sometimes come off. Paul complains that his publishers send him small royalties on his books. He survives mainly from the money for the film right on three novels.

He feels he is unable to leave Tangier. He believes if he does he will not be allowed to return. Has he a persecution complex? Yet his autobiography has not been suppressed here, and there are criticisms of the regime in it. He first came to Tangier in 1935 with the composer Aaron Copland who he believes is the best American composer of his time, influenced directly by Stravinsky. He was himself a composer of note and has written two symphonies. He tells me that Charlie Barton's story of the twelve injections he (Paul) got for rabies after he had been bitten by a dog is exaggerated. In fact, Paul caught the dog and had put it in the pound for a month where he brought it food every day. In the end, the dog was found to be free from rabies. Paul says children today need discipline. But injustice will be remembered if administered by parents.

15 January

When I leave my hotel room this morning I see a cat on the couch in the corridor with six tiny newly born kittens tugging away at her. Cat comfortably settling herself. Manager comes. Makes a slight *tch tch* noise. I hope he doesn't feel that I disapprove of the little darlings. But I don't want to be also seen as sentimental by saying 'Lovely little pussies' etc as the kittens moan and push each other away to get a nipple. When I come back three hours later the kittens are gone and Mummy is mournfully meowing on the couch. I close my eyes and I think of them being drowned. It is so dreadful but at the same time it's something I think I should like to watch sometime. Life there. Life

---

* Born Buckinghamshire, 1916; educated at Downside. Early member of André Breton's surrealist movement in Paris. Later in Tangier a close friend of William Burroughs, whom he greatly influenced. He returned to Paris, where because of his association with the peace movement and his artistic connections he was constantly sought out by young writers and artists.

gone. I know it would horrify me. But some thrill as if I was in control, or really as if I was safe and those poor creatures weren't. I notice today in the market the great tranquillity of the hens as they lie in the arms of the women who offer them for slaughter. Like doves.

19 January

Meet Bowles at 2.30 in his apartment. We drive out to the road to Cape Spartel in his car, a blue Mustang. His Arab chauffeur is a hefty bloke who takes on all comers on the road. We stop to see the house where Paul lived with Aaron Copland in the Thirties, both of them working on their music. The chauffeur drops us at the Roman Road which runs along the spine of a hill overlooking the sea but then insists on accompanying us, walking a few yards behind. When I ask Paul why he can't stay in the car, Paul says something to him in Spanish but he insists on staying with us. Exquisite sun. Marvellous day. Wind mild. Grass bright green. Seagulls like floating diamonds. Spangled effect of the underparts of their bodies in the sun. Then we come across the goats. Lovely pastoral creatures. Horrific sound. Dogs barking. My heart jumps. I remember being chased by a horde of these animals some time ago and learning later that many of them were rabid. However, no dogs appear this time.

Down below the blue sea. On the edge little white houses here and there. Paul says he would like to live in one of those. Back to his flat for a delicious tea served by his servant, Mrabhat. He is here to make cakes for Paul's birthday party to which to my delight I am invited. Though Mrabhat cannot read or write his folk-stories are known to a wide audience. Paul has tape-recorded them and translated them and they have been published in many languages. Mrabhat, who has been a successful professional boxer as well as a gymnast and swimmer, frequently dives off heights which horrify Paul. He laughs and arches his back to show how he lands after one of his dives. Plays football every day. But he has the smoky eyes of a kif taker, blurred, whimsical, tolerant.

'I am old at forty-five. I have lived hard. If you have lived easily you can be young at seventy. When I was at a book fair in Amsterdam Yevtushenko, the Russian poet, said to me, "The Moroccans are at war with socialism because they are fighting Libya and Algeria". I said, "We are not. We are fighting Soviet Russia."'

Yevtushenko took this as an insult and put up his fists. Mrabhat says he just pushed the big man who towered over him (he is almost seven feet) on the chest but the press reported it as a real ding-dong. This encounter became a world story and he was rung up and badgered by reporters almost every day. When Paul tells of how Mrabhat's stories are resented by the Arab population as they feel he is stealing them from them, I remind him that J.M. Synge had much the same objection from his countrymen when he used their conversation in his plays. Some of the audience were so shocked at hearing themselves talk that they broke up the Abbey Theatre on the first week of *The Playboy of the Western World* in 1908.

Paul has the calm of an Irish monk. Knowing of his interest in psychic matters I tell him about George Russell (AE) who in 1882 on top of Kilmashogue (three miles from my house) described seeing an aircraft pass by within a few inches of him. Russell maintained that he understood in an instant everything that was in the pilot's mind. Paul is inclined to accept this. He has always revered AE, but not known as much as he would like about him. There is something of AE's spiritual touch about Paul, though his small neat figure in the polo-neck jumper couldn't be less like Russell's bearded bulk.

The cat, who has been waiting for him, now strolls in. Then scratches his head with his leg just like a dog and gallops into the next room for a drink of milk.

I remark that I am convinced that certain people go mad once a month with the moon. Bowles looks the word up in the dictionary, lunar-lunacy. While we're talking about hysteria, a gleam comes into his eye. 'Wait till I get you something that'll interest you.' He scurries into the bedroom and comes out with a cassette tape. It is a recording of James Jones, the American evangelist, speaking to his congregation in Guyana just before he persuaded them to commit mass suicide by drinking cyanide administered by him. Jones induced lawyers, doctors, academics and businessmen to allow him to invest their money and then persuaded them to come and live in the Guyanan jungle where he formed a commune. On the night of the carnage he stood in the middle of the bodies of 700 people whom he had persuaded to kill themselves and then shot himself.

Each evening, he would address the 'family' beginning with the words 'Father says', Father being of course himself. It is to one of these allocutions that Paul wants me to listen. In it, Jones is deriding Western culture. Starting off with a casual chuckle and accelerating into a cacophony of laughter, he keeps on for some minutes, hysteria holding him to it, generating a sound not yet heard on land or sea. Still his voice doesn't break. Bowles looks at me to see my reaction.

'Isn't that something? Takes you where you've never been before, doesn't it?'

We agree that somewhere in that astonishing, prolonged howl lies an essence which if it could be analysed would tell us more than any biography could.

I ask Paul about Port Moresby, his character in *The Sheltering Sky* whose passivity seems similar to that of Mersault, the protagonist in *The Outsider*. Bowles said he hadn't read Camus at the time he worked on *The Sheltering Sky*. But he considers Mersault's fatalism as reflecting an Arab culture, though Mersault himself is French. In Algeria, colon and native are affected by indigenous conditions and Bowles believes that this can actually affect physiognomy as well. For instance, he points out that the *pieds-noirs* have shirt collars larger by one and half inches than those worn in mainland France.

Paul's flat is neat, well-kept. No junk. Everything in place. He is a fastidious dresser and not a little fond of smart clothes. It is ironic then that he could have been acclaimed as 'a cult figure for the beats'. Certainly Ginsberg, Corso and Kerouac have come out to see him in Tangier on a number of occasions and declared their allegiance. But though Bowles thinks Kerouac had a significant influence on the novel, more even than Burroughs, he is emphatic that he himself 'never was a beat writer.'

20 January

Off home. Usual anxiety as I enter the airport – not flying, about which I don't give a fiddler's. There is some awful deal in Morocco about bringing out dirhams. I am never able to comprehend whether I am in the right or the wrong but this time I haven't had time to change my dirhams back and am bringing them in my wallet to change at home. Luckily the green Irish passport carries me through and I crash out on the plane till we reach London. On landing I find at the airport bank that dirhams cannot be changed outside Morocco. Another win for the Tangierines.

1978

Overworked. So exhausted unable to remain in bed. Want to do everything at once. In the throes. Anxiety. Then when I go out I lose my wallet. Galvanized. Ring police and two others who may be able to help. Substantial sum missing. Nevertheless, definitely feel much better. Shock treatment?

Strolling among the crowds today, I think that my love of drifting aimlessly may derive from the Latin element (Catholic) in our culture and that, as I grow more engrossed in the work ethic, I may become bored with doing what I am doing now.

On number 15 bus tonight, city-bound. Snowing in the street. An old lady on crutches arrives at the stop just as the conductor is about to hit the bell, he ignores her and the bus moves off. I say to him 'Don't leave her in the snow. Couldn't you let her on?' He shouts at me he'll get the police if I don't sit down. I don't want a row as I am intent on trying to get the poor thing on board, so I content myself with saying how would he feel if it was his mother being left behind.

A few hundred yards on he stops the bus at Rathmines police station and brings the sergeant on board. I tell him what has happened and say I'm not going to leave the bus. The driver then orders all the passengers off the bus and drives off. I accompany the sergeant into the station where I make a statement. The whole thing is outrageous of course. But what is really shaming is that none of the passengers except one offered to back me up. This was a young American student at the Royal College of Surgeons in Dublin who accompanied me into the station and corroborated what I said.

20 February

A Garda calls at the house today to serve me with a summons for district court No. 3. I am to be prosecuted for being abusive to the conductor on the bus and impeding him in the course of his duty. Flabbergasted. Both I and the student have made unequivocal statements on the spot about what happened. Clearly someone doesn't like me. Important thing now to find the College of Surgeons student. I am being set up, and because of the pusillanimity of the other passengers I may make the headlines in a most unpleasant and unfair way.

5 March

Micheál MacLiammóir died yesterday. At the removal almost the entire acting fraternity. Charlie Roberts, the actor, says 'Standing room only' as they come into the church. The fellow next to me kept saying 'Hail Mary, etcetera, etcetera.' Thought how I hadn't called Micheál in the last month: 'I'll give you a ring.' Last time in our café near Mountjoy Square. His sparkling wit. How kind he was to write about Daddy when he died.

Always deep sympathy for the underdog. Politics meant nothing to him. He once told me that after Michael Collins' death he made up his mind to have nothing more to do with public affairs. He had met Collins only once, on a car journey to Howth.

The taxi man said when I drove off: 'Your old friend is gone.' He used to drive Micheál to a masseur in Ranelagh. 'Don't let them fool you,' Micheál had said to him a few months ago, 'old age is awful.'

Church, state, judiciary, barristers, surgeons, working-class people, actors, musicians, writers, all there, some of them weeping. Remember walking with him through the great squares of Edinburgh, with their grey granite palaces, during the 1956 Festival when Micheál had finished playing in the *Hidden King*, a bad play but a perfect vehicle for his gifts. The critics had raved about him and journalists from around the world had been mesmerized when he answered questions at press conferences in five languages.

'The Irish people have taken away my telephone,' he declared as I walked him to his hotel one night, and indeed they had. He and Hilton couldn't pay their bills. He would insist he wasn't known

outside Ireland except for playing Judge Brack opposite Peggy
Ashcroft in *Hedda Gabler*. I tried to reassure him but it wasn't until ten
years later that he would receive world recognition for his mould-
breaking *The Importance of Being Oscar* one man show. 'I shall retire to
4 Harcourt Terrace and sit under a maple tree to sip green tea and read
Little Women,' he said jauntily as he swept through the swing doors of
his hotel. He loved an anonymous Gaelic poem written in praise of a
chieftain of his clan who had died and whose verse could have been
about Micheál himself.

> A noble man has left us.
> He was without envy.
> His like shall not be seen.
> He was loved for himself.

10 March

This afternoon in the fading light a little old lady coming along
Earlsfort Terrace stopped me. She asked me for four shillings. I gave
her a pound. Pink skin, blue eyes, no bitterness in her face. Said she
slept in the Morning Star hostel.

'We have to get out in the day time though. The chapels are where
we sit then. They're warm.'

She had been born and reared on a farm in Roundwood, Co.
Wicklow, which had fifteen cows. Now she will get buns for her tea
with the money I have given her. Headscarf and suede shoes. I looked
back to watch her as she was going away. She seemed as if she was
hardly moving through the cold rain. I ran after her and gave her five
pounds. She didn't want to take it. She felt she had deceived me as she
would get tea at 6 pm in the hostel. Sadness of sadness.

12 March

I have got onto the Royal College of Surgeons registrar, who knew
my old man and he has found the student who was on the bus when
the incident occurred. I met the lad today in the Shelbourne for tea.
It turns out he is Canadian. Has a clear memory of what happened
and will swear up in court. Rush of anger thinking of the swine on
the bus who shambled off like sheep when they were ordered, without
a bleat. Later on I talk to a Senior Counsel chum. I tell him what has

happened and my concern that I am being set up. Says he will talk to
someone and see what is on the file.[*]

17 March, Pittsburgh

Tonight will speak at a Book and Authors dinner in Pittsburgh about
The Troubles – 1912–1922 (Bobbs-Merrill), my latest book. Other
authors to speak are Sir William Stevenson MC, DFC and Dr Malachi
Martin.

Thrilled to meet Bill Stevenson. Had heard all about him from
Monty Hyde[†] who wrote his biography some years ago, *The Man
Called Intrepid*. Stevenson is a Canadian who ran the British Secret
Service in North America during World War Two. He was a flying
ace in the Great War, and became a millionaire shortly after, when he
invented and merchandized a new form of wireless photography. He
worked in tandem with the legendary 'Wild Bill' Donovan in New
York from 1940 onwards, and Monty Hyde came over to join him
from the English Secret Service. Stevenson is small in stature, and neat
on his feet. He took up a mock boxing stance as soon as he saw me
and I remembered that Monty had told me Stevenson had once won
the world light-weight amateur championship. Asked him, of course,
about this. He laughed modestly and said that he had won the
Canadian light-weight championship but when he was in Paris after
the First War he had fought for a World Championship title.

'There were so few able-bodied men left to fight. I won by a
street.'[‡]

He told me he had been going to talk tonight about his Secret
Service operation in North America, but as he learned the theme of
the presentation was 'love' he will now talk about 'Madeleine', a
British woman spy who he believes sacrificed her life for humanity.[§]
Dr Malachi Martin,[¶] a former Jesuit who acted as an advisor to Pope

---

[*] A week later the file was returned with instructions that there was no evidence on
which a prosecution could be brought.

[†] Harford Montgomery Hyde: see 21 August 1970, note.

[‡] He didn't add that he won the title again in 1923 when presumably the able-bodied
were not as thin on the ground.

[§] I had met 'Madeleine' (Cynthia) with Monty Hyde in Dublin some years before.

[¶] A brother of Professor F.X. Martin, the splendid Augustinian who in the early Sixties
led a series of massive protest marches in Dublin against the city fathers' decision to
destroy ancient Scandinavian sites.

John XXIII for four years, will talk about love as a force against hate in the context of his participation in exorcisms as described in his recently published *Hostage to the Devil*.

My own contribution will stress how love can turn into hate, if the state, whose function it is to see the rule of law applied, fails to deal with injustice. The refusal of the House of Lords to pass the Irish Home Rule Acts, presented to it by Parliament three times in 1912–14, is a prime example.

'You Americans faced a similar situation in 1964 when black people were demanding their civil rights. But your Supreme Court and the American conscience rose to the challenge and you had an evolution not a revolution.'

2 April, New York

On New York TV with Margaux Hemingway.* Also on the panel a doctor who is a fan of Oliver St John Gogarty's fantasy in fact *As I was going down Sackville Street*. Hemingway is tall and just misses being gangly. When a discussion comes up about exclusivist policies which are invading the American medical profession and their treatment of senior citizens I manage to slip in a reference to Maud Gonne in her old age, which tees me up to recite Yeats's poem to her *When you are old and grey and full of sleep* in my droopiest voice. A poem is a neat way of grabbing the limelight in a chat show, and a bonus this time was that Ms Hemingway was good enough to say afterwards that it had blown her mind.

11 April

Talk at Gotham Book Mart to Frances Stellof's literary group. Questions afterwards which allow some horror in the audience to stand up and call me a 'nasty Irish writer who didn't make it at home'. Not content with this he asks 'How high did you jump as a pole vaulter. Your own height?' A pox on him.

Miss Stellof's cat[†] once again waltzes around the wainscoting, trying to upstage me, but has apparently taken to the drink since I was here last, and falls off quite fluthered. Easily dealt with this time.

---

[*] Actress granddaughter of Ernest Hemingway.
[†] See 20 April 1973.

12 April

Slightly frightened-looking man on bus being gazed at by a lovely girl with an adoring look. Later Long John Nebel radio show. On air from twelve midnight to six in the morning. Has a vast listenership. Three guests sit around the microphone throughout the night and talk with Long John who hosts a phone-in. The show is unique and is held together by the presenter's extraordinary ability to create an interest in his listeners about almost anything, and to spot what will make good radio journalism. At 3.00 am a lady phones in: 'We sleep by day to wait up for you Long John.' Cokes, hamburgers, sandwiches and coffee are supplied through the night to keep us awake. At one stage there is a discussion about Irish-Americans. I say there are two types, 'bog-Irish' and 'lace curtain Irish'. Someone rings in with a third, 'cut-glass Irish', who apparently have Waterford glass on the table and real fruit in the bowls. After some character on the phone has asked: 'Long John, do you go down on dogs?' I ask the presenter does he get much of this filth. He says he does, but there is a three-second time lag, so the technician must have been asleep for this one.

I emerge in the streets a little after 6 am. Empty, except for the huge skyscrapers and the seagulls who waddle around before gridlock sets in. It is hard to believe I have spent an entire night speaking on the radio to millions of people I don't know. Hasn't taken a feather out of me. Feel chipper. Hope when I get back to the Chelsea I'll crash out. I do.

15 April

In P.J. Clarke's on Third Avenue a wide-eyed sylph from a Southern Irish suburb is attempting to defend some of the activities of the travelling people at home, pointing out that they do have a trade if one wants to make use of it. 'If you have a dent in a saucepan the tinkers will fix it.' 'Yes,' says Milton Machlin who is with me, 'but if your wallet happens to be sticking out that won't stop them from stealing it.' This is followed by his usual explosive Russian giggle.

17 April

Tonight Liam Maguire in the Lion's Head. He works for Aer Lingus in the luggage section and is over here on trade union business. I know Liam from Groome's Hotel, the Dublin late night drinking spot, where he is nearly always to be found after midnight. What is remark-able is that he lives the life of a carouser though his lower body is par-alysed from a car crash. He is now in his thirties and has retained the good looks which he had before his injury. Despite being imprisoned in a wheelchair he has become an influential trade union negotiator. Politically, he is a convinced Marxist who contains a cold fury, which occasionally erupts and then – wham! bam!

We remain good friends despite having different views on Northern Ireland and are given to ferocious arguments with each other on the subject. Later Liam asks me back to his hotel room on Fifth Avenue and 40th for a drink and Malachy McCourt, the Limerick-born film actor and radio star, joins us. These days Malachy has developed an almost patriarchal appearance with an attractive bushy fair beard and sparkling amused blue eyes. Runs a successful bar called the 'Bells of Hell' where the film actor Richard Harris spends a lot of time and has become very much a New York personality.

Once he has negotiated his wheelchair into the room Liam is an excellent host. He tells us to take what we want from the drinks cabinet. 'Isn't Aer Lingus picking up the tab?' Anyway, aren't we dis-tinguished visitors. We talk about some of the figures who drink in Groome's after hours. Charlie Haughey (who had his nose broken there), John Hume, Jim Kelly, the Belfast Republican tried and acquitted in the Arms Trial, every actor and director in the city worth his salt, and out of town ones such as Sean Connery, Robert Mitchum, Kim Novak and John Ford. Out of context I make a remark about a leader of the 'Stickies' [breakaway IRA group] which Liam takes exception to. Suddenly a titanic row erupts. Liam's argu-ment is that we have no right to campaign for a United Ireland until we have succeeded in remedying social injustice in our own part of the country. Without wishing to excuse the leaden foot of social progress, I remark that Liam's position smacks of a cop-out and takes no account of the indefensible denial of civil rights to the National-ist community in the North. Soon we are both trading clichés and yelling at each other. Suddenly Liam takes a run at me in his wheel-chair, narrowly missing, but hitting the walls as I skip aside ('Don't hit me with the wheelchair in your arms' I almost shout but don't). Catch a glimpse of Malachy's appalled face, his head bowed like a Cistercian monk at the Folies Bergère. He has clearly been long enough out of Ireland to have forgotten the way Dubliners can go about an argu-ment. It has never occurred to me not to go full-throttle against Liam simply because he is in a wheelchair. He is aware of the local rules and plays to them. With a roar to Malachy telling him that the McCourts, once a notable Ulster clan, are now totally washed out, I make a graceless exit.

As I walk back to the Chelsea Hotel I remember someone telling me that when Liam is going out of his skull from tension he will sometimes hoist his wheelchair off the footpath and join the traffic. Then his real kick is to turn and face the cars and plunge into them at full-tilt against the flow.*

24 April

Lunch with Sean Carberry of the Irish Tourist Board. A marvellous publicist who has key columnists of the New York press in the palm of his hand. While at lunch he has to keep in constant touch with a lecturer at New York University, Terry Moran, who is down with flu. (Sean stands in for him at lectures.) As he walks me back to the Chelsea, we pass a shop in the window of which there are cats hanging by their paws on trapezes.

'Swinging cats,' says our Sean.

27 April

Chelsea Hotel. George Kleinsinger has shown me a piece of music which he said is part of a score of the only musical work that

---

* Later I wrote 'Sisyphus Wins':

Call no man happy who is not dead
But of this one it must be said:
His case is not so easily analysed,
In a wheelchair and paralysed.
He's out there rolling with the traffic;
Yes, it is a little melodramatic
But the footpath's crowded with people
    walking
Which reminds him of – oh don't be
    talking.
But hey, what's happening to this bozo?
Is he going to drive against the freeflow?
He's turned his wheelchair and is facing
    out,

Christ, he's off with a mighty shout.
Arms pumping he swerves through the
    gullies,
Destabilizing commuter bullies;
Face on fire and flushed with freedom,
This is the way to make them heed him.
He's said goodbye to the dreary
    pavement,
Doesn't give a damn what the gods
    meant.
He's left them now without a function,
Himself in command at the next
    junction.

Leonardo da Vinci ever wrote. The trouble up to now is that it has been indecipherable. George, however, has read that Leonardo did mirror writing. So working with a hand-held looking glass, he thinks he has deciphered an air close to the one Leonardo thought up, and wants me to work with him to put words to it. First of all he has me lilt the tune in gobbledegook; meaningless words churned out just to catch the beat and not inhibit the flow. For some reason (connected with consonants George says) certain words are verboten. 'Pearl', 'secret', 'soar', for example. Anyway, we will work on it for a week. One thing we are firmly agreed on is that it won't be called 'The Smile'.

As I am leaving I am curious to know where George's pet skunk has gone. It turns out it bit him last month and had to be put down. I point out that the last time I was here the animal bit Doris Chase (a girlfriend of George's) twice but George says that that was different.

1 May

This is from today's *Daily News*. Marion Bermudez of Arizona State University has won her first bout in the featherweight division of the men's Golden Gloves Boxing Championship. Her opponent was so badly beaten up that he had to be helped out of the ring after the first round. Miss Bermudez had arrived with her lawyer, and though the President of the Arizona Boxing Association tried to stop her getting into the ring, he was legally out-foxed.

'What the hell could we do? We asked her to strip for the medical. I thought this would stop her, but she stripped just like the rest.'

The guy she's going to fight in the next round really has the wind-up. And so does his coach.

'My boy may quit if he loses. He was on the school wrestling team last year, and he had to wrestle with a guy with one arm and no legs, and now this.'

12 May, Dublin

Letter from Olive Reid.

PO Box 1558
Salisbury
Rhodesia

Dear Ulick

Thanks for *A Terrible Beauty is Born.** The style is so flowing.
Very necessary to myself in the sere and yellow, rather American
I feel. What a delightful book. I cannot put it down. It covers
this rather overworked subject in such a light fashion without
those endless notes, references and dry legal jargon. To me, far
better than Gogarty or Behan. Have yourself and Jonathan Cape
had a divorce? If alive, he must be a hundred. I've just finished
Jean Genet's two very way out books, all written in the nick.
Very mad but beautiful writing. A friend brought them from
Athens.

I've moved into a hotel in Salisbury where there are some
young gentlemen of diverse nationalities. One from the Emerald
Isle gave me the Sunday paper and your picture was the first thing
I clapped my eyes on. Not to be outdone, Aquinas sent me
another one from London with no caption. The one in the Irish
papers relates to the Fitzwilliam Tennis Club centenary, which
you wrote to me about.

The room I have in the hotel is that of a Somerset Maugham
novel, lacking only the fan in the centre of the ceiling. All the
rooms lead off from a balcony. You can imagine the old colonial
style. This hotel is very camp indeed. Last Wednesday I came
home about 1.30 am and heard sounds from a room opposite. It
was a gent from Germany protesting vigorously that he would
pay 'Ten dollars later on'. A dangerous speech if ever I heard one,
considering he had not one, but as it turned out, three dark ladies
in his room. I was highly amused as the night porter came up and
after much screaming got them out, sans the dollars, I would
imagine. In the struggle, however, they had lost their wigs. I
learnt later they came back this morning to collect them, as
bright as buttons. The German gent looks a little sheepish.

---

* See 21 August 1970, note.

Congratulate Bill Williams.* I can just picture him on the bench. How goes Rory O'C?† He very kindly got my old driving licence to enable me to get one here. Very good at this sort of stroke. I could not remember my address in Pembroke Lane, but he did. He tells me he is very proud of his ex-client as most of the rest did not 'make it' as he puts it. He's got something there, Deo Gratias.

15 May

Dear Olive

I was so glad to get your letter of the 20th April. As I read about Rhodesia every day in the newspapers I keep on wondering what has been happening to you. I see in tonight's paper that fifty blacks have been killed in a confrontation with the Army. It is a relief to see that you are in a position to get out when you want.

I was sorry to hear about your Great Dane, Rory. I remember the way you were totally involved with Christy Mahon.‡ He really was a little monster. I recall very clearly when I was winning an argument with you, one of the ways you avoided giving in was by talking to Christy Mahon. The little bastard would wag his tail, look up at you, delighted at the attention being paid to him, and of course you would read this as an indication that he actually understood you, and was backing you up against me. Needless to say I didn't concur.

I think I told you that Bill Williams has become a judge; but since he has become one, he's turning out to be like Lord Norbury, the eighteenth-century hanging judge at Green Street. He gave a fellow three years recently in Galway for shoplifting. The guy nearly had a hysterectomy and, of course, everybody is up in arms: while Bill is now known as 'The Butcher' on the Circuit.

Do you know that Dublin has grown to almost a million people. I wonder would you recognize some of it if you saw it now. Stephen's Green is a shambles. Where the Russell Hotel

---

* A Law Library silk who had just become a judge.
† Her Dublin solicitor.
‡ Olive Reid's sealyham when she lived in Dublin in the Fifties. See 5 October 1971, introduction.

was is now just a gaping wall and nothing has been put up in its place. From the College of Surgeons down to the Gaiety Theatre has been bought by property speculators; even the Georgian house owned by Dr Emmet, Robert's father, is under threat. They are not able to build at present, and in the meantime it has been taken over by rag-shop short leases in general filth.

The drinking here is quite abnormal. More than any other country I have been in. What I see in Dublin life with young people drunk makes New York seem like a convent. They took the breathalizer test off here about a year ago because it was found to be unconstitutional. The result was killings on the roads went up by more than 100 people. In other words it means that there must have been more than 100 drunks on the roads and, simply because the police weren't able to arrest them, they killed the unfortunate people who got in their way.

I didn't think you would be interested in my tennis book. But I shall get a copy and send it out to you. It is out of print at present. But I have asked Fitzwilliam to get you one. Needless to say, you did scent something devious in the book even from afar. Maybe it sneaked into the Rhodesian newspapers. I discovered that one of the founders of the Club was a notorious murderer. He was a man called Vere Goold, who actually reached the finals of the British Tennis Championships in 1878. He was a typical Dublin stroller who had an easy job in Dublin Castle. Most of his afternoons were spent playing tennis. Rather like my own barrister afternoons spent pole-vaulting out in Belfield when I wasn't dodging my training sessions by taking time off with you in Pembroke Road. Goold later married a rich French lady and they both went to live in Monte Carlo. There he did in some harmless Swedish heiress and was travelling around the golf clubs with her body in the trunk when he was intercepted by the police. He later died, I think, on Devil's Island. Anyway I found a very handsome portrait of him, tennis racket and all, standing in Fitzwilliam Square when the Club was founded.

Dear old Micheál* did die at last. It is quite true to say that he was dying for the last year or two. I think he could see a little to read but, certainly in public, he always had to feel his way around.

---

* Micheál MacLiammóir. See 5 March 1978.

Though heroically he did come to plays. He had a fantastic send-
off. As always the Irish adore you when you are dead. Everybody
turned out from Church and State. The President who resigned
two years ago, a really smashing guy, Cearbhall O'Dalaigh, came
up from Kerry to speak at Micheál's grave. [Alas, only three
weeks later O'Dalaigh himself died of a heart attack. He too, in
common with Micheál, had a great love of the Irish language as
well as a great heart.]

It was great to hear from Aquinas again. He seems as camp as
ever. It's nice to know he's offered you a camp too, if you need
it. I'm pretty sure though unless things get very bad in Rhodesia
you won't have to leave. That may well happen as it is what happened in Ghana and other places, in that a black majority will
take over slowly. If that happens I'm sure you won't suffer. You
were always well in with blacks in London anyway – ahem.
Seriously though, I think they should possibly regard Irish
people as different from English, especially if you play your cards
properly. I know this all sounds like hurler on the ditch advice
but I am trying to see it against the general trend of what has
happened elsewhere.

Yours
Ulick

22 May, Dublin

Books beside my bed, read in the last fortnight:

The Death and Resurrection of Mr Roche (play by Thomas Kilroy)
Woodbrook by David Thomson
Hitler's Children (about the Baader-Meinhof group)
Helter Skelter (about Charles Manson)
Irish Journey by Heinrich Böll
The Life of Lord Northcliffe by Frank Owen
Irish Love Poems in English by Sean Lucey
Ancient Irish Sagas by Eleanor Knott
Marcel Proust, volume two by George D. Painter
The plays of Ernst Toller
Evelyn Waugh and his World by David Pryce-Jones

Is reading a disease?

4 June

Nanny recalls her grandfather who fought in the Crimean War and shows me some of his campaign medals. Then the other day I learned that Annie's father was a gamekeeper on Colonel Tottenham's estate in Woodstock, Co. Wicklow. How is it one knows so little about these things. I knew it in a vague way, like shadows flickering in the nursery fire.

12 June, Belfast

This entry is an account of a visit to Belfast, accompanied by Paul O'Dwyer* and Trevor West.† We were meeting leaders of the Protestant paramilitaries there. Though it is long I have not abridged it, because of the relevance of the matters discussed to current circumstances.

Up to Belfast with Trevor West and Paul O'Dwyer. Jim Fitzpatrick‡ had sent a car for us. As we passed through the Belfast streets we saw the troops standing with their rifles at street corners. Paul remarked that they were more visible last time he was here. When we got to Fitzpatrick's office we waited for him to arrive to drive to his house. A tall elegant man with well-groomed grey hair. He drove us to his home in the professional belt of Belfast. Fine house with Victorian fenestration and tall chimneys. Big rooms. Lots of paintings by Northern artists. Paul Henry, Arthur Armstrong, Humbert Craig, William Conor. How is it that the North has produced so many of Ireland's finest painters? I noticed not one but two portraits of Thomas More, the English martyr and lawyer. A danger sign?

The Northern voice is naturally soft. Much more so than the Dublin one with its often sarcastic undertone. For instance, when Jim Fitzpatrick mentions Trevor's name it has more of a purr sound than it would have in the South, where it can sound sometimes like a neutered yelp.

Fitzpatrick had arranged for us to see Andy Tyrie, Commander of the Loyalist UDA, and he called him on the phone to check the time.

---

* President of New York City Council. Lawyer, nationally known as a civil rights figure in the USA.

† See 2 February 1970, note.

‡ Owner of the *Irish News*, the paper with the second biggest circulation in Northern Ireland. A Catholic and prominent businessman.

Mentioned my name and Trevor's. We both tried to signal to him that Andy had already met Paul but Jim politely ignored us. When he put down the phone he told us that he couldn't mention Paul O'Dwyer's name on the telephone for security reasons.

He then outlined for us the essence of the plan for an independent Ulster, which he supports. It would involve the Six Counties breaking with both the Republic of Ireland and the United Kingdom and creating a self-governing Ulster Republic. He outlined the nature of the talks that the Northern Unionist barrister, Desmond Boal QC, has been having with Sean MacBride SC. Their aim is to secure a cease-fire from both the main paramilitary organizations, the Loyalist Ulster Defence Association and the Nationalist IRA. The UDA are prepared to proceed, but the IRA are not as enthusiastic. Their military council feel they could not sell it at this time to the army, although they themselves are in favour of talks. The feeling at grass roots IRA is that if they negotiated another cease-fire it might end up in a situation where they would have gained nothing politically, and at the same time it would not be possible to reactivate the movement to the same efficiency as it has at present. Their argument is that in 1975 they negotiated a cease-fire with the British on the grounds that there would be a statement of intent by the Government to leave Northern Ireland sometime in the future. No such statement has emerged since then and the IRA feel hesitant about making any commitment in the future. The last meeting where there was an attempt to bring the parties together took place in Sean MacBride's house in Dublin on the night of last year's elections in June. It is felt, however, that Desmond Boal could now bring Paisley some part of the way with him and that a deal might be worked out with the Provisional IRA.

Jim Fitzpatrick then gave us his assessment of the Ulster Defence Association and Ulster Volunteer Force, the two main Loyalist paramilitary groups. Andy Tyrie is the commander-in-chief of the UDA and John McKeague of the UVF. [Ulster Volunteer Force]. They both have more or less the same aim, which is to provide a military campaign for a Loyalist constituency.

After this briefing we drove to an arranged meeting with John McKeague, the UVF commander, and arrived at a house in a lower middle-class area in the ground floor of which was a small printing firm. There had been two fire attacks on the house, in one of which McKeague's mother had been burned to death.

McKeague was waiting for us with Sam McClure, a UDA

Commander. McKeague was small, good-looking with pale-blue eyes. If you had met them in another context, he could have been taken for a successful Belfast businessman. Pleasant. Certainly there was no impression of a working-class killer. Yet McKeague was in charge of the UVF battalion out of which came the notorious Red Hand Gang who methodically killed Catholics on a sectarian basis. Also, he has formed a Praetorian guard of young Belfast lads who accompany him wherever he goes. He is homosexual and some of these young guerrillas, as well as being trained marksmen, are accomplished sodomites.

We were brought up to a room upstairs and introduced to his committee. One of them, George Allport, his second-in-command, looked like a retired British major. He came from Clonakilty in the South but had moved to Belfast in 1922 after the Black and Tan War (later Paul O'Dwyer said he had reservations about Allport but I didn't).

McKeague proudly showed us the flag of the new movement. It was the cross of St Patrick on a white background and in the middle the Red Hand of Ulster. He and McClure spread it out for us so that we could see its full splendour. Father Alec Reid,* the Redemptorist priest who has done a lot of fine work bringing paramilitaries of both sides together, was the next to arrive, followed by Father Desmond Wilson. Both have succeeded in securing the trust of the Protestant paramilitaries where politicians have previously failed. It is clear that the UVF men present have a high regard for them. There was a good deal of banter between the two and a warm feeling one would not have expected. It was almost as if, having been separated for so long, the two groups had discovered the existence of a specific personality and humour which as Belfast men they shared.

One of them said jokingly: 'When we have an independent Ulster we'll make sure that Father Alec will be made a Cardinal.'

Allport said to Father Desmond Wilson: 'Do you believe, Father, there should be separation between Church and State in Ireland?'

Des Wilson's reply was emphatic. 'I believe that there should have been separation between Church and State long ago. Now, don't get me angry and spoil my day.'

Allport has already been involved in negotiations with the American Congressional Committee of One Hundred and Twenty

---

* In 2001 Fr Reid remains a key figure in negotiations between the two sides in Northern Ireland.

who have asked him to address them. The Ancient Order of
Hibernians are coming over from America for their Annual General
Meeting which this summer they have decided to stage in Killarney
and the UVF may be represented there. American Hibernians form a
strong nation-wide organization with somewhat uncompromising
views on Irish nationalism. My own feeling about the Irish-American
community (having had contact with them over the last fifteen years)
is that they would be so attracted by the idea of breaking the link with
England and the prospect of an independent Ulster even though it
would not be under the jurisdiction of Dublin that they might go
along with the idea. McClure and McKeague then, between them,
outlined their policies based on documents and articles and on semi-
nars held to discuss the proposal. McKeague said that there was a
strong feeling among Loyalists that they had been constantly betrayed
by the British, and that whoever their friends were they were not to
be found in Westminster. They had also come to recognize that to a
large extent the Unionist leadership had been controlled by a group
who were not in sympathy with Protestant working-class people.
(The Unionist party is largely controlled by big business and the professional classes topped up by the landed gentry, and has exploited the
working-class Loyalist population since the founding of the statelet.)
Breaking the link with Britain could result in a shift of class power.
There had been clearly some hard-nosed thinking. President Carter's
recent offer to provide financial aid to a reformed Northern Ireland
raised their hopes. Paul, however, felt it was naive to think that
American businesses would invest in Ireland simply because Carter
had promised it. At present they needed extra industry in New York,
where he was President of the City Council, and they were now
finding it difficult to attract investment. However, it was possible that
Marshall Aid type funds might be made available to Northern Ireland
if the circumstances were favourable. His view was that if an
Independent Ulster could induce nationalists to stop looking to
Dublin, and Unionists to stop looking to Westminster, it could generate a positive impetus in the USA.

I questioned McKeague about the guarantees the minority
Nationalist population could expect under an autonomous Ulster
Parliament. He gave an interesting reply. The elections he said would
be conducted on a proportional representation basis which would
ensure a strong input from any minority party and would prevent
single party domination. The most likely form of government for

some years would be a coalition. This seemed to me to be a form of power-sharing and McKeague emphasized that's just what it would be, power-sharing under a different name but a power-sharing agreed on by Ulstermen themselves and not from an outside source. Progress could be made through referendums. Alec Reid felt that if a referendum was to be taken it would have to be put to the 32 Counties to see if it would be acceptable to them. In such circumstances Alec felt that the Provisionals could find common cause with the proposal. McClure added that in his view the recent statement by Roy Mason (Secretary of State for Northern Ireland) that the Provisionals were beaten was a stupid one, as well as being unhelpful.

As we went downstairs Alec Reid thanked us for coming along. 'Well, it's all in the hands of God.' I made an appointment to see Des Wilson later on in Dublin that month. Before I left I had a good chat with McKeague. I found we had a mutual admiration for Jimmy Young, the Belfast comedian who can make Ulstermen of all backgrounds laugh at their own shortcomings.

George Allport then drove us down to the Park Hotel. When we were going in two toughs in black jackets passed us on the way out. Inside there was a smallish heavily built man sitting down waiting for us. He had a moustache, dark glasses (through which you could see blue eyes), olive skin and black hair. This was Andy Tyrie, the legendary Commander of the UDA. He was with a small fellow whose name I didn't get but who was clearly a minder. Tyrie brought us upstairs, to a room which looked like a private one in a pub. I wondered if any of our hosts had guns on them for protection (Trevor told me later that that is why they wear leather jackets, because they can hide the guns under them. Jim Fitzpatrick carries a gun for safety and has taken shooting lessons.) It's rather humbling to think that in Belfast, all these people have been going around for years with their lives at risk while down South we simply don't have an idea of the fearful dangers to life and limb in Northern Ireland. After all, only two years ago John McKeague was shooting Catholics (innocent ones) for no other reason than that of religion. Yet when we meet him now he turns out to be a bright, interesting human being.

Andy Tyrie told us that in a period of two years he had travelled a long way and had come to recognize that there was a built-in system of social injustice in the Northern Ireland state which affected both the Loyalist and Nationalist communities. He felt that some of his followers had come to this conclusion and could accept the proposals for an Independent Ulster. He said he would like to make a propaganda film to be shown to his commanders which would explain to them the advantages of such a solution. He thought that if Ulster became independent (and McKeague had agreed on this) it could become a wealthy state. They were looking these days at the South and were impressed with how the resources available were being used as a springboard for international investment. Paul pointed out that there were 4000 people employed at the Asahi plant in County Mayo. Tyrie spoke of many Ulster people's fear that if they were governed from the South they might never get their full pension.*

He added that the proposal would contain the same built-in protections for minorities that the American system did. He is in favour of an elected President à la United States. He told us that the UDA committee at present were studying various constitutions including those of America and France. They had recently been contacted by the French Consul here after he had seen them on television, who had offered to help with any information they might require about the constitution of the Republic of France. Paul asked Andy Tyrie about his telegram to Senator Edward Kennedy asking him to come to Northern Ireland to get an overall view of the situation there. Tyrie said that he understood very well how Ted Kennedy might not have been impressed by this if he had read about it in the newspapers without his having previously been in touch with him. No matter how vague their intentions may be, it is interesting and to an extent encouraging that both Tyrie and McKeague are looking to America for a solution rather than to Britain. Tyrie, in fact, claimed he was disenchanted with the British in relation to their handling of Northern Ireland, saying they had told so many lies to the paramilitaries that they could no longer be relied on. On the other hand, he did believe Jack Lynch when the Irish Taoiseach said he had secured from Jim Callaghan a guarantee against total integration into the UK. Lynch was regarded by Tyrie as an honest man. Tyrie claimed that there had been changes in UDA policy. Under his and some others' influence sectarian killing had stopped and, no matter how the war went, it would be between soldier and soldier. When asked for a reason why an independent Ulster State should not fall into the hands of Loyalist extremists and result in a regime even more extreme than the Stormont one, he replied:

---

* The Southern economy at this time was not as strong as that of the UK.

'The South are on our border. If the British were gone we would have to behave ourselves. Also the essential financial aid coming from the United States and Europe would literally depend on the capacity of a new Northern State to function without limiting Civil Rights in any way.'

They were working on a discussion paper on the subject. They hoped Paul could get circulation for it in the United States when it was finished. Paul replied that any such document would have to be submitted to the raw and perhaps inhibited scrutiny of the UDA soldiers before it could have an effect. Glen Barr, the Derry politician, could act as a middle man. Tyrie was hoping Barr might get him onto a course at Harvard on constitutional law so that his knowhow would not be suspect at grass roots level. They wanted to develop their own political ideas in consultation with the paramilitaries themselves and put an end to war. They were reluctant to take on board too many abstract theories.

One thing they did want was a constitution for the new state. In discussion groups while interned in Long Kesh they had recognized the necessity for this.

Paul replied that if UDA representatives came to New York, he would provide lawyers to work with them on a constitution for an Independent Ulster. [Some months later Andy Tyrie and John MacMichael went to New York, and working with legal experts provided by Paul, did indeed draft a constitution for what they hoped would be an independent Ulster State.]

Next thing a sweet old lady, very tiny, came in with cups of tea. She winked knowingly at Andy Tyrie. It turned out that some weeks previously she had been giving out hell about the paramilitaries to Mairead Corrigan of the peace movement without knowing that it was Tyrie who was standing beside her. Tyrie told us this with great good humour and then remarked that the only way she could make it up to him was by marrying him, and the reason she wasn't likely to was that women were too selfish and just took men's pay packets. She replied that a woman she knew had been deserted by her husband and had brought up her four sons and educated them. After 25 years the husband turned up and she took him back. Paul remarked amid laughter that it was a shrewd move by the wife for the husband was now in a position where his life depended on a household of which she was totally in control. As I looked around the laughing faces I thought, here were two Northern Ireland Protestants, a Dublin Catholic, a

Cork Protestant, a Mayo American and a Protestant Belfast working woman all joking with one another, because we had in common an Irish sense of humour and the levelling of class consciousness that it can bring about.

15 June, Dublin

Visited Kathleen Behan* at Sybil Hill, a splendid home for the old, run by American nuns in Raheny, a suburb of Dublin's northside. I wanted to ask about a painting of her by Sarah Purser, a fine Irish painter of the 1890s and first half of the twentieth century, who had used Kathleen as a model. I had hoped to identify the painting and had brought Kathleen some photographs of portraits by Purser. Kathleen remembered Sarah Purser as rather cross and

'like Madame Markiewicz not at ease with ordinary people. Madame Gonne [Maud Gonne] was the opposite when I worked for her as a receptionist – very nice.

'I got five shillings for posing for Sarah Purser. Mrs Tom Clarke [wife of the executed Tom Clarke, signatory of the 1916 proclamation] told me that in prison Madame Markiewicz and Maude Gonne were always talking about bloodshed.

'There were a lot of ladies like them – upper class in prison with us. Madames, they called themselves inside at the time, and they used to have their own parties, which they got working-class girls to prepare. One Halloween, Lizzie Twigg, who was in the fourth battalion of Cumann na mBan [the Women's IRA], got fed up laying out the barmbrack and sweets for the Madames and ate the whole lot herself. Oh there was a terrific row.'

Now for the moment; I showed Kathleen a photograph of the Sarah Purser painting which I thought might be of her. I knew she'd say yes or no, as she had rejected two previous ones I had fetched up. This was a painting of a beautiful young girl, eyes half-closed, which could have come out of a good Paris studio at the turn of the century.

'That's me,' she said simply.

Mission accomplished.

---

* Brendan Behan's mother. See 17 July 1970, note.

22 June

Eason's. Signing session for a new paperback edition of the Brendan Behan biography. Middle-aged lady comes up. Obviously wants to lay her egg.

'I know things you don't know. I knew them that knew Mattie Harris,* your Grandfather.'

'Great-grandfather,' I say tersely.

A bit too sharp perhaps, as she didn't buy a book and is just coming out with the familiar stance of some Irish people to tell me she knows more than I do (when in fact she probably knows nothing at all), and then decides to depart with a conspiratorial look.

Another eccentric country girl says with wild eyes, 'You're a lovely handsome Irish gentleman and I am trembling to be near you.'

Then John Cowley the actor comes in with his dotey little wife, Annie who is a star in *The Riordans*, a TV soap, and was once married to Louis Dalton, the playwright and actor who holds a record at the Abbey for the longest run of a play (*This Other Eden*). She has a good luck message from Chris O'Neill who manages some of my work and who is a star in the soap. I ask her if Chris is as thin as ever.

'Chris O'Neill,' says Annie, 'has as much flesh on him as would be left on a tinker's stick after a beating.'

7 July, Co. Clare

Sean White† drives me to Ballyvaughan, Co. Clare. Fine Stations of the Cross in the church by Sean O'Sullivan RHA in pastel, and stained glass windows by A.E. Child. Then to Laban Church built by Lady Gregory. W.A. Scott designed the local school at her invitation in 1892. This is Irish Literary Renaissance land and Edward Martyn lived nearby at Tulira Castle in the next county to his cousin George Moore. I have come to visit Count de Basterot's grave at nearby Duras. This strange man was a contemporary of Proust, the Goncourt brothers and Huysmans in Paris but chose to live part of his year here. He had an Irish connection with the Lynch family through whom he was related to Edward Martyn. [Martyn, who lived nearby at Tulira Castle,

---

* Matt Harris, MP for East Galway. Also on the Supreme Council of the Irish Republican Brotherhood. Responsible with Michael Davitt for promoting the New Departure, which brought the Physical Force movement into the political arena in 1879 under Parnell.

† Professor Sean White, by now Director of the College for Irish Studies.

was passionately interested in drama and it was his money that funded the Irish Literary Theatre which later became the Abbey Theatre.] De Basterot's summer villa stands in a clearing at the edge of a harsh stony beach, relieved only by the dancing sea light. It was in this villa that Yeats and Lady Gregory, on a visit to Edward Martyn, conceived the plan for a national theatre. This plan would create a 'quick forge and working house' for John Millington Synge, Lennox Robinson, Padraic Colum and Sean O'Casey as well as Yeats and Lady Gregory.

In the graveyard we locate a huge vault in which de Basterot is buried and which, in French fashion, has a lengthy family pedigree inscribed on it. One ponders on why this French intellectual should have chosen to live between Paris and this wind-blown isthmus nearly one hundred years ago. Suddenly a very old man seems to have materialized beside us. He tells us that he knew 'the Count' in his old age when he was confined to a wheelchair. When we ask what was the nature of the illness, he lowers his eyes and tells us it was brought on by 'sexual excess'. Then he conjures up another figure from the past: the Count's companion, whom he refers to as 'Budget', who took him out for jaunts in his wheelchair.

'Budget killed the Count – poisoned him. At the funeral the horses refused to pull the coffin until Budget left the church.'

Sean and I are mystified. Who could 'Budget' possibly be? Then it struck me that Paul Bourget, the French novelist, was a regular visitor to De Basterot's home at Duras. Bourget? Budget? Could it be that an icon of the Paris right had polished off our eccentric Count?

23 July, Dublin

Rather cold. So boring. Hard to get to grips with work. Maybe I should have canalized my energies into one form – poetry perhaps. All you want is pen and paper beside you until your poem is finished. With me these days it takes me hours to get all my books and 'tartels' (as Nanny calls them) together before I can even begin on plays and biographies.

21 August, Leixlip

Charles Lysaght* drives me to Leixlip for dinner. It's Mariga's invitation. I'm not sure what the relationship is at present between her and

---

* See 13 August 1972.

Desmond. With regard to friends, I shift my mind into neutral whenever there is a marital dispute. It's not just that it's a matter between
themselves, it's that they are the only people who can even remotely
understand the chemistry involved.

Dinner in the library. Of course the right place to have it, why
didn't one think of it before. Among the party of ten is John Jolliffe,*
whom I met seventeen years ago, when he came to Ireland encouraged by Mariga, and having got a whiff of Georgeenianism, was
forever held enthralled. Jolliffe has a vivid recollection of barely
getting his bags unpacked before finding himself wafted to the Gate
Theatre by Mariga and myself. Micheál MacLiammóir was playing in
The Importance of Being Oscar, and we'd insisted that Jolliffe see this
fine production before it went to Australia. Much to his surprise he
found himself, shortly after the play ended, walking up one of the
Dublin mountains to the Hellfire Club. As he puffed along in our
wake, he has a memory of Mariga being amused at my comment that
the colonial experience has made the English adept at adapting lifestyles, and at how well he was able to keep up with our 'goat-like
steps'.

'It was so exhilarating to see the twinkling panorama of the lights
of Dublin spread out far below, with the wonderful spring smell of
new grass and thyme.'

I had told him I wasn't sure how long that 'panorama' was going to
last.

'"We have heard the chimes at midnight," Sir John. In a few years
you will be more likely to smell car exhausts than thyme at the Hellfire
Club and find the city floodlit below you. Sally is gone from
Ha'nacker Hill, and from what I can see she ain't a-comin' back.'

> Wind and Thistle for pipe and dancers,
> And never a ploughman under the sun.
> Never a ploughman. Never a one.'

25 August, Dublin

Today get confirmation that the Japanese business community here
will sponsor the production of Noh plays of mine. They will be presented at the Dublin International Theatre Festival in October. Ring

---

* Hon. John Jolliffe, author and publisher, born 1933.

James Flannery, the director, in Atlanta, Georgia, telling him that everything is on target for rehearsals at the end of September.

6 September

James Flannery and myself meet the composer, Archie Potter, to discuss a score for my Noh play* *Deirdre*. Potter has piercing blue eyes and the pale complexion of an alcoholic off the drink. He speaks in incredibly long paragraphs which can evolve into declamatory orations. For instance when I emphasized to him that to meet the rehearsal schedule (which includes dance, mime and chorus) his musical score would definitely have to be ready before the 5th of October, he perhaps thinking I was implying unreliability because of his 'habit' took offence, paused for a second and then embarked on a reply, delivered in the quiet voice of a Mafia chief directing a gin run. At first it seemed that what he was talking about had no relevance, but as he reached his peroration his meaning came into place with the snap of a sprung trap as he finally captured what he wanted to say.

'When Talleyrand chose Neukomm to write the anthem for the opening of the Congress of Vienna, he knew that he was by no means the best composer available. After all, Beethoven would be present at the first meeting of that Congress, the patron of which was a Russian Count whose name means the same in Russian as mine in Irish. Admittedly, Haydn was dead but Schubert was still alive. Yet it was the lesser musician, Neukomm (who later went to America and achieved unremembered fame) that Talleyrand, always a perfectionist, chose to compose the anthem which opened the Congress. Why? Because he knew that Neukomm would deliver on time. So do I.'

---

* My Noh plays were the first in English since Yeats wrote *The Only Jealousy of Emer* and *The Dreaming of the Bones* in 1919. The Noh play, which combines verse with chorus, music, dance and mask, anticipates what in the second half of the twentieth century became known as 'total theatre'.

Unlike the Greek plays, Noh drama contains no plot or movement of character to achieve catharsis. Its object as a dramatic form is to create a mood in the audience which is connected with the Buddhist belief in reincarnation and *satori* (enlightenment). It is difficult to define precisely the trance-like state which the Japanese Noh playwrights sought to induce and which they called *yūgen*. But the sixteenth-century dramatist Seami gives this description: 'To watch the sun sink behind a flower-clad hill, to wander on and on in a huge forest with no thought of return, to stand upon the shore and gaze after a boat that goes hid by far-off islands, to ponder on the journey of wild geese lost among the clouds.'

The next three weeks were taken up with rehearsals for the Noh plays.

25 September

One of the new difficulties in trying to stage a Noh play is that it is impossible to implement the choreography required unless the actor has begun to learn it at a very young age. However, I have brought over Ms Sachiyo Ito, a Japanese choreographer who trained in Tokyo, to teach the cast the rudiments of Noh dance. The actors have been chosen for their ability to move. It is an exciting experience to see hints of the form overtaking the actors. We are using an orchestra of bodhrans [Irish drums] and tin whistles to replace the Japanese drums and flutes, which form the orchestra for Noh in Japan.

At rehearsals, Sachiyo makes the actors clean the floor every day, as Noh is a form of religious ceremony and the performing area must be spotlessly clean. You can see actresses sitting in the lotus position. Others moving across the room as if they were floating on water.

28 September

How these days have passed. The smell of onions and macrobiotics in the Golden Dawn.* Going in daily, listening to the different groups chanting, dancing, acting. Sachiyo cleaning the floor in subdued fury, when some newcomer has trodden on it without taking shoes off. Christopher Casson† is fascinated by the Noh movements that Sachiyo demonstrates and the mystical content of the art. I sometimes find him in a corner rehearsing a movement on his own. Classical profile in repose when kneeling. First run-through of show.

Martin Dempsey's powerful baritone voice moves everyone when as Sir Roger Casement in the Noh play *Submarine* he leaves the ship to set foot in his beloved Ireland. The electronic score by Jolyon Jackson conveys the sound of the submarine (which had brought Casement from Bremerhaven to Ireland) submerging to the seabed in a series of pings, pongs and gurgles which gradually turn into the sound of the Irish uillean pipes as Casement wades through the surf

---

* We rehearsed on the spacious top floor of this vegetarian emporium in Eustace Street.

† Gate Theatre actor, son of Dame Sybil Thorndike and the actor Sir Lewis Casson.

to the Irish shore. Occasionally we hear other electronic pings which now become the song of skylarks soaring in the sky.*

7 October

Opening night at the Edmund Burke Theatre for the Dublin Theatre Festival. House full. At end, there is no clapping. Silence. Is this as it should be? Trance. However, I am relieved when a form of clapping breaks out like wind blowing through the leaves. Sean MacBride here, whose mother played the part of Cathleen ni Houlihan in the first dream plays written by Yeats presented by the Abbey Theatre in 1901. Mentions that he knew Frank Ryan and Sean Russell, the protagonists in *Submarine*. They were under his command when he was Chief of Staff of the IRA.

Mariga sits on her own at the back. Is impressed. 'How nice to actually understand what the actors are saying for a change. I was born in Japan and Mama used to bring me along to Noh plays. She would give me an idea of what was going on but that's all. It's very clever of you.'†

27 October

Drinking with sports writer on *Irish Times*, Paddy Downey, whom I meet at the Arts Club. We are discussing Maud Gonne's beauty. He says tentatively with some shyness, 'Had she not large hands that were not beautiful?'

---

* Later when the plays were in performance Christopher Casson said that this scene ranked among four great moments in theatre he had seen:

'The final entry of Roger Casement in *Submarine* when I played in the Chorus provided that perfect combination which gives you an eternal quality where you don't think of going anywhere, a point which covers the whole district of time. The larks are singing as Casement lands on the shore and there is very beautiful music by Jolyon Jackson. The other scenes that gave me this sort of moment were my mother as Hecuba in *The Trojan War*, Ernest Milton in *Timon of Athens* and Anew McMaster as *Oedipus Rex* in his last entrance.'
† I never knew till this night that Mariga had been born in Japan. But then I never knew till a long time after I met her that she spoke five languages fluently or that she was a princess and the great-grand-niece of Elizabeth, Empress of Austria. Once after she'd introduced her father to me I asked her what he did. 'Oh, he's a car salesman,' she replied. (Prince Albrecht von Urach at that time had cousins on the throne of Bavaria, Saxony, England and Monaco). This was not reverse snobbery. It simply was that Mariga was without a defined sense of class distinction. She used to say 'As a socialist I believe that not everybody has the same talents and so we have to pool our resources.'

2 November

Lunch with Sean MacBride. MacBride who has recently done a magnificent job for the UN in setting up the Namibian State is not optimistic about the situation in Northern Ireland. I say while it's not a perfect parallel nevertheless the similarities between the situation now and that in 1914 are alarming. In 1914 John Redmond, a patriotic Irishman,* lost the leadership of Nationalist Ireland when after he had been betrayed by the postponement of the enacted Home Rule Bill, he tried to conciliate Parliament by committing Ireland to the Allied cause. My point is that Hume is in a not dissimilar position, as his party supported the constitutional campaign leading to the Sunningdale Agreement which fell apart when the British Government failed to confront Unionist thuggery.

Meet John Hume by chance in the Arts Club in the evening. I mention the 'Redmond' dilemma that I talked about with Sean MacBride. It's clear that John is not unaware of the dangers underlying the Northern situation if the present trend is not contained. He agrees that internment is counterproductive. I refer to it in conversation as 'the camps' and this gives him an idea. He says the term 'camps' is emotive and intends to use it in future in hopes that it will suggest other camps – Auschwitz, Dachau etc.

7 November

At the Olympia Theatre to see Julian Beck and Judith Molina with their Living Theatre. Tonight they do their version of Euripides' *Alcestis*. A number of the cast come on stage stark naked. What's more, they occasionally leave the stage and sit among the audience. One choleric Colonel Blimp in front of me nearly has a fit when a beautiful girl with flowing fair hair but without a stitch on her sits on his knee. 'If you don't desist and go, I'll call the police,' he shrieks at the young lady who nevertheless continues to stroke the hair on the back of his head.

10 November

Meet Judith and Julian in the Shelbourne for tea. Taut ascetic faces. Despite the lechery with which they are associated, they have more

---

* Leader of the Irish Party at Westminster.

the appearance of medieval mendicants than licentious actors, as is often the case with those who try to rid the world of cant.

9 December

Leixlip Castle. Mariga Guinness a little tipsy. She keeps beseeching Constantine Fitzgibbon not to hit me. Considering he's fluthered too, it's most unlikely that he'll do so. But even if he does, he probably won't land a punch. He's writing a book about the Salem witches he tells us. I suggest 'Miller's Daughter' for a title.

Arts Club later. Conversation with the artist, Paddy Collins.*

Collins: 'We are tyrannized by our art.'
Me: 'We are happy slaves.'
Collins: 'We have to do it.'
Me: 'We refuse to do anything else.'

Collins tells me that he ate slugs and snails for a while when he was penniless, then talks with extraordinary relish about a rabbit he killed and ate. Maybe he was so used to slugs and snails that rabbit made a gourmet dish. When he was a young man, he was stuck in Wexford town without the price of a pint. He often slept in the railway station.

10 December, Dublin

Walking home from Dobbin's Restaurant about 10.30 pm. Go up by Baggot Street [a long wide Georgian street leading into Stephen's Green]. Peggy Gilmartin is standing looking out under the Georgian portico of her house. One of the most beautiful women I've ever seen is Peggy. When I was a boy I could never understand why she wasn't a world-famous film star. She and her husband Tommy are among the last of the medical specialists to live in these fine Georgian streets. She asks me in for a drink saying Tommy is upstairs. House wonderful. Plaster ceiling work by Michael Stapleton, walls packed with paintings by J. Arthur O'Connor, Augustus John, Orpen. Tommy says it was my father who persuaded him to take up the presidency of the

* Winner of the national award of the Guggenheim Award Exhibition (1958). In 1984 he was made a 'Saoi' ('Wise Man') by Aosdana, the Academy of Irish artists, writers and musicians. This is the highest honour Aosdana can confer.

Royal College of Surgeons Association. When he didn't leap into the gap and another less desirable candidate was about to take the post Daddy met him one day and said 'I won't speak to you again if you don't take it.' We talk about a well-known four ball at Portmarnock Golf Club, Jack Coolican, Mick Burke, Paul Murray and Daddy. Coolican, who was club wit, once told Tommy about a patient who complained of impotence but nevertheless could achieve in a solo performance what he referred to as 'ten orgasms a day'. 'You'd envy a fellow like that, wouldn't you?'

Lots of chat. Tommy tells me that when he was putting Micheál MacLiammóir under anaesthetic, the actor always insisted on keeping his make-up and toupee on during the operation. Peggie comes up with an even better one about Norman Scott, Jeremy Thorpe's erstwhile love, who was well known in Baggot Street. He had a flat opposite the Dail (where he was said to have carried on a relationship with a prominent member of an Irish political party) and circulated in the coffee shops and pubs. She said Scott was good-looking enough but was always whingeing 'No one loves me' and would hover around her offering to carry her groceries home. He had a crush on Dara O'Loughlin, a handsome young jazz player, who wasn't interested and once threw a plate of food at him in Mrs Guy's restaurant.

1980–1981

Arrive at Chelsea Hotel. Bump into George [Kleinsinger]* in – guess where – the elevator. He's accompanied by a beautiful girl in her twenties, tall, slim, fit and with raven-black hair. Looking at her with his white teeth shining in a dazzling smile, George says:

'My new wife, isn't she beautiful?'

'Yes, indeed, when did you marry her, George?'

'I don't remember.'

They've just come back from swimming together in the YMCA across the road. She tells me she talks to herself under the water. Also they take a reefer or two before they get in to swim.

'I took mescaline on Fire Island before I knew you,' she says to George.

'Such a time does not exist,' replies he, smiling seraphically.

At present George (sixty-three) has hurt his leg so he can't play tennis. He should have limped from the lift but it would be a not inaccurate account of his leaving it to say that he floated out, wafted on the arm of his nymph.

When I go down to see Stanley Bard [the Chelsea owner] in his office, he is agog.

'Isn't that something?'

'How long have they been married?'

'Two months. He can barely make it down the stairs every morning. It'll kill him.'

Stanley tells me that my friend Roderick Ghuika† has died. Roddy was a fine sculptor who, though he was educated at Eton and Oxford and his father was Crown Prince of Romania, hadn't a tosser. The Chelsea, as for others, had become a womb where he could hide when he was hard-up. He used to sleep in other people's rooms and when his credit ran out, he would take off till things got better. This time, though, he hopped the twig before he could come back. Stanley,

---

* See 22 June 1971, note.

† See 24 June 1971.

who is a totally decent human being, is dismayed that Roddy didn't ring him because he would have let him have his room back. Now he believes the poor guy just hadn't the price of a phone call.

17 March

St Patrick's Day parade. At the Irish Tourist Board's headquarters on Fifth Avenue, we have breakfast, bacon and eggs, black pudding, soda bread and tea. This is an 'Ulster Fry', a dish peculiar to Ireland's fourth province.

The St Patrick's parade takes eight hours to pass the reviewing stand and I have no intention of seeing the last band pass. I take off to play squash at the Racquet Club with Carl de Gersdorff whose family have been here so long they still own slices of Manhattan. My horror, then, as we go down Park Avenue to see a creature approaching us in a green Derby hat and swallow-tailed coat and with a face that would not have been out of place in a Punch cartoon. He greets us with a knowing wink to establish a spurious intimacy and raises the whiskey bottle he is holding to his mouth to take a gigantic swallow. When he's recovered his breath, he looks at us sadly, points to the depleted bottle and says, 'Each man kills the thing he loves.' As we walk into the Racquet Club, I say to Carl: 'You know that's from Oscar Wilde's poem *The Ballad of Reading Gaol*.' He didn't know, but it put the Emerald Isle back in perspective and the spring back in my stride.

At seven o'clock to the Players Club for the St Patrick's Day dinner, in its splendid building in Gramercy Park. The Club was founded by Edwin Booth, the doyen of American nineteenth-century actors, and is the equivalent of the Savage Club in London or the United Arts in Dublin. I am filling a gap that has come at the last moment in the St Patrick's night programme because Art Carney, the Broadway star who was scheduled to make the key-note presentation, has been taken ill. Martin Gable, President of the Club, has asked me to stand in. Of course, it's going to spoil my evening, but Martin's wife, TV chat show host Virginia Graham, has been awfully decent to me and I owe her a few. But this audience! Showbiz people and actors make the worst audiences for an after-dinner speech. There's nothing they don't know about timing and, if your internal watch is off, boy do they give you the mitt.

I kick off with a few Behan one-liners, going so fast they don't have time not to laugh and then suddenly, click! I'm in. A matter of luck.

When chemistries meet, you're on your bicycle. They have to come to you in spite of themselves. But if a gap grows, it takes a lot to close it, and once you start trying to make them laugh, you're already in the mulligatawny. When I have done, a gentleman who looks vaguely Chinese stands up and says approvingly:

'Follow that, Art Carney.'

Surely I've seen him before. It turns out he is Warner Oland, the Russian-born movie star who became world-famous as the Chinese detective Charlie Chan. He tells me his father built the Manchurian Railway and he grew up with a governess who used to read him Dostoevsky.

20 March, New Orleans

A trip to talk to the Ladies' Club of Audubon Park. Managed to take the morning off in the French Quarter, sunk in the past under beautiful balconies of wrought iron, recently shined up and painted. Went into a second-hand bookshop on the quays and found a play by Rabindranath Tagore, whose plays influenced Yeats. Also a book by Ernest Rhys, fin-de-siècle poet which includes reminiscences of Ernest Dowson, Francis Thompson, Aubrey Beardsley and Oscar Wilde. Munch! Munch! I'll have a good read in the plane which is two hours in the air before it reaches New York. Should we judge cities by their second-hand bookshops?

I visited the United States in spring 1980 for rehearsals of the three Noh plays The Grand Inquisitor, Submarine *and* Deirdre *which had been premièred at the Dublin International Theatre Festival in 1978. I have dealt with this event in some detail under that year, and have therefore kept the account of the New York production to a minimum. The US première was presented by Jean Erdman at the Theatre of the Open Eye on 82nd Street.*

Jean had pioneered modern theatre in New York for three decades and won a Tony award in 1962 with a stage adaptation of Joyce's Finnegans Wake *entitled* The Coach with the Six Insides. *Herself a celebrated dancer, Jean found that Yeats's verse plays written after the Noh fashion were suited to her vision of total theatre which was to bring masks, music, dance, chorus and verse together on the stage as drama. It was not certain however what New York audiences would make of* Deirdre, *a tale from the fifth century BC, and* Submarine, *a play about the return of Sir Roger Casement from Germany in 1916, both performed in a style deriving from sixteenth-century classical Japanese drama.*

5 April, New York

Casting today. I see a strange sight outside the rehearsal room. The corridors are filled with people, some sitting on the floor, like refugees in a famine relief centre. This is what is called here the 'cattle call'. (There are more unemployed actors in New York than in any other city in the world.) As soon as it is known that auditions for a new play are being held, Equity members flock to the spot. Michael J. Pollard, a friend who has won an Oscar for his supporting role in *Bonnie and Clyde*, is here. At the auditions when the director asks why he wants to work in this production. Michael replies with his slightly vacant grin:

'Because I like Yeats's poetry and [pause] I like Ulick.'

For whatever reason, a number of actors have chosen for their audition piece the opening speech from *Richard III*. As one after another comes in and assumes the familiar hump, the thought runs through my mind, should this be called the 'camel call'. One of the last to come in is a young thing who does some mime lying on the floor writhing snake-like and fanning out her arms. When asked what it is she is representing she replies, with a slightly indignant look as if we should have known:

'A poem, of course.'

'Yes, but which one?'

'*The Song of Wandering Aengus*. Yeats.'

'Wow!!!'

20 April

Jolyon Jackson, the young Dublin composer who has written the electronic score for *Submarine*, is enjoying himself here no end. He's quite frail but he's a wow with the girls. I thought they'd be put off by his shyness and very upper-class accent. Not at all. 'Gee, I'm crazy about him, he's like a little leprechaun. Such a pixie' is what you hear from some of the beautiful girls who are working on the play. I'm pleased for Jolyon, whom I made some effort to bring over here, knowing how much contact with the New York musical scene would mean to him. He has Hodgkin's disease, a form of leukaemia, and has to undergo therapy every three months or so.

4 May

Ran today at the New York Athletic Club. The indoor running track is useful for fitness, though ten laps to the mile is tedious. Taxi-driver who brings me home is a Dublin aficionado. Though not Irish he learned a lot about us from Irish maids in the house where he grew up on Rhode Island. He has lived in Dublin for a while and been most impressed by an Electricity Supply Board guy he got to know there, who lived in a company bungalow. There was a greenhouse in the garden which your man wired up to the free electricity and grew enough marijuana to have got half the country stoned.

9 May

Opening Night. Three curtain calls, though I'm not sure what this means, especially in a Noh play where the audience are expected to sit stunned at the end, having hopefully glimpsed eternity in a flash. Malachy McCourt [New York chat show host] says 'serenity and intensity'. Joseph Campbell the anthropologist[*], John Cage[†], and Donald Keane, an academic who specializes in the Noh, are not, I think, displeased. We go over afterwards for dinner to the Witches' Hut in German Town, about three blocks away. Sit next to Joseph Campbell who is much in the public eye at present. He has recently presented a television series, broadcast on the National networks, entitled *The Hero in Man* in which he traces the heroic personality through Ulysses and Cuchulain down to Siegfried and Roland. He tells me his four books of mythology will be reviewed by J.K. Galbraith next month in the *New York Times*. He's not without his enemies, though. I am to look out for a review by Max Lerner which

---

[*] Husband of Jean Erdman and a director of the Theatre of the Open Eye. I had been a Joseph Campbell fan for years. He was the co-author of *A Skeleton's Key to Finnegans Wake*, which in 1944 (four years after Joyce's work was published) provided a guide to the Joycean labyrinth. More than half a century later, it is still the best analysis of *Finnegans Wake* there is. It is remarkable how accurately he and Henry Morton Robinson identified the structure of the work without any hints to guide them. Campbell reminded me he was after all an anthropologist and Joyce intended his hero, Humphrey Chimpden Earwicker (Here Comes Everyone), to be a universal figure, transcending time, race and religious belief. Some search.

[†] Composer, who once presented a new work by coming onstage and opening his hand from which a butterfly emerged. The audience were expected to listen to the sound of the wings.

will be a tough one, and he's been dodging his editor at Dartmouth Press for some time for the same reason.

11 May, leaving New York

Trunks packed for the quays where the *Queen Elizabeth II* is berthed. Instead of flying home I have worked a wheeze with the Cunard Line to give me a free trip, first class and a state room, in return for a performance of my Brendan Behan one man show. They have an excellent theatre on board, in which the ship's resident professional company present plays by Noël Coward, Terence Rattigan, Alan Ayckbourn and the like. I've also managed to have my performance scheduled for the first night of the trip so it means I'll have the show over with before we are out in mid-ocean and can relax. Delightful state room. Plenty of space. Already waves of release are flooding my limbs. First thing, I look to find where the gym and swimming pool are. Feels exciting to have both within a few yards of your door. The *QE2* is enormous. I can run round the deck five laps to the mile.

After lunch a girl hoves to. American. Anne Marie Payne is her name. She knows a lot of the crowd in the Gotham Book Mart* and has read some things of mine. Also can quote Pushkin in Russian. Play table tennis with her. Then walk on deck. Lots of gossip about Gotham. Knows Andreas Brown, the boss, and maintains there is a gay clientele upstairs in the bookshop. I wouldn't be surprised; though Frances Stellof still owns the shop and says she is leaving it to a Hebrew university. Anne Marie tells me that when she was younger, for about six months she did the gay scene with the bookshop boys. But lesbians began to bore her and she returned to the fold.

14 May, QE2

Interesting French girl walking on deck. Tells me her husband writes operettas but she doesn't like the world of the stage. She has read Gautier, Céline, Apollinaire. Admires the actor Pierre Fresnay and surprisingly, Robert Brasillach, the poet who was condemned to death in 1945 after his trial as a collaborator. He was a fine poet and it's good to meet an admirer of his, who can separate art from politics.

---

* See 20 April 1973.

15 May

Last day on board. I feel as if my head has been dusted and swept. We haven't had newspapers for five days. In that time I haven't been near a telephone. I've decided to get a taxi from Southampton to Exeter from where I can fly to Dublin in forty minutes.

7 September, Dublin

Tonight at the Arts Club, Barney Mulligan* (seventy-five) tells me he leaves the club most nights about 1.30 am and goes home 'by rail'. I am puzzled by this as he lives just five doors up the street. But what Barney means to convey is that he feels his way along the railings of Fitzwilliam Street until he reaches his house. No matter how spifflicated he may be, this method ensures that he can be in bed a few minutes after he has left the club bar. The only difficulty is that if a gate is left open Barney can take a header down the basement steps. But he claims the hard stuff relaxes him so that he has never been hurt yet in a fall. In fact, he's been known to give a running commentary on his descent as he tumbles down. Barney maintains he perfected this technique in the London squares when he was a civil servant there in the Twenties.

Quite a figure our Barney was then in the acting world. He tells a ripping tale about the impresario J.B. (Jack) Fagan and Sean O'Casey during the rehearsals for the London première of O'Casey's *The Plough and the Stars* at the Fortune Theatre in which Barney was playing the part of Needle Nugent. Eileen Carey, a beautiful model and actress, had been brought in at short notice to replace Kathleen O'Regan as Norah Clitheroe and was rehearsing with the cast, O'Casey and Fagan watching from the auditorium. Barney overheard Fagan say after some time:

'It's no good, she won't do.'

'She'll have to do,' said O'Casey.

'You're letting your heart rule your head, Sean,' Fagan told him.

'It's not my heart that's ruling me Jack, it's me balls.'

Sarah Allgood, who was playing Bessie Burgess, exited in high dudgeon, though her sister Molly, a harum-scarum, who had been

---

* Dublin civil servant who was transferred to London in 1920 where he worked in the Ministry of Supplies. He moonlighted in the West End theatre with the Irish Players, a breakaway Abbey group which included Sydney Morgan, Sarah Allgood, Arthur Sinclair, Harry Hutchinson and Marie O'Neill.

Synge's lover, and the foremost tragic actress of the Abbey, collapsed in laughter. The beautiful girl did get the part and subsequently became Mrs Sean O'Casey. Lucky Sean.

The taxi-man on the way home asks me a question as a literary man. He's read two books about Oliver Cromwell recently and he can't make out which one was authentic. In the first book Cromwell loved flowers and animals and was a patriot. In the second he killed people and stabled his horses in a church. Could I tell him, the taxi-man asked, which version was the right one?

'Neither,' I told him, 'for if we understood Cromwell, we'd understand the English, which no one has ever done, so why should we be the first to do it?'

16 November

Sunday: meet Leland Lyons, Provost of Trinity, coming out of Provost's house at the bottom of Grafton Street. He lives by right in the centre of the city so the Green which is nearby is his natural choice for a constitutional. A combination of my short sight and his natural shyness means that we greet each other with a last-minute yelp of recognition.

Something of a hero of mine is Leland Lyons who is in the tradition of the great Trinity all-rounders. An exceptional historian whose lives of Parnell and of John Dillon MP have become classics, he has won a number of Irish squash championships and is a fine cricketer. We chat for a minute or two about an essay he has written recently on Thomas Davis, the Trinity patriot who in the 1840s became the first man to recognize what Irishmen of both cultures have in common. Is he wondering what tradition I belong to, in an untidy long overcoat, unshaven on a Sunday morning, carrying a loose bag of sports togs, heading for Sunday lunch in a hotel. As I open the Sunday papers at lunch I realize why he may have been mildly embarrassed. He had resigned as Provost just a few hours before. Lee Lyons embodies all the qualities that a four-hundred-year-old university like Trinity should require from their Provost. One wonders are they embattled. Are the moneylenders moving in? Are the cobbled squares and the Georgian porticoes to be auctioned off to the highest bidder? Will this last bastion in an almost destroyed city fall to whatever moneylenders can pressure a Provost to surrender his sacred trust?

2 December, Alicante

Off to Alicante today. I have spent extended periods in the last four years in Tangier, Spain and Malta, working on my Literary Renaissance book which is already overdue for Hamish Hamilton. I now have the seven biographical portraits of the leading figures of the era done* but I have to make them come alive as characters. And then find some way to have them move against each other, while I create a narrative and remain at the same time solidly on a bedrock of fact.

I nipped out to Alicante last year to case the joint.† There's an excellent residential hotel where I can stay. The city has few tourists, that is foreign tourists. Spaniards tend to come down to Alicante for a break or holiday. But though Benidorm is only forty miles away, the overflow from that sink doesn't seep in here. A place with few English-speakers is just what I want so that I don't waste time in excessive chat.

I'm loaded with trunks as I have to bring almost a library with me, since many of the books I require wouldn't be available in Spain. As usual, Iberia Airways balls things up for me. When I change at Madrid, they put me on the wrong plane and leave me off at Barcelona, instead of Valencia. Siberian Airways they ought to call it. When I get to my room in the Estudio Hotel, Alicante, it takes me about two hours to unpack as I have to put masses of manuscripts and books in different parts of the room.

4 December

Out to San Juan beach in a dinky little train that bowls along and is so cheap that one would have thought everyone would use it. This is not so, though. Socially, this train is for the lesser breeds. On the promenade I notice women with inordinately high stiletto heels who pick their way along like flamingos on a beach. When I come back, tea with Graham Kingsford-Smith, the British Consul in Alicante. He is half-Spanish. His father came to Alicante before the Civil War and married a local girl. He's mad about soccer and played on an English universities side. On my last visit I asked him could he find me a typist and now he has kindly secured one for me.

---

* See 1 January 1978, Tangier.
† This trip was made possible through the late Liam Galligan, a friend and prominent Irish businessman in London.

7 December

Short walk on the sea front. Energetic but uneasy. I still have to find a form to bring the book alive or I will come back once more with an unfinished manuscript as I did from Malta, Tangier etc. I have three years behind me now. As I see the work, the book could become huge which is not what I want. Where is the key? DREAD. I can't abandon it. The difficulty is I can only assess a project (and the time it will take to complete it) as I see it unfolding before me. I need a structure to come out of the material rather than impose one on an unruly collection of facts. Am I fastened to a dying animal for another five years? God! Dinner today in my room and downstairs for coffee in the restaurant on the front where I am now. Almost afraid to go up to my room (11.30 pm) to start my second session.

8 December

Partial boredom. To write as I do requires being able to live by oneself. As long as I don't get a cold. Spent three hours at Kingsford-Smith's today, who has a cold and I hope I don't catch it. Still haven't got a typist after all. Take an hour's walk in San Juan. Anxiety gnawing at me. Back to meet Kingsford-Smith and wife again. Am absolutely terrified of getting their colds. Remind myself to stop thinking of the book in between work.

12 December

It is impossible to record the despair and confusion that writing can cause. There are times when nothing at all seems possible. One has to turn one's whole world upside-down and concentrate on one aim. Anxieties are at their height. I keep flashing back to awful moments in Torre Blanca, Soto Grande, Malta. This afternoon, went for a walk to San Juan beach. When would the conductor ask for the fare? If he'd come round and ask, it would stop the agony of waiting for him. Feel rotten, yet very good 45-minute walk. Bus back. Ring Laurie Cunningham, striker at Real Madrid, about going up to do a piece for the *Sunday Times*.

24 December

As I walk to the house of Graham Kingsford-Smith for dinner, the sun is quite blinding. Nice tang in the air. Blue sky. Still insecure about my book. Hope I'll be able to keep going. What to do in between work. Isolated all evening with pen.

About eight guests at the Consul's including very pretty American girl. Delicious lamb, sherry trifle, fresh vegetables. Turkey available if required. Kingsford-Smith full of useful Spanish information. Asked to propose a toast to the Queen, I hesitate because of Republican views, but decide that not even the most cherished convictions should be allowed to supersede the rules of hospitality. I propose a toast to Her Majesty, Queen of England and the King of Spain.

25 December

Christmas Day. Last night, finished the introduction. Fell asleep last Tuesday after dinner and a half-bottle of rosado. No meal at all tonight because no restaurants were open. When I went for a walk this morning, I made one of those discoveries that one only can do when one is travelling on foot. At the end of a very long street, there were a lot of trees. Behind them I found the most exquisite gardens. In the middle of them was a funfair out of a scene two centuries ago.

18 January 1981

I have been reading E.L. Doctorow's *Ragtime*, based on the life of the socialist Emma Goldman, and *The Agony and the Ecstasy* by Irving Stone, which claims to be a biography of Michelangelo, to see if I could find a literary form which would help me with my book. These two are written as 'faction', a fashionable device where the author purports to present the facts but allows himself complete licence as to how he makes use of them. Conversations can be invented, character traits imposed and situations concocted to suit whatever whim grabs the author. I came upon this passage halfway through *The Agony and the Ecstasy*:

'What fell on your nose, Michelangelo?'
'A ham.'
'From a butcher's rack? Did you forget to duck?'

'The way the people on Vesuvius forgot to run from the lava: it had covered them before they knew it was coming.'
'Have you ever been in love?'
'. . . in a way.'
'It's always "in a way".'
Her body stirred in its gown, causing a sibilance of the silk. Her fashionably shod foot rested lightly against his calf. His insides somersaulted.

As did mine. So farewell Irving Stone. Back once more to fettle at the forge.

22 January

Have spent the last two days trying to get the Celtic circus up and going. The plan is to have my characters move against one another as they would in a novel. But their conversation must come from attributable sources. Likewise their activities must be bound irrevocably to the wheel of truth. What I need now is to bring my characters to life so that the reader can feel he is meeting them for the first time when he encounters them in the book. Then the circumstances which will move the characters back and forth so that we may be afforded glimpses of their personalities will not be invented ones but taken from life and capable of revealing aspects which I do not think could be brought out in a work of fiction.

24 January

Note on tonight's work. Terribly depressed after rereading my Lady Gregory section. Dull, which is one thing her ladyship was not. Then Yeats typescript arrives back. Reads quite well but I think that it's overwritten. Then get back to Lady Gregory and George Moore. Not too much to be changed with Moore. But the big question is Synge. Where does he come in? It's all so in the air. You have to search and search and not lose patience.

Today had two-mile walk. Don't feel the same sense of exhilaration as I used to at the end of it. I have to walk back to Alicante from San Juan after missing the tiny train.

1 February

Hardly dared to write this. But last night as I dictated what I'd set down for the evening, the machine began to move and I sensed a storyline. Will it work? I won't know until I've gone over it again, and not perhaps even then. This is what makes it so scary. All those generalizations are out there like gale winds beating against the mind and one has to accept their impact and try and give them shape on the page. Perhaps I have a structure. Is it there? I was so exhausted beginning last night, didn't want to continue. Despite anxiety, got the plan on paper. And then immediately began to worry about another manuscript and so on.

5 February, Madrid

Up to Madrid for the *Sunday Times* to see Laurie Cunningham. Two years ago he became one of the first English soccer millionaires when he was transferred from Manchester United to Real Madrid. He lives in a mansion with Moorish turrets with his girlfriend. His training regime is awesome and he is convinced there would be a strike in English football if they had schedules like this. Every Thursday the whole team has a check-up from a bone surgeon, a cardiologist and a brain surgeon. When I ask what do they need a brain surgeon for, he points to three scars on his face made by football studs and which he got when going up to head the ball.

Afterwards I visit the Real Madrid stadium which holds 120,000 spectators. Gymnasiums, swimming pools, physiotherapy centres are part of the complex. It even includes a shrine where, before a match, players can pray for victory to their patron, Our Lady of Paloma, whose image, if you press a button, obligingly pops up from behind the altar.

23 February, Alicante

Tonight at 7.30 pm wait in the hotel lobby for Leopoldo Martin, an English teacher at the University of Alicante. He doesn't turn up. The manager is walking up and down uneasily. Coming down in the lift, someone has said something in Spanish about Civil War. They were agitated.

I go to the Ciero restaurant to eat suckling pig. I've ordered it when the owner comes over and says:

'Have you got your passport with you?'

'No, why should I?'

'You should get back to your hotel. We're closing up.'

He returns to the door and shuts it. What is happening? Not a sinner in the streets. No trains. I walk back to Estudiotel. Ring Graham Kingsford-Smith. He says there has been an attempted *coup d'état* in Madrid, led by Antonio Tegero, Commander of the Civil Guard, who has just burst into Congress and stopped a debate on the appointment of the new prime minister Calvo Sotelo. The rebels have mounted machine guns and fired over the heads of the deputies.

I go out onto the street again to see if I can find a bar that is open. I see only one person, a man waiting for a bus. When I find a café, the lady behind the bar sells me a glass of rosado. Doesn't have much to say for herself. Then when I ask for a second glass she says they are closing. The old lady who is the owner apologizes, 'It is very regrettable. *Buenas noches*.' I wonder are there army units waiting to rise in support. I notice a man outside phoning agitatedly from a public telephone box. All the other bars seem to be closed. Have to say that before I left the hotel a woman warned me not to go out. I paid no heed as I didn't think anything serious was up.

Absolutely nobody out. A police car stops at the traffic lights. I look at them. They look back but drive on. It strikes me that when a coup occurs, how very few people may be aware of it. It's simply a shift of power. Who rules? Who elects? Who imprisons? A great number of people say to themselves it's none of their business and go about their daily work as before. Things however are different now from forty years ago when Franco organized his coup from the Canary Islands. Today everybody can watch TV to see what is actually happening. By the time I get home it's 11.30 pm. Go up to the TV room. Most of the people there are residents of the hotel. Upper-class, many of them retired. They are watching TV without turning a hair almost as if they were at mass. There is a little flurry however when the King comes on and makes his speech to the nation. He says he will not tolerate this usurpation of the people's rights. Tegero and the Civil Guard have been ordered to withdraw. Appreciative murmur from the watchers. A few of them get up and leave the room. There is an absence of emotion. Everything is well. The King has spoken. Later I learn the Motorized Division of the Spanish Army commanded by Lieutenant-General Milans Bosch is now in the streets of nearby Valencia with jeeps and police cars and there are tanks and soldiers on the way.

When I come downstairs for breakfast I find the affair is all over. It seems the King's address did have an effect. I ring Kingsford-Smith:

'I must say the King did behave very well indeed,' he says.

I reply that, while I am sure the King would be pleased to learn that he did have Her Majesty's Consul's approval, what I actually heard His Majesty say on television was that the administration of law and order had been transferred to the army until the crisis was over and the democratic process restored; so it wasn't just giving the Royal assent to a bill for the preservation of the Giant Panda. Graham a little miffed.

Ventured out to have morning coffee at 9.30. Glorious day if a little cloudy. High summer heat in the offing later on. Walk to shops I know. No one seems put out. Come back to find Leopoldo* there. Greatly excited. He has the newspaper *Ja*, with a picture of Franco's former Minister of Defence who is among the rebels arrested. Also Suarez the Prime Minister whom he admires for his courage. Apparently Suarez, who was addressing the Cortes when the rebels entered, remained unmoved and simply asked them politely what they were doing there. The rebels belong to a group called 'The Galaxies', so named because they used to meet in a café of that name. He shows me the Catholic daily paper *Ja* with the headline: 'National disgrace'.

Two young girls ask can they borrow the paper. They are what Leopoldo calls '*pasatos*', college dropouts.

Leopoldo is excited that the system has stood the test. I tell him about last night in the television room at the hotel and how the whole atmosphere changed as soon as the King came on to speak. He is now a keystone in the democratic process. It seems to me that Unamuno would have had something to say about the situation so we buy a paperback of *Del Sentimiento Tragico della Vida* to scan it. In the bookshop the television is on. The announcer tells us that the Mayor of Madrid, an anti-Francoite, has had a heart attack. No wonder. He may have heard the distant drums and thought the Falange were on the march again.

In the streets you see people listening to their radios. Relief in their faces. Just to have had a whiff of revolution in their nostrils and then the following morning to emerge into the clean air of freedom is a funky trip.

---

* See 23 February.

6 April, Dublin–Westminster

Westminster, to see Michael Foot.* The Labour Party have just announced they will support the Tory policy of refusing to meet the demands of Maze prisoner Bobby Sands†, who is on hunger strike. I am an admirer of Foot's work on Swift and Byron and regard him as the last of the essayists in the tradition of Desmond MacCarthy, G.K. Chesterton and Cyril Connolly. Also as a pacifist with the radical tradition of a famous family behind him, I feel he may be receptive to a new view.

First Michael makes the point that the Irish Government refused concessions to IRA hunger strikers in Port Laoise prison similar to those demanded by Sands. I tell him all these issues have now been resolved in the Republic. He then argues that if the British Government give in, it will act as a recruiting drive for the IRA. I say on the contrary that if the Government let Sands die for something as trivial as refusing to wear prison clothes it is this which will ensure a rush to Republican ranks. Terence MacSwiney's death in 1920, after 73 days on hunger strike in Brixton Jail, was what provided the then IRA with a respectable pedigree on a world level.‡ Criminals don't die on hunger strike. Michael is somewhat upset. He says the majority in the North have to be listened to. I reply that this majority has been determined by an artificial boundary, and doesn't represent the whole of the people of Ulster and certainly not the whole of the people of the island.

Point out too that Bobby Sands has a constituency as he's just been elected MP for Tyrone/Fermanagh. This sends Michael over the top. 'They held a gun to his head, they held a gun to his head,' he says excitedly. I don't know who he is talking about until it turns out he is referring to Frank Maguire, the Nationalist candidate who withdrew in favour of Sands. (This is a yarn put out by the dirty tricks brigade.

---

* Became leader of the Labour Party in 1980.

† 1954–81; sentenced in September 1977 to fourteen years for destroying a furniture factory. Died on 5 May 1981, the 66th day of his hunger strike. He has become an international icon.

‡ Terence MacSwiney was Lord Mayor of Cork in 1920. Arrested and jailed, he swore that if he was not released, he would not leave prison alive. After he had begun his hunger strike, he was taken to London. His refusal to take food, which resulted in his death, was observed day by day throughout the world. 'It is not those who can inflict the most suffering but those who can endure the most who will prevail' was his own assessment of what he set out to do.

Maguire has a Republican background but withdrew because he thought Sands a better candidate.)

I put it to Michael that the Labour Party should have no difficulty with a compromise on the hunger strike. Harold Wilson condoned serious breaches of law seven years ago when he bowed to Loyalist bullies who had threatened to paralyse the province.

'What could we do,' says Michael.

'You could have brought in the army to enforce the law.'

'I'm surprised at you, a Nationalist, asking an English politician to use the army against Irishmen.'

I say I'm not speaking on behalf of Nationalists, I'm speaking on behalf of Irishmen who are looking for justice. The government of which Michael was a Cabinet member in 1974 should have used troops to enforce the law. By not doing so they gave currency to the view that England would never enforce the law against Unionists.

'What is this! Shoot strikers, shoot strikers?' Michael's voice goes up a decibel.

'Is it more awful than killing Catholics?' I ask. 'If Protestants break the law, you simply refuse to deal with them. But for Catholics in a similar situation you pull the trigger.'

Michael likes Yeats a lot, so I think I'll use the poet's words in my defence, as Yeats himself had Pearse 'summon Cuchulain to his side' in the GPO.* The idea of the hunger strike as a form of pacifist protest appealed to Yeats, especially when he learned that it was used by the poets in ancient Ireland to confront the King. In a play he wrote on a hunger strike,† the chief poet of Ireland (Seanchan), having installed himself at the palace gate, proceeds to starve himself to death as a protest against ill-treatment of poets. I quote to Michael Seanchan's dying words which seem relevant to the present goings-on.

> 'When I and these are dead
> We should be carried to some windy hill
> To lie there with uncovered face awhile
> That mankind and that leper there may know
> Dead faces laugh – King! King! Dead faces laugh.'

---

* In the poem *The Statues*:

> When Pearse summoned Cuchulain to his side,
> What stalked through the Post Office? What intellect,
> What calculation, number, measurement, replied?

† *The King's Threshold*. Abbey Theatre, November 1905.

Michael is too het up to pay much attention. I am disheartened as I admire him a lot as a torchbearer for freedom and social reform and now even he appears to be parroting establishment views.

30 April, Dublin–Edinburgh

Take Nanny for a walk. We go down Templemore Avenue to Rathgar Church. I watch her tiny neat figure cross the road. Once we enter the church, she remembers immediately where the font is to bless herself, which I do as well. We kneel down and say a prayer. A priest hearing confessions in a side aisle. Nanny approaches the shrines around the church; the Sacred Heart, St Anthony, the Little Flower, Our Lady. All present and correct. But one of the confession boxes, my favourite one, has been moved. Painted a different colour too. At an empty niche we debate as to whether it was St Bernadette or St Aloysius who used to be there. Here as a boy I used to embark on such enthralling trips. After we had done our rounds we genuflected and walked out under the choir loft where in the year 1878 James Joyce's father, John Stanislaus, met his fellow chorister May Murray, whom he would later marry. I wanted Na to take a bus home. We're about a mile from the church. But though she's almost ninety, she won't hear a word of it and insists on walking.*

I have my bags packed and a taxi ready to take me to the airport. Off to Edinburgh to speak at a literary week, organized by Colm Brogan, a recent acquaintance. He is a young columnist on the *Glasgow Herald* and has read English at Cambridge where his uncle was a well-known political scientist. He has been following my career from afar for some time and has formed a very much exaggerated view of my prowess.

At a public debate in St Celia's Hall later on, the author Bernard MacLaverty says that entertainment is not literature. Margaret Drabble says the opposite. Melvyn Bragg is in the chair. Whole thing lacklustre. It's not helped either by local brain-box Owen Dudley Edwards, son of a decent professor of history at University College, who seems to have gone the way of most Irish academics who go native when they get to Britain. Afterwards, Colm Brogan takes us to a restaurant. He has some zany idea about going back to my room to drink a bottle of champagne which he has very decently ordered

---

* See appendix 2, 'Requiem for a Nanny'.

in advance as a token of his regard for me. But I'm starving after laying my egg and it's the last thing I want to do. This annoys him more than one could have imagined, and for the rest of the night he remains sullen. He has been kind to me and wishes to promote me in Scotland as an Irishman who can help inject some life into Scottish nationalism. But clearly he sees me through rose-tinted glasses as a mixture of Oliver St John Gogarty, Compton Mackenzie and Augustus John, with Leonardo da Vinci thrown in for good measure. As I leave later in the night, I hear him entertaining other guests with well-meant but grotesque versions of feats I am supposed to have accomplished.

4 May, Dublin

Extract from letter sent from me to Michael Foot today, after I had read in the *Irish Times* that Don Concannon, the Labour shadow Minister of State, has visited the Maze prison to inform Bobby Sands that the Labour Party now support the Tory Government's refusal to meet the demands of the hunger strikers.

One wonders will they ever learn in England. Sands will die and be succeeded by another striker. When the third is gone, the British government will give in – maybe. The insanity of it all. Bobby Sands being forced to dress in prison wear when less than a hundred yards away in the same jail, because of a difference in the date they were arrested, prisoners who are inside for offences more serious than Sands' are wearing their own clothes.

Robert Ballagh* rings to say Bobby Sands died this morning. As soon as I get off the phone, ring up the sculptor Yann Goulet† to ask him to make a death mask. No reply.

Watch Bernadette Devlin‡ on the news. Fantastic. Masterful. Advocacy, authority and passion. Attractive-looking. Conveys a sense of absolute sincerity. She says she would give the Ulster Defence Association gunmen who shot her and her children the same status in prison as that now demanded by the IRA.

---

* Distinguished Irish painter. Founder of the Irish National Congress.

† A Breton who had done some of the best public sculpture in Ireland at that time.

‡ See 31 May 1974, note.

I meet Derek Warfield of the Wolfe Tone Band in the Arts Club. Suggest a ballad on Bobby Sands which he could set to music. He said if it's done, it must be done immediately. At the Arts Club, Fr Des Wilson is there. Heated. He says the Brits should get out and that's the long and the short of it. I said, if they did, we'd prosper down here. Northerners believe in a day's work.

At eleven o'clock, send a taxi to James Power,* the sculptor who lives on the northside. The driver returns half an hour later.

'There's no reply. I nearly knocked the door down.'

5 May

I ring another sculptor, Peter Grant. Still no luck. Then another, John Behan, not at home. Finally get Goulet. He will do it for a fee which he names. A fine artist but a dicey political record. He can't go back to France as he is wanted there as a collaborator.

6 May

Spend morning trying to get hold of the Sixty Eight Committee† to finance the Goulet project. Also, it is essential to get permission from the Sands family to have a mask taken. I have asked Gerry Adams‡ to discuss it with the Sands relatives, that is Bobby's mother and two sisters. Lunch at the Unicorn. I see Brian Friel§ and Seamus Heaney deep in conversation. Cute Northerners. Brian, though, has a passionately nationalist outlook, which in a crisis he has no hesitation in asserting. Seamus not inclined to comment. Sheepy-eyed Seamus.

Later run in Trinity with Trevor. Six sprints. Back home to do some work. Gerry Adams rings. The coast is clear. The family have agreed to let Goulet do the death mask. Gerry adds: 'It's OK for you

---

* He was away and his sisters don't answer the door.

† A civil rights committee formed by campaigners of various backgrounds in 1968.

‡ Outstanding figure in the Republican movement. In 1983, as leader of Sinn Fein, he won the seat for West Belfast in the Westminster elections. He later entered into negotiations with John Hume, leader of the SDLP, which resulted in a consensus and led to the IRA ceasefire in August 1994. He is seen by many as in the Parnell mould of persuading revolutionaries to examine constitutional alternatives.

§ Regarded by many as one of the greatest living playwrights. Among his best known plays are *Translations*, *Dancing at Lughnasa* and *Philadelphia, Here I Come!*

down in Dublin. You don't have to argue the way I do on these matters.'

7 May

Go to meet Yann Goulet at 5.30. He has just come back from Belfast with his driver from the Sixty Eight Committee. A row blew up over a delay in bringing him a cup of tea. Result. Home empty-handed. Remind myself that the Bretons, like ourselves, are Celts.

17 July

What a lousy summer, though according to the television, England is having good weather. Coming up the stairs this morning at 7 am, after going down to get a drink of water, I got a glimpse of myself in the mirror on the first landing. Hair wild. Not old-looking, but in my Knights of the Campanile sweater* which I'd put on for the cold, I look distinctly odd. I was up very late last night as I met John Hume at the Arts Club. He liked the piece that I had written in the *Sunday Tribune* on Rev. Martin Smyth,† whom I'd gone up to see in Derry. John tells me that he has an affection for Smyth, despite his exalted position in the Orange Order. He says the thing now is to hit the Brits with everything we have and our biggest weapon is the United States. He does not agree with my suggestion that an independent Ulster would be worth considering. He would prefer a federation with local powers to pass acts in Protestant areas which would be sympathetic to the culture of those living there. He says he thought that a blood-bath would have occurred after the Sunningdale Agreement broke down. Now, he thinks it won't happen. The Unionists will just reorganize.

18 July

Woke up late. I have two things to do, march to the British Embassy in a protest on behalf of the hunger strikers and then finish a run at the Oscar Theatre of my Behan show. Didn't know it was already 10 am because my watch had stopped. I thought it was 8 am.

---

* Trinity College sports club whose colours are dark-blue, light-blue and pink. Similar to Vincent's in Oxford and the Hawks in Cambridge.
† A Westminster MP and former Grand-Master of the Orange Order.

Walk to the Shelbourne Hotel in Stephen's Green where I have a sandwich. Then meet Gerry Jones* and Mickey Mullen† as arranged in the Unicorn. Later we stand outside the Shelbourne as the marchers gather. Run into my cousin, Carroll, the American TV star who is staying in the hotel. He looks uneasy. I ask him is he going on the march? 'My dogs won't let me.'

I think what have his dogs got to do with it and then remember he is talking American slang and means his feet are sore. It is a neat side-step from his stance as a declared supporter of the left twenty years ago. Kevin Boland,‡ Matt Merrigan§ there. Also see Bruce Arnold, writer. Not in the march himself ('certainly not'), but his son is. We walk down Nassau Street. No chance of escape if the fuzz move in. Gerry Jones says he could arrange to protect himself if attacked, whatever that means. Walking past Merrion Square, he offers useful advice:

'Never go down a lane. You're cornered.'

Mickey Mullen says the police are losing the run of themselves, getting bold, making claims that are unrealistic. They have come to him to ask him to form a trade union. Then, when he wasn't keen, they said with a veiled threat, 'You could be arrested for talking to us.'

Now, as we're marching, there are stewards running up and down telling us to link arms but to keep order. 'Stand on your dignity, don't panic.'

It seems inevitable that there will be some confrontation. Gerry offers more combat advice:

'Keep your hands over your head, if batoned.'

Bernadette Devlin is at the front of the march. I shake her hand. She's overweight through lack of exercise, because she hasn't been able to walk properly since she was shot two months ago.¶ She's on

---

* Then a director of the Jones Group, one of the richest construction firms in Ireland. He took an active part in the Troubles in 1969 and went up to Belfast with a rifle to defend Nationalists during the Loyalist attacks on the Falls Road. Recognizable by his black eye-patch and striking looks.

† General Secretary of the Irish Transport and General Workers' Union.

‡ Former Minister for Defence in the Jack Lynch Fianna Fail Government. Resigned in protest against the decision to prosecute ministers in the Arms Trial of 1969.

§ Former General Secretary of the Workers' Union of Ireland.

¶ Bernadette had been attacked by Loyalist paramilitaries who broke into her house six weeks before and shot both her and her children while they were hiding under the bed.

crutches, with her injured leg strapped up behind her. Now we're just to the left of the Royal Dublin Society. Further on the same side there is the old Masonic Girls' School and a large lawn of about an acre in size on which the British Embassy stands. I pick out the side door of a house on our left to climb over it if a riot starts.

I have a press pass but I sense that violence of some kind is likely with the police lined up as they are. They have arranged themselves in a phalanx across the road and we are not allowed to pass this. They have situated themselves on the main road just before it branches off on either side, so confrontation seems inevitable.

I see Mickey Mullen pushing his way through from the back. He looks nervous. I know he has a heart condition and he's plucky to be here. I hear someone in front say: 'Six will be allowed.' A delegation from the march will hand in a letter to the Embassy and I am asked will I be part of it. We are brought in through formidable iron gates. Bernadette is with us along with two women colleagues, obviously well schooled in protest. As we approach the front door of the Embassy, Bernadette leads with her entourage one of whom knocks at the door. I can't see what's happening just now. I hear a scuffle. Bernadette's entourage begin to squeal like stuck pigs.

'Bernadette, Bernadette, they'll kill you.'

It seems she asked to speak to the Ambassador and when told she could only see the First Secretary, replied:

'My mother told me always to ask for the man of the house if I knock at a door.'

With this she went, crutches and all, through the doorway into the foyer. Now she is stretched on the floor, surveying the scene with her crutches scattered beside her.

'Bernadette, Bernadette.'

The girls are now screeching as if she were dying. Some are hauled out of the porch. One in a neck-lock. A young baby-faced guard is trying to calm them. He's not a good negotiator. I go to Inspector John Hogan, a distinguished-looking man, more like a successful surgeon than a Branch man, and I suggest he should ask the Embassy to talk to the delegation. I go over to Bernadette who greets me:

'I'm sorry for shouting at you early on.'

I say 'You know you're not' and squeeze her hand reassuringly. I go out through the door to the lawn with Mickey Mullen. He says quietly that he thinks that Bernadette and her group meant to squat inside the Embassy. I go back to Inspector Hogan and ask that he get an Embassy official to come out, which would defuse the situation. Then I hear thumps in the distance. Bernadette knowledgeably says 'That's CS gas.' Police come to tell us things are very bad in the street outside the Embassy. Stones thrown from the back of the march have landed on the marchers in front. Because of the position of the police barricades, it has, as I thought, been impossible for marchers to escape down side streets. They had only two options, to go back or push forward past the barricades. When the stones from the back started to fall on marchers at the front, they took the latter course and the battle began. The wounded are now being carried on stretchers into the large field at the back, where a battalion of the army are on the alert to go into action if the riot escalates.

(The Oscar Theatre where I have to perform tonight is only a few hundred yards away down Serpentine Avenue. But to get there is another matter. I must be in the dressing room in an hour.)

The Superintendent asks us would we like to visit the injured. Mickey Mullen says no.

'That's not our business. We're here to deliver a protest.'

I have another idea. Through loud hailers we could ask the crowd outside to disperse provided the Embassy will agree to receive our deputation. The young cherubic policeman refuses to listen. He becomes abusive and personal. I tell him to fucking well listen. He won't. I call him a bowsie and he walks off. I put our plan to the Inspector. I ask him to let me talk to the Embassy people. He says he will try.

5.30 pm

The police tell us that there is a crowd of over 500 in Sandymount Avenue who won't move. Will we go out and speak to them. This is the offer that Cherub-face relays to us but he may be trying to get us out so they can shut the gates and not let us back. I say I'll only go if the deputation is received by the Ambassador. Another blow. Mickey Mullen has to leave. Now I'm on my tod. If things turn nasty, I can get a hiding. On the other hand, if I go, Bernadette and her entourage will be on their own.

I sit down and lean on my umbrella like Rodin's Thinker. What am I going to do. It's almost time for curtain-up at the Oscar Theatre. Bernadette starts to draft a statement for the six o'clock TV news. I lend her my pen. I walk back to commiserate with a policeman, bleeding from the nose, who is walking alongside one of the stretchers. Two sergeants, friendly.

At the back, about 500 soldiers are sitting on the lawn. Relaxed. A policeman says to me: 'I hope you're proud of yourself.' I ignore him. Some police hail me in friendly fashion. One says though:

'I'm surprised to see you with them. You and Michael Mullen are looked up to. You give this crowd respectability.'

I tell him that I had to join in a protest against British policy on the hunger strike issue. He says:

'What about the blackguardism?'

One of his colleagues, with a mottled face, says you can't give in to them:

'It will be your house next or mine.'

I say concessions should be made where there has been injustice in the first place. I have a regard for police but this time they have been put in a false position. I mention that I have practised as a barrister and have come in contact with many fine members of the force. The mottled-faced fellow walks off. They have had a tough time. The policeman with the cheerful face asks me why I am not on the *Late Late Show*.

When I get out of the Embassy, I turn left up Simmonscourt Road. I meet two policemen on either side of a dazed lad whom they are dragging along. His head is badly cut and he's bleeding. He looks nervously at the policemen and says nothing. I stop and take their number.

'What are you looking at?'

'Nothing.'

'Well then fuck off. You shouldn't be on the road.'

Aggressive. Cut of a bully. I out-stare him. As he goes he says to a colleague:

'That's Ulick O'Connor.'

I think how the system is disintegrating when police enforce bad laws.

When I finally arrive at the Oscar, I phone the *Sunday Tribune* and RTE and read out Bernadette's statement, that she's given me, to an RTE journalist. (It was not used.)

Good audience at the show, especially considering the disturbances nearby.

Read press reports in the late editions on what has happened. Horrifying. The police have batoned the crowd and hit people lying down. This is what I foresaw two weeks ago could happen if the Fine Gael coalition got back. Police could be encouraged to seek confrontation. Down Sir!

25 July, Stephen's Green Club, Dublin

Meet with Ronan Keane,* Donal Barrington† and James Cawley. We are a foursome who dine together every three months. Three barristers and a solicitor. When called to the bar we had been admonished on our memorials not, in any circumstances, to consort with attorneys, but we have made an exception in the case of our friend Cawley. Our sole rule is that there are no rules, except one – guests are not allowed. Now we are sitting in the drawing room, waiting for Keane to arrive. Noll Gogarty‡ sitting across the room with James Meenan, Dean of the Economics Faculty in University College, Dublin. Noll quite tipsy. Says he likes the bust of Joyce, currently on display, which a centenary committee of which I am chairman propose to erect in St Stephen's Green. I say I'm glad he approves. But then he pulls a neat one by saying the reason he likes it is because it makes Joyce look mean.

'He was mean to my father when they were students together.'

Joyce's daughter Lucia has died this week in Northampton asylum, so I think it might cool things down to mention this. Noll says he used to play hockey there when he was at Oxford.

'There were ladies in long dresses on the side-line shouting "I hope the winners win."'

Jim Meenan says:

'Noll only remembers that he was at Oxford because they have started winning the boat-race.'

Noll was on the Western Circuit when I joined it in the Fifties and he has great yarns of the roistering life there. To be drunk in court then was no crime, as the judge was often drunk himself. Once, an inebriated Lord Hemphill, pleading for a client in a drunk driving

---

* Senior Counsel; later Chief Justice of Ireland.

† Senior Counsel, later Judge of the Supreme Court.

‡ Oliver Duane Gogarty, Senior Counsel. Son of Oliver St John Gogarty. Practised at the Irish Bar from 1936. Very much his father's son, and his wit did the rounds of the Law Library.

case before Judge Wyse Power (also under the influence), was told:

'It's no use Lord Hemphill. Your client was as drunk as a Lord.'

'Well, he wasn't as sober as a judge.'

'Case dismissed.'

'Equity' Smith* was another who made substantial contributions to the upkeep of the Licensed Vintners Association while on circuit. Noll, before he took silk, was usually deputed to see the old boy on the train for Dublin. On one occasion after he had poured Smith into his first-class seat and was waiting on the platform for the train to start, he saw the door of the carriage open and Smith place a new pair of boots carefully on the platform. Another trencherman was the father of the Circuit, Neville Denning, whom Noll recalls once stood up to address a jury:

'I wish to base my address on an intrinsic proposition of Law.'

There was a long pause.

'I'm afraid I have forgotten it, my Lord.'

He consulted with the second silk who was like himself in the twilight zone: no reply.

'Mr Denning, would you be thinking of the Law of Retrospective Necessity?' said the Judge helpfully.

'Indeed, I was my lord,' replied Denning who with dropped eye, squashed nose and crooked finger usually managed to remain inscrutable when the pressure was on.

Noll is now falling asleep, which I am not unhappy to see, as I have been afraid that he might try and join us. We have a private room which we go to, telling the head waiter not to let our whereabouts be known.

26 July, Dundalk

Drove up to Dundalk today with Liam Tuohy and Paddy Ambrose to play in a soccer match against the Army. Liam has played inside forward for Newcastle and for Ireland and Paddy for Shamrock Rovers and on the famous Irish team which beat England, Scotland and Wales in the same year. I have to identify myself at the gate of Custume Barracks. (Dundalk is only a few miles from the Border and

---

* Reginald Smith, Senior Counsel. The name 'Equity' derived from the legal maxim 'Equity knows no law'.

is known these days as 'El Paso' as IRA men are reputed to take time off from their activities over the border to relax in the bars and coffee-shops.) The names of the team were taken three times before we finally got to the officer in charge. Did a lot of stretching beforehand so as not to pull a muscle. John McCarthy, the young Protestant rector of Dundalk, is at right-half for us. Our mutual friend Trevor West is at left-half. I like playing against the Army. They always give you a fair shake. When one of them lands me a severe kick in the calf he says with genuine concern, 'Very sorry.' At half-time the Army full-back addresses me in similes, 'Do you have to charge like a brutal ram?'

Score 3:1.

On the way back we stop in Dundalk, at a smart supermarket. See well-dressed kids in working-class area. Financially independent now at sixteen.

After we start again for home Paddy Ambrose gives a fascinating account of pigeon-racing which is the chief passion of his life. As a young footballer of international class, he was never keen on going to England to make his name as it would have meant leaving his beloved pigeons behind. Brought over by Norwich FC for a trial when he was seventeen, he performed well, but back in Dublin he began to think of his pigeons and what would happen if he became a star. He was so afraid Norwich would come after him that he hid down in Cork for a year till he felt sure the search had been called off.

26 August, Dublin

Came in last night at 2 am. From the landing, I direct my voice to Annie's room where she is asleep, 'Breakfast at 8.30 am.' Voice from sleep: 'Breakfast at 8.30.' I know it will be there on time. Served my mother and father. Now serves me. Mystery in these materialistic days.

14 September, Northern Ireland

Head towards Belfast with Trevor West.* We are paying a visit to Long Kesh, the internment camp which houses paramilitary prison-

---

* Senator Trevor West. See 2 February 1970, note.

ers both Republican and Loyalist. Trevor has wangled it so that we can meet Gusty Spence, a former Company Sergeant in the Royal Ulster Rifles. Spence was in right at the start of the Northern Ireland troubles. In 1966 he and two other Ulster Volunteer Force Loyalists forced their way into Malvern Street Bar, Belfast and shot dead three Catholics. This was a sectarian killing to let the Teagues know their place.

At the prison there is a slight difficulty. Trevor said in his application that I am a relative of the prisoner. This is so that Gusty will not lose out on the number of non-relatives he can see every month. The warder on duty is not too happy with my second name. (In Northern Ireland Catholic names are usually distinguishable from Protestant ones.) He looks down at the sheet of paper and then says, his face brightening a little:

Warder: 'Is Ulick a Scandinavian name?'
Me: (eagerly) 'Yes it is.'
Warder: 'Away in, so.'

Scandinavian to the Loyalist mind-set invokes sound Protestant stock. Saved by the Nordic bell. We wait in the visitors' room for Gusty to come down. He comes in, an erect military looking-man with mild blue eyes wearing the blazer of the Royal Ulster Rifles.

Gusty Spence* has the image of a callous killer. But he is said to be a changed man after fourteen years in prison, and has even learned the Irish language. The silver ring (*fáinne*) in his buttonhole attests to this. It turns out that Gusty is acquainted with Cardinal O'Fiach, the Catholic Archbishop of Armagh, and thinks highly of him.

---

* In the Seventies he became leader of an interesting group of Ulster Protestant activists. Members were drawn largely from the lower middle and working classes, and were in reaction against the current policies of the Unionist Party whose leadership had tended to come from the landed gentry or the middle classes. Trevor and I had been booting around the idea of a separate Ulster State for some time, which would involve both Britain and the Republic of Ireland giving up their claims over the territory of the Six Counties. This geographical unit would then be ruled by a government elected democratically from all the people of Ulster. Such a solution would have the advantage of taking the British element out of the equation, which many people, including Trevor and myself, believe is the prop which supports the whole ramshackle administration in Northern Ireland.

'I'm very fond of his Eminence.'

'Why?'

'He's straight.'

'Gusty, I don't call him his Eminence. I am a Republican. I don't like titles.'

'Well, he's his Eminence to me.'

'What do you and Tom O'Fiach talk about?'

'That's between me and him. Sometimes we talk about tobacco.'

'Tobacco?'

'Yes, "baccy". One day he broke his pipe in here and I gave him a new one, the Matt McQuaid type, that stops you dribbling. Another time I gave him "baccy", that we grew in here. We used to put poteen* in it. When he took a draw on the pipe, I saw his eyebrows go up. A few days later, I got a message "Will you send out more of that strong tobacco."'

Gusty makes a motion with his hands as if smoking a pipe. It seems that Gusty and Tom O'Fiach write to each other on a regular basis. I ask Gusty how does he get the letters delivered.

'The UVF. A fellow on a bicycle goes down from here to the Cardinal's Palace in Armagh.'†

We had been with Gusty about an hour when a warder came in to say that our time was up. Gusty asked the warder to request the Governor to allow him an extra half an hour of his visiting time. I was pleased at this, as it showed that our friend didn't think we were wasting his time. I was fascinated too as I have always looked on Loyalist activists in Northern Ireland as Irishmen who have one way of looking at things. They want union with Britain and think it is best for Ireland. We want separation because we think it is best for Ireland, and our Northern cousins too, if they only knew it.

A short while after the warder came back to say it was no dice, the Governor wouldn't budge. Gusty was unfazed. With a disarming smile he said to the warder, 'Tell the Governor I said he is a gentleman.' Then, ignoring his jailer, he went on to discuss the chances of the Northern Ireland football team in the next World Cup.

---

* A very powerful alcoholic drink distilled from potatoes. Illegal.

† I questioned Cardinal O'Fiach about this when I met him at the Arts Club a few weeks later. He assured me that it was so. A man would arrive about once a month at Ara Coeli from the UVF and collect the Cardinal's letter for Gusty.

15 October, Dundalk

At a service conducted by the Church of Ireland Archbishop of Armagh, Dr George Simms,* I find myself in the pulpit waiting to read a hymn. It is a translation I have done from the Swedish of an eighteenth-century Lutheran Archbishop, J.O. Wallin. I chose this hymn, *Where is the Friend*, because it has a theme found in early Irish poetry – that the divine image is reflected in the beauty of nature.† It is hard to get the fineness of the original over in English but I feel my spin is near enough. When I finish, Isabel, the rector John McCarthy's wife, has her choir sing the hymn in my translation and very beautiful it sounds too.‡

After a pleasant lunch in John's house with Trevor buzzing around, the Archbishop offers me a lift to Dublin. I'm very much in favour of chauffeur-driven cars because they allow you to chat away while someone else toils at the coalface. I find, however, that George Simms is driving his own car and does not have a chauffeur. We have always got on well with one another. Years ago I taught his son Nicholas to box.

On the road he shocks me when he tells me he is going to retire at the end of this year. The strain of the Northern troubles has been too much. I ask him would he not reconsider in any circumstances. He says no. I think the answer is simply that George Simms, a thoroughly

---

* 1910–91; ecumenist and world authority on the Book of Kells.
† There are many similarities between this eighteenth-century Swedish hymn and Joseph Plunkett's poem *I see his Blood upon the Rose*. When they are placed side by side the resemblance is such that it suggests Plunkett may at one time or another have read Wallin's poem. For his role in the Irish Rebellion in 1916, Plunkett, who was one of the leaders and a signatory to the Proclamation, was executed.

I see his blood upon the rose	I hear his Voice where summer winds are breathing,
And in the stars the glory of his eyes,	
His body gleams amid eternal snows,	Where forests sing, and where the river's seething.
His tears fall from the skies.	
	Its splendour fills me, and where that Voice is,
Joseph Plunkett.	
	My heart rejoices.

J.O. Wallin, translated by UO'C.

‡ Later that year the school choir where Isabel teaches music entered for the Great Britain Choir Contest and came second with the hymn *Where is the Friend*.

decent man, is so heartbroken by the antics of a section of Orangemen
and Loyalists who claim to represent his church that he just can't take
any more.

7 November, Dublin

Eileen Pearson [a friend of mine and Christy's] rings. Christy Brown[*]
is dead. Choked to death during a meal at his bungalow in
Glastonbury. When I heard two years ago that he'd moved to England,
I had already written Christy off. It had seemed ludicrous to have relo-
cated as he did four years ago to Kerry where he and his wife Mary
bought a house. Christy's roots were in Dublin and he needed the
oxygen of family life and his own people around him to enable him
to breathe. Kerry would have seemed like Alaska to him. But
Glastonbury, ye gods, was the North Pole. Even moving to
Rathcoole, Co. Dublin, about four miles from Stanaway Road where
he grew up in Dublin, was I thought a bit far from his rearing. He had
built a house there for his sister and her husband and then put an addition on for himself. After he married Mary, a dental assistant from
London, things gradually went downhill. It was a daring experiment
which didn't work. Mary was so often away in London, leaving him
lonely as only someone locked up in a twisted body can be.

I feel sure she was fond of him, but she didn't fully grasp what was
at the centre of his life, which was to craft words in his own way. I
remember her at the wedding. Quite sexy. Christy lolling in a wheelchair, drinking brandy through a straw.

'Christ! This means another funeral. I'm bound to catch a cold.'

I remember when I opened Christy's first painting exhibition thirteen years ago. The canvasses which he'd painted with the brush held
in his toes were startling. They had a sort of primitive Spanish touch,
painted by an artist who himself looked as if he came out of an El
Greco painting. In my speech I said what a pity it was that his mother
(who had died a few years before) couldn't have been here to see
Christy's triumph.

'She *is* here,' Christy insisted from his wheelchair.

For a moment, it seemed she was.

---

[*] See 30 May 1970, note.

APPENDIX I

Table-talk of Eoin O'Mahony ('The Pope')

Presently the 'Pope' remarked on the vestigial remains of an estate in the distance:

'Ah . . . that must be Rathmogerley Castle. I knew his Lordship's brother well. He was said to be the love child of the Earl of Drogheda and his mother, Lady Rathmogerley, when his Lordship was with the Heavy Brigade in the Crimea. He had survived the charge of Balaklava, having got among the Russian guns at the end of the fatal sally. Indeed, he could display in later years (when Master of the Ward Union Hunt) the scorch marks, from the gunpowder of the same artillery, on the lace cuffs he had been wearing that day with his hunting pinks . . . It was unfortunate about the uncle,' the 'Pope' continued. 'He had been related by marriage to the Fitzroy-Carews and had been a major with the twelfth Lancers serving beside Churchill at the battle of Omdurman in 1898. His wife Nellie (she was famous for her home-made marmalade – hers was a secret recipe, handed down by her family who were themselves, on the spindle side, direct descendants of the last chaplain to Mary, Queen of Scots) became strangely infatuated with James Elroy Flecker to the extent that the major ('Galloping Depravity' as he was known), in a fit of pique, turned his affections to his dogs – ten couples of basset hounds he kept in his luxurious kennels near George Moore's, the novelist's house in Ely Place. There was a tragic outcome and an ensuing scandal so severe that it almost toppled Gladstone's second government when the major was made to stand trial on charges of carnal knowledge of one of the hounds in the back of his landau during the running of the Irish Grand National at Fairyhouse. Despite learned counsel's plea for the defence when it was argued that the dog had not only willingly accepted his master's *amours* but warmly returned them, Lord Chief Justice Baron Palles was moved to give his celebrated ruling that has since become enshrined in the constitution of many lands – *In the case of bestiality, mutual consent is not a good defence . . .'*

John Ryan, *Remembering How We Stood*, Gill & Macmillan (1975)

APPENDIX 2

Requiem for a Nanny by ULICK O'CONNOR

Ann Bell died in August 1984.

I

I saw from the water bus,
Like a dot on the piazza,
An old lady emerge
From the gloom of San Giorgio.

It reminded me of you
Who fifty years before
Taught me the Stations of the Cross
In our church at Rathgar.

Taught me to 'salute'
Priest – and parson too –
For you were from Tyrone
Where that was the thing to do.
Yes, I was brought up well
By Nanny, Ann Bell.

II

For you, the Church of the Three Patrons
Was a temple of delight,
Tented by that soaring roof
You made your own rite.

Loosed your mind from time to time
To join in the liturgy's swell,
The delicious strangeness of the Latin,
Accept the discipline of the bell.

When in your ninetieth year
I took a chance and walked you down
(It didn't take a feather out of you,
You wanted to walk home on your own),

We went round the familiar altars,
Murmured to the Little Flower,
Touched the feet of St Anthony,
Knelt for the Holy Hour.

It seemed like before, except
That beside you, I was an empty shell,
Not feeling in that silent nave
The peace that enveloped you like a spell.

III

On your way out
I glanced at the organ loft
Where Joyce's father met his wife
And thought of that devious poet,

But was careful not to mention it,
Even in a passing phrase,
For I knew you thought him responsible
For most of my wayward ways.

Ulick O'Connor, *All Things Counter*, Dedalus
Press (1981)

Notes on Frequently Mentioned Persons

ANNE BELL (1900–92)

Came to Fairfield Park as my nanny when I was five. One of the last of her breed with a code of rules, which she exercised with some severity, but also fairness, over her charges. My younger brothers and sister and I adored her. She stayed with the family until she was ninety-two. She was from Cookstown, County Tyrone, and had a certain no-nonsense quality about her that is associated with the Northern Irish. Her personality was such that subsequent generations, children and grandchildren, when they met her, fell under her spell just as we had.

She and our housekeeper Annie were immensely capable women; dignified and with a devotion and loyalty of a sort rarely found today.

PAUL BOWLES (1910–98)

I first met the novelist Paul Bowles in Tangier in the Sixties and was captivated by his roving mind and wide-ranging conversation. He had a strong influence on a generation who really knew very little about him. The Beatnik writers, Kerouac, Ginsberg, Corso and others, regarded him as an exemplar, but he was never quite sure himself why this was so. Bowles was a remarkable artist who, while he had an uncommon command of language, nevertheless relied on his unconscious instinct to guide him as to which way his characters would proceed. He was wonderful company with his darting mind and sense of humour, always on the alert for whatever he might snatch from 'this most excellent canopy, the air' and pin it on the page.

BOB BRADSHAW (1922–92)

Because Dublin pub talk figures so much in the literature of James Joyce, Sean O'Casey, Flann O'Brien and others it has its own special currency in twentieth-century literature. It drew its pith and strength from a type of working man who savours language as others might good food or drink. Davy Byrne's, The Bailey and the Lincoln Inn were well-established in the Thirties and later McDaid's and Grogan's were the places one could find the best talk. It was in the former I met Bob, a fine-looking jobbing builder with a constant and voracious interest in life as it was lived on a particular day. He would often express himself at the pub counter in what was to my mind startling and original prose.

ANNE BRADY (b. 1915)

My housekeeper from Ballyronan, Newtownmountkennedy, Wicklow where her father was gamekeeper for Major Tottenham on the Woodstock Estate. Came to Fairfield Park in 1939 as housekeeper and cook during her twenties, when I was nine. A superb chef and, with her Titian hair and bearing, distinctive-looking, she became an adjunct of the family. Part of her charm came from her strong character, which she did not feel it necessary to assert in any way.

GREGORY CORSO (1928–2001)

Gregory was one of a famous trio, with Jack Kerouac and Allen Ginsberg, of what were regarded as prototype Beatniks. I think he liked me because I could do conjuring tricks and quote Yeats at length. In the Sixties and Seventies I used to meet him a lot in the Chelsea Hotel where we would talk for hours on whatever subject had lately come into his ken. I ran into him again, by chance, five years ago in Rome and remarked how well he was looking. He said it was all due to methadone, which he had been prescribed and which had helped him to put new energy into his verse. The only drawback was that he had to go to sleep by ten. I thought of him as a sort of New York Jean Genet.

MONK GIBBON (1896–1992)

Poet, memoirist, novelist. He and Padraic Colum were among the last significant figures of the Irish Literary Renaissance to survive into the Eighties. His beautiful prose is what he will be most remembered for. A cousin of Yeats and Ninette de Valois and an intimate friend of George Russell (AE), he brought me into an environment where literature and art were preeminent, ranking even above the natural passion for politics rampant among the Irish. A close friend with whom I had many literary tussles, none of which lessened our friendship in any way.

THE HON. DESMOND AND MARIGA GUINNESS

These two created an enchanted world in Leixlip Castle, County Kildare, just outside Dublin. They also created a public awareness of the destruction of country houses in the eighteenth-century city which was about to commence. Both made an inestimable contribution to Irish life. Also tremendous fun to be with. To set out on an adventure with them was like the launching of the boat in Tennyson's *Ulysses*.

JACK LYNCH (1917–1999)

One of the icons of Irish sport and regarded as among the three greatest players ever in the national game of hurling. Tall, powerfully built, fair and good-looking, Jack Lynch exercised a national authority when he was elected Taoiseach in 1966. It was the beginning of the troubles in Northern Ireland and there was a danger that a civil war situation similar to that of 1922 might break out. In my view Lynch played an important part in preventing this. Popular recognition of his contribution was apparent in the general election in 1977 when his party Fianna Fail won the largest majority ever in Irish history. He was not at his best in his second term, however, mainly, as I believe, because of a physical ailment. He had had to undergo an operation for his heel and the surgeon had, in Lynch's words to me, 'butchered' his leg. This deprived him of the opportunity for regular exercise, which he needed to maintain the calm and determined stance he had demonstrated in public office. In 1979 he lost the leadership of the party in circumstances which, I think, would not have arisen had he been in the full of his health. Our relationship was based on the confidential work he had asked me to do in relation to Northern Ireland as Chairman of his Steering Committee. With hindsight, I believe that the trust he placed in me might not have been unrelated to the mutual code we shared as sportsmen.

MICHEÁL MACLIAMMÓIR (1899–1978)

Actor, linguist, playwright, set designer. Founder with Hilton Edwards of the Dublin Gate Theatre and the funniest and most brilliant conversationalist I have ever known. His knowledge of music, art, theatre and literature made him an invaluable companion as one's imaginative horizons began to expand. I thought of him, with his multiple gifts, as someone out of the Quattrocento and when he played Iago to Orson Welles' Othello in the well-known film, he seemed not at all out of place against the backdrop of Renaissance Venice.

VIVA

Viva Superstar. Born Susan Hoffman. Had a meteoric rise to fame when Andy Warhol decided to promote her as one of his superstars under the name Viva. The louche atmosphere surrounding the making of those early films, especially *Blue Movie* and *Lonesome Cowboys*, had obscured the fact that Viva came from a professional family in up-State New York and had been to a French convent finishing school to complete her education. I found her as bright as a button when I met her in the Chelsea Hotel and full of originality, which she would express in an amusing conversational style. She made her name in a period of quick and rapid change and the full impact of her innovative improvisatory acting style has, perhaps, never been adequately assessed.

TREVOR WEST (b. 1939)

Sportsman, biographer, professor of mathematics at Trinity College Dublin and friend, Trevor is a son of the late headmaster of Middleton College. From the time we were in our early thirties, we trained together in the College Park at Dublin University to keep fit, and played soccer, cricket and squash when it took our fancy. We both developed a keen interest in the divided part of our country, Northern Ireland. Trevor with friends in the Loyalist community and I with ones among the Nationalists worked together to develop common interests with both sides. He represented Dublin University for twelve years in the Irish Senate. Has written a fine biography of Sir Horace Plunkett, the founder of the Irish Co-operative Movement. As well as being a Fellow of Trinity College Dublin, he is a graduate of Cambridge University where he played cricket for St Catherine's College.

Index

Abbey Theatre, Dublin: Dowling on, 8–9;
author's Behan play performed at, 80,
92–3, 218–19; style, 154; founded, 273;
Yeats's *Cathleen ni Houlihan* produced at
(1901), 277
Abrahamson, Leonard, 58
Abrahamson, Max, 58
Acton, Sir Harold, 221
Adams, Gerry, 302 & n
Agadir, 232–3
Agate, James, 181
Aherne, Maureen, 239
Albaret, Céleste, 180–1
Albert, Mrs (of San Francisco), 83
Alfvén, Hugo, 197
Algren, Nelson, 75 & n, 76–7, 90,
188
Ali, Muhammad, 167–8, 216
Alicante, 291–7
All in the Family (US TV programme),
82
Allende, Salvador, 83
Allgood, Sarah, 289
Allingham, William, 203
Allport, George, 266, 268
Ambrose, Paddy, 309–10
Amery, John, 44 & n
Ampthill, Christabel, Lady, 193 & n
Anderson, Lindsay, 16
Andersson, Gerd, 56
Andrews, David, 175 & n
Anglo-Irish Treaty (1921), 148–50
Anne, Princess, 16
Annie (housekeeper), 37, 210, 310
Anson, Lady Elizabeth, 16
Antheil, George, 197
'Aquinas' *see* Torey, Thomas

Arnold, Bruce, 304
Arrington, Sailor (boxer), 216
Arts Club, Dublin, 5–6, 21n, 48, 277–9, 289,
302, 303
Ashcroft, Dame Peggy, 253
Ashton, Sir Frederick, 120 & n
Asquith, Herbert Henry, 1st Earl of Oxford
and Asquith, 97 & n
Attlee, Clement, 1st Earl, 132

Bacall, Lauren, 213–14
Bach, Jeannie, 170
Bacon, Francis, 119–20
Baldwin, James, 79
Baldwin, Stanley, 1st Earl, 96
Ballagh, Robert, 301
Ballyvaughan, Co. Clare, 272
Bard, Milton, 166
Bard, Stanley, 80–1, 86, 165–6, 283
Baring, Maurice, 84
Barr, Glen, 270
Barrington, Donal, 125, 161, 308
Barrington, Jonah, 6, 8, 15, 27
Barton, Charlie, 244
Basterot, Count de, 272–3
Baudelaire, Charles, 122–3
Beardsley, Aubrey, 22
Beardsley, Mabel, 187
Beaton, (Sir) Cecil, 156, 238n
Beauvoir, Simone de, 75–6n
Beck, Julian, 278
Beckett, Jim and Margot, 204
Beckett, Samuel, 53, 137–8, 146, 204, 231–2;
Waiting for Godot, 77n
Bedford, Patrick, 42, 49
Behan, Beatrice (*née* ffrench-Salkeld), 32–33 &
n, 34

Behan, Brendan: as 'Regency Buck', 5;
  practical jokes, 9; author's biography of, 15,
  28, 32–5, 38–9, 47, 50, 61, 68, 71, 81, 99,
  115, 186, 272; MacLiammóir quotes, 22;
  sexual proclivities, 32, 35, 68, 69n, 72;
  patronizes McDaid's, 47n; reputation in
  USA, 72, 89; in Paris, 79; author's one man
  play on, 80, 85, 92–3, 119n, 127, 154,
  200–1, 218–19, 288, 303; in New York, 81,
  87; Kleinsinger composes Lament for, 87;
  rugby-playing, 132; friendship with Philip
  Corley, 187; Ginsberg and, 189; The
  Hostage, 34
Behan, Brian, 33n
Behan, Carmel, 33n, 38
Behan, Dominic, 33n, 34–45
Behan, John, 124, 190, 302
Behan, Kathleen (Brendan's mother), 33 & n,
  38–9, 121–2, 271
Behan, Rory, 33n
Behan, Seamus, 33n, 38–9
Behan, Sean, 33n
Behan, Stephen (Brendan's father), 33 & n, 39
Beit, Sir Alfred, 39 & n, 40–1
Beit, Clementine, Lady (née Mitford), 39n
Belcher, Muriel, 119–20
Belfast, 264–71
Bell, Ann (Nanny), 32, 37, 177, 195–6, 198,
  202, 229, 264, 300; death and requiem
  poem for, 317–18
Bell, Clive, 68
Bell, G.K.A., 228n
Belton, Paddy, 177
Benjamin, Walter, 122
Bergen, Edgar, 82–3
Bergin (Dublin chauffeur), 145
Bergner, Elisabeth, 24–5
Bermudez, Marion, 259
Bernhardt, Bill, 117–18, 123–4
Berrigan, Father Dan, 79 & n, 85–6
Berrigan, Father Phillip, 79n, 85–6
Bertolucci, Bernardo, 140
Betjeman, Sir John, 221
Betts, Joey, 47
Birley, Annabel (née Bury), 44
Blackwood, Lady Caroline, 158 & n
Blue Movie (film), 85n, 139–40
Blunden, Sir William, 118
Boal, Desmond, 265
Boland, Kevin, 304
Booth, Edwin, 284
Bosch, Lieutenant-General Milans, 296

Bourget, Paul, 273
Bourne, Laurie, 226
Bouverie, David, 84
Bowles, Jane, 239
Bowles, Paul, 234, 240 & n, 243–7
Boyle, Harris, 199
Bradford, Roy Hamilton, 174
Bradshaw, Bob, 143–4 & n, 146–7, 155,
  179–80, 199
Brady, George, 61
Brady, Liam, 191
Bragg, Melvyn (later Baron), 300
Brasillach, Robert, 288
Brenan, Gerald, 67 & n, 68
Brendan (O'Connor; play), 154
Breslin, Jimmy, 188
Breton, André, 244n
Brewster, Barry, 27
Brien, Alan, 35
Broad, David, 119–20
Brogan, Colm, 300
Brooke, Rupert, 170
Brown, Andreas, 288
Brown, Christy, 28 & n, 144, 314
Brown, Georgia, 119n
Brown, Mary, 144, 314
Brown, Nick, 86
Browne, Nick, 212
Browne, Monsignor Patrick, 226–7
Brugha, Cathal (Charles William St John
  Burgess), 149 & n
Brugha, Rory, 175
Burgess, Charles William St John see Brugha,
  Cathal
Burgess, Guy, 44
Burke, Mick, 280
Burlington Hotel, Dublin, 146
Burroughs, William, 88, 188–9, 243–4, 247
Bury, Lady Mairi, 42–3
Byrne, Gay, 70 & n, 182, 218

Cage, John, 287 & n
Cain, Herb, 83
Callaghan, James (later Baron), 269
Campbell, James, 10
Campbell, Joseph, 287 & n
Campbell, Michael, 9–11
Campbell, Patrick, 9n
Camus, Albert, 247
Canning, Father Pat, 11
Cape, Jonathan, 260
Capote, Truman, 134

Carberry, Sean, 258
Carey, Eileen (Mrs Sean O'Casey), 289-90
Carney, James, 5
Carpenter, Edward, 2
Carrier, Robert, 119n
Carroll, Paul Vincent: Shadow and Substance, 193n
Carson, Johnny, 109
Casement, Sir Roger, 21 & n, 196, 238, 276, 277n, 285
Casement, Thomas, 21
Casson, Christopher, 24, 276, 277n
Casson, Sir Lewis, 24
Castletown, Co. Kildare, 39-40, 157-8, 193
Cavett, Dick, 71-2, 109
Cawley, James, 224, 308
Century Club, New York, 90
Chaffee, Susie, 189-91
Charlemont, James Edward Caulfeild, 8th Viscount, 45, 121
Charles, John, Archbishop of Dublin, 99
Chase, Doris, 259
Chelsea Hotel, New York, 74, 80-1, 85-9, 165-6, 169, 171, 188, 256, 258, 283
Chesterton, G.K., 84, 225
Chicago, 75-8, 167
Child, A.E., 272
Childers, Erskine (the younger), 170 & n, 176
Churchill, Sir Winston, 97, 214n
Clan na Poblachta, 220
Clarke, P.J., 89, 256
Clarke, Shirley, 80, 85
Cleveland, Ohio, 75
Clonmore and Reynolds (publishers), 29n, 30
Cocteau, Jean, 243 & n
Colley, George, 105, 107-8, 162, 175
Collins, Michael, 62, 148-9 & nn, 161n, 179, 238, 252
Collins, Paddy, 279
Colthurst, Captain Bowen, 98n
Colum, Padraic, 73 & n, 154n, 236, 273
Compton, Denis, 228
Concannon, Don, 301
Connection, The (film), 80
Connery, Sean, 257
Connolly, Lady Louisa, 158
Conway, Jimmy, 191
Coolican, Jack, 280
Cooney, Patrick, 224
Cooper, Ivan, 105
Copland, Aaron, 244-5
Corish, Brendan, 132, 133n

Corley, Philip, 186-7
Corley, Tom, 186
Cornforth, John: The Inspiration of the Past, 60n
Corrigan, Mairead, 270
Corso, Gregory, 85, 88-9, 166-7, 171-2, 188-9, 247
Corvo, Baron see Rolfe, Frederick
Cory, William, 203
Cosgrave, Liam, 132, 133n, 145-6, 159, 176, 182, 210
Cosgrave, Louie (née Flanagan), 16
Cosgrave, Mary, 159
Cosgrave, William Thomas ('Boss'), 15-16, 159
Council of Ireland, 160
Coveney, Terry, 231
Coward, Noël, 21, 24-5
Cowley, John and Annie, 272
Coyle, Marion, 224
Craig, Edward Gordon, 22, 154
Craig, Maurice, 203
Cromwell, Oliver, 290
Cronin, Bart, 105, 107, 109, 181
Crosby, Bing, 116
Crossman, R.H.S., 96
Crowningshield, Mary, 169
Culliton, Gerry, 100
Cunningham, Laurie, 292, 295
Curley, Taitsie, 121-2
Curley, Walter, 121-2, 210-11
Currie, Anne Ita (Anita), 160, 178-9
Currie, Austin, 105, 127n, 145, 161, 174, 178
Cusack, Cyril, 11 & n, 17
Cusack, Paul, 120
Cusack, Sinead, 11n

Dallas, Texas, 133
Dalton, Louis, 272
Daly, Father Edward (later Bishop), 108-10, 126-7
D'Arcy, Father Martin, 224, 234
Dark Lovers, The (O'Connor; play), 193 & n
Davie, Michael, 223
Davis, Thomas, 290
Davitt, Judge Cahir, 219-20
Davitt, Michael, 220, 272n
Dawson Lounge (pub), Dublin, 151
Day Lewis, Daniel, 28n
Deirdre (O'Connor; Noh play), 275, 285
Dempsey, Martin, 276
Dennehy, Tim, 105
Denning, Neville, 309
Dermody, Frank, 63

Derry (Londonderry), 105, 126–7; 'Bloody Sunday' shootings (1972), 107–10, 118, 171
de Valera, Eamon, 26, 62, 147–50 & nn
de Valois, Dame Ninette, 197
Devlin (McAliskey), Bernadette, 177 & n, 301, 304–7
Devlin, Patrick, 159–60, 174, 176
Dickens, Charles, 123n
Dickey, James: *Adventure*, 79
Dillon, John, 290
Doctorow, E.L.: *Ragtime*, 293
Donleavy, J.P., 190, 214
Donnelly, Mrs (Nanny's former employer), 195
Dorr, Noel, 105, 117
Douglas, Mike, 173
Douglas, Sharman, 214
Dowling, Vincent, 8
Downey, Paddy, 277
Doyle, Vincent, 146
Drabble, Margaret, 300
Dream Box, The (O'Connor; play), 69n
Dreiser, Theodore, 75n
Drennan, William, 45
Drogheda, Charles Garrett Ponsonby Moore, 11th Earl of, 84 & n, 239
Dublin: churches and religious orders in, 91n; Huguenots in, 131 & n; bombings in, 173–4; rebuilding, 239, 261–2; population, 261; July 1980 protest march in, 303–8
Dublin International Theatre Festival, 41, 92, 274, 277
Duddy, Jackie, 110
Dugdale, Rose, 211n
Dun Laoghaire, 91–2
Dundee, Angelo, 216
Dunn, Lady Mary, 83–4
Dunne, Sister, 34
Dunsany, Edward John Moreton Drax Plunkett, 18th Baron of, 6
Dwyer, Michael, 215

Eastman, Hal, 233
Edgar, Don, 123–4
Edmund Burke Theatre, Dublin, 277
Edwards, Bob, 124
Edwards, Hilton, 21n, 22, 49, 62, 187, 252
Edwards, Oliver, 152
Edwards, Owen Dudley, 300
Egan, Sister Jogues, 85–6
Ekland, Britt, 5
Elliot, Anne, 52
Elliot, Gordon, 52, 57

Ellman, Richard, 186
Emmet, Robert, 214–15
English, Mick, 100–1
Ensor, Tony, 100–1
Erdman, Jean, 285
Euripides: *Alcestis*, 278
Evans, Revd Arthur, 243
Evans, Godfrey, 118
Evergreen Review, 77n
Exorcist, The (film), 77, 137

Fagan, J.B. (Jack), 289
Fanning, Aengus, 203 & n
Farrell, James T., 75n, 188
Farson, Dan, 119–20
Faulkner, Brian (*later* Baron), 160, 174–5
Feehan, Colonel Matt, 147
Fitt, Gerry (*later* Baron), 105, 145
Fitzgerald, Lord Edward, 17
Fitzgerald, Jack, 231–2
Fitzgerald, Jim, 155, 158
Fitzgerald, Lady Pamela, 17
Fitzgerald (Trinity College Dublin groundsman), 13–14
Fitzgibbon, Constantine, 279
Fitzpatrick, Jim, 264–5 & n, 268
Fitzwilliam Club, Dublin, 6, 177, 196, 217, 218–19 & n, 223, 231, 260, 262
Flanagan, 'The Bird', 159 & n
Flannery, James, 41 & n, 275
Fleming, Sir Alexander, 151
Flynn, Mannix, 230–1
Foot, Michael, 298–301
Ford, John, 257
Francis, Arlene, 170–1
Francis of Assisi, St, 22
Franco, General Francisco, 296
Franks, Denis, 63, 71 & n
Frascati, Blackrock, 17–18
Fraser, Lady Antonia, 59
Fraser, Hugh, 59
Freddie, Prince (of Buganda), 234
Friel, Brian, 302 & n
Fuller, Bill, 121
Furness (house), Co. Kildare, 62

Gable, Martin, 284
Gageby, Douglas, 224
Galbraith, John Kenneth, 287
Galilei, Alessandro, 157n
Gallagher, Eddie, 211n
Galligan, Liam, 291n

Ganly, Eileen, 20, 113–14

Gardner, Isabella, 140, 169–70

Gardner, Rosie, 141–2, 169n

Garnett, David, 203

Garrison, Jim, 135–6

Gate Theatre, Dublin, 21n, 22, 62, 157

Gavilan, Kid, 168

Gebler, Ernie, 190

General Elections (Ireland): (1972), 132; (1977), 224

Genet, Jean, 56, 260

Gerrity, Ned, 83

Gersdorff, Carl de, 284

Ghuika, Roderick, 89–90, 140, 169, 172, 188, 217; death, 283–4

Gibbon, Philly, 151

Gibbon, William Monk: friendship with author, 9 & n, 10–11, 18–19, 94, 197; relations with Yeats, 18–19; on George Moore, 19–20; on Proust, 94–5, 180–1; puritanism, 95 & n; and wife's prosecution for careless driving, 113–15; author's disagreement with, 150–1; eightieth birthday party, 210–11; at Fitzwilliam Club party, 218–19; at filming of *Ulysses*, 229; *Alphabet of Morality*, 211–12; *Inglorious Soldier*, 97–9 & n; 'Notes on the Meditation of Love', 150

Gibbon, Winifred, 18, 94, 113–15, 150

Gibraltar, 92

Gide, André, 181n

Gilbey, Anthony, 234

Giles, Johnny, 191, 196

Gill, Pierce, 165

Gilmartin, Peggy, 279

Gilmartin, Tommy, 279–80

Ginsberg, Allen, 85, 88, 188–9, 247

Givens, Don, 191

Glenavy, Beatrice, Lady (*née* Elvery), 9 & n, 10–11, 18, 20–1

Glenavy, Gordon Campbell, 2nd Baron, 9n, 10

Gogarty, Oliver Duane ('Noll'), 308–9 & n

Gogarty, Oliver St John: and Mabs Moltke, 7; author's biography of, 9n, 98–9, 186; wins Gold Medal at Taillte, 18–19; writes to Lady Londonderry, 45; author writes TV script on, 100; author's one-man play on (*The Last of the Bucks*), 154, 158–9, 185, 225; depicted in Joyce's *Ulysses*, 154n, 204, 228; Yeats on, 154n; at Renvyle House, 225–7; TV film of, 225, 228–32; limericks and parodies, 226–7; presents swans to

Liffey after escape from kidnap, 227n; loses libel action, 232–3; and Irish Literary Renaissance, 236; *As I was going down Sackville Street*, 255; *Golden Stockings*, 229

Goldman, Emma, 293

Goldman, Milton, 165

Gonne (MacBride), Maude, 7n, 8 & n, 156, 161n, 271, 277

Goold, Vere, 262

Gorges, Desmond Patrick Michael, 15–17, 32, 35

Gorges, Meehawl, 17

Gotham Book Mart, New York, 141, 255, 288

Goulding, Sir Basil, 192, 219

Goulding, Lingard, 118

Goulding, Valerie, Lady, 192

Goulet, Yann, 301–3

Gowrie, Alexander Patric Greysteil Ruthven, 2nd Earl of ('Grey'), 40–1

Graham, Godfrey, 228

Graham, Virginia, 81, 284

Grand Inquisitor, The (O'Connor; Noh play), 285

Grant, Peter, 302

Graziano, Rocky, 72n, 76

Greaves, George, 235–6, 239, 241–3

Greene, Graham, 189

Gregory, Augusta, Lady, 225, 236, 272–3, 294

Grey, Francine, 85

Griffith, Kenneth, 182

Grogan, Vincent, 6

Guinness Book of Records, The, 200

Guinness, Desmond: at Leixlip Castle, 6–7 & n, 59–60; slimming, 8; and Mick Jagger, 24; invites author to Castletown, 39; buys Castletown, 40; tennis-playing, 40–1, 193; friendship with author, 47, 63; discusses father, 59; marriage relations, 274

Guinness, Mariga (*née* Princess von Urach): at Leixlip Castle, 6–7 & n, 273, 279; and Georgian conservation, 17–18, 25; correspondence with author, 24; broadcasts, 25; in Holland, 36, 40; in Norway, 36–7, 117; Nancy Mitford and, 38; at Castletown, 40; friendship with author, 47, 63; qualities, 60; Padraic Colum asks about, 73; entertains Sir Oswald Mosley, 95–6; in Russia with Jullian, 202; marriage relations, 274; attends Noh play, 277; family background, 277n

Guinness, Marina, 47, 63

Guinness, Patrick, 8
Gysin, Brion, 244 & n

Hackett, Joe D., 196 & n, 219
Hamill, Pete, 85
Hamilton, Gervaise, 233, 240–1
Hamilton, Hamish (publishers), 28, 185–6, 232, 291
Hamilton, 'Rat' (solicitor), 219
Hardcastle, William, 32
Harding, James, 181
Harlech, David Ormsby Gore, 5th Baron, 214
Harris, Matt, 220, 272
Harris, Richard, 257
Harte, Paddy, 177
Haughey, Charles, 58, 101, 224, 257
Haverty, Joe, 27
Hawn, Goldie, 190
Heaney, Marie, 48
Heaney, Seamus, 48, 72n, 302
Hearn, Lafcadio, 67 & n, 134 & n
Heath, (Sir) Edward, 132, 145, 160, 173
Hemingway, Margaux, 255
Hemphill, Martyn, 4th Baron, 309
Herbert, David, 238–9 & n
Herrema, Riede: kidnapped, 211 & n
Heyerdahl, Thor, 55
Hingerty, Don, 100 & n
Hintlesham Festival, Suffolk, 119
Hoffman, Abbie, 75
Hogan, Inspector John, 305–6
Hogan, Maurice, 223n
Holden, Bill, 9–10
Holland, Aileen, 25
Hone, Evie, 26
Hone, Nathaniel, 26
Hopkins, Gerard Manley, 152
Hopkins, Thelma, 182
Horrocks-Taylor, Philip, 101
Housman, A.E., 95
Hume, John: in Social Democratic Labour Party, 105, 146, 185; assaulted in Dublin, 124; at author's Behan show, 127; meets Jack Lynch, 127; arranges author's meeting with Edward Kennedy, 143; at Dungloe meeting, 145–6; and Sunningdale Agreement, 160–1; contributes to *Irish Liberation*, 165n; in Northern Ireland Executive, 174; resists Conor Cruise O'Brien's attacks, 179; in Dublin, 257, 278, 303; negotiates with Gerry Adams, 302n

Hurst, Brian Desmond, 32–3
Hyde, Harford Montgomery ('Monty'), 41 & n, 42–5, 254

Inglis, Brian, 137n
IRA (Irish Republican Army), 161–2, 200, 298, 310
Ireland Act (1949), 132
Irish Association, 160
Irish Georgian Society, 6n
Irish Liberation (ed. O'Connor), 165n, 167
Irish Players, 289n
Irish Republican Brotherhood, 220

Jackson, Jolyon, 276, 277n, 286
Jagger, Mick, 23–4
Jameson, Derek, 33
Jersey City, New Jersey, 216
John XXIII, Pope, 255
John, Augustus, 225, 279
John of the Cross, St, 68, 69n
Johnston, Denis, 9n, 14 & n
Jolliffe, John, 274
Jones, Gerry, 304 & n
Jones, James (evangelist), 246–7
Jones, James (novelist), 79
Jordan, Peggy, 48
Joseph, Irene, 33
Joyce, James: tribute to George Moore, 19n; piety at school, 34; Virginia Woolf writes on, 53; Marsh seeks Civil List grant for, 97n; author lectures on in New York, 141; stays in Martello tower with Gogarty, 228; in Irish Literary Renaissance, 236; bust of, 308; *Dubliners*, 6; *Finnegans Wake*, 287n; *Stephen Hero* (dramatized), 155; *Ulysses*, 19n, 42n, 154n, 189, 204, 228
Joyce, John Stanislaus, 300
Joyce, May (née Murray), 300
Joyce, William ('Lord Haw-Haw'), 44 & n
Juan Carlos I, King of Spain, 296–7
Jullian, Philippe, 201–2 & n

Kane, Michael, 124
Kavanagh, Patrick, 12n, 47n; *Soul for Sale*, 94
Kavanagh, Ronnie, 100, 107
Keane, Donald, 287
Keane, Ronan, 150–1, 308
Kearney, Peadar, 33n
Keating, Sean, 144
Keelan, Dr Pat, 155
Keeler, Christine, 186–7 & n

Kelly, Jim, 257
Kelly, Luke, 191
Kelly, Stephen, 181
Kennedy, Basil, 42, 44
Kennedy, Edward, 143, 165n, 269
Kennedy, John F., 133, 135
Kennedy, Robert, 143 & n
Kennelly, Brendan, 13 & n
Kerouac, Jack, 85, 244n, 247
Kiely, Benedict, 72 & n
Kildare Street Club, Dublin, 17, 30–1
Kingsford-Smith, Graham, 291–3, 296–7
Kingswell, Dickie, 132
Kleinsinger, George, 87 & n, 188, 258–9, 283
Kolkhorst, 'Colonel' George, 221–2
Kranstam, Henning, 120n
Kyle, Jack, 192, 231

Lagercrantz, Olof, 51, 53–5
Lalor's (pub), Dublin, 222
Lamb, Henry, 62
Lamb, Lady Pansy, 62
LaMotta, Jake, 72
Lancaster, Sir Osbert, 221
Land League (Irish), 220
Last of the Bucks, The (O'Connor; play), 154–5, 158, 185, 225
Last Tango in Paris (film), 140
Late Late Show (Irish TV programme), 63, 70, & n, 111, 152, 156, 182
Lavery, Hazel, Lady, 42, 156, 238–9
Lavery, Sir John, 42, 239
Law, Andrew Bonar, 118–19
Lawrence, Gavin, 15
Lawrence, John, 15–6
Le Fanu, Sheridan, 202
Legge, Hector, 204
Leixlip Castle, Co. Kildare: author visits, 6–7, 12, 23, 59, 63, 193, 273, 279; building and design, 60n; Mosley visits, 95–6
Lemass, Sean, 179
Lenihan, Brian, 108–10, 175
Lennon, John, 133
Leonard, Hugh, 155
Lerner, Max, 287
Leslie, Sir Shane, 177
L'Estrange, Garry, 177
Lewis, Al Blue, 167
Lifar, Serge, 156
Lifestyles (O'Connor; poems), 186
Liston, Sonny, 168
Littlewood, Joan, 34

Living Theatre, 278
Lloyd George, David, 1st Earl, 44, 148
Loach, Ken, 16
Lohr, Marie, 24
Londonderry, Charles Stewart Henry Vane-Temple-Stewart, 7th Marquess of, 41 & n, 45
Londonderry, Edith Helen, Marchioness of, 42, 45
Longford, Edward Arthur Henry Pakenham, 6th Earl of, 21n, 62–3
Longford, Elizabeth, Countess of, 62
Longford, Francis Aungier Pakenham, 7th Earl of, 62, 63
Long Kesh (internment camp), 310
Los Angeles, 81
Lovesey, John, 186, 194
Lutyens, Sir Edwin, 225
Lynagh, Michael, 192
Lynch, Jack (Taoiseach): author meets, 105, 124, 174, 176, 182; and Northern Ireland situation, 105, 125, 159, 175–6; and 'Bloody Sunday' killings, 108–9; addresses Oxford Union, 126; Hume meets, 127; loses office in 1973 election, 132, 159; Hume praises, 160; and Dublin bombings, 174; letter to New York Times, 177; and Haughey, 224; negotiates with Callaghan, 269
Lyons, Leland, 290
Lysaght, Charles, 118, 273
Lyttelton, Andrew, 16

McAliskey, Bernadette see Devlin, Bernadette
McAllister, Sister Liz, 85
MacAnna, Tomás, 80, 92, 154–5, 170
MacAonghusa, Prionsias, 44
McArdle, Johnny, 139
MacBride, Major John, 8 & n, 161n
MacBride, Sean, 161 & n, 179, 219–20, 265, 277–8
McCabe, Charlie, 83–4 & n, 209
McCann, Hugh, 126
McCarthy, Isabel, 199, 313
McCarthy, Revd John, 199, 310, 313
McClure, Sam, 265–8
McCourt, Malachy, 7, 86, 89 & n, 188, 257–8
MacCurtain, Tomas, 144
McDaid's (pub), Dublin, 47, 146
MacDonagh, Thomas, 20
MacDonald, Ramsay, 45, 96
McDowell, Robert Brendan, 12 & n

McEntee, Margaret, 187
McGiver, John, 82
McGowran, Jackie, 136–8
McGuinness, Norah, 9 & n, 10
McGuire, Edward, 198 & n
Machlin, Milton, 256
McKeague, John, 265–9
McKenna, James, 120–1, 124–5
McKenna, Siobhan, 32, 119n, 136, 218
Mackey, 'Gurrier', 47
Macklin, Milton, 79–80, 86
MacLaine, Shirley, 85
MacLaverty, Bernard, 300
MacLiammóir, Micheál: co-founds Gate
    Theatre, 21n, 22, 62; friendship with
    author, 21–3, 49, 187; manner, 21–2;
    Coward mocks, 25; disagreement with
    author, 50; eye operation, 60; and Eileen
    Ganly, 114; records speech for NBC,
    157; death, 252, 262–3; reputation, 253;
    in The Importance of Being Oscar, 274;
    keeps on make-up during operation,
    280; plays in Yeats's translation of Oedipus,
    178
McMahon, James (of CIE), 108–9
McMahon, James (Under-Secretary, Dublin
    Castle, 1919–21), 147
McMaster, Anew, 24, 277n
McMaster, Marjorie (née MacLiammóir), 24–5
MacMichael, John, 270
McPhillips, Joe, 234–5
Mac Stiofain, Sean, 125
McSweeny, David, 69n
MacSwiney, Terence, 298 & n
McWhirter, Norris and Ross, 199–200
'Madeleine' (Cynthia; British wartime spy),
    254
Madrid, 295
Maguire, Frank, 298–9
Maguire, Liam, 256–8
Mahaffy, John Pentland, 154n, 225, 237
Mahon, Christy, 261
Mailer, Norman, 79, 85
Manning, Mary, 197
Marais, Jean, 244n
Markiewicz, Constance, Countess, 271
Markpress Committee, 181
Marsh, Sir Edward, 97
Martin, F. X., 254n
Martin, Leopoldo, 295, 297
Martin, Dr Malachi, 254
Martyn, Edward, 91, 236, 272–3

Marvell, Andrew, 88
Marx, Bill, 212
Mason, Roy (later Baron), 175n, 268
Masters, Edgar Lee, 81
Mattello, Roberto, 138
Matthews, (Sir) Stanley, 152
Mayhew, (Sir) Patrick, 169
Meenan, James, 308
Merrigan, Matt, 304
Michelangelo Buonarroti, 293
Midnight Cowboy (film), 82
Miller, Arthur, 81
Milton, Ernest, 277n
Mitchum, Robert, 257
Mitford, Nancy, 37–8
Mogambo (film), 156
Molina, Judith, 278
Moloney, Johnny, 131
Moltke, Countess Mabs, 7 & n
Monaghan: bombings in, 173–4
Monaghan, Kevin, 151
Moore, Brian, 48
Moore, George, 10, 19–20, 73, 94, 236, 240,
    272, 294; Avowals, 241; Celibates, 5–6; Hail
    and Farewell, 19n; The Lake, 228n; A
    Mummer's Wife, 19; The Untilled Field, 6,
    19n
Moore, Patricia, 239
Moran, Terry, 258
Morgan, Cliff, 192
Mosley, Diana, Lady (née Mitford), 95n
Mosley, Sir Oswald, 95–6 & n
Mountstewart (house), Co. Down, 41–6
Moylan (Dublin tailor), 154
Moyne, Bryan Walter Guinness, 2nd Baron, 59
    & n, 60
Mrabhat (Paul Bowles's servant), 245–6
Mullen, Karl, 192
Mullen, Mickey, 304–7
Mulligan, Andy, 107, 192
Mulligan, Barney, 289 & n
Mulligan, Paddy, 27
Murphy, Tom, 147
Murray, Paul, 280

Nanny see Bell, Ann
Nebel, Long John, 256
Nehru, Jawaharlal (Pandit), 9n
Neukomm, Sigismund (Austrian composer),
    275
Newman, Randy, 216
New Orleans, 133–6, 285

New York, 71, 74–5, 79–81, 85–90, 133, 138–41, 165–71, 188, 212–17, 255–9, 283–8
Nicolson, (Sir) Harold, 95n, 96, 202n, 239
Noh plays, 274–7, 285–7
Norman, Frank, 33
Northern Ireland: unrest in, 59, 105, 107–9, 117, 123–4; proposed restoration of Parliament in, 132; election for Executive (1973), 145; Assembly, 159–61, 168, 174; author edits book on, 165n; strike (1974), 173; Unionist-Nationalist conflict in, 174; Assembly dissolved, 175–6; killings and violence in, 181, 200; proposed independent Ulster State for, 212–13, 265–70, 278, 311n; Loyalist groups in, 265–9, 311–12; IRA hunger strikes in, 298–9, 301; see also Derry
Novak, Kim, 257
Nowlan, Kevin, 36 & n, 40

Obolensky, Alice (Astor), 240
Obolensky, Ivan, 240
Obolensky, Prince Serge, 239
O'Brien, Conor Cruise: political ambitions, 132–3, 162; as Minister for Posts and Telegraphs, 133n, 182, 209; and human rights case in Strasbourg, 145; hostility to John Hume, 160, 179; career, 176n; dislikes Nationalist ideas, 176; dismisses Markpress, 181; made Minister for Information, 182; loses seat in 1977 election, 224
O'Brien, Edna, 52–5, 190
O'Brien, Flann see O'Nolan, Brian
O'Brien, Noel, 131, 194
O'Brien, Toby (Agency), 15, 32, 35
Observer (newspaper), 223
O'Casey, Eileen, 193
O'Casey, Sean, 193, 236, 273, 289–90
O'Connell, Daniel, 95n
O'Connell, John, 125
O'Connor, Andrew, 111–12
O'Connor, Carroll, 82, 304
O'Connor, Donagh, 196
O'Connor, Frank, 203–4
O'Connor, Garry, 196
O'Connor, Hugh, 82
O'Connor, J. Arthur, 279
O'Connor, James, 134n
O'Connor, Marilyn, 134–5
O'Connor, Maureen, 90
O'Connor, Michael, 133 & n, 134–6
O'Connor, Sir Nicholas, 90

O'Dalaigh, Cearbhall, 210–11, 263
O'Dwyer, Paul, 264–6, 269–70
O'Faolain, Sean, 6, 203–4
Offering of Swans, An (film), 225n
O'Fiach, Cardinal Tomás Séamus, 311–12
O'Flaherty, Gerry, 32, 93–4
O'Flaherty, Liam, 203
O'Halloran, Brian, 107
O'Hanlon, Patrick, 145
O Hanrachain, Padraic, 105, 107, 117–18
O'Kelly, Kevin, 126
Oland, Warner, 285
O'Loughlin, Dara, 280
Olympia Theatre, Dublin, 178, 278
O'Mahony, Eoin ('Pope'), 12 & n; table-talk, 315–16
O'Neill, Chris, 272
O'Nolan, Brian (Flann O'Brien; Myles na Gopaleen), 47n; At Swim-Two-Birds, 204
Ophuls, Marcel, 188
O'Regan, Kathleen, 289
O'Reilly, Alpho, 42
O'Reilly, Anthony J., 148, 192 & n, 196
Orlofsky, Peter, 188–9
O'Rourke, Father Joe, 85
Orpen, Sir William, 26, 225, 279
Osborne, Walter, 26
Oscar Theatre, Dublin, 303, 306–7
O'Shea, Jack, 9
O'Sullivan, Archie, 61–2
O'Sullivan, Colm, 28, 219
O'Sullivan, John, 105
O'Sullivan, Sean, 272
O'Sullivan, Seumas, 236
Oswald, Lee Harvey, 136
Oxford, 126

Painter, George, 94–5, 180
Paisley, Ian, 265
Pakenham, Thomas, 59
Paris, 106–7
Paris Review, 214
Parker, Carey, 143
Parnell, Charles Stewart, 73, 220, 290
Partridge, Frances, 83n
Pasternak, Boris, 146
Pater, Walter, 94
Paul VI, Pope, 69n
Payne, Anne Marie, 288
Pearce, Sir Edward Lovett, 157n
Pearse, Patrick, 20, 299
Pearson, Eileen, 314

Pearson, Noel, 155, 158
Pembroke, Reginald Herbert, 15th Earl of, 239
Perkins, Max, 90
Perrott, Patrick, 21
Perry, Lionel, 91, 221
Peters, Charlie, 172
Peters, Mary, 182
Pim, 'Josh', 219
Pittsburgh, 254
Players Club, New York, 284
Plimpton, George, 214, 217
Plomer, William, 203
Plunket, Aileen, 5
Plunkett, Sir Horace, 14n
Plunkett, James, 225–6 & n, 230, 231
Plunkett, Joseph, 20; I see his Blood upon the Rose, 313n
Plunkett, Blessed Oliver, 195
Pollard, Michael J., 189, 286
Potter, Archie, 275
Pound, Ezra, 161n, 235
Pound, Omar, 234
Power, Arthur, 5 & n, 6
Power, James, 302
Power, Judge Wyse, 309
Prentice Hall (US publishers), 71
Presley, Elvis, 227
Price, Linda, 69 & n
Project Theatre, Dublin, 193
Proust, Marcel, 94–5, 180
Provisional IRA ('Provos'), 162
Pryce-Jones, Alan, 221
Purser, Sarah, 26, 271

Quartet (publishers), 199
Queen Elizabeth II, RMS, 288
Quinn, Gerry, 192

Racquet Club, New York, 74–5, 217
Radiguet, Raymond, 243
Raft, George, 173
Rand, Mary, 8
Raymond, Gary, 33
Reardon, Mike, 86
Reavey, George, 146–7
Redgrave, Lynn, 133
Redmond, John, 278
Reid, Father Alec, 266, 268
Reid, Olive, 96–100, 115–16, 260–1
Renvyle House, Ireland, 225, 226
Requiem for a Nanny (O'Connor; poem), 317–18

Reynolds, Paul, 90
Richards, Shelah, 9 & n, 10, 15, 20
Richardson, Damien, 152
Roberts, Charlie, 252
Robinson, Cecil ('Bomber'), 50
Robinson, Henry Morton, 287n
Robinson, Lennox, 273
Robinson, Peter, 50
Roche, Butch, 230
Rochford, Justice Alfred, 114
Rolfe, Frederick (Baron Corvo): Hadrian VII, 17
Romeo and Juliet (ballet), 56
Rosse, Anne, Countess of, 61
Rosset, Bernard (Barney), 57, 77–8 & nn, 165n
Rosset, Mary, 78
Rossmore, William Westenra, 7th Baron, 17
Rowsome, Leo, 48
Ruskin, John, 13
Russell, George (AE), 236, 246
Russell, Sean, 277
Ryan, Fran, 277
Ryan, John, 12n, 34; Remembering How We Stood, 316
Ryan, Phyllis, 193 & n
Ryan, Ritchie, 204

Sackville-West, Vita, 202, 239
Sai Chin, 70 & n
Saint Gaudens, Augustus, 73
Salkeld, Cecil, 34
Salkeld, Celia, 34
Salkeld, Florrie, 34
Sandberg, Margot, 55, 57
Sandberg, Wili, 52, 55–8
Sandburg, Carl, 75n
Sands, Bobby, 298, 301–2
Sandycove, Dublin, 228
San Francisco, 83–4
Sartre, Jean-Paul, 76
Schlesinger, Alexandra, 213–15
Schlesinger, Arthur, 214
Schultz, Shelly, 109
Scott, Norman, 280
Scott, W.A., 272
Searle, Ronald, 202
Seattle, 71
Seeger, Alan, 170
Seeger, Pete, 70
Sellers, Brian, 5

Sellers, Peter, 5
Shaw, Colonel Clay, 135–6
Shaw, George Bernard: *The Doctor's Dilemma*, 131; *John Bull's Other Island*, 157
Shaw, Irwin, 214
Sheed, Wilfred, 81
Shelton Abbey, Co. Wicklow, 30
Sheridan, Jim, 28n, 230
Sheridan, Peter, 230
Simms, George, Archbishop of Armagh, 313
Simms, Nicholas, 313
Sinclair-Stevenson, Christopher, 185–6
Sinclair-Stevenson, Deborah, 185
'Sisyphus Wins' (O'Connor; poem), 258
Sixty Eight Committee, 302–3
Sjöman, Vilgot, 57–8
Skeffington, Francis Sheehy, 98n
Smith, Brendan, 41
Smith, Harry, 140 & n
Smith, Jean Kennedy, 85, 213
Smith, Paul ('Pauline'), 187
Smith, Reginald ('Equity'), 309
Smith, Stephen, 214–15
Smyth, (Judge) Esmonde, 177
Smyth, Revd Martin, 303
Smyth, Sammy, 174
Sotelo, Calvo, 296
Southern, Terry, 9
Spain, 291–7
Spence, Gusty, 311–12
Spiegel, Sam, 214
Stapleton, Michael, 18, 279
Stellof, Frances, 141, 255, 288
Stephens, James, 18, 225, 236
Stevenson, Sir William, 254
Stockholm, 51–9
Stoker, Bram, 26n
Stoker, Frank, 219
Stone, Irving: *The Agony and the Ecstasy*, 293–4
Strachey, Lytton, 6, 237
Strong, (Sir) Roy, 16
Strutt, Toby, 222
Stuart, Francis, 72n
Stuttgart, 200–1
Suarez Gonzalez, Adolfo, 297
Submarine (O'Connor; Noh play), 196, 276–7 & n, 285–6
Sunday Independent, 223
Sunday Mirror, 41, 124, 156, 567
Sunday Times, 194, 196, 199, 292, 295
Sunday Tribune, 303, 307

Sunningdale Agreement (1973), 160–1, 169, 303
Sutor, John, 72
Sweetman, Jack, 231
Swift, Jonathan, 131, 193–4
Swift, Patrick, 47n
Synge, John Millington, 236, 246, 273, 290, 294
Synnott, Pierce, 62, 234

Taillteann Games, Co. Meath, 18 & n
Talleyrand, Charles Maurice de, 275
Tallon, Don, 118
Tangier, 233–47
Tara Hall, Sandycove, 18
Tchelitchew, Pavel, 156
Tegero, Antonio, 296
Teresa of Avila, St, 68
Terrible Beauty is Born, A (O'Connor; republished as *The Troubles*), 45, 254, 260
Thomas, Dylan, 75, 81, 94, 178
Thorndike, Dame Sybil, 24
Thorpe, Jeremy, 280
Times, The: author writes for, 15–16, 25n
Timmons, Eugene, 175
Tobin, Brian, 50
Todd, Judy, 115
Tomalin, Nicholas, 123–4 & n
Tone, Wolf, 95n, 215
Topping, Ken, 44
Torey, Thomas ('Thomas Aquinas'), 97–9, 260, 263
Tracy, Honor, 68
Treacy, Ray, 191
Trefusis, Violet, 44, 202 & n, 239
Trelease, Dolly, 222
Trimble, David, 145n
Trinity College Dublin: sports at, 13–14, 26–7, 191
Troubles, The – 1912–1922 (O'Connor) see *Terrible Beauty is Born, A*
Tulira Castle, Co. Galway, 272
Tullynally Hall, Co. Longford, 62
Tunney, Dick, 231
Tuohy, Liam, 309
Tuohy, 'Rasher', 152
Twenty-four Hours (BBC TV programme), 32, 37–8
Twigg, Lizzie, 271
Tyrie, Andy, 165n, 264–5, 268–70

Ulster Defence Association (UDA), 126 & n, 174, 265, 268–9
Ulster Volunteer Force (UVF), 265–7
Unamuno, Miguel de, 297
United States of America: author reports Derry shootings in (1972), 108–10, 118; support for Northern Ireland, 267, 269–70, 303; author tours: (1971), 71–91; (1973), 133–43; (1980), 285; *see also* New York
Urach, Prince Albrecht von, 277n

Vane, Major Sir Francis, 98n
Vangsaae, Mona, 120n
Vidal, Gore, 241n
Vietnam War, 79
Viva Superstar (Susan Hoffman), 85–6 & n, 139–40, 166–7
Voight, Jon, 82
Volkova, Vera, 52
Vonnegut, Kurt, 90

Walden, Louie, 85n, 139
Wallace, Hilda, 218–19
Wallin, Archbishop J.O.: *Where is the Friend* (hymn), 313
Warfield, Derek, 302
Warhol, Andy, 85n, 139
Washington Post, 212–13
Watson, Patrick Burgess, 27
Watt, Peter, 185
Waugh, Alec, 235, 240–1 & n
Waugh, Evelyn, 221, 223–4, 235, 240
Waugh, Victoria, 240
Welles, Orson, 21n, 22, 57
West, Trevor: career, 14n; sporting activities with author, 14, 204–5, 212, 302, 311; friendship with author, 119, 227, 313; proposes independent Ulster State, 212–13, 265; visits Belfast, 264–5, 268; visits Long Kesh, 310–11
Wheatcroft, Geoffrey, 38
Whelan, Joseph, Bishop of Owerri, 155
White, Jack, 44
White, Sean, 105, 107–10, 181, 210, 272
White, Stanford, 74n
White, Terence de Vere, 99, 223–4 & n
Wicklow, Eleanor, Countess of (*née* Butler), 31, 92

Wicklow, William Cecil James Philip John Paul Forward–Howard, 8th Earl of: friendship with author, 29–31 & n, 68, 91, 221–4; death, 221; and author in Tangier, 235; as cousin to David Herbert, 239
Wilde, Oscar, 21n, 22–3, 25n, 32, 154n, 201; depicted in *The Importance of Being Oscar*, 23, 274
Wilkinson, Max, 90–1
William III (of Orange), King, 44
Williams, Judge Bill, 261
Williams, Emlyn, 61
Wilson, Father Desmond, 266, 302
Wilson, Harold (*later* Baron), 299
Wolfe, Charles, 203
Wolfe, Thomas, 81
Wood, Ernest, 210, 220
Woolf, Virginia, 53
Wyeth, Andrew, 57

X, Miss, 47–8

Yarnton Manor, Oxfordshire, 221
Yeats, Lily and Loly (WBY's sisters), 18
Yeats, William Butler: and Shelah Richards, 9n, 15; dislikes Monk Gibbon, 18; MacLiammóir on, 22; writes to Lady Londonderry, 45; praises Padraic Colum, 73n; on Hopkins, 152; and Abbey dramatic style, 154; teaches Sean MacBride, 161n; translation of *Oedipus*, 178; supposed fascism, 179; dedicates *The Death of Cuchulain* to Ninette de Valois, 197; sees ghost at Renvyle, 225; at Gogarty's swan ceremony, 227n; in Irish Literary Renaissance, 236, 239, 294; and founding of Irish national theatre, 273; Noh plays, 275n, 285; *Cathleen ni Houlihan*, 277; *The Dreaming of the Bones*, 275n; *The King's Threshold*, 299; *The Only Jealousy of Emer*, 235, 275n; *Oxford Book of Modern Verse* (ed.), 154n, 230; *The Statues*, 299; *When you are old and grey and full of sleep*, 255
Yevtushenko, Yevgeny, 245–6
Young, Jimmy (boxer), 216
Young, Jimmy (comedian), 268

Zale, Tony, 76
Zola, Emile, 19n